IBM Sametime 8.5.2 Administration Guide

A comprehensive, practical book for the planning, installation, and maintenance of your Sametime 8.5.2 environment

Gabriella Davis
Marie L. Scott
Thomas Duff

BIRMINGHAM - MUMBAI

IBM Sametime 8.5.2 Administration Guide

First published: November 2011

Production Reference: 1091111

Published by Packt Publishing Ltd.
Livery Place,
35 Livery Street,
Birmingham B3 2PB, UK.

ISBN 978-1-84968-304-3

www.packtpub.com

Cover Image by David Gimenez (bilbaorocker@yahoo.co.uk)

Credits

Authors
Gabriella Davis
Marie L. Scott
Thomas Duff

Reviewers
Susan Bulloch
Mitch Cohen
Carl Tyler

Acquisition Editor
Dhwani Devater

Development Editor
Hyacintha D'Souza

Technical Editor
Kedar Bhat

Project Coordinator
Vishal Bodwani

Proofreader
Jacqueline McGhee

Indexer
Tejal Daruwale

Graphics
Valentina D'silva

Production Coordinator
Aparna Bhagat

Cover Work
Aparna Bhagat

Foreword

Allow me to be the first to congratulate you for purchasing this book. Sametime 8.5 is a very different product from previous versions of the product. What once was a simple offering that provided secure instant messaging with some web conferencing capabilities has now evolved into a robust, flexible, sophisticated communications platform. This book, written from the perspective of a Domino Administrator, will help you get the most out of this platform.

For reasons I can't fully explain, the major innovations in Sametime seem to come with the "dot five" releases and 8.5 was no exception. Consider, for a moment, this partial list of enhancements:

- Completely new Online Meetings that have been ranked as one of the best web conferencing solutions on the market.
- A seamless user experience that integrates meetings into the Sametime Connect Client. Quick and easy access to meeting rooms and ability to invite others through drag and drop.
- Zero-download browser access to meetings for those who prefer to operate without a rich client.
- A new unified infrastructure that leverages industry standard codecs and protocols for better audio and video performance and interoperability.
- Bandwidth Management tools to provide an optimal experience while protecting the network.
- Standards based firewall and NAT Traversal for audio and video to make rich communications easy outside the enterprise.
- The ability to replace Sametime's native audio / video with those from our partners, turning the Sametime Connect Client into first-class end points for leading room and tele-presence systems.
- Telephony middlware that delivers advanced functionality (single number service, intelligent call routing, a softphone experience unqiue in the industry) regardless of the complexity of the underlying telephony infrastructure.
- Zero-download browser-based instant messaging and Web 2.0 APIs to easily embed Sametime services into web apps.

- Mobile clients for the latest, hottest smart phones and tablets.
- A modern, flexible product architecture with consolidated management of all the components.

As Sametime has matured into a full unified communications platform, the skill set required to plan, deploy, and manage it has also evolved. *Chapter 2* , *Chapter 3* , and *Chapter 9* will introduce you to the various servers that make up the product family. This componentized architecture is one of the ways that 8.5 is different from previous iterations of Sametime. It provides much more flexibility by allowing you to deploy more or less of any given capability to suit your specific needs. But that flexibility also requires you to make new decisions and, in conjunction with the earlier chapters, rely on *Chapter 5* (planning considerations) to step you through the thought process.

Another key change to Sametime has been the migration to WebSphere Application Server (WAS) and DB2 for all new servers. WAS is a different animal from Domino and, in *Chapter 4* , the authors have provided a 'Rosetta stone' for Domino admins. It is an excellent resource and well worth the time to thoroughly digest.

The remaining chapters step you through the process to install (*Chapter 6*) and secure your environment (*Chapter 7*), customizing and delivering clients (*Chapter 10* and *Chapter 11*), integrating with other software (*Chapter 8* and *Chapter 10*) and interacting with the outside world (*Chapter 9*).

Of course, Sametime 8.5 is not the end of our journey. Just as the industry has migrated from collaboration to unified communications, social business looms on the horizon. Social forms of interaction — micro-blogging, status updates, blogs, and wikis — are rapidly becoming strategic forms of business communications. In many instances, they have taken the place of the phone call and voicemail as they provide access to knowledge when the expert isn't or can't be available. Blending social concepts with today's rich forms of communications (such as video), the explosion in mobile devices and tables (such as the iPad), new delivery and business models (such as the cloud), and managing the resulting governance and compliance challenges will be our focus as we look towards the future of Sametime.

John Del Pizzo
Program Director and Head of Product Management, IBM Sametime

twitter: jrdpizzo
linkedin: linkedin.com/in/johndelpizzo
johndel@us.ibm.com

About the Authors

Gabriella Davis lives in London, England and is Technical Director at The Turtle Partnership, an IBM Business Partner, for the past 16 years. Starting out as a cc: Mail administrator and a Lotus Agenda user, she has continued to work with mail systems and Lotus software and has stayed true to her admin roots ever since. She now focuses on designing and tuning infrastructures and integrating mail and collaboration products for small and large enterprises alike. Gabriella was recently named an IBM Lotus Collaboration Champion for Collaboration Solutions https://www.ibm.com/developerworks/mydeveloperworks/profiles/user/GabDavis. Gabriella's blog can be found at http://blog.turtleweb.com.

A lot of people deserve my thanks for this book ever getting written not least Tom and Marie for asking me to work with them and showing extraordinary patience. To my friends Andrew Pollack and Rocky Oliver who encouraged me many years ago to share what I knew. Life would not be as fun without the support of some of the smartest women you could meet, the incredible Nerd Girls: Susan Bulloch, Jess Stratton, Amy Blumenfeld, Teresa "Kitty" Elsmore, Maureen Leland, Mary Beth Raven, Jennifer Stevenson, Marie Scott, Kathy Brown, Francie Tanner, Eileen Fitzgerald, and Kathleen McGivney. Thanks also to the Lotus Community and the many smart people in it who may not realize it but raise the bar every day, make me love what I do and who I'm lucky to call friends, especially Carl Tyler, Paul Mooney, Warren Elsmore, Bob Balaban, Chris Miller, Ben Langhinrichs, Bill Buchan, Rob Novak.

Thanks to all at Turtle but especially Mike Smith and Samuel Gee, who worked around me for 9 months without a complaint. To my parents Berry and Graham Hedley, who never gave me an option to not try my hardest at anything, I love you both.

Above all to my husband Tim Davis for his talents with a cocktail shaker in an emergency and for loving me.

Marie L. Scott is the Director of Email Services at Virginia Commonwealth University in Richmond, Virginia. She holds a bachelor of science in biology from James Madison University and a certificate in information systems from Virginia Commonwealth University. Marie has held dual advanced certifications in Notes/Domino administration and development since version 4.0, and she is an IBM Certified Advanced Security Professional for Domino. Marie began working with Lotus Notes in 1996, and she has worked in networking, systems integration, and e-mail systems since 1987. Her primary interest is in Domino administration of complex environments. She has managed large e-mail migration projects including several cloud collaboration projects. Marie has been a speaker at conferences, including Lotusphere, featuring IBM/Lotus technologies. Marie has written for The View (Wellesley Information Services) and Marie and Tom Duff co-authored *IBM Lotus Sametime 8 Essentials: A User's Guide* (Packt Publishing, 2010). Marie was recently named an IBM Champion for Collaboration Solutions: https://www.ibm.com/developerworks/mydeveloperworks/profiles/user/MarieScott. Marie's blog can be found at: http://crashtestchix.com.

I would like to thank the following individuals without whom this book would not have been possible: Gabriella Davis—thanks so much for saying "yes" to this project when we asked. Once again you have pushed me to learn more. I'm glad we could share this "first book" experience! Thank you. Tom Duff—thanks for hanging in there on this project with two administrators. I think you are right on the cusp of being an administrator yourself! As always, whenever you are ready to write again, say the word.

To my friends and colleagues: Connie Whetstine, Joni Snyder, Josie Barbie, Pam McGhee, Diane Talley, Scott Davis, Mitch Cohen, Jason Fortney, Andy Donaldson, Tim Davis, Carl Tyler, Paul Mooney, Warren Elsmore, Steve McDonagh, and Chris Reckling—thanks for providing your special blend of technical support, comic relief, and above all friendship. To the Nerd Girls: Amy Blumenfield, Kathy Brown, Susan Bulloch, Gabriella Davis, Kitty Elsmore, Eileen Fitzgerald, Maureen Leland, Kathleen McGivney, Mary Beth Raven, Jennifer Stevenson, Jess Stratton, and Francie Tanner—thanks ladies for your laughter, wisdom, friendship, and inspiration.

And especially to my parents Joe and Ann Kovalchick, whose unfaltering love and encouragement has been there for me always. Thank you.

Thomas Duff (also known as "Duffbert") is a software developer focusing on Lotus collaboration technologies in Portland Oregon. He started working with Lotus Notes in 1996 in version R3 and has written and maintained hundreds of applications in large enterprises through the years. He also holds Lotus principal development certifications starting at version 4 and going up to version 8, as well as Microsoft and Java certifications. Tom is a prolific writer, both in various industry publications and at his website, Duffbert's Random Musings, at `http://www.duffbert.com`. He also is a frequent speaker at conferences and events focusing on Lotus technologies. Tom and Marie Scott coauthored *IBM Lotus Sametime 8 Essentials: A User's Guide* (Packt Publishing, 2010). You can find his profile at `https://www.ibm.com/developerworks/mydeveloperworks/profiles/user/ThomasDuff`.

For someone who never thought he would write a technical book, somehow I'm now staring at my second one. Thank you to Gabriella Davis, without whom this book would have never been started. I'm glad I was able to be a part of your first book adventure. Thank you also to Marie Scott. Apparently I didn't drive you crazy enough on the first one, as you asked me to be part of this one too. Although we need a bit of a break, I'm ready for the next idea.

For all of you in my online community, thanks for being there when I needed to ask the dumb question, get pointed in the right direction, and finagle an ID and password to your Sametime server to try something out. I really couldn't do it without you.

And for Susan, Ian, and Cam... I promise that I do not have another book lined up and ready to start. I vow to come out of basement more often and discover the art of face-to-face communication... Thanks for putting up with this obsession.

Acknowledgement

The essence of the Sametime product is about collaboration and communication among people and groups. As such, it is not surprising that writing a book about Sametime involves cooperation, communication, and collaboration with numerous people within our personal and professional communities.

Thank you to the team at Packt Publishing for supporting this book and for guiding the three of us through the writing process. Getting our thoughts and words organized and published will make many of our technical colleagues very happy.

We also extend our appreciation to IBM for permitting us to get a jumpstart on this book as beta users of Sametime 8.5.2, especially John Delpizzo, Lilach Ofek, David Marshak, Rob Ingram, and Avshalom Houri.

Thanks to our friends at the Turtle Partnership for use of their valuable server resources as well as our partners in crime at Lucy Sky Diamonds.

Many thanks and kudos go to the Sametime experts we called on to read and review the chapters for readability, content, and accuracy. We received valuable feedback and input on our writing and ideas from various individuals over the course of the months it took to put our words onto the page, including Paul Mooney, Susan Bulloch, Mitch Cohen, Carl Tyler, and Wes Morgan.

And as co-authors, who for most of the project were separated by multiple time zones, we may not have been quite so organized and on schedule without the use of Dropbox. It is a software that just works. And finally to our families, friends, fellow bloggers, tweeters, chat partners, Google+ Circles, and Facebook friends — we thank you for your encouragement and enthusiasm for this project. When things started to drag and we wondered where the next few pages were going to come from, you were there to remind us to keep laughing and keep going!

About the Reviewers

Susan Bulloch has worked for IBM Lotus Software for more than 10 years in software support and development positions. Susan currently works as a Support Engineer on the Lotus Notes Calendar and Scheduling team. She has worked with Lotus Notes and Domino since 1992 as an administrator, instructor, developer, and architect in banking and utility industries. Susan has a Bachelors degree in engineering and a Master's degree in Information Technology. She holds certifications in all current Lotus Notes product releases. Susan is a frequent speaker at technical conferences, including Lotusphere, the View Admin conferences, and at regional user-group conferences worldwide. When not working, Susan likes to annoy insects and buzzards.

Mitch Cohen has 15 years' experience working with Messaging and Collaboration tools, building and managing global implementations of IBM Connections, IBM Sametime, Lotus Notes/Domino, and Lotus Quickr. Father of an eight-year-old girl and two very active three-and-a-half-year-old boys, Mitch and his wife Elisa are never bored. An avid sports fan always rooting for the Mets (baseball) and the Giants (football). Mitch is also a Twitter addict (@curiousmitch) and blogger (http://www.curiousmitch.com).

Carl Tyler is Director of IBM and Microsoft Business Partner Epilio, which delivers applications and turn-key solutions to users of collaboration software such as IBM Lotus Sametime and Microsoft Lync. Carl has over 20 years of experience with collaboration software, including over 9 years at Lotus Development and more than 2 years at IBM Development, UK. At Lotus, Carl was the worldwide knowledge management manager and Lotus Notes R5 international launch manager. He had even worked on various IBM Redbooks and Redpapers. You can often find Carl speaking at Lotus user-groups and other industry events. Epilio offers expertise in developing Sametime plugins and Telephony solutions. A number of free plugins are available from their website at http://www.epilio.com.

I would like to thank my dog Jessie for keeping my feet warm during the cold days of review.

www.PacktPub.com

Support files, eBooks, discount offers, and more

You might want to visit www.PacktPub.com for support files and downloads related to your book.

Did you know that Packt offers eBook versions of every book published, with PDF and ePub files available? You can upgrade to the eBook version at www.PacktPub.com and as a print book customer, you are entitled to a discount on the eBook copy. Get in touch with us at service@packtpub.com for more details.

At www.PacktPub.com, you can also read a collection of free technical articles, sign up for a range of free newsletters, and receive exclusive discounts and offers on Packt books and eBooks.

http://PacktLib.PacktPub.com

Do you need instant solutions to your IT questions? PacktLib is Packt's online digital book library. Here, you can access, read, and search across Packt's entire library of books.

Why Subscribe?
- Fully searchable across every book published by Packt
- Copy and paste, print, and bookmark content
- On demand and accessible via web browser

Free Access for Packt account holders

If you have an account with Packt at www.PacktPub.com, you can use this to access PacktLib today and view nine entirely free books. Simply use your login credentials for immediate access.

Instant Updates on New Packt Books

Get notified! Find out when new books are published by following @PacktEnterprise on Twitter, or the *Packt Enterprise* Facebook page.

Table of Contents

Preface

IBM Sametime 8.5.2 delivers a state-of-the-art enterprise-ready instant messaging, meeting, and conferencing service. This Administrator's Guide navigates through the range of Sametime server components and features, providing you with the essential information required to install, administer, and troubleshoot your Sametime 8.5.2 environment. The IBM Sametime 8.5.2 Administration Guide cuts through the complexity of architecting, installing, and administering all the moving parts of the latest version of Sametime.

With this book, you will have all the information necessary to decide which server components provide the features you need as well as how to install them to get the most performance and maintainability from the software. Starting with an overview of Sametime 8.5.2, you will then dive into each server component, learning what each one does, why it might be needed in your environment, and what you need to have in place to run it. By the end, you will be able to have Sametime running and configured properly for your particular situation. With flexibility comes complexity—but not with this guide. You will learn how different architectures are possible and how to prepare properly for the installation of Sametime. You will learn how to install the servers in the right order so that you can maintain and expand your environment in the future. You will also find out how best to monitor your Sametime environment for issues, as well as how to effectively troubleshoot those problems so that you can quickly get Sametime running again.

The IBM Sametime 8.5.2 Administration Guide is the perfect one-stop resource for learning important installation and configuration details quickly and easily.

What this book covers

Chapter 1, Collaborate in Real Time: Introducing Sametime 8.5.2, teaches you the architecture of Sametime 8.5.2, the hardware and operating system requirements, and what type of licensing is required to run various configurations of Sametime. You will also learn how Sametime 8.5.2 differs from the previous versions of Sametime, and why you would benefit from upgrading to the newest release.

Chapter 2, The Sametime 8.5.2 Servers — Up Close and Personal, introduces you each of the servers that make up Sametime 8.5.2, including the requirements for each one as well as how each might be used in various Sametime environments and how all the servers integrate together.

Chapter 3, Telephony Integration: Working with Sametime Telephony, teaches you how Sametime 8.5.2 integrates telephony, audio, and video to provide a rich communication experience. You will also discover how to add web conferencing to your Sametime environment in order to provide virtual meeting experiences to your users.

Chapter 4, The Infrastructure: Understanding Sametime and WebSphere Application Server Architecture, establishes that integration of IBM WebSphere Application Server (WAS) is the most significant change in the Sametime 8.5.2 architecture. In this chapter, you will gain knowledge about WAS and how Sametime uses it, as well as the concepts behind how WAS is organized. Learn how to configure and deploy WAS in a secure manner.

Chapter 5, Executive Decisions: Preparing for your Sametime 8.5.2 Installation, explains the planning and preparation that are critical for a successful Sametime 8.5.2 deployment. In this chapter, learn about the key decisions that need to be taken into consideration based on how you expect to structure your Sametime 8.5.2 environment. This chapter also covers those choices to allow you to expand and grow your environment in the future.

Chapter 6, Ready, Set, Install: Installing Sametime 8.5.2, guides you through an actual Sametime 8.5.2 installation. In this chapter, discover how each Sametime 8.5.2 server needs to be installed and in what order. You will also gain knowledge about how to verify that each installation step was successful before proceeding to the next one.

Chapter 7, Collaborate Securely: Setting up Authentication and Securing Your Sametime Environment, familiarizes you with the authentication methods for Sametime 8.5.2, and how LDAP, Domino Directory, and Active Directory can be used. In addition, learn how to ensure that your environment is secure from unauthorized users.

Chapter 8, Making it Personal: Using Sametime Business Card, explains that Sametime Business Card offers a convenient way to display information about your various contacts. Learn how to configure the Sametime Business Card feature, how to use different types of data sources to display the contact information, and how to troubleshoot Sametime Business Card if the feature is not working correctly.

Chapter 9, Extending the Sametime Environment: Connecting to Sametime Advanced and Sametime Gateway, teaches you how Sametime Advanced adds additional features into your Sametime 8.5.2 environment, and how it is installed using the Sametime System Console. In this chapter, you will also discover how Sametime Gateway opens up communication with external chat communities such as AOL and Google, the deployment options for Sametime Gateway, and how to install the feature.

Chapter 10, The End User Experience: Preparing for Sametime Client Deployments, illustrates that once your Sametime 8.5.2 servers are installed and running, your attention shifts to the many Sametime client options. Learn about the various Sametime clients, how they are deployed, and how to manage the Sametime client environment through client preferences and policies.

Chapter 11, Collaborate from Anywhere: Sametime 8.5.2 and Mobile Devices, familiarizes you with the options available for using Sametime from mobile clients. You learn how to configure the Sametime environment for mobile access as well as how to deploy various mobile Sametime clients.

Chapter 12, Managing and Monitoring the Sametime 8.5.2 Server Environment, makes you aware that once your Sametime 8.5.2 environment is up and running, you need to keep it tuned to run at an optimal state. Learn how to monitor the different server logs for activity, as well as how the logs are used for troubleshooting issues.

Appendix A, Sametime 8.5.2 Installation Worksheets provides you with a sample set of worksheets to plan and record vital Sametime 8.5.2 environment information in order to make your installation activities flow smoothly, as well as to document your install and configuration decisions.

Appendix B, Sametime 8.5.2 Related Resources provides more information about various aspects of Sametime 8.5.2 by exploring the various links and resources referenced here.

Appendix C, Sametime 8.5.2 Network-Related Resources provides the resources to learn more about how Sametime 8.5.2 interacts with network resources, as well as how to tune your network for optimal Sametime performance.

Appendix D, WebSphere Application Server-Related Resources helps you if you are new to the world of WebSphere Application Server by using the resources to gain a better understanding of this fundamental part of the Sametime 8.5.2 architecture.

What you need for this book

The reader should have a basic understanding of server administration, networking, security, and directory management concepts.

Who this book is for

If you are responsible for installing and administering Sametime 8.5.2, then this book is for you. Regardless of whether you are new to Sametime administration or not, this book will serve as your roadmap for building and maintaining an effective environment. Planning a migration from a prior version of Sametime? This book will help you discover how Sametime 8.5.2 differs and how you work with the new configuration. Even if you already have Sametime 8.5.2 up and running, this guide will answer those questions you may still have of why and how the various server components work, as well as how to grow to meet demand and monitor for a healthy system.

Conventions

In this book, you will find a number of styles of text that distinguish between different kinds of information. Here are some examples of these styles, and an explanation of their meaning.

Code words in text are shown as follows: "9 GB configurable space, plus 1 GB available in /tmp."

A block of code is set as follows:

```
# Sametime.ini Configuration
[Config]
VPMX_CAPACITY=80000
[Connectivity]
VPS_HOST=10.9.2.8,10.9.2.41,192.168.0.100
```

Any command-line input or output is written as follows:

```
Startserver STMeetingServer -username wasadmin -password madeuppassword
```

New terms and **important words** are shown in bold. Words that you see on the screen, in menus or dialog boxes for example, appear in the text like this: "Refer to the **Sametime Meetings** area in the following screenshot".

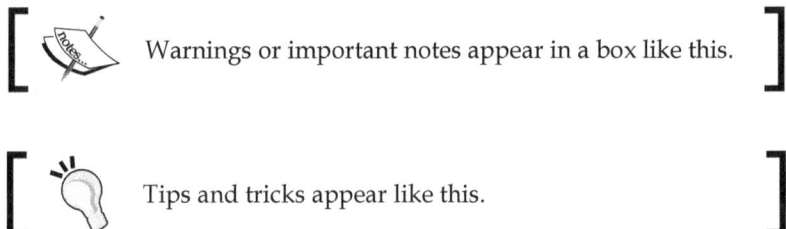

Warnings or important notes appear in a box like this.

Tips and tricks appear like this.

Reader feedback

Feedback from our readers is always welcome. Let us know what you think about this book—what you liked or may have disliked. Reader feedback is important for us to develop titles that you really get the most out of.

To send us general feedback, simply send an e-mail to feedback@packtpub.com, and mention the book title via the subject of your message.

If there is a book that you need and would like to see us publish, please send us a note in the **SUGGEST A TITLE** form on www.packtpub.com or e-mail suggest@packtpub.com.

If there is a topic that you have expertise in and you are interested in either writing or contributing to a book, see our author guide on www.packtpub.com/authors.

Customer support

Now that you are the proud owner of a Packt book, we have a number of things to help you to get the most from your purchase.

Errata

Although we have taken every care to ensure the accuracy of our content, mistakes do happen. If you find a mistake in one of our books—maybe a mistake in the text or the code—we would be grateful if you would report this to us. By doing so, you can save other readers from frustration and help us improve subsequent versions of this book. If you find any errata, please report them by visiting http://www.packtpub.com/support, selecting your book, clicking on the **errata submission form** link, and entering the details of your errata. Once your errata are verified, your submission will be accepted and the errata will be uploaded on our website, or added to any list of existing errata, under the Errata section of that title. Any existing errata can be viewed by selecting your title from http://www.packtpub.com/support.

Piracy

Piracy of copyright material on the Internet is an ongoing problem across all media. At Packt, we take the protection of our copyright and licenses very seriously. If you come across any illegal copies of our works, in any form, on the Internet, please provide us with the location address or website name immediately so that we can pursue a remedy.

Please contact us at `copyright@packtpub.com` with a link to the suspected pirated material.

We appreciate your help in protecting our authors, and our ability to bring you valuable content.

Questions

You can contact us at `questions@packtpub.com` if you are having a problem with any aspect of the book, and we will do our best to address it.

1
Collaborate in Real Time: Introducing Sametime 8.5.2

"Collaborate in real time." What does this phrase mean? We generally think of it as meaning when we communicate and work with others in a seamless and instantaneous fashion. But how do we go about doing that? Today, we have many choices for collaboration, from traditional e-mail or discussion forums to chat communities and near-instantaneous tools such as Twitter. With the ability to connect to the Internet, we can reach anyone with the right tools for our particular situation. For many large enterprises and small companies, the right tool might be instant messaging or online meeting software.

Our focus, here, is on IBM Sametime 8.5.2 software. Sametime is a suite of products that include clients for secure instant messaging, integration with e-mail and calendaring platforms, and connectivity through mobile devices such as Research in Motion Blackberries, Android devices, Apple iPhones, and iPads. Sametime software also includes secure online meeting rooms, persistent chat rooms, and unified telephony connectivity.

Why would a company or organization choose to use Sametime? They might choose Sametime because it closely integrates with their existing collaboration environment—**IBM Lotus Notes** and **Domino**, **Lotus Quickr**, or **IBM Connections**. They may also choose a real-time collaboration system such as Sametime to save money. Online meetings and instant messaging helps save money by eliminating the need for travel costs and long distance phone expenditures, especially if a company integrates Sametime with their existing **Voice over Internet Protocol (VoIP)** system.

Companies of all sizes often find that Sametime has a significant cost advantage over other solutions. It can be deployed on a variety of platforms and hardware with a per-user license cost included in existing Lotus Notes licensing. If a smaller company doesn't have the need to deploy a full web conferencing solution, they can use the online per-user Sametime Unyte product which is tightly integrated with Sametime itself.

A large enterprise might use Sametime because it integrates well with their existing collaboration tools from Lotus to IBM, but it also integrates with tools from other providers such as Microsoft, Avaya, and Tandberg. Sametime's web conferencing solution, including full multi-way audio and video, is extensible with distributed and clustering functionality to support the size and scope of an enterprise-wide infrastructure.

As an administrator of IBM Sametime or Lotus Notes and Domino, you may find yourself in a situation similar to one of the following scenarios. Our goal is to provide you with the resources you require to implement a successful Sametime environment.

- Tim works for a company that currently uses Sametime. The company has recently acquired some new businesses and will be including those subsidiaries in their Lotus Notes and Sametime domain. As they are interested in using some of the new features of Sametime 8.5.2, Tim will be upgrading the company's existing Sametime environment.

- In contrast, Susan works for a company that has only used the e-mail and calendaring features of Lotus Notes. The chief information officer now wants to look at instant messaging and online meeting software. She wants Susan to configure a new Sametime environment to fit their needs.

- David works for a company that has a requirement for secure instant messaging. The company's CEO would like marketing and sales staff to use instant messaging to communicate with customers and coworkers. They would also like to have web conferences among themselves and with customers. However, they have yet to decide whether to manage such a system on their own intranet or to use an online service.

In this chapter, you will learn the following topics:

- What's new in Sametime 8.5.2
- What has changed with regards to Sametime server architecture
- The different types of Sametime clients available in Sametime 8.5.2
- The operating system and hardware requirements for Sametime 8.5.2 servers
- The operating system and hardware requirements for Sametime 8.5.2 clients
- Understanding the different Sametime licenses and what you might need for your environment
- Why you should install Sametime 8.5.2 or upgrade from prior versions

What's new in Sametime 8.5.2

IBM Sametime 8.5 and 8.5.2 introduces many new capabilities to the Sametime product suite. In addition to the numerous features already included with the Sametime 8.x family of clients, Sametime 8.5.2 has extended client usability and collaboration. Let us take a look at a few of those enhancements:

- Sametime Connect Client software is now supported on Microsoft Windows 7.0, Apple Macintosh 10.6, and Linux desktop operating systems including Red Hat Enterprise Desktop (RHED), Ubuntu, and SUSE Linux Enterprise Desktop (SLED)

- A lightweight browser-based client that requires no additional downloads is available for instant messaging for Apple iPhone and iPad users

- A browser-based client is available for Sametime meetings

- Sametime Mobile Client support has been added for Android devices (OS 2.0 and higher), Blackberry 5.0 and 6.0 devices, and Microsoft Mobile 6.5 devices

- Rich text messaging is now available for chats with users connected through the Sametime Gateway

If you deployed Sametime Standard in a previous release or are interested in the online meeting conferencing features of Sametime 8.5.2, then you and your users will be happy to know that meeting attendees now can attend online meetings "instantly" without having to load any additional software in their browser. Meetings start quickly and are retained for future use.

Probably the most significant change for you as a Sametime administrator is the introduction of **IBM WebSphere Application Server (WAS)** as an application hosting platform for Sametime. In previous versions of Sametime, with the exception of the Sametime Advanced and Sametime Gateway features, the Sametime server was deployed on Lotus Domino servers. If you know how to install and manage a Lotus Domino server, then you will most likely be the same individual who will manage a Sametime server as the skill sets are similar.

But with the addition of WAS comes flexibility in server architecture. As an administrator, you have the ability to choose features and configure servers based on your organization's unique needs. The linkage between Domino and Sametime still exists through the Sametime Community Server. So not only can Sametime be sized appropriately for the needs of your organization, it can also run on multiple operating systems and servers as per your requirements.

Some highlights include:

- With the release of Sametime 8.5.2, Lotus Domino 8.5.2 is now supported.

- A Sametime Proxy Server has been introduced as a component of the Sametime server architecture. The Sametime Proxy Server hosts the lightweight browser-based Sametime client. It runs on WAS and is different than the WAS Proxy Server.

- Media Manager Server is another new Sametime server component. This server manages conferences using **Session Initiation Protocol (SIP)** to support point-to-point and multi-point calls and integrates into the Sametime environment through your Community Server. Sametime 8.5.2 introduces support for standard audio and video codec for improved integration in the Sametime client and the Sametime Meeting Center. This allows for interoperability with third-party conferencing systems.

- **Transversal Using Relay NAT (TURN)** server is a Java program that runs in conjunction with the Media Manager Server and behaves as a reflector, routing audio and video traffic between clients on different networks. The technology used by this **Network Address Translation (NAT) Traversal server (ICE)** uses both TURN and **Session Transversal Utilities for NAT (STUN)** protocols and behaves similarly to the Sametime reflector service that was part of earlier versions of Sametime.

- Improved network performance and support for IPv6 networking.

- A new central administration console called the **Sametime System Console (SSC)** for managing Sametime server and configuration resources from a consolidated web interface.

- Sametime Bandwidth Manager is a new optional WAS-based Sametime server component that allows you to create rules and policies that determine the use of audio and video within Sametime. The Bandwidth Manager monitors Sametime traffic and uses your rules to dynamically select codec and quality of video streams as calls are initiated by users.

No matter if you are new to Sametime or a long-time Sametime administrator, our aim is to guide you through the planning, installation, management, and troubleshooting steps so that you can successfully implement and support Sametime 8.5.2 in your environment.

Sametime 8.5.2 server architecture

As we have described briefly, the server architecture for Sametime 8.5.2 has changed significantly from previous versions. Prior to this version, Sametime was a single server installation and ran as an add-in task under a Domino server. It provided both instant messaging and web conferencing features combined into a single server. Although there was a license model that only installed and enabled the instant messaging features (Sametime Entry), the installer was the same if you wanted to include web conferencing functionality as well.

The new architecture still includes a Domino-based component but the Domino server is intended strictly for instant messaging and awareness. All other Sametime functionality has been re-engineered into separate server components running on top of the WAS platform. By moving all but the instant messaging and awareness services from Domino onto WebSphere, IBM has constructed an environment better suited to the needs of enterprise customers who have a high demand for services that require significant non-Domino resources such as audio, video, and web conferencing.

Additionally, the new architecture of Sametime 8.5.2 is about enhancing the client experience, dramatically improving performance, and bringing the technology in line with modern audio, video, and browser standards.

Let us begin by taking a look at the new server components and learning about their role and function.

Sametime System Console

Core to the entire Sametime multi-server architecture is the management interface which runs as a WebSphere application. It is called the Sametime System Console (SSC). The SSC actually plugs into the standard WAS 7.x menu as an additional option.

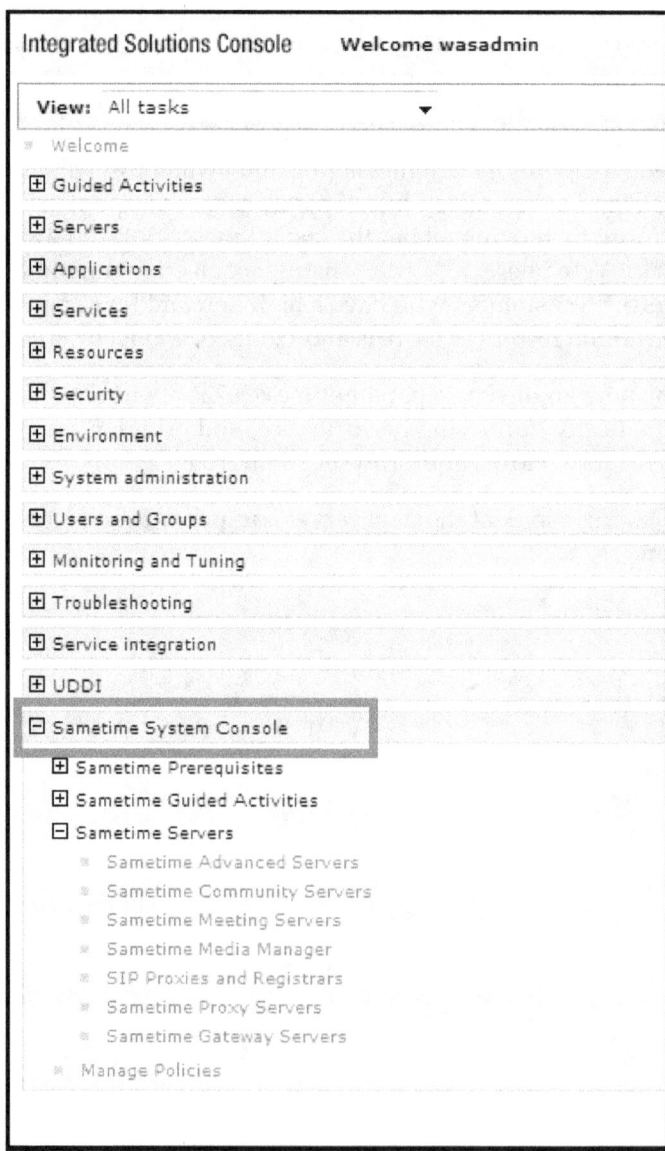

The SSC provides the configuration and management tools needed to work with all the other Sametime components, including the Domino-based Instant Messaging server. It also comes with a series of step-by-step guides called Sametime Guided Activities to walk you through the installation of each server component in the proper sequence. The SSC also has a Sametime Servers section that allows you manage the Sametime servers.

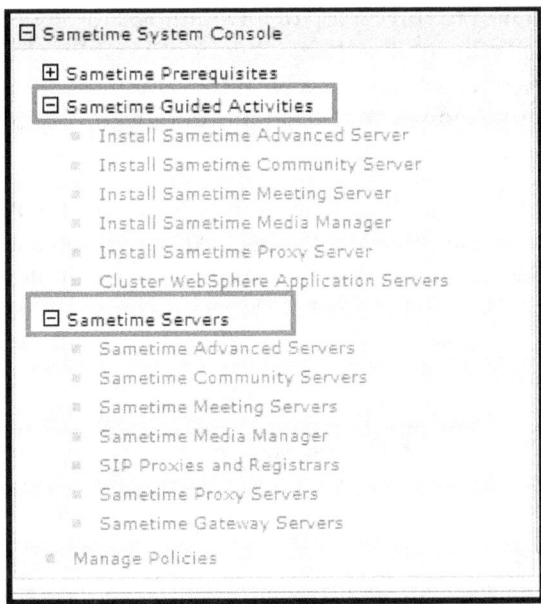

The SSC installs as an add-in to WAS and is accessed through a browser on its own dedicated port. It also uses a custom DB2 database named STSC for storage of its management information.

Sametime Community Server

Sametime Community Server is the instant messaging and presence awareness component of Sametime, which is installed as an add-in task for Domino. It must be installed on Domino versions 8.5 or 8.5.1, but it can work with earlier versions of Sametime already installed in your environment. Keep in mind, however, that pre-8.5.x clients will not benefit from many of the new features provided by your Sametime 8.5.2 servers. If your requirement is solely for instant messaging, then this is the only component you will need installed alongside Domino itself.

The Sametime Community Server "standard" install also includes the original Domino-based Meeting Center. This browser-based component has not been updated in any way from pre-8.5.x versions and is there purely for backwards compatibility and to maintain any existing scheduled meetings. There is no integration or interaction between the Domino-based Meeting Center and the Sametime 8.5.2 Meeting Center(s).

Other than being updated to run on top of a Domino 8.5 or 8.5.1 server, the actual Community Server component has changed very little and includes no significant new features from previous versions. Its browser administration interface and options remain the same. However, if you have deployed the SSC, the native Domino administration is over-ridden.

Following is a chart of the Sametime Community Server infrastructure. Note the optional management of the server by the SSC. Although the use of Domino as a directory is still supported, it is highly recommended you deploy Sametime using a **Lightweight Directory Access Protocol (LDAP)** directory. If you will be deploying other Sametime 8.5.2 components, then your deployment will usually require an LDAP directory to be used.

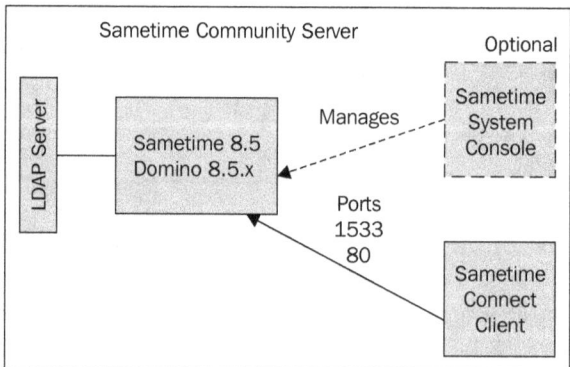

Sametime Meeting Server

The Sametime Meeting server has been completely re-engineered to bring it up to the standards of modern web conferencing solutions. It is also better aligned with IBM's Sametime Unyte online service. The new Sametime Meeting Server (versus the Domino-based Meeting Center) runs as an application under WAS. In addition, as it requires a data store to hold meeting information, it utilizes a dedicated DB2 database for managing the content of each meeting room.

The previous Sametime meeting client was entirely browser-based. To improve performance and functionality for 8.5.2, a rich meeting center client has been introduced which plugs into the Sametime Eclipse environment. A browser interface for meetings is still available but it provides a reduced set of functions.

Sametime Proxy Server

The Sametime Proxy Server re-introduces a lightweight browser-based client for Sametime, which has not been available in versions shipped since 6.5. The new browser client is designed to be lightweight and fully customizable and it is based on Ajax technology and themed using CSS. This allows it to launch quickly and be customized to match your organization's design.

The Proxy Server installs as an application under WAS, although it has no data store of its own and does not require any database connectivity. In the configuration for the Proxy Server, you direct it to a specific Community Server to supply the Sametime services. The following diagram gives a brief overview:

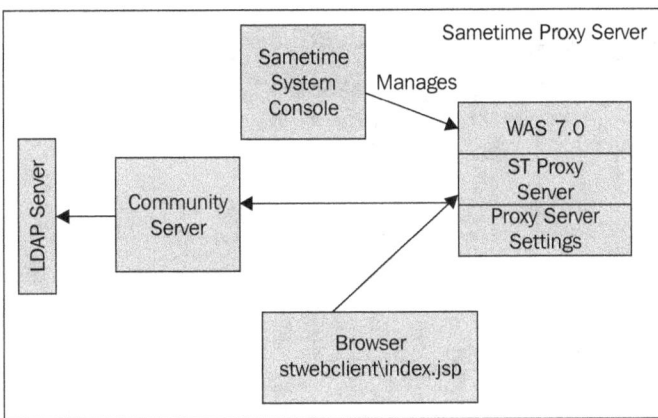

The Proxy Server ships with a default client designed as a JavaServer Page, which can be modified using customizable style sheets. It gives a feature-rich Sametime experience including multi-way chats, browser-based meetings, and privacy settings.

Sametime Media Manager

The Sametime Media Manager takes on the role of providing audio and video services for both the Sametime clients for peer-to-peer VoIP and video chats, and for web conferencing within the meeting rooms in the new meeting center. It is designed to provide services for multiple Meeting Servers and through them for instant meetings from the Sametime client. Installed on a WAS platform, it has no need for a data store and does not require any database connectivity.

The Media Manager is designed to provide a multi-way audio and video conferencing experience using modern codecs; however, it does not support Sametime clients in versions prior to 8.5.2. It is the audio and video "glue" that connects all the other Sametime server elements in 8.5.2.

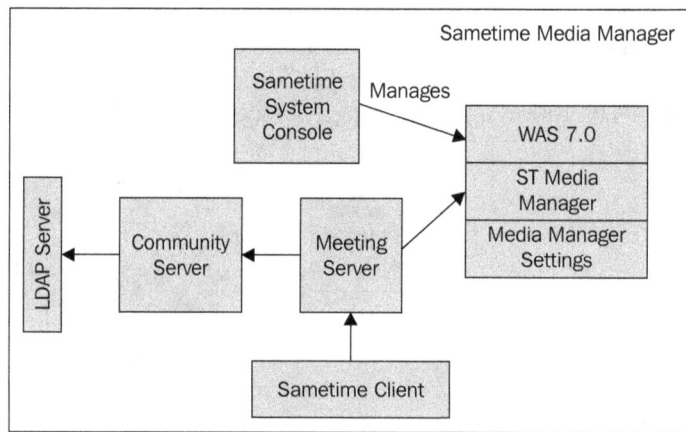

Sametime TURN Server

In its default configuration, the Media Manager creates a SIP connection from itself to the requesting client. However, where the client is not on the same network as the Media Manager, no SIP connection can be made directly. To address this issue, which affects users outside of your firewall as well as those on different internal networks, IBM has introduced the TURN Server with Sametime 8.5.2.

The TURN server uses both TURN and STUN protocols to create a connection with the client. It routes audio and video traffic between itself and the Media Manager, allowing connections between clients across networks. The technology is sometimes referred to as a **reflector** and pre-8.5 versions of Sametime came with a reflector service of their own.

The TURN server is a Java program that runs in a command window on any Windows or Linux server sharing the same subnet as the Media Manager. It doesn't require WAS or any data store but runs with a separately installed IBM Java Virtual Machine (JVM).

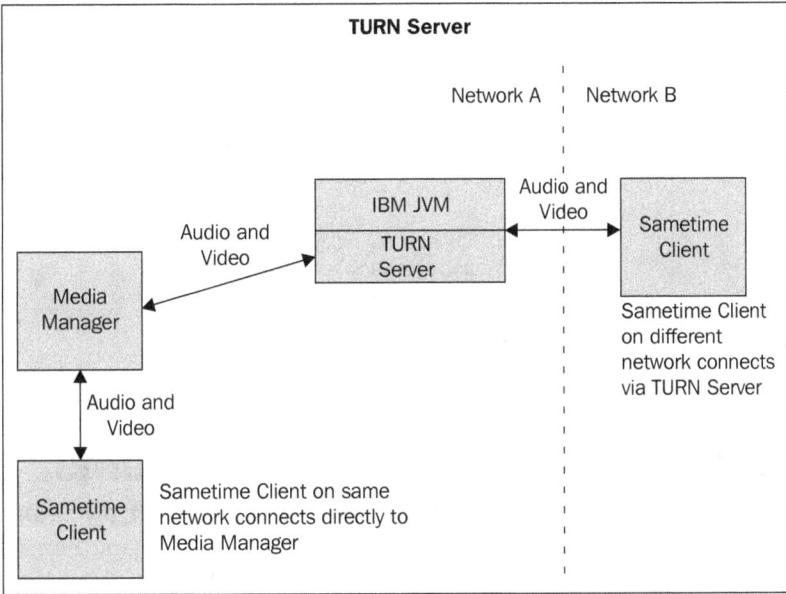

Sametime Bandwidth Manager

The Sametime Bandwidth Manager is a new optional WAS-based component that is designed to help Sametime administrators manage the traffic generated by the Media Manager and its audio and video services. Within the Bandwidth Manager configuration, an administrator can create sites, links, and call-rate policies that define the service provided by the Media Manager. The Bandwidth Manager analyzes its rules when a new call is initiated and instructs the Media Manager on how to service that call.

Among the extremely granular levels of customization available are options for sites to have link rules that constrain the traffic between them. You can also create specific policies that specify the services available to named users or groups during peak and off-peak periods. Depending upon network load, user identity, and call participation, the Bandwidth Manager can be configured to control the bandwidth. It can do this by reducing the audio to a lower codec, reducing the video frame rate, or even denying video completely, informing the user that they should retry at a later time.

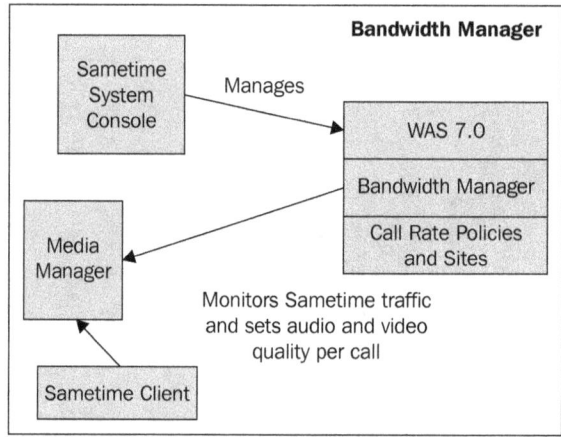

Sametime server system requirements

When planning or migrating to a Sametime environment, as with any other new software or hardware implementation, it is always prudent to plan, plan, and plan! Review the most current release notes for any changes with careful consideration of operating system, disk space requirements, and Sametime or Domino software requirements.

As with other software in the IBM Lotus family of products, the Sametime software and server components will run on different operating systems. For instance, if you have expertise in Linux, you will be happy to find that Sametime 8.5.2 runs on Linux. But if your organization or architecture requires that you run the software on Windows or AIX, then you have the ability to run Sametime on those operating systems as well. The following table provides an overview of the operating systems supported by Sametime 8.5.2 Standard and those components that will run on the specific operating systems:

Operating system	Sametime 8.5.2 Standard server component	Additional information
AIX: **5.3 TL10 POWER System i/p 64-bit or 6.1 TL3 POWER System i/p 64-bit**	Classic Meeting Server; Community Server; Gateway Server; Meeting Server; Proxy Server; System Console Server	Requires 32-bit Domino
Linux: **Red Hat Enterprise Linux (RHEL) 5.0 Update 4 Advanced Platform x86-32 or x86-64 or SUSE Linux Enterprise Server (SLES) 10.0 SP1 or 11.0, x86-32 or x86-64**	Classic Meeting Server; Community Server; Gateway Server; TURN Server; Bandwidth Manager Server; Media Manager Server; Meeting Server; Proxy Server; System Console Server	Requires 32-bit Domino
Solaris: **10 SPARC 64-bit**	Classic Meeting Server; Community Server; Gateway Server; Meeting Server; Proxy Server; System Console Server	Requires 32-bit Domino
SYSTEM i: **i 5.4 IBM POWER 64-bit or i 6.1 IBM POWER 64-bit or i 7.1 IBM POWER 64-bit**	Classic Meeting Server; Community Server; Gateway Server; Meeting Server; Proxy Server; System Console Server	

Operating system	Sametime 8.5.2 Standard server component	Additional information
SYSTEM z: **(Sametime 8.5.1)**	Community Server; Meeting Server; Proxy Server; System Console Server (Sametime 8.5.1 components)	Requires 64-bit Domino Requires 64-bit Red Hat Enterprise Linux Server 5.0 (RHEL) Advanced Platform or SUSE Linux Enterprise Server (SLES) 10.0 SP1 System z
Windows 2003 SP1 /Windows 2003 R2 Enterprise Edition x86-32 or Standard Edition x86-32	Classic Meeting Server; Community Server; TURN Server; Bandwidth Manager Server; Gateway Server; Media Manager Server; Meeting Server; Proxy Server; System Console Server	For IPv6 support, both IPv4 and IPv6 stacks must be enabled
Windows 2003 / Windows 2003 R2 Enterprise Edition x86-64 or Standard Edition x86-64	Classic Meeting Server; Community Server; TURN Server; Bandwidth Manager Server; Gateway Server; Media Manager Server; Meeting Server; Proxy Server; System Console Server	For IPv6 support, both IPv4 and IPv6 stacks must be enabled
Windows 2008 Enterprise Edition x86-32 or Standard Edition x86-32	Classic Meeting Server; Community Server; TURN Server; Bandwidth Manager Server; Gateway Server; Media Manager Server; Meeting Server; Proxy Server; System Console Server	

Operating system	Sametime 8.5.2 Standard server component	Additional information
Windows 2008 / Windows 2008 R2 Enterprise Edition x86-64 or Standard Edition x86-64	Classic Meeting Server; Community Server; TURN Server; Bandwidth Manager Server; Gateway Server; Media Manager Server; Meeting Server; Proxy Server; System Console Server	Requires 32-bit Domino

Additional information about System i requirements can be found at given website: `https://www.ibm.com/support/docview.wss?rs=203&uid=swg21092193`.

The following table summarizes the disk space requirements for the various Sametime 8.5.2 Standard server components. Note that these are only minimum recommendations; you should plan to allow for additional space for growth and any future server upgrades.

Operating system	Sametime 8.5.2 Standard server component	Disk space requirements
AIX	Classic Meeting Server	2 GB minimum
	Community Server	2 GB minimum
	Gateway Server; Meeting Server; Proxy Server; System Console Server	9 GB configurable space, plus 1 GB available in /tmp
Linux	Classic Meeting Server; Community Server	2 GB minimum
	TURN Server; Bandwidth Manager Server; Gateway Server; Media Manager Server; Meeting Server; Proxy Server; System Console Server	9 GB configurable space, plus 1 GB available in /tmp

Operating system	Sametime 8.5.2 Standard server component	Disk space requirements
Solaris	Classic Meeting Server; Community Server	2 GB minimum
	Gateway Server; Meeting Server; Proxy Server; System Console Server	9 GB configurable space, plus 1 GB available in /tmp
SYSTEM i	Classic Meeting Server; Community Server	2GB minimum for each Sametime server; minimum of 4 Disk Drives (arms)
	Gateway Server; Meeting Server; Proxy Server; System Console Server	5 GB free space (3 GB minimum) with a minimum of 6 disk drives with a caching disk controller
SYSTEM z (Sametime 8.5.1)	Community Server	10 GB minimum
	Meeting Server	2.5 GB configurable space, plus 2 GB available in /home, and 1 GB available in /tmp
	Proxy Server	9 GB configurable space, plus 1 GB available in /tmp space
	System Console Server	2.5 GB configurable space, plus 2 GB available in /home, and 1 GB available in /tmp
Windows	Classic Meeting Server, Community Server	2 GB minimum
	TURN Server; Bandwidth Manager Server; Gateway Server; Media Manager Server; Meeting Server; Proxy Server; System Console Server	8.5 GB configurable space, plus 1.5 GB available in %TEMP%

The following table gives minimum memory recommendations. It may be easier to include additional memory in a new server purchase rather than justify additional memory later. So, plan accordingly!

Operating system	Minimum memory (RAM) recommended
AIX	4GB physical memory (RAM) minimum per server component
Linux	
Solaris	
Windows	
SYSTEM i	6 GB physical memory (RAM) minimum for Gateway, System Console Server, Meeting Server and Proxy Server; 4 GB physical memory (RAM) minimum for Community Server and Classic Meeting Server plus 1 GB for each additional Sametime and Domino server

Finally, Sametime 8.5.2 requires DB2 database software and the integration of Sametime with an LDAP server. DB2 software is included as part of the Sametime package. Refer to the release notes for details about specific system requirements, compatibility with LDAP servers, or any other unique requirements you may have for your environment.

Sametime 8.5.2 clients: Something for everyone!

We have discussed many of the nuances of Sametime 8.5.2 servers. Let us now turn our attention to Sametime clients. Sametime 8.5.2 offers not only server architecture flexibility but many client options as well. Companies and organizations can pick and choose how they deploy and provide Sametime services for their users.

Let us start with the Sametime Connect Client. This is the primary Sametime client. If you are already a user of Sametime software, then you may be most familiar with this client. In Sametime 8.5.2, if your environment includes a Meeting Server, then your users will see a new Sametime Meetings section in their client view.

Lotus Notes 8.5.x users with the embedded Sametime client will see it as well. Refer to the **Sametime Meetings** area in the following screenshot:

If you click on the meeting icon, then a new dialog box appears that shows several options for what will be displayed in the **Sametime Meetings** area. **Scheduled Meetings** displays all meeting events, and you can click on the item to quickly join the meeting.

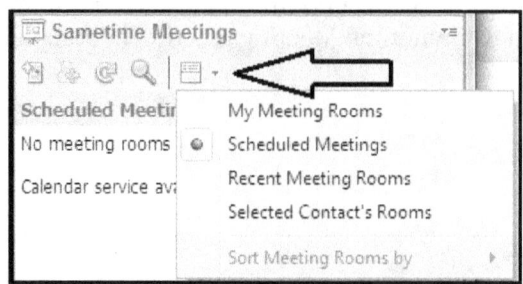

To set preferences for meeting room servers, a new section has been added to the preference list. **Sametime Meeting Rooms** allows users to create profiles for each meeting room server community to which they belong.

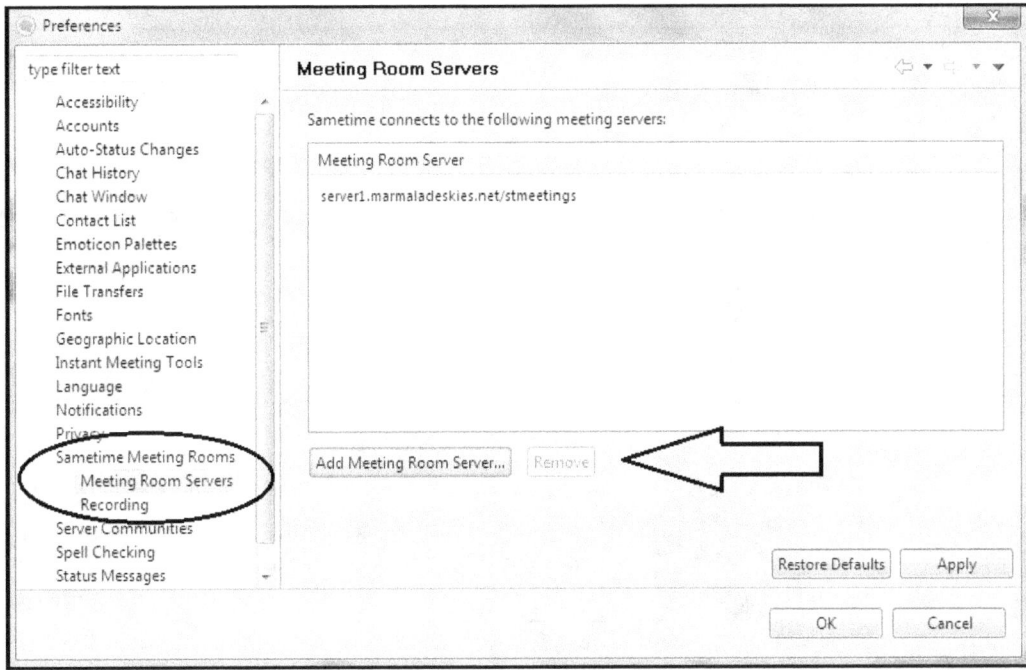

Meetings can also be accessed directly from the new Sametime meeting shelf. In Sametime 8.5.2, meetings are now "virtual conference rooms" in that the meetings are persistent and users will not have to schedule them each time they need to meet online.

The best meeting experience is from the rich meeting client that users simply either access through the Sametime Connect client or the embedded Sametime client by clicking on **Enter Room**. Some new meeting features include:

- The ability to add or invite additional attendees to the meeting, by simply dragging their name from their Sametime Contact list into the meeting room
- Customization of the meeting room layout by dragging areas and resizing
- Photos of participants can be included, and audio and video integration is much simpler to use than in previous versions of Sametime

- Client-side recording of meeting

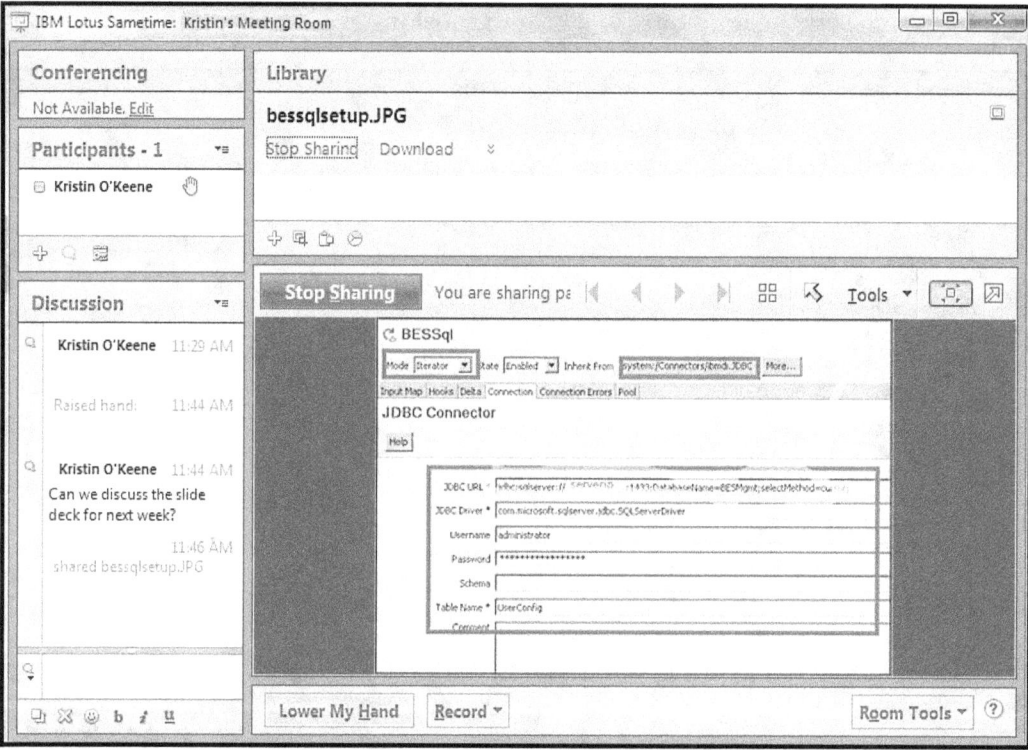

Meeting rooms can also be accessed from a web view which is hosted by the Meeting Server's HTTP proxy. The new web meeting view has a similar appearance to that in the rich meeting room client. However, users cannot modify the screen layout dynamically and there are a reduced set of features. If a user is on the Proxy client, then they will automatically be directed into the browser interface for their meeting as the Proxy client has no rich meeting client available to it. Whichever meeting client you use, you and your users will notice how quickly the meeting rooms load in the browser. In previous versions of Sametime, a Java applet was required to load first. This was sometimes difficult to implement especially when users did not have administrative access to their workstations or were working from kiosks. With the Ajax underpinnings of the new web interface, this is no longer an issue. And meetings are easier to join—with just a single click.

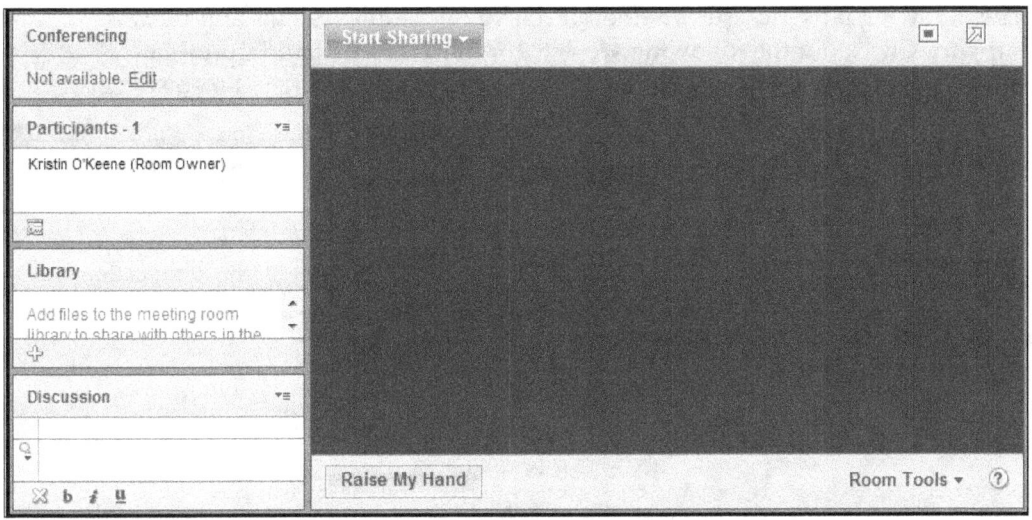

Sametime 8.5.2 introduced a new client—a lightweight browser-based client that can also be used by smartphone clients such as iPhone, iPads, and Android devices. These new Sametime clients include functions such as awareness, online status, business cards, and group messaging.

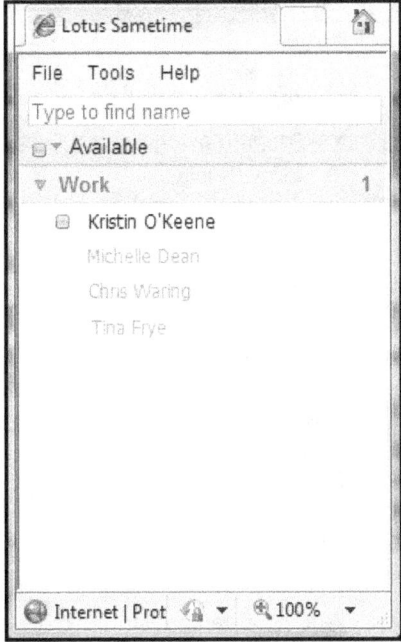

The following table describes Sametime client operating systems and browser support. Check out the following website for more detailed and up-to-date information: `https://www.ibm.com/support/docview.wss?uid=swg27016451`.

Client	Operating system	Operating system releases and browsers supported
Sametime Connect	Windows	Microsoft Windows XP Pro SP2 or later;
		Microsoft Windows XP Pro 64-bit (32-bit certification only);
		Microsoft Windows Vista Business 32-bit (note "Aero" GUI support for all Vista versions);
		Microsoft Windows Vista Business 64-bit;
		Microsoft Windows Vista Enterprise;
		Microsoft Windows XP Tablet PC Edition;
		Meeting Playback: VideoLan Client (VLC) Media player;
		Note: 2 GB physical memory (RAM) recommended, 1GB minimum
Lotus Notes embedded client	Windows	IBM Lotus Notes 8.5.1 FP1 standard (with Sametime 8.5 client upgrade installed);
		Sametime 8.5 supports Meetings calendar integration through Notes 8.5.1 FP1 standard
Web browser	Windows	Mozilla Firefox 2.0 on Microsoft Windows XP Pro, Red Hat Enterprise Linux (RHEL) 5.2, and SUSE Linux Enterprise Desktop (SLED) 10 SP2;
		Mozilla Firefox 3.0 on Microsoft Windows XP Pro and Windows Vista;
		Microsoft Internet Explorer 6.0 on Microsoft Windows XP Pro;
		Microsoft Internet Explorer 7.0 on Microsoft Windows XP Pro, Microsoft Windows Vista, and Microsoft Windows XP Tablet PC;
		Microsoft Internet Explorer 8.0 on Microsoft Windows XP Pro, Microsoft Windows Vista, and Microsoft Windows XP Tablet PC;
		Web client JDK/SDK;
		IBM or Sun JRE 1.5, and 1.6 for Web Conferencing;
		IBM or Sun JRE 1.5 and 1.6 for STLinks API applications;
		Audio/video not supported except in Classic Meetings

Client	Operating system	Operating system releases and browsers supported
	Linux	Mozilla Firefox 2.0 on Red Hat Enterprise Linux (RHEL) 5.2, and SUSE Linux Enterprise Desktop (SLED) 10 SP2;
		Mozilla Firefox 3.0 on Red Hat Enterprise Linux (RHEL) 5.2. Note: Mozilla Firefox 3.0 is not supported on SUSE Linux Enterprise Desktop (SLED) 10 SP2 since the operating system patch is required to run it.;
		Audio/video not supported
	Mac	Apple—Safari 3.2 and 4.0.x on Mac OSX 10.5.x;
		Mozilla Firefox 3.0 on Mac OSX 10.5.x;
		Web client JDK/SDK;
		IBM or Sun JRE 1.5 for Web Conferencing;
		IBM or Sun JRE 1.5 and 1.6 for STLinks API applications;
		Audio/video not supported
Mobile	Windows	Microsoft Windows Mobile 2003 SE Pocket PC;
		Microsoft Windows Mobile 5 PocketPC/Smartphone;
		Microsoft Windows Mobile 6 and 6.1 Standard/ Professional
	Nokia	ESeries
	iPhone	Apple iPhone first generation 3G, 3GS (2.x or higher OS versions) and all supported Apple—Safari browser versions;
		Apple iPod Touch first and second generations with all supported Apple—Safari browser versions
	Android	OS2 and higher
	RIM Blackberry	7100, 8100, 8700, 8300, 8800, 9000, 9530
	Sony Ericsson	M600i, P990i, P1i

The Sametime system offerings

Sametime is not a "one size fits all" offering. You have the power to decide what level of Sametime you would like to license and install based on the feature level that makes sense for your organization. There are four levels of Sametime available: Entry, Standard, Advanced, and Unified Telephony. Each subsequent level adds features to the previous level and determines what options you will have at your disposal.

Sametime Entry: Sametime Entry is the "get your feet wet" version of Sametime. As its name suggests, it provides a basic set of options which include: instant messaging, online awareness, geographic information, screen capture, and Microsoft product integration.

Sametime Standard: Sametime Standard takes instant messaging to the next level by building on the Sametime Entry features to include: file transfers, screen captures, alerts, voice and video chats, web conferencing with video and/or audio as well as screen sharing and chat over VoIP networks; integration with public IM systems such as AOL and Google through the Sametime Gateway system. Some integrated telephony voice options are available with third-party vendor support such as "click to call" and call management. Users can communicate with their Sametime contacts with mobile devices such as Blackberries, iPhones, iPads, Android, and Windows Mobile phones.

Sametime Advanced: Sametime Advanced adds the additional functionality of social networking features in your instant messaging client. Sametime Advanced offers a persistent chat room service, broadcast chat messages, the ability to set up instant surveys, screen sharing, and remote machine control all from within the Sametime client. In addition, in many ways the social networking features of Sametime Advanced act as a real-time complement to those of IBM Connections. Sametime Advanced provides the ability to build communities people can subscribe to, enabling them to share their knowledge amongst a group of like users and send out questions and discussions to those community users in real time.

Sametime Unified Telephony: Sametime Unified Telephony adds "unified communication" functionality. Many organizations are seeking to integrate chat, email, and office applications, with what has typically been only phone-based functionality such as voice mail, call routing, and caller presence. Sametime Unified Telephony adds those features to the Sametime product set.

Feature	Sametime Entry	Sametime Standard	Sametime Advanced	Sametime Unified Telephony
Instant messaging	●	●	●	
Presence awareness	●	●	●	
Persistent group chat			●	
Broadcast			●	
Instant screen sharing			●	
Microsoft Office/Outlook integration	●	●	●	

Feature	Sametime Entry	Sametime Standard	Sametime Advanced	Sametime Unified Telephony
Web conferencing		●	●	
VoIP chat		●	●	●
Video		●	●	●
Support for mobile devices		●	●	●
Interoperability with supported public IM networks		●	●	
Softphone				●
Click to call/conference				●

A more complete list of available options for each Sametime offering can be found at `http://www.ibm.com/software/lotus/products/sametime/versioncompare/`.

Sametime also has the ability to connect with external instant messaging communities through the Sametime Gateway. The Sametime Gateway is an additional server that communicates between your Sametime environment and other messaging environments such as AOL Instant Messenger, Google Talk, and other communities that use the XMPP protocol.

For more information on Sametime Gateway, please review `http://publib.boulder.ibm.com/infocenter/sametime/v8r5/index.jsp?topic=/com.ibm.help.sametime.v85.doc/overview/over_server_gw.html`.

Understanding Sametime licensing

You may be ready to implement or upgrade Sametime. What software licenses are required? Both Sametime Entry and Sametime Standard are at, as of the time of publication, version 8.5.2. Licensing is required for the Sametime server only.

What about Sametime Entry? Perhaps your organization or company only wants to implement instant messaging. Sametime Entry would be a good solution for you. Sametime Entry requires the Community Server component only. To determine what you require for hardware or operating system requirements, review the tables earlier in the chapter for the specific requirements for a Community Server and the operating systems that will support it. Sametime Entry will support connectivity for the Sametime Connect Client, the embedded Lotus Notes client (Lotus Notes 8.5.1 FP2 at a minimum is required) or a Microsoft Outlook enabled client.

Sametime Advanced requires the installation of additional software applications and is currently at version 8.5.2. These additional applications include an LDAP directory, DB2, WebSphere MQ, and WebSphere Event Broker. Licensing Sametime Advanced grants you the license to run DB2 and the WebSphere components.

Sametime Unified Telephony also requires separate licensing and software, and is currently at version 8.5.2. In addition to the Sametime server software, the Telephony Control Server and Telephony Application Server must be installed. This bundles together and installs Tivoli System Automation for multi-platforms, Telephony Application Server Framework, WebSphere Application Server, and Tivoli Directory Integrator. The Sametime Unified Telephony license grants you the authority to run these additional software tools in the bundle.

Why install or upgrade to Sametime 8.5.2?

Should you install or upgrade to Sametime 8.5.2? You or your organization may be reviewing options for a new instant messaging and/or web conferencing system. Perhaps you are considering whether or not to upgrade your existing Sametime servers that are currently meeting your requirements. In either case, there are several key points to consider.

First, if you already have a Sametime environment you should be aware that Sametime 7.5.x is being moved to end-of-life status by IBM in September 2011. What does this actually mean for you? If you are running Sametime 7.5.x or earlier, then you can continue to do so. However, after end-of-life you will no longer be able to get support or fixes for it if you have problems.

In addition, if you are upgrading your Domino environment to the 8.5.x versions, then you will also need to upgrade your Sametime server to 8.5.2 as this is the only version fully supported by IBM on Domino 8.5.x.

Flexibility

Unlike previous versions, Sametime 8.5.2 has been designed to run as separate server components that integrate together. Although the Instant Messaging component remains as a task running under Domino, the other server elements are applications managed by WAS.

WAS is IBM's application management server environment. Deployment, security, clustering, performance management, and availability are part of the benefit of WAS, so applications running under the control of WAS are able to leverage these for their own services. A single WAS server can, and usually does, run several different applications in their own discrete and isolated logical space.

Multiple instances of Sametime Meeting Server or Sametime Proxy Server can be clustered by WAS. The configuration of the servers as well as their running state will be maintained and managed by WebSphere's Network Deployment Manager. Network Deployment Manager is a specific WAS server that manages clusters of servers deployed on secondary hardware. In this way, if one Meeting Server is unavailable, another will take over and provide the same service.

The following Sametime 8.5.2 servers and services run under WAS:

- Sametime Meeting Server
- Sametime Meeting HTTP Proxy
- Sametime System Console
- Sametime Proxy Server
- Sametime Media Manager

You also have the Instant Messaging component running under Domino. To further increase Instant Messaging capacity per server, we can move the Multiplexor service from the Domino server onto its own hardware. The Multiplexor (or MUX) is responsible for connecting client requests to the Sametime Community Server and usually runs alongside the other Sametime Community services. However, the MUX can be moved to separate hardware and doing so will increase the capacity of a single Sametime Community Server tenfold. This is possible because the MUX will maintain a single network connection between it and the Sametime Community Server instead of allowing every client to connect on its own network connection to the Sametime Community Server directly. Using multiple MUX services is a method for improving the reliability and performance of your instant messaging environment.

If you are interested in clustering your instant messaging services, then, as in previous versions, Sametime Community Server can leverage Domino's clustering capabilities to provision its own Instant Messaging cluster, which will support both load balancing and failover.

When designing your Sametime infrastructure, it is entirely up to you how many servers you want to have running the applications and features you need. What follows are some examples of server implementations so you can see how flexible the Sametime server architecture can be.

Example: Instant Messaging only with multiple servers

If your company is interested primarily in instant messaging, then you can deploy Sametime 8.5.2 with only that service. The Instant Messaging infrastructure and deployment in 8.5.2 is very similar to earlier versions of Sametime as it runs on a supported Domino server platform.

In the following example, we have deployed two separate Sametime 8.5.2 Instant Messaging servers, each of which is providing instant messaging services to users in its own region. Both servers in the screenshot are in a shared Sametime Community so users on either server can see each other.

As you will see, only two servers are in use in the following diagram, and there is no failover:

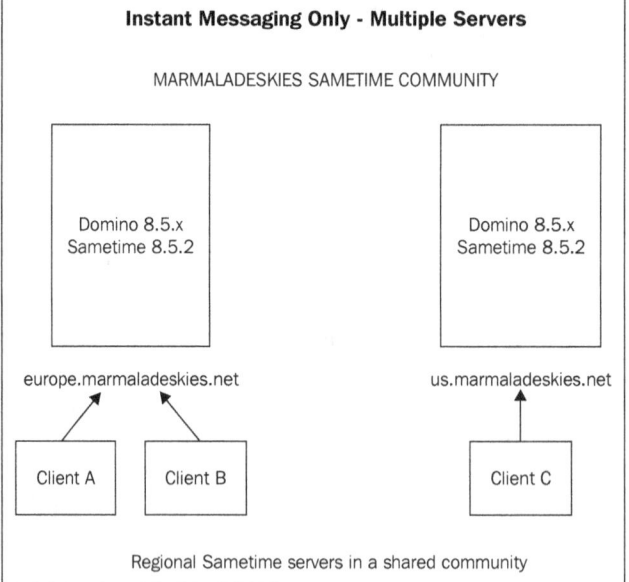

Example: A pilot install

This is the design of the default pilot install of all Sametime 8.5.2 elements as per IBM's documentation. It requires only two servers, one as a platform for Domino and one as a platform for WebSphere. The WebSphere elements, which are all installed onto a single server, require significant combined resources to run concurrently. This configuration is recommended for pilot and test deployments only, and should not be used for production environments.

There is no failover in this design and only two servers. Although the Instant Messaging elements can be expanded with additional servers, the Meeting, Media, and Proxy servers would need to be rebuilt to increase resources.

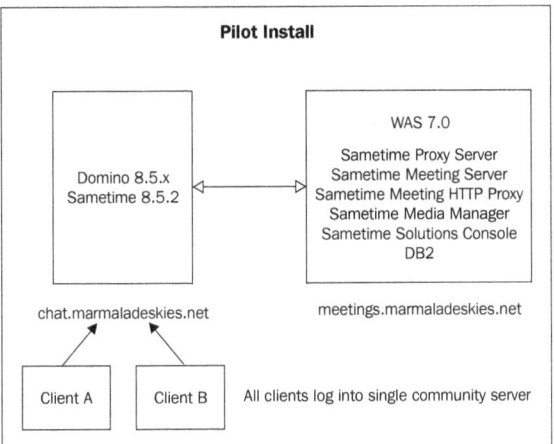

Example: A small install with room for future growth

In this design, the Meeting, Proxy, and Media Manager Servers are installed each on their own hardware. With this scenario, there is the option in the future of introducing additional Proxy and Meeting Servers into the cluster to provide failover services. The Media Manager can now be clustered.

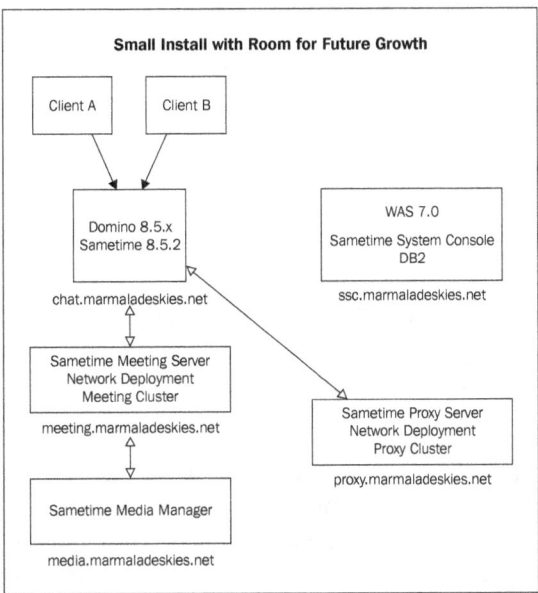

Example: A clustered install with multiple failover

A clustered install with a provision for multiple failover would be an example of the basis for an enterprise-level design. Each component has been installed, where possible, with a cluster mate to provide failover capabilities. As we mentioned previously, the only servers that cannot be clustered are the Media Manager and the SSC itself.

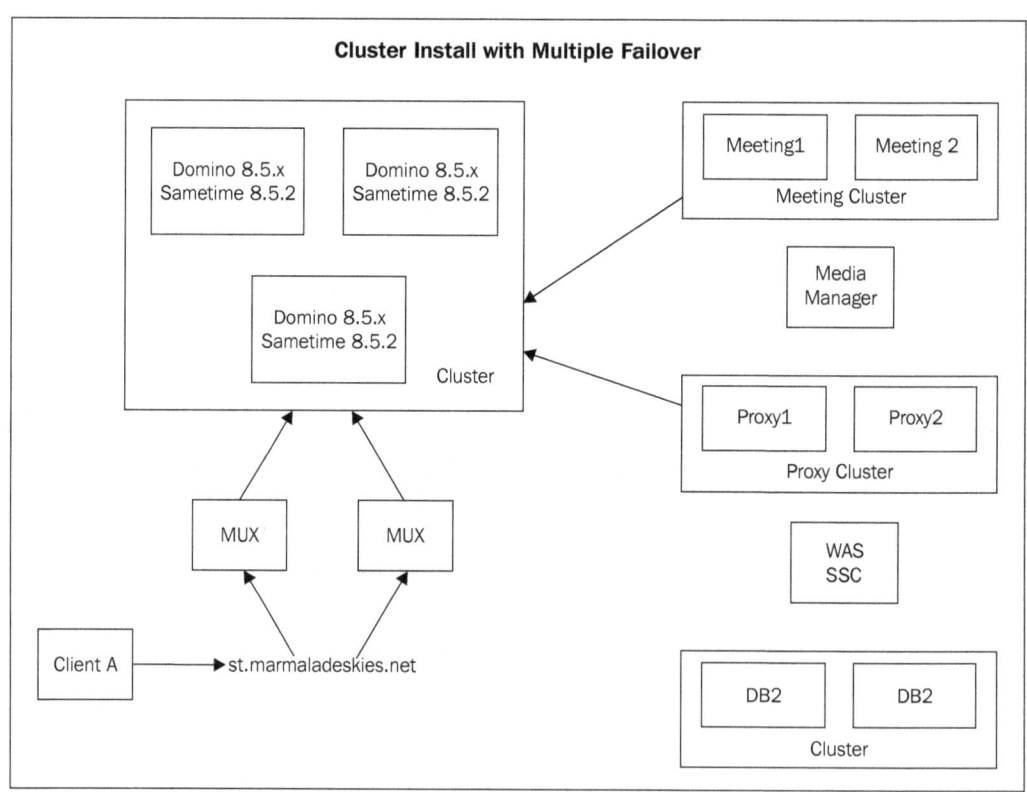

Features

What specific features of Sametime should you consider as targeted reasons for an upgrade or install? As we have already described briefly, the re-design of the Sametime infrastructure in 8.5.2 has also provided the following significant feature enhancements across the board.

- **New Lightweight Client**: The Sametime Proxy Server introduces a new browser-based Sametime client. This client requires nothing more than a supported browser to provide a fast and customizable instant messaging and meeting experience. There is nothing for the user to download or install.

- **Persistent Meetings**: The new Sametime Meeting Server creates meeting places that are persistent with no start and end time and no duration. These persistent meetings places can be re-used repeatedly. For example, you may create a meeting place for a project you are working in, and have weekly reviews of that project in the same place each week. The Meeting Server tracks activity that happened each time in each meeting place allowing you to review previous activity.

- **Improved Audio and Video**: The audio and video services have been separated from the Meeting Server and now run under the management of the Media Manager. The Media Manager supplies audio and video services both to the Sametime clients and to the Meeting Server itself for web conferences. The Media Manager provides audio and video functionality for both person-to-person and multi-way calls. The addition of the TURN server to handle client connections on a different network also now enables the audio and video services through a firewall.

- **Performance Improvements**: The previous Sametime Meeting Center used Java applets and the T.120 protocol, both of which presented problems in deployment. Java applets have always been very slow to download and initiate on the client. Installing Java applets in modern browsers with strict security settings has become increasingly difficult. With advanced HTML5 programming, it has been possible to remove these completely. Additionally, the HTTP protocol is now utilized across the board to provide in-meeting services such as screen sharing and white boarding. The combination of the use of HTTP and HTML5 has dramatically improved performance, client load times, access through firewalls, and reduced network bandwidth consumption. In addition, the new Bandwidth Manager manages the network traffic generated by the Media Manager making it possible to constrain audio and video quality to address network limitations or bottlenecks.

- **Mobility**: There are now Sametime Instant Messaging clients available for a wide and expanding range of mobile devices including:
    - Blackberry 5.0 and 6.0 (9000 and 9350)
    - Sony Ericsson M600/P900/P1
    - Android devices running OS 2.0 and higher
    - Devices running Windows Mobile 5, 6, and 6.5
    - iPhone and iPad OS3 and OS4 use the lightweight browser client, which will also work for many other mobile devices with advanced browsers

- **Telephony**: Sametime 8.5.2 with the new Media Manager can support point-to-point as well as multi-point voice and video calls between Sametime clients and in meetings. It uses the SIP protocol and standard voice and video codecs so it easily integrates with other voice or video systems supporting up to 20 participants in a single meeting.

- We will talk more in a later chapter about Sametime Unified Telephony, which is a separately licensed product from IBM that integrates with your instant messaging and web conferencing environment.

Integration

Sametime and the use of instant messaging are central to many other Lotus products you may already have or are deploying. The Sametime embedded client ships and installs with Lotus Notes and is also available through a browser interface. Sametime functionality such as chatting and online awareness can also be integrated with Microsoft Office products, including Microsoft Outlook.

Frequently, when we talk about Sametime integration we are usually talking presence awareness. Presence awareness is the ability to see if someone is online and if they are, to initiate a chat. In the Sametime embedded client used with Lotus Notes, awareness icons appear in not only in the Sametime sidebar, but also in the mail inbox. Users can click to chat from the inbox, as shown in the following screenshot:

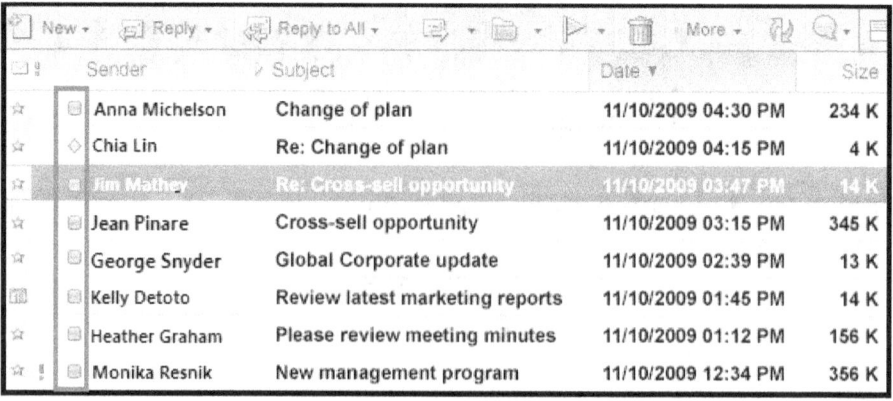

A unified icon set is used across all clients, so for example in iNotes, you will see the familiar online status icon.

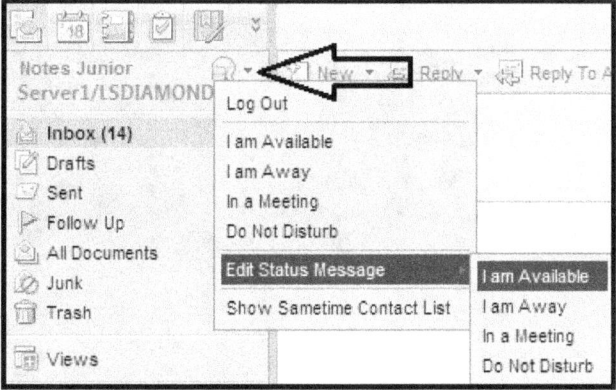

There is Sametime integration in IBM Connections, Lotus Quickr, and virtually every other collaborative solution IBM delivers. Additionally, it is very simple to add Sametime awareness to any web application regardless of the hosting platform. With all of these potential interfaces, consider how "connected in real time" you and your organization might be!

Summary

In this chapter, you learned about the new features of Sametime 8.5.2, both for the server and for the client. You learned about the Sametime 8.5.2 server architecture and how it differs from prior versions. You found what requirements exist for operating systems and hardware configurations, as well as the licensing involved. You saw some sample Sametime system configurations and how each one might work for a particular situation. Finally, you learned the reasons why upgrading to Sametime 8.5.2 is a good idea. In the next chapter you will learn about each of the servers that comprise a Sametime environment, their requirements for server and operating systems, and how they interact with each other.

2
The Sametime 8.5.2 Servers—Up Close and Personal

In versions of Sametime prior to 8.5.2, it was relatively simple to install the Sametime server software. It was a single package that installed quickly, often on top of an IBM Lotus Domino server, and the Domino administrator could easily manage Sametime in addition to their other duties. But with Sametime 8.5.2, the environment has changed significantly. There are now eight different servers that make up a full Sametime 8.5.2 installation and the skills required to install and administer those servers are much more complex.

This chapter will introduce each of the Sametime servers. You will learn the purpose of each server, the operating system(s) on which each can run, how they interact with each other, and the requirements for each server type.

In this chapter, you will learn about:

- Sametime Community Server
- Sametime Systems Console Server
- Sametime Classic Meeting Server
- Sametime Meeting Server
- Sametime Proxy Server
- Sametime Media Manager Server
- Sametime TURN Server
- Sametime Bandwidth Manager Server

Sametime Community Server

The Sametime Community Server is what existing Sametime customers would think of as the "original" Sametime server. In the new 8.5.2 design, the role of the original Sametime server is only partially implemented in the Community Server. Its new role is to provide instant messaging and awareness services, as well as acting as the central point for integration between the Sametime clients and other services on other servers, such as the Meeting and Media Servers.

The online awareness functionality found in products such as Lotus Notes and Microsoft Outlook is provided by the Sametime Community Server, as is the service known as **Sametime Links** (**STLinks**), which is integrated into the Lotus iNotes web-based e-mail client. The Community Server stores the Sametime client user preference settings, presence settings, and privacy settings.

The Sametime Community Server can only be deployed as an add-in task running under an IBM Lotus Domino server and is the only Sametime 8.5.2 component that does not require an installation of IBM WebSphere Application Server (WAS). The Sametime Community Server can be configured to connect to Lightweight Directory Access Protocol (LDAP) for authentication and directory lookup services. This is important if you plan to connect the Community Server to other Sametime server components.

Sametime Community Server by itself provides all the instant messaging and awareness features available within the Sametime clients and the Sametime Meeting Server. These include one-to-one and n-way rich text chats and online privacy settings. The existing meeting services code now known as the "Classic" meeting center is retained in its original form to support companies as they migrate and upgrade, but is not utilized in a full Sametime 8.5.2 deployment.

Installation requirements

Sametime 8.5.2 Community Server installs on top of IBM Lotus Domino. The following versions of Domino, including their patches and fixpacks, are supported for Sametime Community Server:

- Domino 8.0
- Domino 8.5
- Domino 8.5.1
- Domino 8.5.2

If you are installing the Community Server in a brand new environment, you should consider installing the most recent version of Domino. As Sametime is updated, it may no longer support older versions of Domino.

As Sametime 8.5.2 is a 32-bit application, it cannot be installed on top of Domino running as a 64-bit application. However, it can be installed on top of Domino running as a 32-bit application on a 64-bit operating system; so a 32-bit version of Domino with Sametime installed can be run on Windows 2008 64-bit OS. Only zLinux 64 supports and requires 64-bit Domino.

Sametime 8.5.2 Community Server, as with earlier Sametime servers, can be grouped together into a single community of servers. Servers in a community, as well as the users on those servers, can all be seen by each other. Sametime servers in a community need not be running in a Domino cluster.

Sametime 8.5.2 Community Server also supports clustering. Clustering allows multiple servers to provide load balancing and failover capabilities for instant messaging and availability services. Clustering relies on the Sametime Community Server being installed on top of a Domino server cluster and having the Sametime Community services configured for clustering themselves.

To better scale your Sametime Community Server environment, it is possible to separate out the Sametime Multiplexor service, also known as a **MUX**, which handles connection and authentication to the Community Server onto separate hardware. Separating out the multiplexor service can increase the capacity of a single Sametime Community Server by a factor of ten.

The following screenshot is an example of a Sametime Community Server:

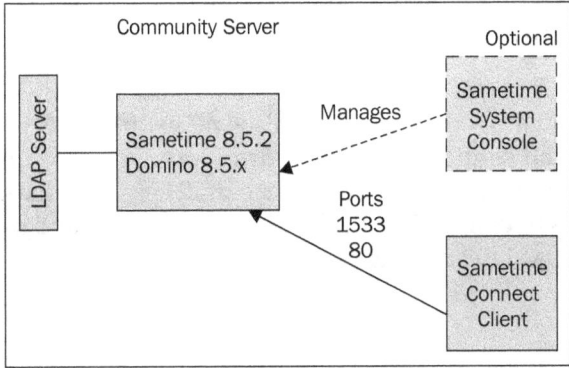

Deployment scenarios

The following are some possible ways you might deploy Sametime Community Servers:

- Jose needs to provide an Instant Messaging server to his company and it should also show an individual's status and business card information when they are online. He has no need for any other web conferencing or meeting services and chooses to deploy Sametime Community Server by itself.

- Lisette has been tasked with providing full web conferencing and meeting services to her company. She will use the Sametime Community Server to provide the functionality of in-meeting chats, showing business card information, and displaying the attendees' online status.

- Valerie wants to add a new Instant Messaging server for a new organization that her company has acquired in another country. She adds a Sametime 8.5.2 Community Server into her existing community of Sametime servers, knowing it allows her existing users on older servers to continue to work with this new site.

- Erika wants to use the online status features in Lotus iNotes and she deploys the Sametime Community Server for that functionality.

Sametime Systems Console Server

The Sametime System Console (SSC) is the administration and management tool that brings together all the other Sametime server elements into a single interface. As Sametime 8.5.2 is comprised of a series of related but independent servers, IBM has developed the SSC as the web-based server tool which can be used to manage all the Sametime servers from a single access point.

The SSC is required to be the first server installed in the Sametime 8.5.2 environment if you intend to install any other servers. This is necessary as its menus include several installation and configuration wizards to walk you through the installation of all the other Sametime 8.5.2 server components. These installation wizards also complete the process of connecting all the disparate servers and server elements, such as LDAP and IBM DB2 databases.

The SSC is an application hosted by WAS and requires a DB2 database be used to store its data. Once completed, the SSC installation inserts a menu at the bottom of the standard WAS menu for management of the Sametime 8.5.2 environment.

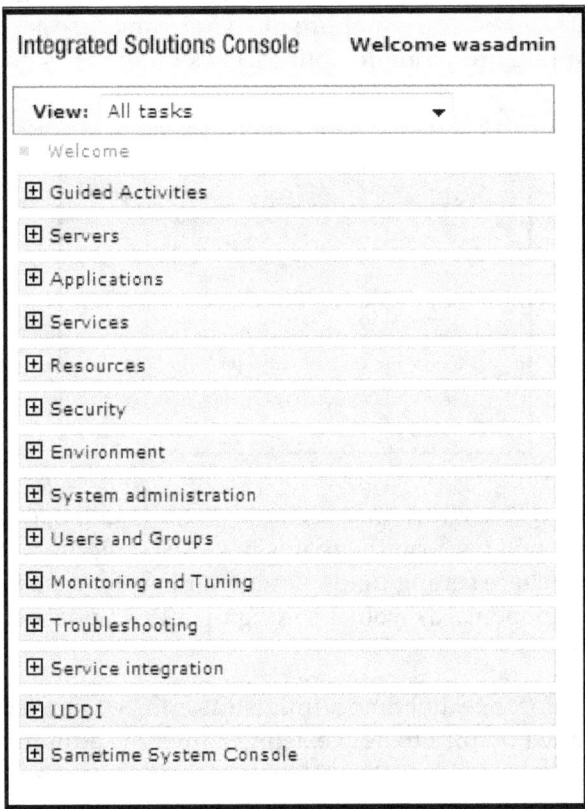

The SSC plugin menu is divided into four sections:

- Sametime Prerequisites
- Sametime Guided Activities
- Sametime Servers
- Manage Policies

Sametime Prerequisites are guided menus for you to add information about your external WAS connections required for Sametime. This includes information such as where to find and how to authenticate with LDAP and DB2 servers. Providing the information to WAS about the LDAP servers and the DB2 databases makes them available for you later when you configure the other Sametime server elements. To review the **Sametime Prerequisite** options, click on the "+" sign to expand the options.

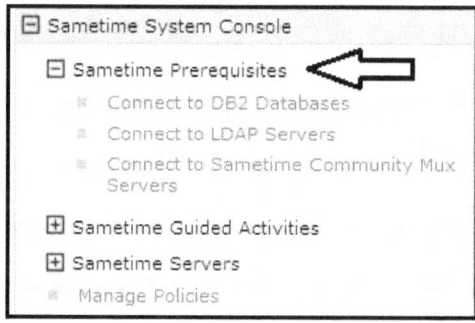

The **Sametime Guided Activities** are a series of wizards in the form of questions that, once completed, will perform the requisite WAS configuration in the background. These include setting up deployment plans for installations of other Sametime server components, as well as setting up a WebSphere cluster with your existing servers.

This avoids the need for the Sametime administrator to be knowledgeable about WAS and was designed by IBM to help existing Sametime administrators transition to the new WAS platform. Click on the "+" sign to expand the **Sametime Guided Activities** options.

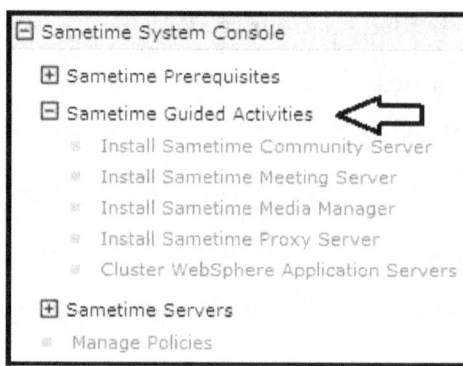

The SSC menu also contains management menus for each of the other server components including the Sametime Proxy Server, the Sametime Meeting Server, the Sametime Media Manager, and the Sametime Community Server. These settings include information on how the SSC should connect to each server, as well as the settings for various server features. Click on the "+" sign next to **Sametime Servers** to view the server listing.

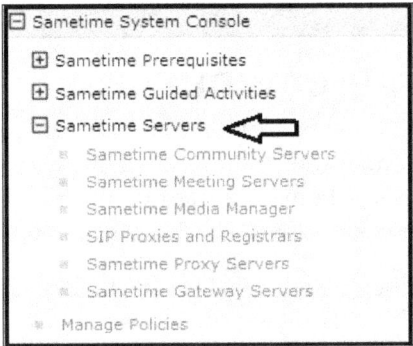

The **Manage Policies** menu helps you configure the features and restrictions that apply to selected users on each server. Policies exist on installation for both anonymous and authenticated users of the Community Server, the Meeting Server, and the Media Manager. Click on **Manage Policies** to view the options.

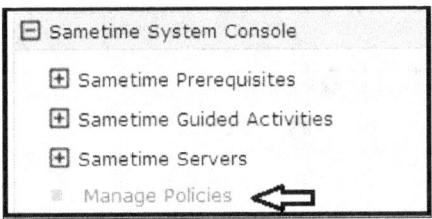

Once the Manage Policies area is expanded, you will see the tabs to modify the settings for instant messaging, meetings, and media manager policies. All these configuration settings, connection settings, and policies that apply to servers are held in the DB2 database for the SSC.

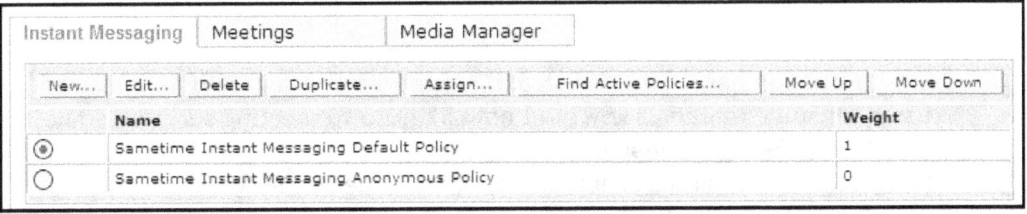

As the SSC contains all the configuration information for each of the different servers, it is also used by each server to understand how to connect to one another. For example, the information is used for connecting the Meeting Server to its corresponding Media Manager, which provides voice and video services. It is also used for connecting the Sametime Proxy Server to its Community Server or Multiplexor for instant messaging services. Because of this interdependence, it is not possible to deploy Sametime 8.5.2 as a complete solution without using the SSC.

Installation requirements

The SSC for Sametime 8.5.2 must be installed on WAS and has a DB2 server in order to store the configuration information. The DB2 server must host a dedicated database that conforms to the schema required by the SSC. This is set up as part of the installation, so this is not something you have to be concerned about configuring.

The Sametime install files include a license for IBM DB2 9.5 Limited Use, which entitles you to install a 32-bit DB2 server on either the Windows or Linux platforms for use exclusively with the Sametime server components. The Limited Use version of DB2 server cannot be installed on a 64-bit Linux operating system. The version of WAS that is supported for all the WAS related Sametime server components is 7.0.0.3. In addition, WAS iFixes are also available and periodically updated to address Sametime specific problems. WAS iFixes can be found at the IBM Fix Central website: `http://www.ibm.com/support/fixcentral/`. It is highly recommended that you should stay current with these updates.

Deployment scenarios

The following are some possible ways you might deploy the SSC:

- Georgio needs to install all the Sametime Server components to provide a full instant messaging, meeting, and web conferencing service for his company. He must install the SSC in order to manage all of the components he is about to install.

- Sheena is planning to only install the Sametime Community Server at this time, but she is considering installing the other Sametime Server components at a later date. She chooses to install the SSC and integrate the Sametime Community Server with the SSC in order to position her environment for future growth.

- Herbie already has a Sametime 8.5.2 Community Server that he has been using for some months. He would now like to add meeting services, so he installs the SSC and registers his existing Community Server with it in order to move forward with a centrally managed Sametime server environment.

Sametime Classic Meeting Server

The Sametime Classic Meeting Server is a portion of the previous Sametime server environment, which has been kept in place to provide backwards compatibility and coexistence support during a company's migration to the new Sametime 8.5.2 Meeting Server environment. Customers that have already deployed Sametime prior to version 8.5.2 will recognize this as the Meeting Server running on top of Domino that provided meeting services to Sametime clients in the past. This is now replaced by the WAS-based Meeting Server in Sametime 8.5.2 but the original Domino-based meeting services are still available for install and licensed for use. These have been renamed Sametime Classic Meeting Server to differentiate the services from those of the new Meeting Server.

The Sametime Classic Meeting Server has not changed significantly from its previous version. In fact, it has been modified very little in recent versions of Sametime. It is the original design, still heavily dependent upon Java applets and the use of older codecs and technologies. The classic meeting services continue to provide the same features as found in Sametime 8.0.2, and are fully supported by IBM as part of your Sametime deployment.

It is important to note that even if the Sametime Media Manager is installed, the audio and video services in the classic meeting center are provided by the Domino-based meeting services, and not the Media Manager itself. The new WAS-based Sametime Meeting Server uses the Media Manager for its audio and video services.

Installation requirements

Sametime 8.5.2 Classic Meeting Server can only be installed as part of a Sametime Community Server installation. The Classic Meeting Server services themselves cannot be installed in isolation. Sametime 8.5.2 Classic Meeting Server is an application that installs as part of the Sametime Standard installation on top of Domino. Sametime Entry does not install the classic meeting center services. Although Sametime Classic Meeting Server can only be installed as part of the Sametime Community Server installation, it is possible to only use the meeting center functionality on that server and have the instant messaging and awareness features provided from a separate Community Server.

Clustering for meetings on the Sametime Classic Meeting Server is only available through the Enterprise Meeting Server product. This is a WebSphere-based solution for providing clustering and load balancing of Domino-based meeting services.

The following versions of IBM Domino, including their patches and fixpacks, are supported for Sametime Classic Meeting Server:

- Domino 8.0
- Domino 8.5
- Domino 8.5.1
- Domino 8.5.2

If you are installing the Classic Meeting Server in a brand new environment, then you should consider installing the most recent version of Domino. As Sametime is updated, it may no longer support older versions of Domino.

As Sametime 8.5.2 is a 32-bit application, it cannot be installed on a Domino server running as a 64-bit application. However, it can be installed on Domino server running as a 32-bit application on a 64-bit operating system so a 32-bit version of Domino with Sametime installed can be run on Windows 2008 64-bit OS. Only zLinux 64 supports and requires 64-bit Domino.

Customization of the Sametime Meeting Center

Meeting Server settings are overall controls that apply to anyone accessing the Meeting center and the limitations in place for meeting users on that server. These include options to enable or disable services such as using whiteboards and polling. The following screenshot shows the customization features for the Classic Sametime Meeting Center. The settings here do not apply to the new WAS-based Sametime Meeting center.

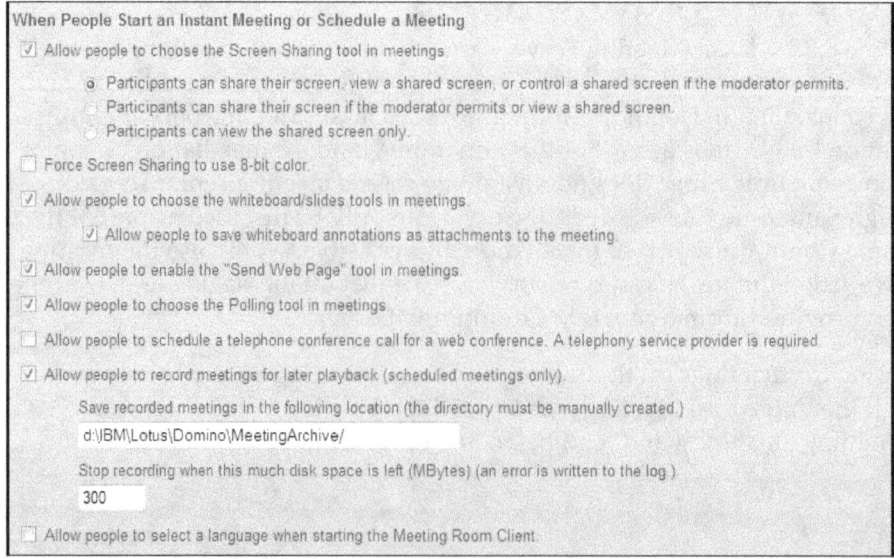

There are also Classic Meeting Server-wide settings to control the user of audio and video and to specify what codecs should be used; but these only apply to the codecs available on that server which are several years old, not to the newer codecs available on the WAS Meeting Server.

In addition to these server-wide customizations, the Sametime administrator can also apply policy settings to restrict or allow features for specific users. Policies for meetings are maintained within the SSC and there is now a specific area under Meeting Server policies that applies to the Classic Meeting Center only. Policies can be created for anonymous or authenticated users, and multiple policies with different settings can exist and be applied to different groups of users.

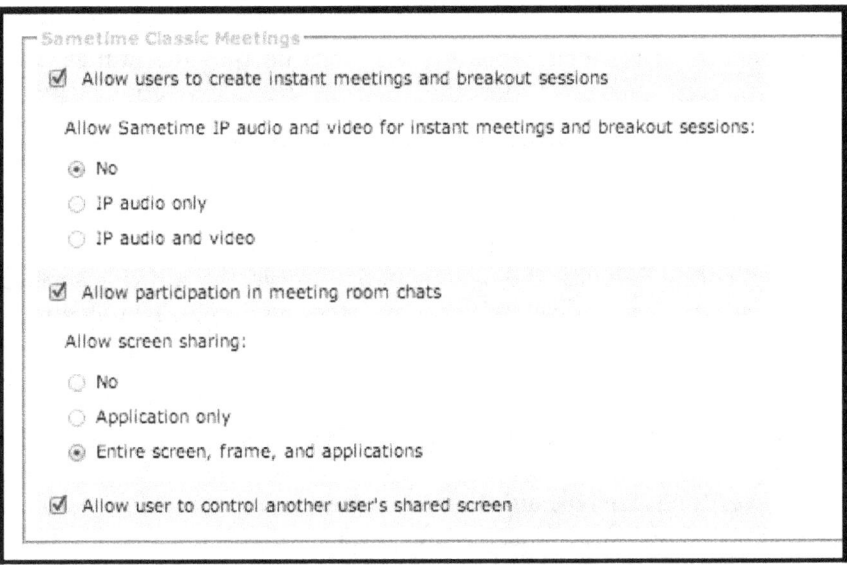

Developers also have the option of customizing the look and feel of the Meeting Center by modifying the Domino design elements such as the Meeting Center Welcome page. There is also a Sametime Software Development Kit (SDK) which can be used for developing and integrating other custom services.

Deployment scenarios

The following are some possible ways you might deploy the Sametime Classic Meeting Server:

- Sam wants to upgrade his servers to Sametime 8.5.2 but he already has numerous meetings scheduled into the future on his Sametime 7.5 meeting center. He upgrades his Community Servers to 8.5.2 and installs a new Sametime Meeting Server on WAS. He can now continue to use the Classic Meeting Server for those meetings that are already scheduled, and start to create new meetings going forward on the new WebSphere Meeting Server.

- Bettina is deploying Sametime 8.5.2 for her head office users but remote users are still on older Sametime clients, and continue to schedule meetings using their Classic Meeting Servers. All users need to attend these meetings so Bettina continues to support the use of the Classic Meeting Server until all Sametime clients at all sites are upgraded.

Sametime Meeting Server

The Sametime Meeting Server is the new Sametime server for meeting services that replaces the previous Domino-based Sametime Meeting Server. The Meeting Server itself has been entirely redesigned to be faster as well as easier to use.

Unlike the previous versions of Sametime, Meeting Server meetings are now persistent and no longer have start times or durations. A meeting exists from the moment it is created until you choose to delete it. It also tracks multiple visits and activities over time. This behavior is akin to a meeting space where attendees can visit and revisit over time to discuss and track progress on a project. This is very different than the previous behavior of meetings, which acted as calendar appointments and only existed for a specific moment in time. Once a meeting is created in Meeting Server, you can go into the meeting at any time and continue where you left off.

IBM has focused on removing many of the elements that made the previous Domino-based meeting server slow to use. This includes such things as Java applets (which have been replaced throughout) and the use of inefficient protocols such as T.120 (which has been replaced with HTTP). As well as improving performance, this aids in ensuring connectivity through a firewall.

The new Meeting Server is also enhanced by the addition of a new Meeting Center client. The dedicated rich meeting client is embedded into the Sametime Connect application or the Lotus Notes application to provide fast launching of meetings and access to all the features of the Meeting Server itself. There is also a browser client for the Meeting Center which accesses the same meetings but with more limited functionality than the rich client.

Installation requirements

The Sametime Meeting Server can only be installed from the SSC by first configuring an LDAP server, then creating and configuring a new DB2 database, and finally setting up a deployment plan to link the installation of the Meeting Server to each of those components. The DB2 database used in this installation is different than that used by the SSC, but resides on the same DB2 server. This means that prior to beginning the install of the Meeting Server, the following must be in place:

- Sametime 8.5.2 System Console
- Supported LDAP Server
- DB2 Server and dedicated Meeting database

In addition it is advisable to have at least one Sametime 8.5.2 Community Server installed and, if audio, video, or web conferencing is required, a Media Manager Server. Both of these elements can be installed after installing the Meeting Server but you may experience unexpected missing features without them.

The Sametime install files include a license for IBM DB2 9.5 Limited Use, which entitles you to install a 32-bit DB2 server on either the Windows or Linux platforms for use exclusively with the Sametime server components. It is not necessary to have a dedicated DB2 server for each Meeting server as you can use a single DB2 server as the host for all your Sametime-related databases. The Limited Use version of DB2 server cannot be installed on a 64-bit Linux operating system. The version of WAS that is supported for all the WAS-related Sametime server components is 7.0.0.3. In addition, WAS iFixes are also available and periodically updated to address Sametime specific problems and are available on the IBM Fix Central website: http://www.ibm.com/support/fixcentral/. It is highly recommended that you stay current with installing these updates.

Sametime 8.5.2 Meeting Server also supports clustering using Network Deployment for WebSphere. In a clustered Meeting Server environment, you would have multiple Meeting Servers with identical configurations. They would all use the same DB2 database or a mirrored version of it. All users attending a meeting must be using the same server. This means that clustering is only supported for disaster recovery and failover, and not for load balancing.

The following are supported LDAP servers for the Sametime Meeting Server:

- Lotus Domino 6.5.3
- Lotus Domino 7.0
- Lotus Domino 8.0
- Lotus Domino 8.5
- Lotus Domino 8.5.1
- Lotus Domino 8.5.2
- IBM Tivoli Directory Server 5.2
- IBM Tivoli Directory Server 6.0
- IBM Tivoli Directory Server 6.1
- IBM Tivoli Directory Server 6.2
- Microsoft Active Directory 2003
- Microsoft Active Directory 2008
- Microsoft Active Directory Application Mode 2003
- Novell eDirectory 8.6

An example of a Meeting Server installation follows:

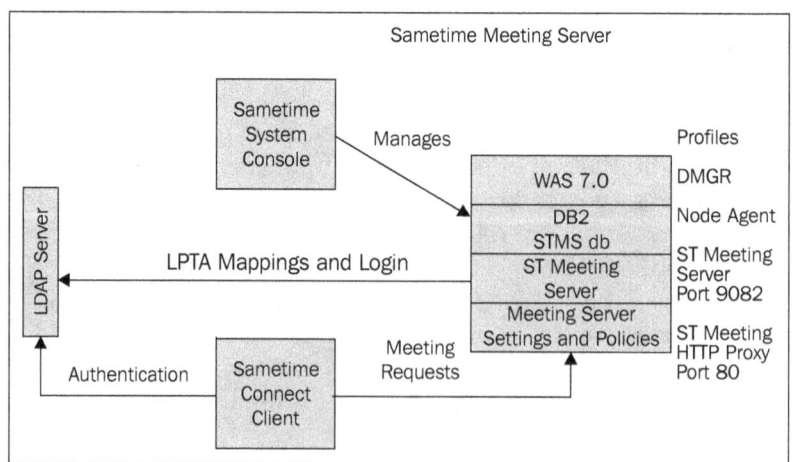

Customizing the Meeting Server

Currently, customization of the Meeting Server is available in two areas: server-wide settings and policies. Server-wide Meeting Server settings are accessed through the SSC menu.

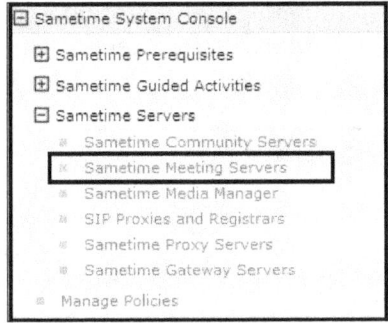

The settings here include:

- File attachment types that can be uploaded into meetings
- Requirements for passwords on all meetings
- Guest access options
- Search options
- URL for the Sametime Proxy Server that provides web browser meeting services

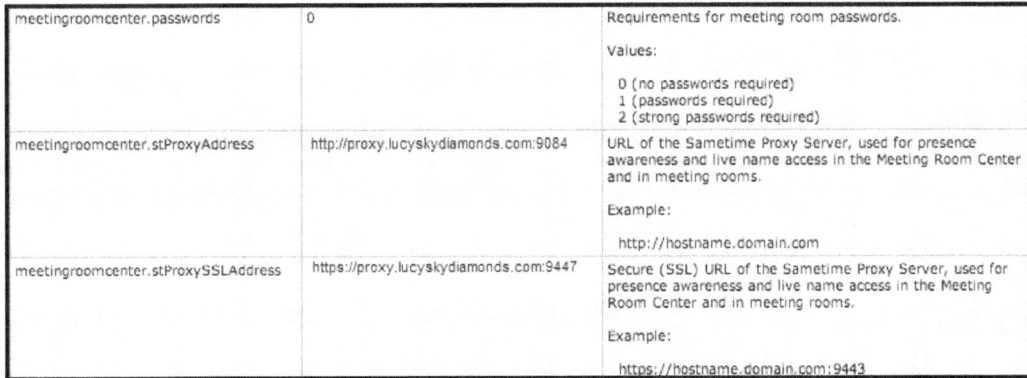

meetingroomcenter.passwords	0	Requirements for meeting room passwords. Values: 0 (no passwords required) 1 (passwords required) 2 (strong passwords required)
meetingroomcenter.stProxyAddress	http://proxy.lucyskydiamonds.com:9084	URL of the Sametime Proxy Server, used for presence awareness and live name access in the Meeting Room Center and in meeting rooms. Example: http://hostname.domain.com
meetingroomcenter.stProxySSLAddress	https://proxy.lucyskydiamonds.com:9447	Secure (SSL) URL of the Sametime Proxy Server, used for presence awareness and live name access in the Meeting Room Center and in meeting rooms. Example: https://hostname.domain.com:9443

In addition, there are policy settings that allow the Sametime administrator to customize the features available for anonymous or authenticated users.

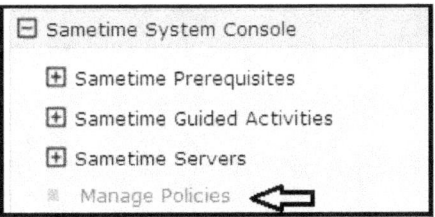

Multiple policies can exist for authenticated users and applied by name or group. Default policies for anonymous and authenticated users are created during installation.

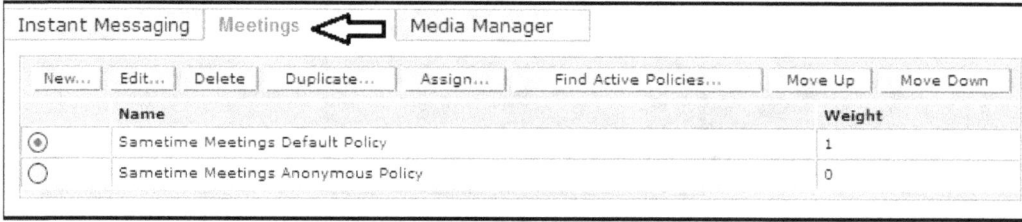

Policies control all the settings that are available for the Classic Meeting Server as well as those for the new Meeting Server. This includes whether meetings are searchable or hidden, as well as size management for uploads and individual meetings.

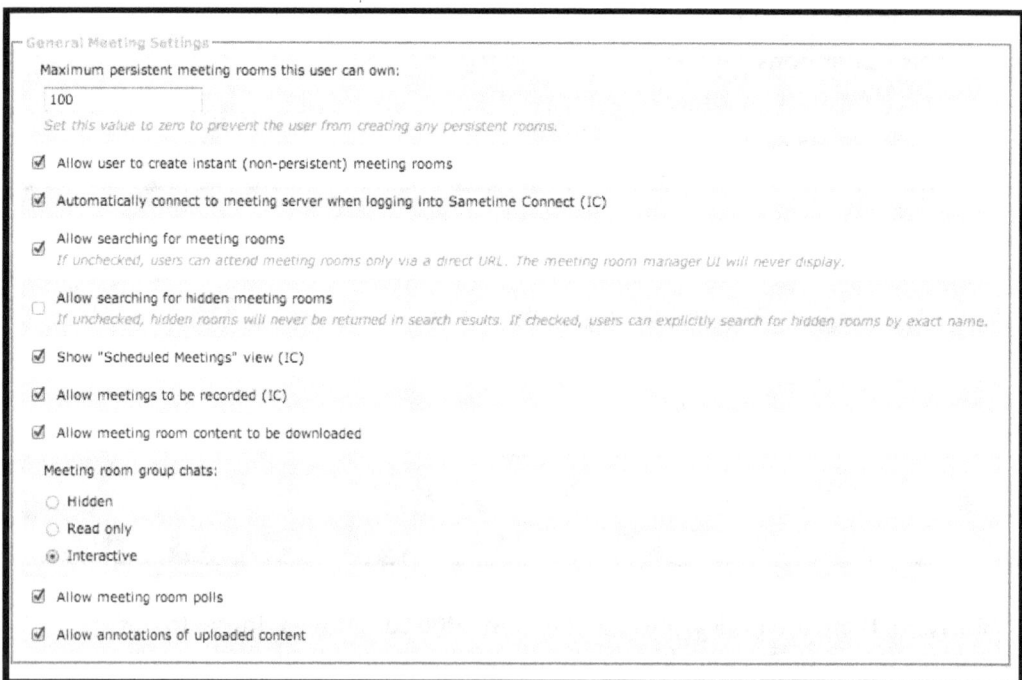

Additionally, there are settings to control behavior when screen sharing:

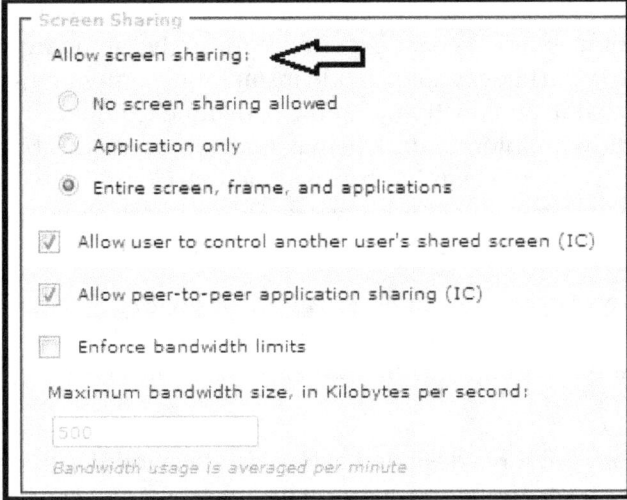

This configuration menu allows you to set whether or not you want to allow screen sharing, as this may be a security concern in your environment.

Customization of the look and feel and extension of the features of the Sametime Meeting Center is currently limited; although there is now a publicly available SDK for working with the WAS-based Sametime Meeting Server at the following website: `http://www.ibm.com/developerworks/lotus/downloads/toolkits.html#sametime`.

Deployment scenarios

The following are some possible ways you might deploy the Sametime Meeting Server:

- Mary Jean would like to provide a way for her Sametime 8.5.2 Connect users to create and attend feature-rich meetings directly from their clients without needing a browser. She installs the Sametime 8.5.2 Meeting Server so her clients can create and access meeting spaces using the new rich Meeting Client.

- Rosalie would like to provide Meeting services for her marketing team to share and work on project documents with their suppliers. She installs a Sametime 8.5.2 Meeting Server which allows the Marketing team to create their own meeting spaces to work with suppliers.

Sametime Proxy Server

The Sametime Proxy Server is a new Sametime component that provides a full feature-rich instant messaging client experience through a standard web browser. The Sametime Proxy Server cannot provide instant messaging or awareness services itself. It must be used in conjunction with the Sametime Community Server. Most importantly, it acts as an intermediary between browser requests from a client and the services provided by the Domino-based Sametime Community Server. The Proxy Server hosts the Sametime client for browsers and provides name awareness for Sametime meetings, business cards, and custom applications.

The Sametime Proxy Server can connect to and work with a Sametime 8.5.2 Community Server or any supported Domino-based Sametime server. It does not require the instant messaging or awareness services themselves to be generated from an 8.5.2 server.

The Sametime Proxy Server is designed using Ajax JavaScript calls to handle client requests and style sheets for layout. The use of style sheets makes the interface customizable, enabling a customer to brand the application as needed. The use of Ajax makes the browser application not only fast to run but also leaves a small footprint on the Sametime Community Server.

In addition, the functionality of Sametime Proxy Server can be used to replace the use of STlinks — the component previously used for Sametime client awareness in the Lotus iNotes e-mail web client — and the Java applet-based awareness toolkit that shows online status of web application users. Sametime Proxy Server is based on Ajax JavaScript calls, which require less overhead for the client and the server than the earlier Java applets. Currently, Lotus Domino ships with a version of web-based e-mail that still uses the older Sametime applets for online status.

Installing a Sametime Proxy Server provides you with a third client option for Sametime alongside the Sametime Connect desktop client install and the embedded Lotus Notes client.

Installation requirements

Sametime 8.5.2 Proxy Server must install as a WAS application on top of WebSphere 7.0.0.3 as with the other WAS-based Sametime servers. It is also expected that you have installed the SSC in order to complete its installation and ongoing management. As the Sametime Proxy Server is only an interface to the Sametime Community Server, you must also have an existing Domino-based Sametime server already installed in your organization for its connection.

The Sametime Proxy Server can be clustered through Network Deployment for WebSphere. In a clustered environment, multiple instances of the server exist with identical configurations, and users can access any of the servers. The Proxy Server can also connect to a Sametime Multiplexor instead of directly to a Domino-based Sametime Server, allowing it to utilize the Community Server's high availability and clustering features.

The Sametime Proxy Server requires that the Sametime Community Server or Domino-based Sametime server support LDAP authentication and not just Domino authentication. This means that prior to beginning the install of the Meeting Server the following must be in place:

- Sametime 8.5.2 System Console
- Supported LDAP Server
- Sametime 8.5.2 Community Server or any supported Domino-based Sametime Server configured to authenticate using LDAP

In addition, the supported browser clients for using the Sametime Proxy Server are:

- Microsoft Internet Explorer 6
- Microsoft Internet Explorer 7
- Microsoft Internet Explorer 8

An example of a Proxy Server installation follows:

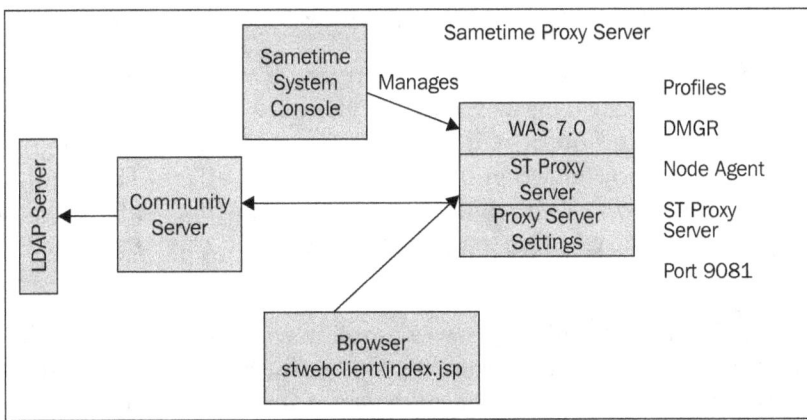

Deployment scenarios

The following are some possible ways you might deploy the Sametime Proxy Server:

- David wants to allow his roaming users access to an instant messaging client even when they are outside of the office. He deploys a Sametime Proxy Server and connects it to his existing Sametime Community Server environment. His users can now connect to their instant messaging environment from virtually any browser and platform wherever they are located.

- Mike wants to give access to Sametime instant messaging for some internal users who do not have Lotus Notes, without having to deploy another application to the desktop. He installs Sametime Proxy Server and adds a URL to the company intranet site that allows any user to connect to the instant messaging environment through a browser on their computer.

- Lisa is having problems with her web-based applications which are using online awareness and experiencing slow response time. She installs Sametime Proxy Server and replaces her use of STLinks applets throughout her applications with Ajax functions that use the Proxy Server instead.

Sametime Media Manager Server

The Sametime Media Manager is a new set of server components that are designed to offer high quality web conferencing, video, and audio capabilities when in Sametime 8.5.2 meetings or when using Sametime 8.5.2 clients.

The Media Manager is designed for extensibility and integration with other third-party conferencing systems as it uses the standard Session Initiation Protocol (SIP) for point-to-point and multi-point calls. It also supports a wide range of standard audio and video codec that other providers can utilize. The Media Manager is designed to support up to a maximum of twenty people in a web conference. This setting is in place for bandwidth management reasons and can be adjusted by the Sametime administrator.

In Sametime 8.5.2, the Media Manager works solely with the Sametime 8.5.2 Connect clients and with the Sametime 8.5.2 Meeting Center for WebSphere, but not with the lightweight web browser client. It also does not support earlier clients. For this reason, Sametime 8.5.2 clients cannot make voice or video calls to users on earlier client versions.

In the Media Manager, secure transmission of data is enabled by default. You have the option to choose **Transport Layer Security (TLS)** or **Security Sockets Layer (SSL)** when configuring the server. TLS transport is recommended for media encryption.

The Media Manager Server is itself divided into three separate components:

- The Conference Server is core to the provisioning of audio and video conferences as it handles all the point-to-point and multi-point requests and connections from clients. It integrates directly with the client and handles the server workload. Multiple Conference Servers can be created to better handle workload but they must all be clustered as a single cluster under a single SSC.

- The SIP Proxy and Registrar handle the forwarding of SIP messages to their destinations. The Proxy and Registrar can also be clustered but only as a single cluster under a single SSC. The SIP Proxy Server is a different server component than the Sametime Proxy server.

- The Packet Switcher handles the traffic generated by media streams between endpoints. Its job includes the monitoring of audio streams to be able to dynamically switch the video through voice-activated switching. Multiple Packet Switchers can exist to handle demand and do not need to be clustered. The Packet Switcher requires access to LDAP and a range of media ports for audio and video.

In a small installation, these three components would be installed on one server. In a larger installation, some of the elements would be clustered and appear in multiple instances as part of a single Media Manager.

The following is an example of a Media Manager architecture:

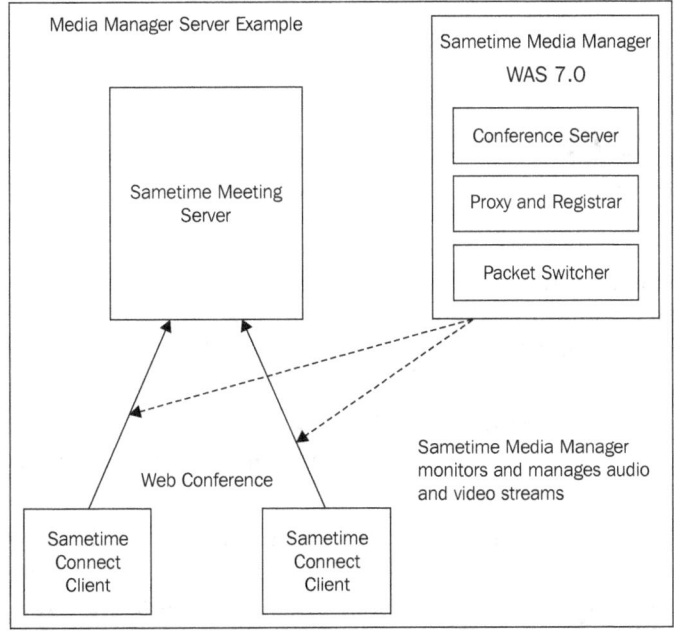

Installation requirements

Sametime 8.5.2 Media Manager must install as a WAS application on top of WebSphere version 7.0.0.3 as with the other WAS-based Sametime servers. It also requires that you have installed the SSC in order to complete its installation and ongoing management.

The Media Manager provides services to both Sametime 8.5.2 Connect clients and to the Sametime 8.5.2 Meeting Center client. One of these clients must be installed in order to use the Media Manager. The Media Manager does not support browser-based clients including either the Proxy web client or the Meeting browser client. It also does not support pre-8.5.2 Sametime Connect clients or the Classic Meeting Server on Domino. This means that prior to beginning the install of the Media Manager, the following must be in place:

- Sametime 8.5.2 System Console
- Supported LDAP Server
- Sametime 8.5.2 Connect client
- Sametime 8.5.2 Meeting Server (required if you want to use in conferencing meetings)

In a small server deployment all three components of the Media Manager would be installed as single instances on a single server. In larger enterprises, where web conferencing is in demand, it may be necessary to create a cluster of Conferencing services and Proxy and Registrar services as well as multiple Packet Switchers, each on their own hardware.

Deployment scenarios

The following are some possible ways you might deploy the Sametime Media Manager Server:

- Valerie has deployed Sametime 8.5.2 Connect clients to her internal desktop users and would now like them to have video and audio conferences with each other. She installs the Sametime Media Manager to enable conferencing for chats.
- Graham has installed the Sametime Meeting Server for his executive team to hold team briefings. He installs the Sametime Media Manager so those briefings can include broadcast of live audio and video.
- Ignacio wants to provide the ability for users to create their own meetings using web conferencing from their third-party conference bridge. He installs the Media Manager server and adds his own conference bridge information to Sametime user preferences.

Sametime TURN Server

The Sametime TURN Server, otherwise known as the NAT Traversal Server, is a new Java-based program that works in conjunction with the Sametime Media Server. The TURN Server addresses the issue the Media Server has in sending audio and video content to clients on a different network than itself. The TURN Server acts as a reflector service for the Sametime Media Server, creating a connection between the client and server SIP Proxy Registrar and directing audio and video traffic from the Media Server to the client. Without the installation of the TURN Server, clients on different networks or outside your firewall will not be able to attend web conferences or hold audio and video calls.

Installation requirements

The Sametime TURN Server provides a simple reflector service. It has minimal configuration as its role is simply to route the audio and video traffic. It depends upon the configuration of the Sametime Media Server for its settings. The TURN Server is a simple Java program that does not require any installation but it does need access to IBM's Java Virtual Machine (JVM) to run. IBM's JVM is built into Notes, Domino, and WAS.

The TURN Server must be set to run on the same network as your Media Server. The following screenshot shows the TURN Server running in a command window:

Deployment scenarios

The following are some possible ways you might deploy the Sametime TURN Server:

- Vancho has installed the Sametime Media Server to allow his users to conduct peer-to-peer audio and video chats. Users located at other sites cannot join in these calls. He installs a TURN Server to enable all his sites to participate in audio and video chats.

- Magda would like her product development department to be able to have web conferences with customers. She has put the Media Server and TURN Server in her DMZ to enable everyone, both inside and outside the firewall, to join a web-based meeting.

Sametime Bandwidth Manager Server

The Sametime Bandwidth Manager was introduced in Sametime 8.5.2 and is designed to help administrators control the network traffic consumed by audio and video services. Working in concert with the Sametime Media Server, the Bandwidth Manager can be configured with call rules that define everything from the codec used for an audio call to the frame rate for video traffic. The server monitors the audio and video being generated on the network and uses rules, defined by the Sametime administrator for bandwidth usage at each site, for links between sites and for users to customize each call as it is initiated. In this way, a call between two users at the same site can have different resource allocation than a call between users across sites. Similarly, the Bandwidth Manager can dynamically adjust the quality of audio or video assigned to a call during peak periods. It can also deny access to services entirely during periods of heavy bandwidth usage, informing the user that the system is too busy and to try again later.

Installation requirements

Sametime Bandwidth Manager must be installed on a WAS server but it is not installed as part of the SSC's Guided Activities. It uses a DB2 database and must have a DB2 server available to create its dedicated database. The DB2 server can be the same one used for other Sametime components. Unlike other Sametime components, the installer for Bandwidth Manager does not create a database for you and this must be done manually on the DB2 server. Similarly, the install of the Bandwidth Manager Server itself is a separate process, where the server is installed on top of an existing WAS server and then federated into the SSC for management.

The Bandwidth Manager can be installed as a stand-alone server or in a cluster. As its role is the monitoring of network traffic through the Media Manager, you will need to place the two server components (Media and Bandwidth Manager) adjacent to each other on your network.

The Sametime install files include a license for IBM DB2 9.5 Limited Use, which entitles you to install a 32-bit DB2 server on either the Windows or Linux platforms for use exclusively with the Sametime server components. The Limited Use version of DB2 server cannot be installed on a 64-bit Linux operating system. The version of WAS that is supported for all the WAS-related Sametime server components is 7.0.0.3. In addition, WAS iFixes are also available and periodically updated to address Sametime-specific problems. WAS iFixes can be found at IBM's Fix Central website: http://www.ibm.com/support/fixcentral/. It is highly recommended that you should stay current with these updates.

Deployment scenarios

The following are some possible ways you might deploy the Sametime Bandwidth Manager Server:

- Ivy would like to enable audio and video services for meetings but is concerned about the increased traffic on her network, especially as people will attend meetings from many different locations. She installs Bandwidth Manager and configures call routing rules to give priority to meeting traffic during peak hours and to send a lower quality audio and video to those attending from another network.

- Magnus is receiving complaints from his users that at peak times the quality of audio during calls can be unreliable. He installs the Bandwidth Manager and configures it to reduce the audio codec during peak times.

- Rafael would like to only allow access for video chat to his executive team. Using the Bandwidth Manager, he creates call rules that deny access to video services for everyone except his named executives. The remaining users can continue to make audio calls.

Operating system options

Now that we have discussed each of the individual Sametime servers and their roles, it is important to remember that you have some flexibility on which operating systems you use to install and deploy Sametime 8.5.2. Some of the individual servers may only run on certain operating systems, while others can take advantage of multiple options. We have provided the following table as a reference:

	Proxy	Community	System Console	Classic Meeting	Meeting	Gateway	Media Manager	TURN Server	Bandwidth Manager Server
AIX									
AIX 5.3 TL10 POWER System i/p	X	X	X	X	X	X			
AIX 6.1 TL3 System i/p	X	X	X	X	X	X			
IBM System i									
IBM I 5.4	X	X	X	X	X	X			
IBM I 6.1	X	X	X	X	X	X			
IBM I 7.1	X	X	X	X	X	X			
LINUX									
RHEL 5.0 Update 4 x86-32 / x86-64	X	X	X	X	X	X	X	X	X
SLES 10.0 SP1 / 11 x86-32 / x86-64	X	X	X	X	X	X	X	X	X
Solaris									
Solaris 10 SPARC	X	X	X	X	X	X			
Windows									
2003 SP1/ 2003 R2 Enterprise / Standard 32/64Bit	X	X	X	X	X	X	X	X	X
2008 / 2008 R2 Enterprise / Standard 32/64bit	X	X	X	X	X	X	X	X	X

Summary

In this chapter, you learned about each of the Sametime servers that make up a full installation of Sametime 8.5.2. You learned about the installation requirements, as well as the dependencies between each of the various servers. You also learned about the different operating systems you can use for each of the Sametime 8.5.2 servers. In the next chapter, you will be introduced to the telephony features of Sametime 8.5.2.

3
Telephony Integration: Working with Sametime Telephony

In addition to its excellent messaging and collaboration features, Sametime supports the ability to make audio and video conference calls to people in your Sametime community. Sametime also has the capability to integrate into your organization's phone system to allow you to call your contacts regardless of whether they are online or away from their computer. This capability often referred to as "unified communications", means that you can maintain a single point of control for all your communication instead of bouncing between various systems.

The following are some examples of scenarios where a company or organization might want to integrate telephony into their Sametime system:

- Phoebe is upgrading her Sametime 7.5 environment to Sametime 8.5.2, and her company is interested in integrating their VoIP system with Sametime 8.5.2.

- Miguel has been asked if the users of his Sametime 8.5.2 environment can make calls to another organization that uses Skype to make and receive international calls.

- Maria has a requirement to be able to make voice and video calls involving three or more people. She needs to understand which Sametime 8.5.2 server components are needed to support this feature.

- Chia works for a company with offices across several countries. The company wants to integrate their current telephony vendor's plugin with Sametime.

In this chapter, you will learn:

- What is unified communication and telephony
- What telephony options are available for Sametime
- What is Sametime Unified Telephony (SUT)
- How Sametime 8.5.2 connects to telephony products
- How to add audio, video, and conferencing to your Sametime client
- The role of Media Server when using audio and video calling
- How client-side plugins work in Sametime 8.5.2
- How to add web conferencing to the Meeting Center
- How to use third-party web conferencing services with Sametime

Unified Communication and Telephony

Unified Communication (**UC**) is a term used to describe the integration of communication technologies, such as voice or phone communications, with multi-media technologies such as VoIP, video conferencing, and social media communication like instant messaging. Technology vendors may use the term "Unified Communication" to describe a particular software or hardware product, or a family of products. What is consistent across vendors is the concept that all forms of communication may be "unified" so that the user has the flexibility to pick and chose those components that best serve their needs without having to install several disparate components themselves.

Telephony is a term frequently used when discussing unified communications. To many people, the word "telephony" is synonymous with VoIP. However, there are many differences between the two terms. It is important to understand the different options available to you in order to define your requirements for a voice or unified communication system.

Telephony systems use traditional telephone company infrastructure such as handsets, speakers, receivers, and transmitters. Telephony solutions are often designed and integrated by telephony vendors, or they may be developed by customizing solutions commonly available in the marketplace. In comparison, VoIP is a technology that converts analog voice into digital data for transmission. VoIP systems use either computer microphones and speakers or VoIP-compatible handsets. Many modern handsets can support both telephony and VoIP traffic.

Features enabled by these integrated solutions can include:

- **Click to call**: A user selects a contact from their instant messaging client and calls their designated handset. Calls can use either microphone and speakers or handsets. These types of calls utilize traditional telephony functions like mute, hold, and transfer.

- **Telephony presence**: Using custom icons, a user can see at a glance if one of their contacts is on the phone.

- **Web conferencing**: Users can connect to an external third-party web conferencing solution to provide multi-person audio and video calling using phone handsets and regional call-in numbers.

- **Multi-party calling**: Users can call multiple people into a single audio meeting by clicking on the names in their contact list. Calls are directed to their phone handsets, and features like mute and adding new callers are available.

Telephony options available in Sametime

There are a number of different telephony terms and technologies applicable to Sametime 8.5.2. In addition, IBM has a separate large enterprise Sametime product called SUT, which is designed to complement Sametime itself, as well as a client-side soft phone product called Sametime Unified Telephony Lite. There is some confusion as to what telephony options are available in Sametime 8.5.2 Standard in comparison to those added by using SUT or Sametime Unified Telephony Lite. We will discuss the features available with Sametime 8.5.2 Standard first.

Several audio and video options are available with Sametime 8.5.2. Your choice of which one to use depends on what services your company or organization requires and how you wish to deploy them. The Sametime 8.5.2 Connect and embedded clients themselves can initiate audio and video calls, but only with the aid of the Sametime Media Manager, which must be installed. If you want to connect to a third-party conferencing service, then a separate client or server-side plugin must be deployed. None of the audio and video services require a Sametime Meeting server to be installed, unless you need web conferencing specifically in meetings.

The Sametime 8.5.2 Connect and embedded clients support several different methods for audio and video integration. Plugins have been developed to connect directly to telephony services provided by companies such as Vonage and Skype. These plugins use no other Sametime services and require no specific Sametime server installations.

The same clients can leverage Sametime integration points such as SIP or the **Telephony Conference Service Provider Interface (TCSPI)** to make audio and video calls. For example, a client-side plugin can enable the Sametime client to act as a SIP client and endpoint, with audio and video delivered by a third-party service. Alternatively, instead of deploying client-side plugins, the Sametime 8.5.2 Connect client together with the Sametime Media Manager can use a custom **Service Provider Interface (SPI)** adaptor, developed using TCSPI, to connect to an external service offering audio, video, and conferencing facilities.

In summary, the options are:

- Standard:
    - Point-to-point audio and video using Sametime Media Manager.
    - Multi-point audio and video using Sametime Media Manager.
    - Web conferencing within the Sametime Meeting rich client using Sametime Media Manager.

- Custom:
    - Client-side plugin using third-party networks and technologies.
    - Client-side plugin using SIP and offering click to call, multi-person calls, mute, hold, and transfer. This works in the Sametime 8.5.2 Connect and embedded clients only. It is not supported in the browser or proxy clients.
    - Server-side TCSPI adaptor connecting to third-party systems offering multi-way audio and video, telephony presence awareness, teleconferencing numbers, and more. The adaptor can be used by the Sametime 8.5.2 Connect and embedded clients as well as the Sametime Meeting Center.

 It is very important to be aware that the underlying infrastructure behind audio and video services has been completely redesigned for Sametime 8.5.2. The Sametime 8.5.2 Connect and embedded clients cannot participate in audio and video calls directly with older Sametime clients for this reason.

Sametime Unified Telephony

As we mentioned previously, SUT adds additional telephony features on top of a Sametime 8.5.2 installation. SUT is an entirely new Sametime product that shipped alongside Sametime 8.5.2. Although it complements the standard Sametime 8.5.2 Standard services, it is licensed separately and is not a requirement for use of audio and video services within Sametime 8.5.2.

The SUT solution is a combination offering of software, hardware, and services from IBM and a small number of third-party telephony partners. It is designed to connect multiple high-end **private branch exchange** (**PBX**) and telephony systems in use at a single company. IBM often demonstrates the SUT software by showing a Sametime user transferring calls between their headset, desk phone, and mobile phone as the client dynamically detects the user's location and determines the best routing for the call.

SUT is designed by IBM to deliver a high return on investment for very large enterprises with multiple telephony systems and a distributed office network. The complexity of the technology and deployment is currently appropriate to only very large enterprises and, as a separate product, is outside the scope of this book. The following table provides a brief comparison of features included with Sametime 8.5.2, those added with vendor plugins, and those added with the use of Sametime 8.5.2 Unified Telephony.

	Lotus Sametime 8.5.2 (Standard)	Lotus Sametime 8.5.2 (Standard) with vendor plugins	Lotus Sametime 8.5.2 (Standard) with Lotus Sametime 8.5.2 Unified Telephony
Voice functions			
Click to call computer (VoIP)	X	X	X
Click to call voice		X	X
Click to call multi-parties		X	X
Phone availability awareness	X	X	X
External audio integration with Sametime Meetings		X	X

	Lotus Sametime 8.5.2 (Standard)	Lotus Sametime 8.5.2 (Standard) with vendor plugins	Lotus Sametime 8.5.2 (Standard) with Lotus Sametime 8.5.2 Unified Telephony
Sametime client functions			
Drag and drop additional users	X	X	X
View invited user status	X	X	X
Mute/unmute controls (self)	X	X	X
Moderator controls (mute/unmute/end call)	X	X	X
Preferred device/ number		X	X
Forward calls to another person			X
Transfer call from one device to another			X
Presence aware incoming call rule sets			X
Call history			X
Merge calls			X
Phone book			X

Sametime Unified Telephony Lite client

The Sametime Unified Telephony Lite client was introduced in Sametime 8.5.2 and provides a standards-based SIP connection from the Sametime Connect client or embedded Sametime client to many voice and video systems. The following screenshot shows the Lite client from the Sametime Connect client:

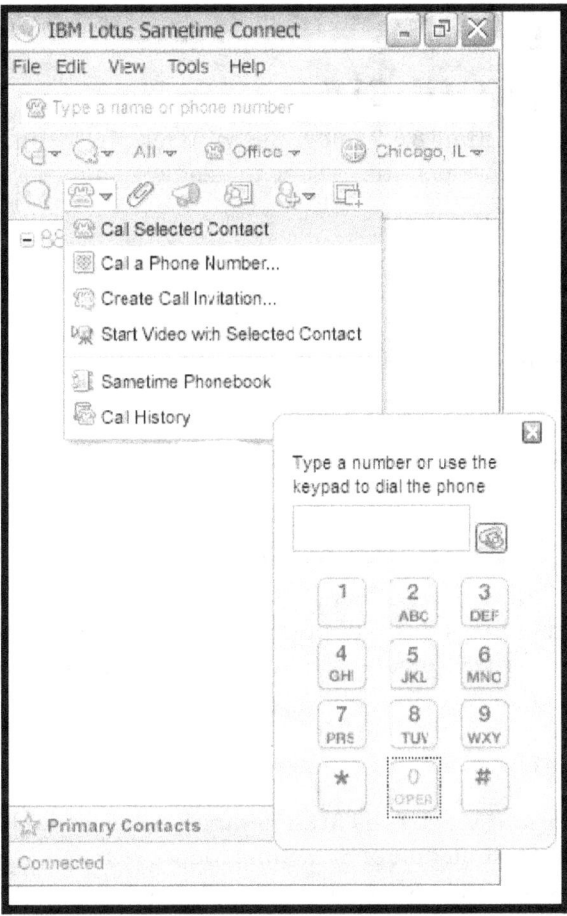

The SUT Lite client creates a SIP session with the Sametime Media Manager in order to allow the client to make and receive audio and video calls across external numbers and systems. Any system providers to be utilized by SUT Lite must first be certified by IBM. The following is current list of certified and under review providers:

Vendor	Category	Model/Version	Status
Avaya	PBX	Aura 6	In progress
Cisco	PBX	8.5	In progress
Cisco	Gateway	VCS 6.1	Completed
Dialogic	Gateway	DMG 6	In progress
Polycom	MCU	RMX Version 7.1+	Completed
Radvision	MCU	Scopia V. 7.5	Completed

Connecting Sametime 8.5.2 Connect to telephony products

Let us examine how Sametime 8.5.2 integrates with telephony products. There are several types of audio and video integration available:

- Point-to-point audio and video
- Multi-point audio and video
- Web conferencing with Sametime Meetings
- Client-side plugins not using Sametime technology
- Client-side plugins using SIP
- Server-side TCSPI adaptor

Point-to-point audio and video

Point-to-point audio and video is where a Sametime client initiates a voice or video call with another Sametime client. Although the ability to do person-to-person calling is available in earlier versions of Sametime, it has been completely rewritten in Sametime 8.5.2 to be more robust and support n-way conversations. For this reason, only calls between Sametime 8.5.2 Connect and embedded clients will work, while calls to or from earlier client versions will fail.

Management of voice and video calls in Sametime 8.5.2 is through Sametime Media Manager. Without the installation of Sametime Media Manager, the menu options and preferences for voice and video calling are not available. The Media Manager itself is managed by the SSC, and Media Manager requests from the Sametime 8.5.2 clients come through the Sametime Community Server. Therefore to utilize point-to-point audio and video, you need to install and configure the following standard Sametime elements:

- DB2 to support SSC
- Sametime 8.5.2 System Console
- Sametime 8.5.2 Community Server
- Sametime 8.5.2 Connect or embedded client
- Sametime Media Manager

There is no requirement for the Sametime Meeting server itself to be installed. This is only required if you want to attend meetings and have voice and video available in those meetings.

In the following diagram, you can see how point-to-point calls are handled.

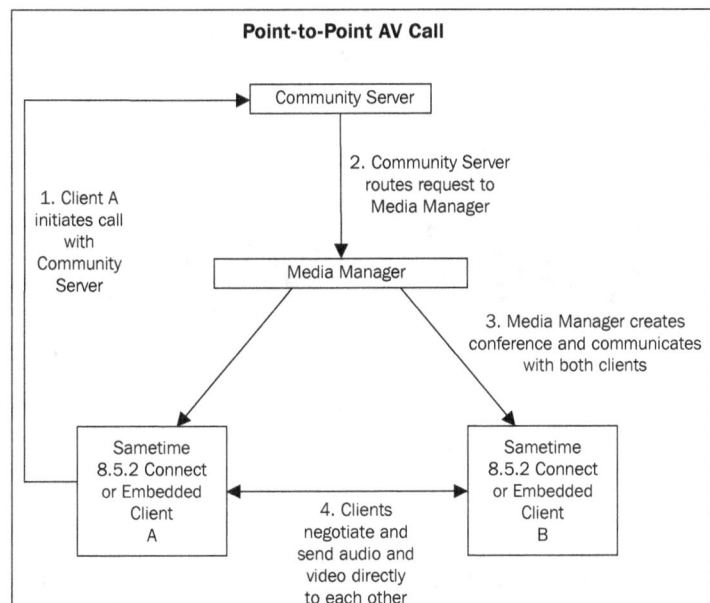

The steps are:

1. The client initiating the call selects the person they wish to call from their Sametime Contact list.

2. The request to voice or video call that person is sent as a request to the Community Server.

3. The Community Server routes that request to the Media Manager.

4. The Media Manager creates a conference and connects directly to both Sametime clients to join them into it.

5. Once joined, the two Sametime clients send all their audio and video traffic directly to each other, bypassing both the Media Manager and the Community Server.

6. Once the call is terminated, the Media Manager terminates the conference.

Multi-point audio and video

Multi-point audio and video or n-way conferencing is available directly from the Sametime 8.5.2 Connect and embedded clients. The term "n-way" refers to the ability to add additional conferencing participants to a single conference call.

The following screenshot shows a multi-way VoIP call initiated by the Sametime 8.5.2 client:

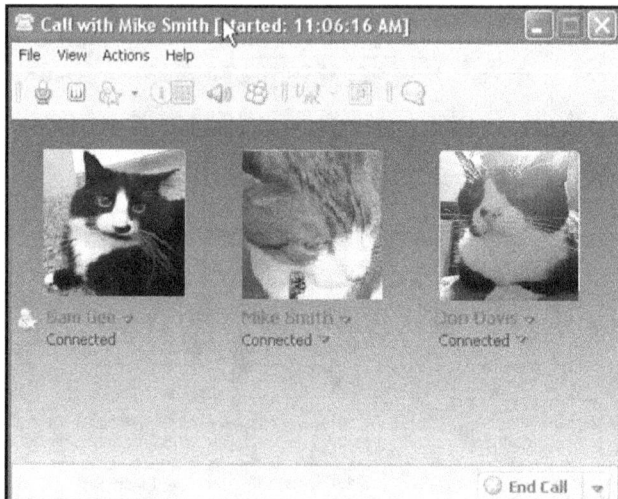

The Sametime 8.5.2 Connect and embedded clients also support n-way video. As you can see in this example, four participants are on the call, with two showing video images.

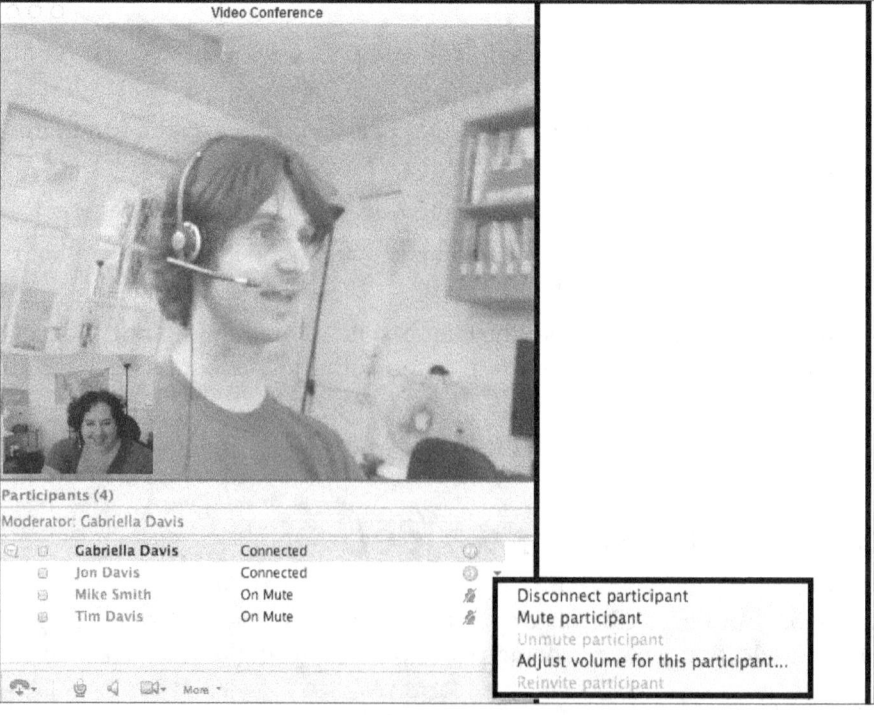

By design, the audio and video in n-way conferences is managed by the Sametime Media Manager and is not peer-to-peer. The role of the Media Manager is to monitor the audio and video streams from all connected clients and route traffic from the current speaker to the other attendees.

The Media Manager uses **Voice-Activated Switching (VAS)** to determine the current speaker and to route their video stream to others accordingly. The use of VAS is very effective if all clients who are not speaking remember to mute their lines. Otherwise, the Media Manager has to attempt to differentiate between multiple live audio streams of differing quality and volume. If there are too many audio streams with voice activity, then the Media Manager cannot successfully determine which video stream to designate as live.

The use of n-way audio and video from the Sametime client requires the deployment of Sametime Media Manager but not the deployment of Sametime Meeting Server. Once again, without an installation of Sametime Media Manager, the menu options and preferences for voice and video calling are not available.

The Media Manager is managed by the SSC. Media Manager requests from the Sametime 8.5.2 clients come through the Sametime Community Server. Therefore, to utilize n-way audio and video, you need to install and configure the following standard Sametime server and/or client components:

- DB2 to support SSC
- Sametime 8.5.2 System Console
- Sametime 8.5.2 Community Server
- Sametime 8.5.2 Connect or embedded client
- Sametime Media Manager

In the following diagram, you can see how n-way audio and video calls are handled:

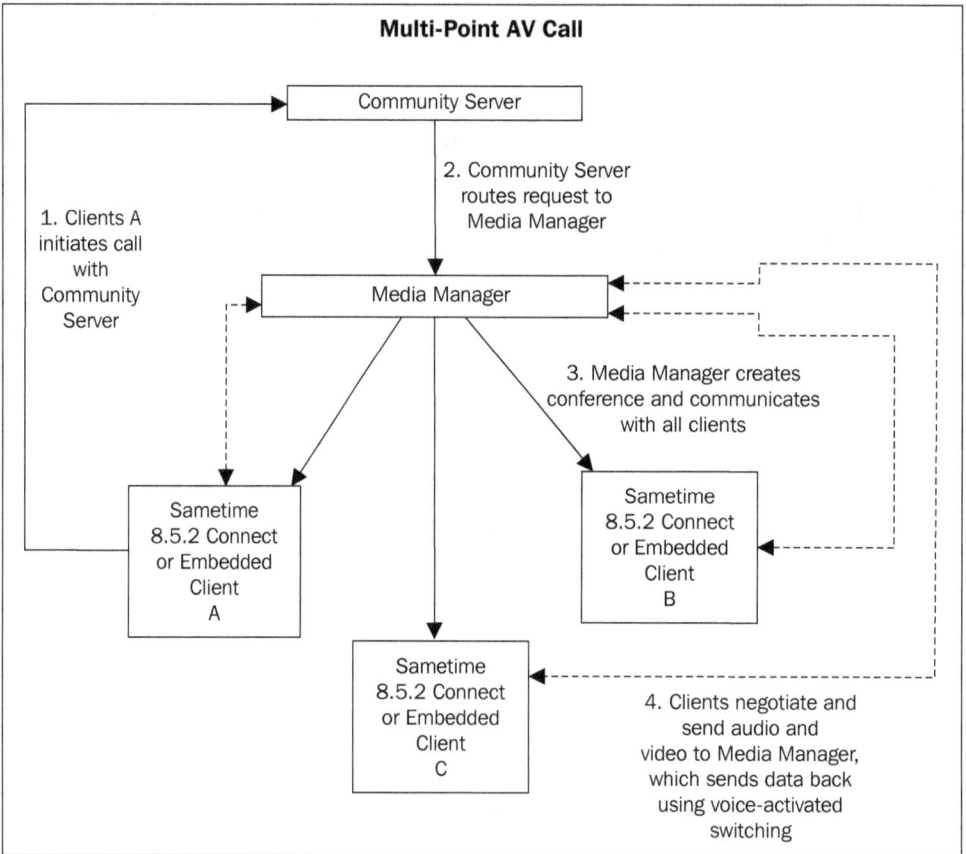

The steps are:

1. The client initiating the call selects the people from their buddy list.

2. The request to voice or video call those people is sent as a request to the Community Server.

3. The Community Server routes that request to the Media Manager.

4. The Media Manager creates a conference, connects directly to all Sametime clients who were invited, and then adds them into the conference.

5. Once joined, the Media Server monitors all client audio streams for activity. All audio streams are routed to each client.

6. When the Media Manager detects activity on a specific audio stream, it makes that user's video stream live and routes that traffic to all other attendees.

7. Once the call is terminated, the Media Manager terminates the conference.

8. It is important to note that client traffic in n-way calls is not peer-to-peer.

9. If a user adds a third person to an existing person-to-person call, the traffic for that call will immediately change from being peer-to-peer to being routed through the Media Manager. This is seamless to everyone attending the conference because the Media Manager is in control of the call at all times.

Web conferencing within Sametime meetings

Web conferencing in Sametime meetings is available through integration between Sametime Meeting Server and Sametime Media Manager. The Sametime Classic Meeting Server still offers voice and video integration in its meetings but the Classic Meeting Server uses older codecs and protocols. For the purposes of this book, we are discussing the new web conferencing features in Sametime 8.5.2 only.

The Sametime Media Manager provides web conferencing services to any meeting held on the Sametime Meeting Server. Meetings are now called **meeting places** and are persistent. Persistence refers to the meeting place remaining in existence after the meeting is over. The meeting owner, who creates the meeting, determines if it will have audio and video capabilities. In this way, a meeting definition is created and the Meeting Server knows to contact the Media Manager should anyone new enter the meeting room. Audio and video capabilities can be added to a meeting at any time.

The Meeting Server itself provides no audio or video capabilities. All of these capabilities come from the Media Manager. The job of the Meeting Server is to initiate the conference with the Media Manager. The Media Manager will then connect directly to any attendees in the meeting and manage their audio and video streams.

As with n-way client conferences, meeting conferences require the Media Manager to monitor all audio streams. The Media Manager also determines which is the active video stream and selects which audio stream is currently active. The use of VAS in meetings makes it important that anyone who is not speaking should mute their line. This will help the Media Manager to accurately determine which audio stream is currently active. To benefit from audio and video capabilities in browser-based meetings, you must also deploy the Sametime Proxy Server, which is responsible for handling awareness and client connections for browser-based clients.

The following screenshot shows two video participants in a Sametime meeting. The Room Owner is currently sharing an image:

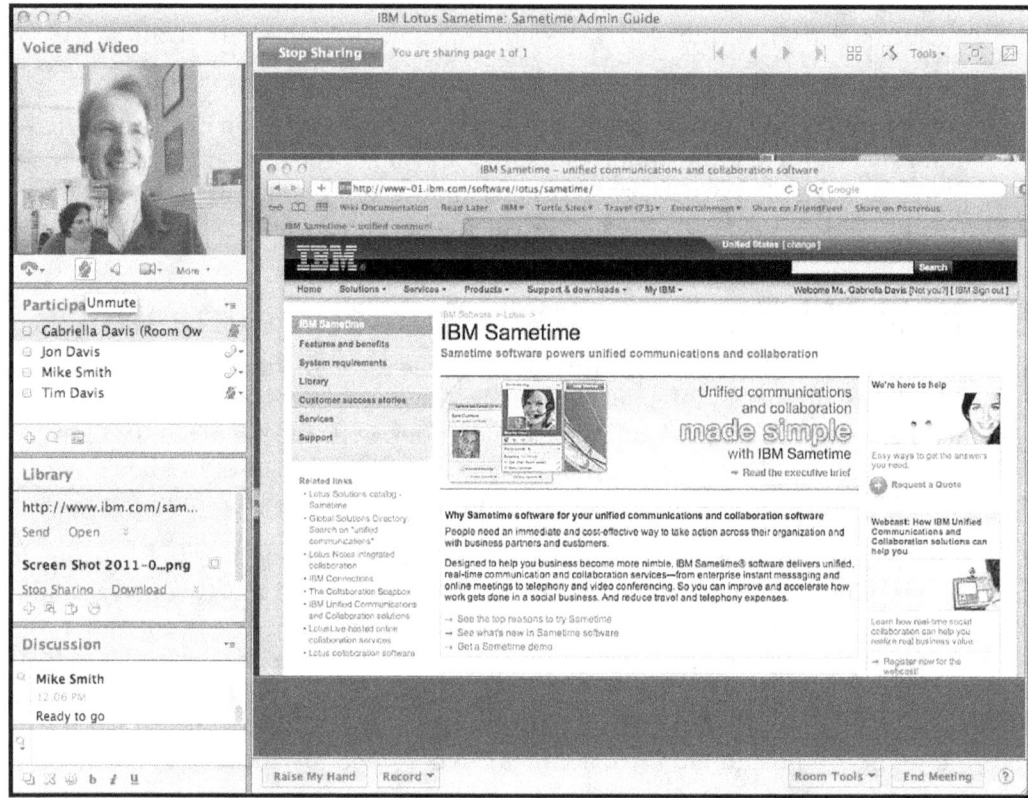

To utilize web conferencing in meetings, you need to install and configure the following standard Sametime 8.5.2 elements:

- DB2 to support SSC
- Sametime 8.5.2 System Console
- Sametime Community Server
- Sametime 8.5.2 Connect or embedded client
- DB2 to support Sametime Meeting Server
- Sametime 8.5.2 Meeting Server
- Sametime Media Manager
- Sametime Proxy Server (optional and used only when attending meetings through a web browser)

A Sametime Community Server does not have to be installed for meetings but must be installed for audio and video to work properly. This is because presence awareness is required to enable the Media Manager to route the audio and video traffic to clients correctly.

In the following diagram, you can see how audio and video conferencing works in meetings for stand-alone and embedded clients:

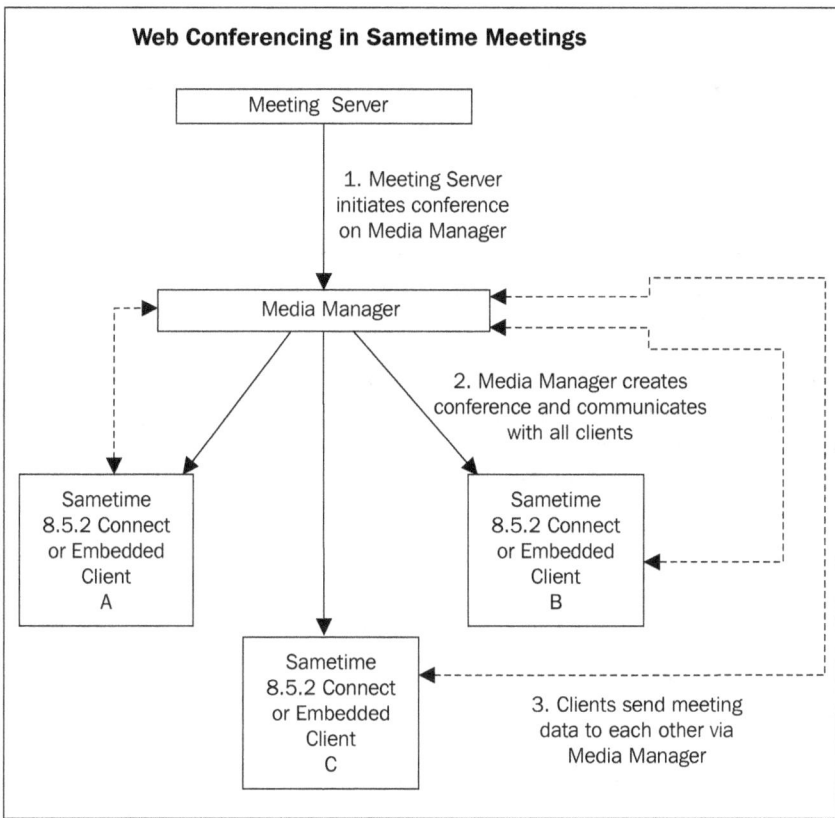

The steps are:

- The meeting owner creates a meeting from their Sametime 8.5.2 Connect or embedded client, specifying that the Sametime conferencing service should be used for attendees

- The Meeting Server stores the details of the meeting in the DB2 database and waits for people to join

- When anyone enters the meeting room, the Meeting Server contacts the Media Manager directly and asks to start a web conference

- The Media Manager initiates a new conference and attempts to connect to anyone who is online in the meeting room to monitor their audio and video streams

- The Media Manager uses VAS to determine the current speaker and direct the traffic from their video stream to the meeting room clients

Client-side plugins not using Sametime technology

Client-side plugins are Java applications installed in the Eclipse framework supporting the Sametime 8.5.2 Connect and embedded clients. As these plugins are using the Sametime client as their host environment and are not integrating directly with any of the Sametime server elements, they are entirely independent of any server requirements.

Client-side plugins are often custom developed or provided by telephony providers and connect to specific services. For example, there is a client plugin to connect to Skype as well as one to connect to Vonage. These are not designed specifically for Sametime but are Java-based applications that connect to external services.

To utilize a client-side plugin, you need to install and configure the following standard Sametime elements:

- Sametime 8.5.2 Connect or embedded client
- Third-party client-side plugins
- Sametime Community Server

The behavior of each client-side plugin will differ according to the service to which you are connecting, as well as how the plugin is developed. Regardless, the client program will connect and authenticate directly with the external service.

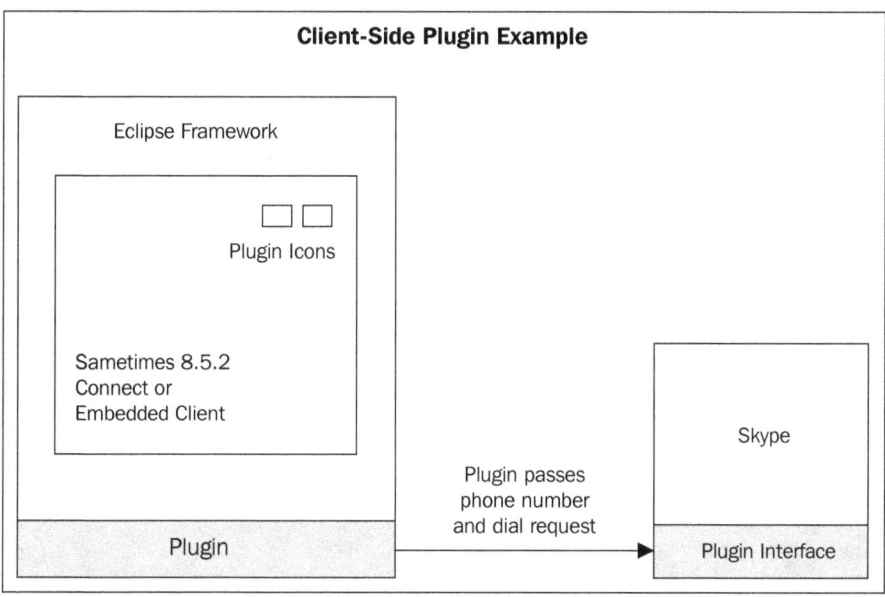

Client-side plugins using SIP

Client-side plugins using SIP are developed with the Sametime client-side API. These custom applications are designed to connect the Sametime client directly to the SIP interface of an existing endpoint. Many of the features you might want to have deployed in the client are only available from the client API.

To utilize a client-side plugin using SIP, you need to install and configure the following standard Sametime elements:

- Sametime 8.5.2 Connect or embedded client
- Sametime Community Server

The behavior of the client-side plugin depends entirely on what you would like it to do. For instance, a click to call plugin using SIP needs to connect directly to a SIP endpoint to send instructions, such as with a PBX system:

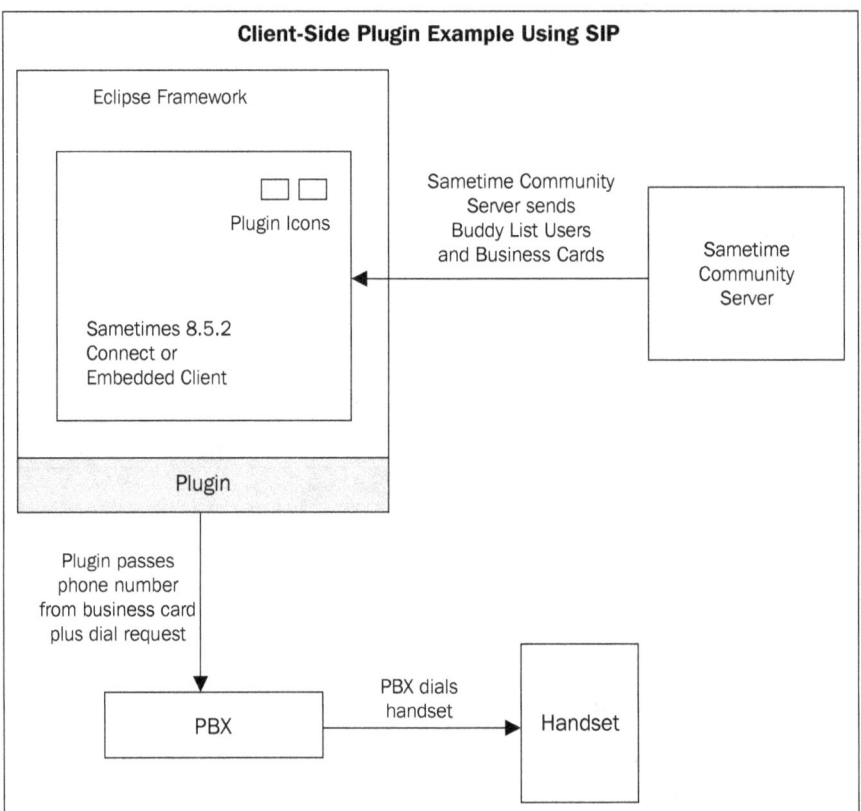

Server-side TCSPI adaptor

TCSPI solutions are developed with the Sametime server-side API and an API from any third-party telephony provider with which you wish to connect. These TCSPI solutions are either already developed by existing telephony providers and can be plugged directly into your Sametime server environment, or they are custom developed to integrate with your own telephony system using that system's APIs.

TCSPI solutions have been available since Sametime 3.0. Many of them will still be supported on Sametime 8.5.2 or supportable with some updates to meet new API requirements. If you already have a TCSPI solution in place, then you will want to include the testing of that solution in a Sametime 8.5.2 server environment as part of your upgrade planning.

TCSPI functionality in Sametime 8.5.2 can include:

- Click to dial audio calls to external devices such as telephones or web conferencing systems
- Point-to-point and n-way audio and video conferencing and client-side user interface extensions
- Support of SIP-enabled multi-point control units acting as conference-aware audio and video endpoints

To utilize a TCSPI solution, you need to install and configure the following standard Sametime elements:

- Sametime 8.5.2 Connect or embedded client (if conferencing is required from within instant messaging)
- Sametime 8.5.2 Community Server
- Sametime Media Manager
- Sametime Meeting Server (if conferencing is required in meetings)

The behavior of a TCSPI solution, for example when making a conference call, is as follows:

- Sametime client initiates a request for a conference call to some users in its buddy list
- The request is converted into dial numbers and directed to the TCSPI adaptor on the Sametime Media Manager
- The TCSPI adaptor on the Media Manager connects to the third-party conferencing system
- The conferencing solution creates the conference call, dials the buddy list members, and sends confirmation back to the Media Manager
- The Media Manager sends an update to the Sametime client connecting it to the active conference call

The following diagram shows a TCSPI adapter connection to a Sametime Media Manager Server:

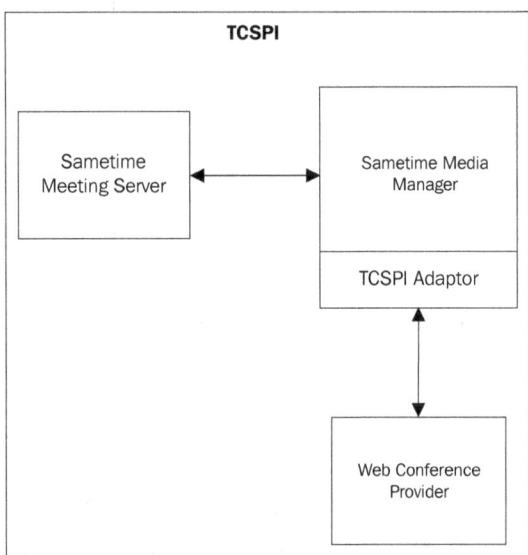

As of Sametime 8.5.x, the TCSPI solution is installed onto the Sametime Media Manager. In earlier versions of Sametime, TCSPI solutions were installed onto the Domino Sametime Server. The Media Manager can support two TCSPI adaptors, one for audio and one for video (which includes audio). This means you can have services to both a voice conference system and a separate video conferencing system available from the same Media Manager. The TCSPI adaptor installs into the **Conference Manager** component of the Media Manager and the Conference Manager itself can be clustered. However, only two external TCSPI adaptors can exist in a single Sametime Community.

Adding audio and conferencing to your Sametime client

Adding a new conferencing solution to your client is managed from your Sametime client preferences. In the **Preferences** menu, there is an option for **Telephony** and **Audio and Video**. This menu will be blank if you don't have an active camera and microphone or if you cannot connect to the Media Manager. You may not be able to connect to the Media Manager if you are connected to Sametime from outside your company or organization's firewall and your company has not configured a TURN server. The **Audio Conference Solution** titled **Sametime Audio/Video** conferencing is the built-in Media Manager conferencing system we have already discussed.

If there is a TCSPI adaptor installed on the Media Manager for your Sametime community, then you can click on **New** and add the call-in details in order to use the TCSPI adaptor in calls from your Sametime client, and also to allow for setup of audio and video-enabled meetings.

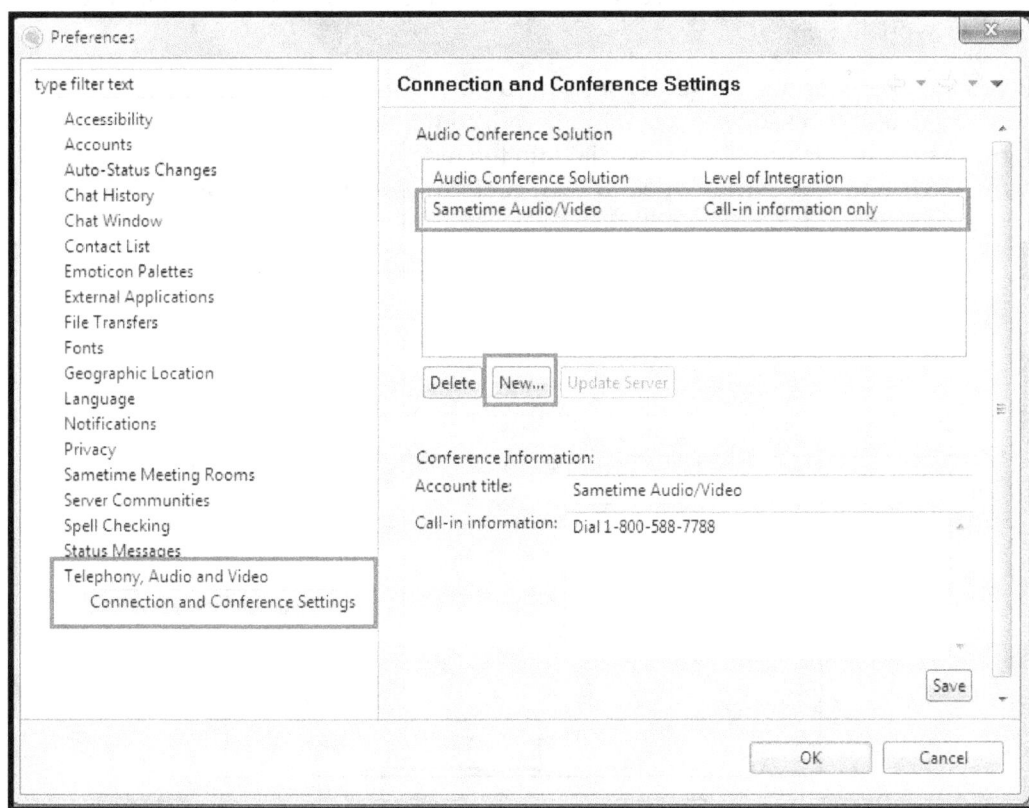

Adding web conferencing to the Meeting Center

When creating a new meeting, you now have the option to decide if the meeting will use audio or video for web conferencing. If you want to use web conferencing, then you have following three options:

- Using the built-in Sametime audio and video computer-based conferencing with the Media Server

- Third-party web conferencing services

- TCSPI solutions

If you configure Sametime to use the built-in Sametime audio and video conferencing components, then a conference attendee cannot call into the meeting room using a telephone. When they join the meeting, they have to click on the **Meeting Join Call** icon. They will then select their computer to join the call, assuming that they have the necessary audio and video hardware pre-configured on their workstation.

If your company or organization uses a third party for conferencing services, this service can also be used with a Sametime web conference. With the third-party service, a telephone can be used to dial into the meeting. The following screenshot shows an example of setting up your own conference dial-in information to an external system outside of Sametime for a specific meeting:

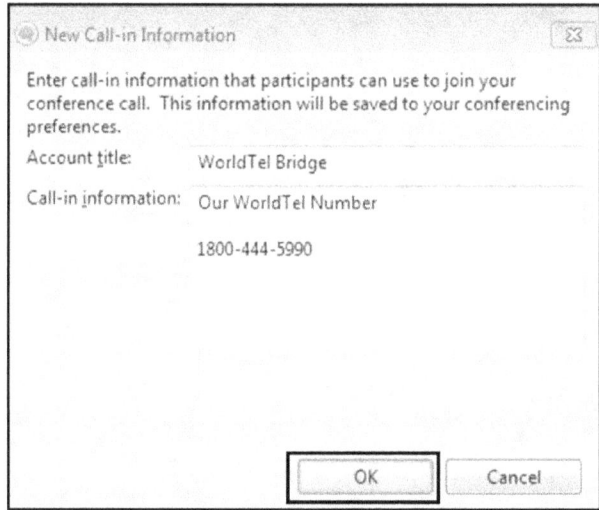

A final option is to use a third-party conferencing solution made available through a TCSPI Media Manager install, which will be available in your meeting room preferences. The following screenshot shows where you can select the audio solution for your meeting:

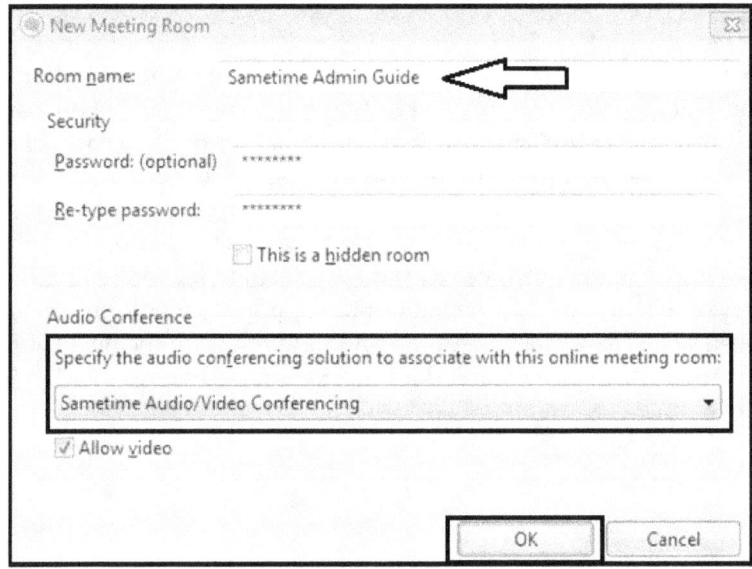

The following table describes options that are available with Sametime client plugins, TCSPI plugins, TCSPI-Sametime plugin combination, the SUT Lite client, and finally using SUT and the Sametime client. An "X" indicates what service is provided depending on the plugin. An "*" indicates which service is provided natively.

	Client plugin	TCSPI	TCSPI–client plugin combo	SUT Lite client	SUT–client plugin combo
Click to call	X	*	*	X	*
Telephony presence	X		X		*
Sametime web conferencing		*	*		
Call management	X	*	*		*
Advanced call management	X		X		*
Transfer calls	X		X		*
Office integration		*	*		*
Voicemail	X		X		
Integrated soft phone	X		X	X	*
Video integration	X	X	X	X	X

Summary

In this chapter, you learned about what constitutes unified communications and telephony and what telephony options are parts of Sametime 8.5.2. You learned about the SUT product, as well as how Sametime 8.5.2 connects to various telephony products under different configurations. This includes point-to-point and multi-point audio and video calls, web conferencing in Sametime meetings, and client-side plugins. You learned how server-side adaptors are used to connect to various telephony systems. You learned how your users can add audio and video to their Sametime client preferences. Finally, you learned about the options for configuring your Sametime Meeting Center to include audio and video calls. In the next chapter, you will learn about WAS and what it does in a Sametime environment.

4
The Infrastructure: Understanding Sametime and WebSphere Application Server Architecture

In Sametime 8.5.2, the majority of the server elements have been moved from the IBM Lotus Domino platform to WAS. Understanding this component of your Sametime infrastructure is important regardless whether you are an experienced Domino administrator, experienced WAS administrator, or new to either system. As you will soon discover, many of the decisions regarding the implementation of a Sametime 8.5.2 environment center on WAS, its requirements, and how it is deployed. No matter the level of your WAS skill set, this chapter will introduce you to the required concepts and how they impact Sametime planning, as well as describing how WAS fits into the Sametime server architecture.

The following scenarios describe examples of environments where you would need to deploy a Sametime server on the WAS platform:

- Phoebe is the administrator of a Sametime 8.5.2 Instant Messaging environment and she wants to introduce audio and video calling for her connected Sametime users. She installs a Sametime Media Manager under WAS to provide audio and video services to her existing IM Clients.

- Yasser works in marketing and needs to be able to hold meetings with his team and external suppliers without deploying additional client software. He installs Sametime Meeting Server under WAS which enables him to invite attendees into the browser-based meeting center.

- Carmelo has rolled out Sametime Instant Messaging to all his users who are logging on using the Notes embedded client or the Sametime desktop client. He would now like external contacts to log in to Instant Messaging, but does not want them to install Notes or the Sametime desktop client. He installs Sametime Proxy Server under WAS. This enables his external contacts to use a standard browser to log in to the instant messaging environment and retain a rich client experience.

In this chapter, you will learn:

- What is WAS
- Why Sametime now requires WAS
- The meanings associated with WAS terms and concepts
- How to configure WAS directory options and how they relate to security
- How to deploy WAS and why you need multiple servers in your Sametime environment

Introducing WebSphere Application Server

IBM WebSphere Application Server (WAS) is a software platform designed to provide a management environment in which J2EE applications can run securely. WAS performs this management function for various IBM software applications such as Sametime and Lotus Quickr J2EE. In the case of Sametime, each of the Sametime server elements that run under WAS, such as Sametime Meetings, Media Manager, and Proxy Server, are separate J2EE applications with their own rules, security, and behavior. It is important to know that WAS by itself does not provide any functionality to a user beyond what the application installed under it provides.

What does this mean? First, many things that a Domino-based Sametime administrator may expect to see are not part of WAS. There is no mail engine; if you wish to send internet email from an application you must tell WAS where to find a SMTP server so the application can use it to send the email. Similarly, there is no built-in data store with WAS. IBM Sametime applications must use DB2 but WAS in general is designed to connect to any JDBC-compliant database system including SQL and Oracle. IBM supplies a limited use license of DB2 for Sametime servers on WAS to use as the data store, or you could also use your own DB2 deployment if it meets system requirements.

WAS is designed to let multiple and often unrelated applications run under a single server management environment with entirely different configurations. It is able to keep each configuration isolated from the other. The configuration files for an application are stored as XML files on the file system where WAS is installed, and each application will have to separately define its own data store, directory, and security.

The following diagram is a simple example of a WAS management environment running two J2EE applications such as Sametime Meeting Server and Sametime Proxy Server. In this instance both servers are using the same LDAP directory.

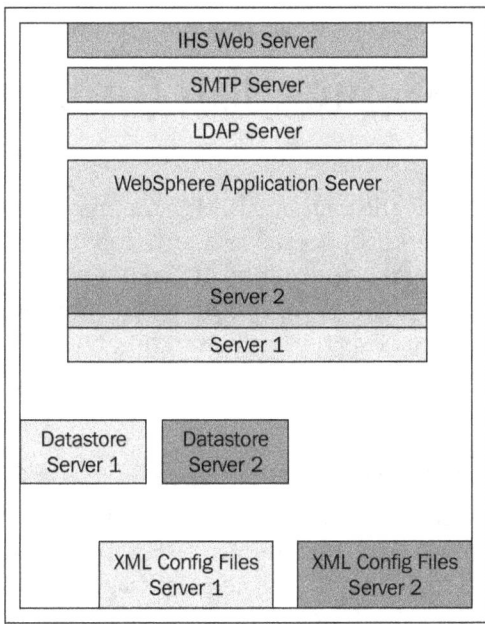

So WAS, a software component of the IBM Sametime infrastructure, does not in itself provide IBM Sametime services. Those come from the J2EE applications such as Sametime Meeting Server, Media Manager, and Proxy Server that are installed under WAS. However, because WAS is the management environment for Sametime applications, the installation of Sametime requires you as a Sametime administrator to understand how WAS is structured to help with your infrastructure planning and ongoing management.

Why is WebSphere Application Server used with Sametime?

WAS provides Sametime 8.5.2 with the application server base to allow Sametime to be customized in many ways. WAS provides scaling, multiple deployment models, consolidated system management, consolidated security, network management, and clustering that was not as robust in previous versions of Sametime. Once you understand the basic concepts described in the following section, you will be better prepared to set up the proper Sametime server configuration that best fits your own environment.

WebSphere Application Server concepts and terms

To understand how to install and manage IBM Sametime under WAS, we first need to understand a few basic server concepts and terms as they apply to the structure of WAS itself and how it manages applications. It is not within the scope of this book to provide a full explanation of all WAS concepts and components. We will discuss those concepts that provide a basis for understanding how the IBM Sametime products install and behave in a WAS environment.

Deployment Manager

Every application or server installed under WAS must be part of a **cell**. During the installation of an application that runs under WAS, you are prompted to identify the cell to which an application belongs. Each cell also has a single Deployment Manager process, which is responsible for management, configuration, and authentication of the application. The Deployment Manager process retains the configuration for all servers in its cell and updates the **node agent** with the latest configuration information for each server. A Deployment Manager shares a cell with a series of **nodes**. The following screenshot shows the admin client for a WAS server known as the **Integrated Solutions Console (ISC)**:

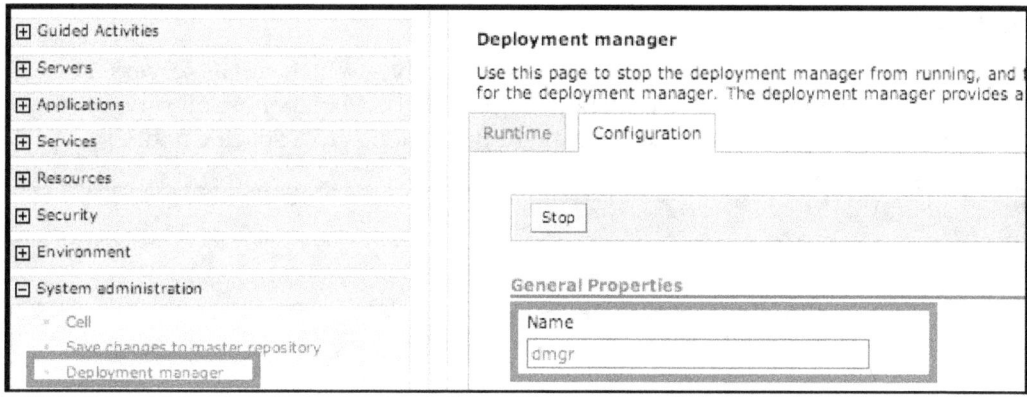

Node

Every application server that is installed with WAS is also identified as being part of a node. A node will often be a dedicated physical server or a server running in a **virtual machine** (**VM**). In many cases, especially with smaller Sametime environments, there will be several nodes on one physical server or VM. The Sametime Meeting Server installs as a node, as does the Sametime Proxy Server, but they are separate nodes from each other, even on the same machine.

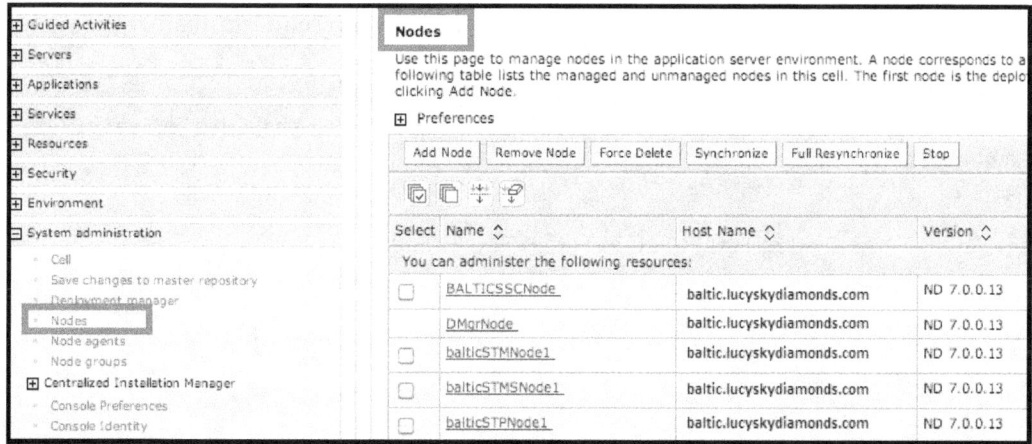

Server

Within each node, we have the applications themselves which run as servers. For example, the Meeting Server, Proxy Server, and Media Manager are all servers. A server is under the control of the node agent that belongs to a specific node.

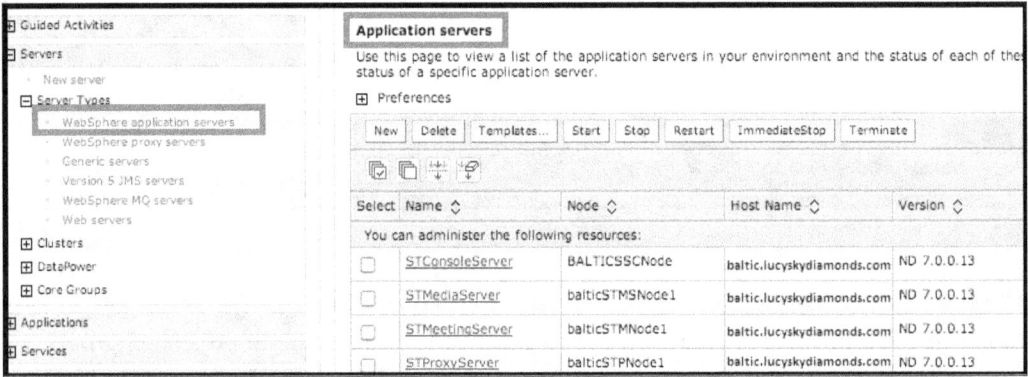

Node agent

To manage the servers in the node, WAS also needs to have a node agent. A node agent is another server instance with a specific role. It updates the server with the latest configuration information and performs start or stop requests against the node.

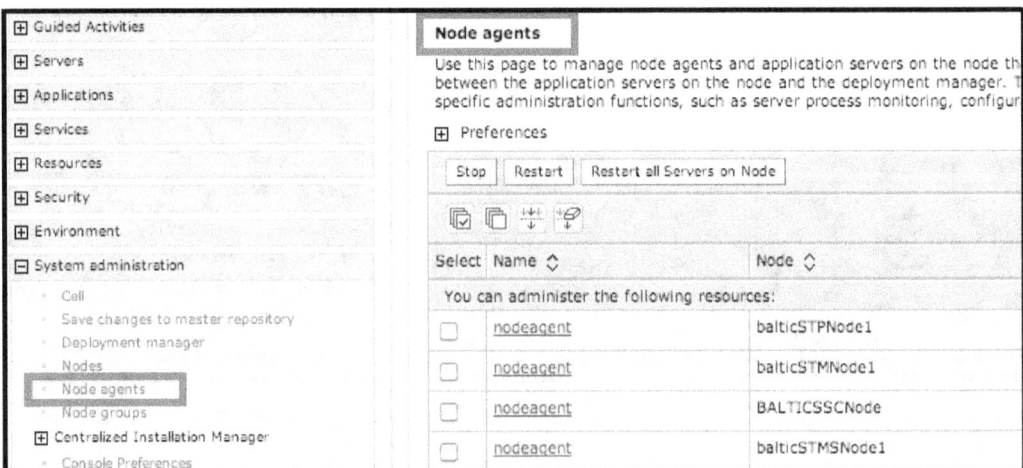

Cell

The grouping of multiple nodes into one management area is called a cell. Tying this all together we can see:

- A single WAS server may have several cells
- A cell will contain a Deployment Manager server
- A cell may have several nodes
- Each node will contain a node agent
- Each node may also contain multiple servers

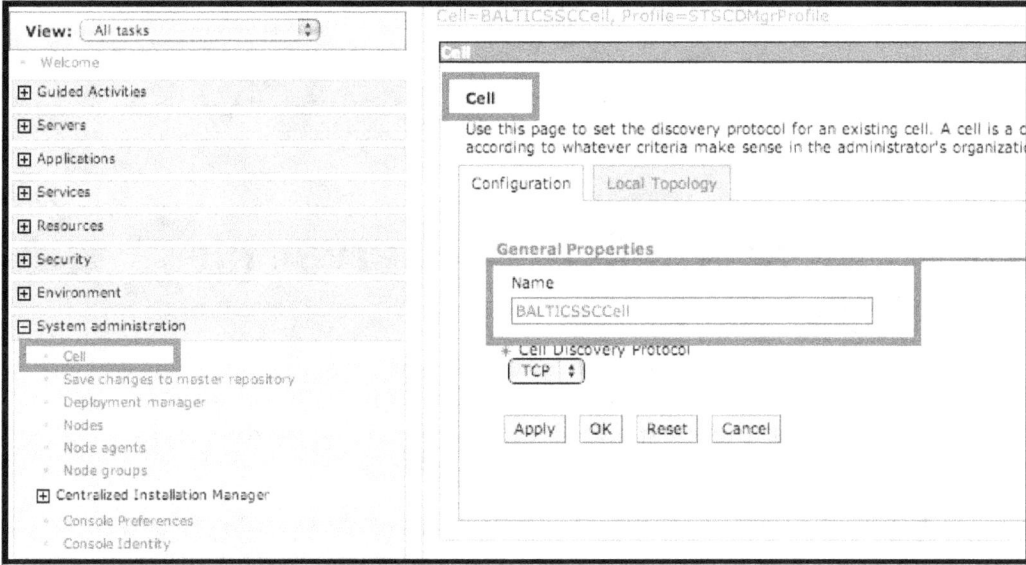

In Sametime 8.5.2, if we install every Sametime application onto one machine in a single cell we will have the following:

- 1 cell
- 1 Deployment manager
- 4 nodes (SSC, Proxy Server, Meeting Server, and Media Manager)
- 4 node agents, one per node

- 5 servers (Meeting Server also includes an http meeting proxy server)

WebSphere Application Server file locations

WAS has a very specific directory structure that matches many of the concepts we previously discussed. Because the directory structure is standardized, it makes it easy for you to find the information you need by traversing the directories.

Appserver or WebSphere home directory

Our starting point is always what is referred to in IBM documentation as the **WebSphere Directory**. This is actually the directory, called appserver, where WAS is installed.

In a standard Linux install, this directory is found at: /opt/ibm/websphere/ appserver.

In a standard Windows install, we strongly recommend modifying the default path on install from: c:\program files (x86)\ibm\websphere\appserver to instead be <drive>:\ibm\websphere\appserver.

There are several reasons for this, not least of which is that the WAS directory structure is deeply nested underneath the **appserver** location, and you may hit Windows file path length limits (which can be limited to 256 characters). We would also strongly recommend against using an install path that contains a space such as '**program files**'. The space in the directory name can often lead to hard-to-find syntax errors in configuration files.

So having established our starting point of `appserver` as our WebSphere directory, we know that all the information we need with regards to our specific Sametime servers is located underneath this directory.

Profiles

The `profiles` directory is the next directory of interest to us under the `appserver` directory. A **profile** is a set of files that define the environment for an application. This includes the `.xml` files that instruct WAS how to run and secure the application itself. A `profiles` subdirectory will contain all the information regarding a specific node so there may be multiple `profiles` subdirectories per machine.

For example, the default Meeting Server profile directory will contain not only the details for the Meeting Server but also its node agent and often the Meeting HTTP Proxy. The Meeting HTTP Proxy provides access to the meeting server through a browser interface on standard port 80.

Therefore, the `profiles` directory contains subdirectories referencing every profile on the server. For example, the following screenshot displays the contents of the `profiles` directory on a small Sametime server named Baltic where all applications are installed. You can see directories for each node as well as for the Deployment Manager itself.

```
     Directory of C:\IBM\WebSphere\AppServer\profiles
28/02/2011   18:46   <DIR>          .
28/02/2011   18:46   <DIR>          ..
02/03/2011   13:38   <DIR>          balticSTMPNProfile1
02/03/2011   19:48   <DIR>          balticSTMSPNProfile1
27/02/2011   19:44   <DIR>          balticSTPPNProfile1
26/02/2011   12:58   <DIR>          STSCAppProfile
25/02/2011   21:46   <DIR>          STSCDMgrProfile
```

In this example where every server is installed into the same cell:

- **balticSTMPNProfile1** is the Sametime Meeting Server node
- **balticSTMSPNProfile1** is the Sametime Media Manager node
- **balticSTPPNProfile1** is the Sametime Proxy Server node
- **STSCAppProfile** is the SSC node
- **STSCDMgrProfile** is the Deployment Manager for the entire cell

Each `profiles` directory contains all the details about the behavior and configuration of an application in the application's own node subdirectory. The structure of each subdirectory under each `profiles` directory conforms to a standard pattern, but as IBM Sametime administrators, we are primarily concerned with three of the subdirectories under each profile.

Logs

The `logs` subdirectory contains the log files for each node. If a profile contains multiple nodes, then there will be multiple directories under `/logs` for us to review, each one matching the name of a node.

If we take the IBM Sametime Meeting Server as an example, then we can see in the following screenshot that there are directories for the three nodes that appear in that profile:

- **STMeetingServer** is the application itself
- **meet_proxy** is the web proxy for the Meeting Server
- **nodeagent** is the node agent that supports both of the above nodes

```
    Directory of C:\IBM\WebSphere\AppServer\profiles\balticSTMPNProfile1\logs

01/03/2011   21:47   <DIR>          .
01/03/2011   21:47   <DIR>          ..
28/02/2011   18:48               646 AboutThisProfile.txt
09/03/2011   16:52         2,097,152 activity.log
09/03/2011   16:52                 0 activity.log.lck
28/02/2011   19:19            28,101 addNode.log
09/03/2011   14:33   <DIR>          ffdc
28/02/2011   18:58               224 iscinstall.log
02/03/2011   13:38   <DIR>          meet_proxy
06/03/2011   06:55   <DIR>          nodeagent
28/02/2011   21:57             3,107 serverStatus.log
02/03/2011   13:36   <DIR>          STMeetingServer
```

In each of the three subdirectories, there are additional log files relating to the activity of each node. As IBM Sametime administrators, the four files in each subdirectory of primary interest to us are:

- **startserver.log** — the server activity as it last attempted to start
- **stopserver.log** — the server activity as it last attempted to stop
- **systemout.log** — a continual report of server activity as you would usually expect to see on a server console
- **systemerror.log** — any errors being thrown by the node

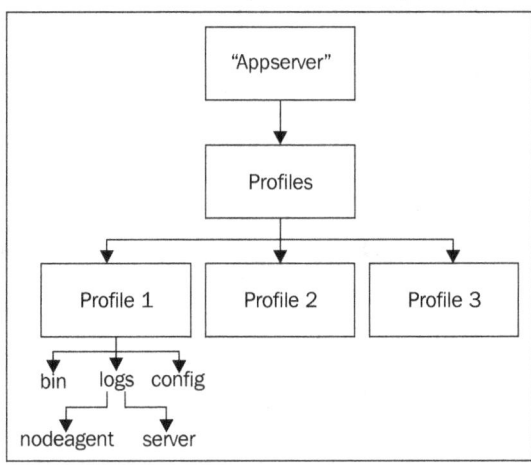

Config

The `config` directory under each profile contains the configuration information that instructs WAS how to deploy and secure the node or application. This configuration information is stored as `.xml` files and in normal circumstances you would not interact with the files directly. It is essential that these files are backed up as these contain configuration and security-related information.

The structure of the subdirectories under each profile's `config` directory also conforms to a consistent pattern:

- The `/config` directory contains a subdirectory called `/cells`
- In `/cells`, we find a directory for every cell that exists on the WAS server
- In each specific `/cells` there is a subdirectory called `/nodes`

- In `/nodes` we find directories for each Node

- In each `/nodes` directory we find directories for each server

```
Directory of C:\IBM\WebSphere\AppServer\profiles\balticSTMPNProfile1\config\cells\
BALTICSSCCELL\Nodes\balticSTMNode1\servers


02/03/2011   13:35   <DIR>        .
02/03/2011   13:35   <DIR>        ..
02/03/2011   13:35   <DIR>        meet_proxy
28/02/2011   19:11   <DIR>        nodeagent
28/02/2011   19:11   <DIR>        STMeetingServer
```

It is worth noting that the directory structure under `/nodes` for all but the Deployment Manager profile is a bit misleading. In the Deployment Manager profile, the `/nodes` directory contains subdirectories for each application, and it stores files containing their configuration information. When you update configuration details in the Sametime Solutions Console, the details are saved here and picked up by the Deployment Manager on restart. However, in the other profiles such as the Meeting Server or Proxy server, these directories are empty.

The preceding screenshot shows that we have drilled down into the profile for the Sametime Meeting Server, and so the only configuration we should see is that of the Sametime Meeting Server. However, as all the Sametime server elements are installed in the same cell in this instance, the directory listing under `/cells` shows all five nodes.

```
28/02/2011   19:18   <DIR>        .
28/02/2011   19:18   <DIR>        ..
28/02/2011   19:18   <DIR>        BALTICSSCNode
28/02/2011   19:18   <DIR>        balticSTMNode1
28/02/2011   19:18   <DIR>        balticSTMSNode1
28/02/2011   19:18   <DIR>        balticSTPNode1
28/02/2011   19:18   <DIR>        DMGrNode
```

- **BALTICSSCNode** — the Sametime Systems Console

- **balticSTMNode1** — the Sametime Meeting Server

- **balticSTMSNode1** — the Sametime Media Server

- **balticSTPNode1** — the Sametime Proxy Server

- **DMGrNode** — the Deployment Manager for the cell

Four of the /nodes directories do not contain server information. Only the **balticSTMNode1** Meeting Server node under the balticSTMPNProfile1 profile has actual configuration files and servers listed. In this way, each profile contains its own /config directory which stores only the files relevant to that profile, and which are updated from the master records stored in the Deployment Manager profile.

Why should you be familiar with the directory structure? Understanding the directory structure will help you implement the appropriate backup and disaster recovery procedures.

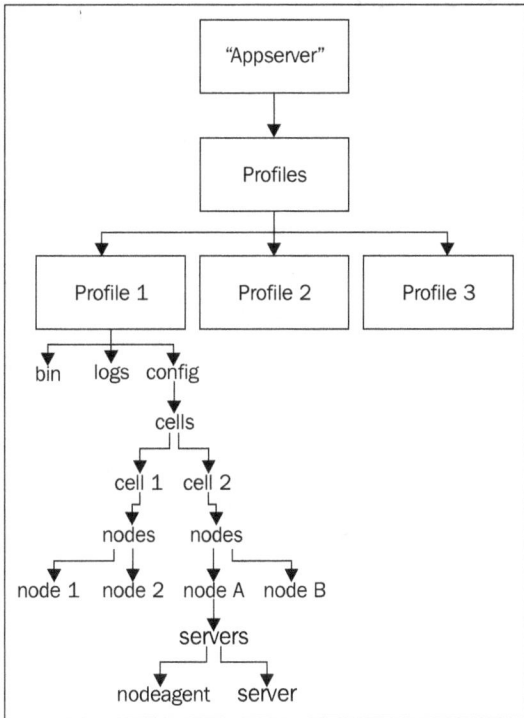

Bin

The /bin directory under each profile contains the batch files used for starting, stopping, and interrogating the application outside of the WAS ISC administrative interface. In each /bin directory, there are a series of batch files used to manage the servers in that node. These include the following:

- **Startserver** — to start a named server
- **Startnode** — to start a node agent
- **Stopserver** — to stop a named server
- **Stopnode** — to stop a node agent
- **Serverstatus** — to review the status of all servers in that node
- **BackupConfig** — to back up the configuration for that node into a file

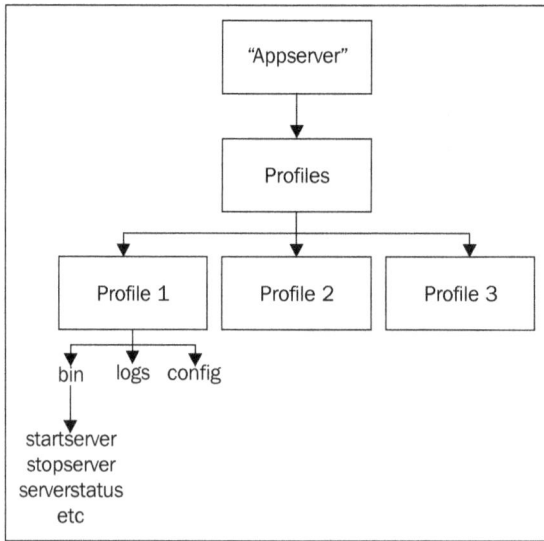

Each command will prompt for an administrator name and password for each server instance but you can pass parameters on the command line such as:

- **-username [username]**
- **-password [password]**

Therefore, to start the Sametime Meeting Center, you would issue the following command string where **wasadmin** and **madeuppassword** are our respective example username and password:

```
Startserver STMeetingServer -username wasadmin -password madeuppassword
```

WAS security

In a WAS environment, there are two separate security mechanisms you will be using. The first mechanism is the security of the WAS environment itself, which includes the WAS administrator user ID that has rights to manage the configuration of the server once it is built. The second mechanism is the security of the application, which is managed within the application itself.

During initial install of an application, such as Sametime Meeting Center, you are prompted to create a name and password for the administration account that is used to set up the server you are installing. In the following screenshot, we are creating an account called **wasadmin**.

For every WAS application you install, such as the Sametime Proxy Server, the Sametime Media Manager, and the Sametime Solutions Console, you are prompted to create an administrative account during install. It is important to note that this account only provides administration rights for that specific server. The account you create can be given whatever name you want, but it must be unique across any directory you want to use. This means you cannot use any name that might also appear in your LDAP environment.

The user ID you create during install is stored in a local repository for the application server only. If you install all your Sametime servers using the same credentials, then you are actually creating multiple, unique copies of those credentials. Each one is located in the local repositories of the servers you installed. Because they are unique user IDs, there is a unique password associated with each one.

Once the server is installed, the WAS ISC for each server allows you to manage that account. The following screenshot is the ISC for the SSC showing the administrative account **wasadmin** that was created during install:

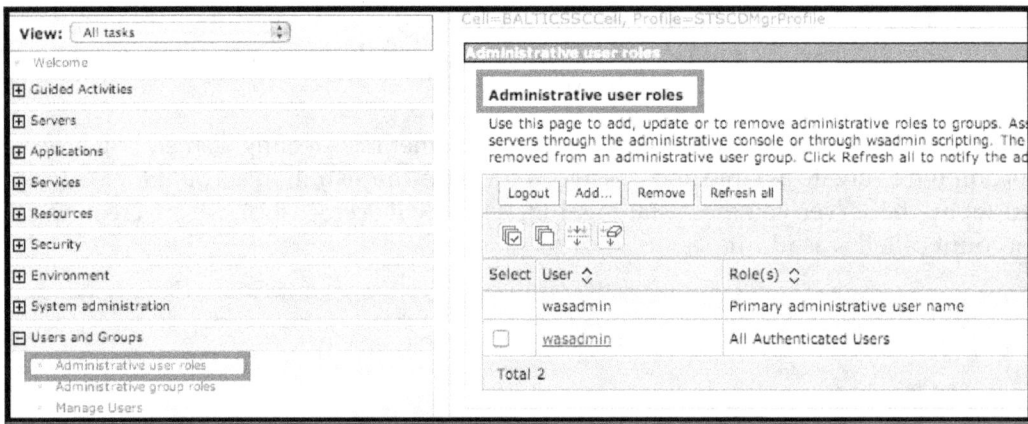

Once the application server is installed, it will have its own levels of security, which are managed within the application itself or within the WAS server instance. For example, we can drill down into the Sametime Meeting Server application in the ISC to set additional Meeting Server administrators beyond the original administrator account created during install.

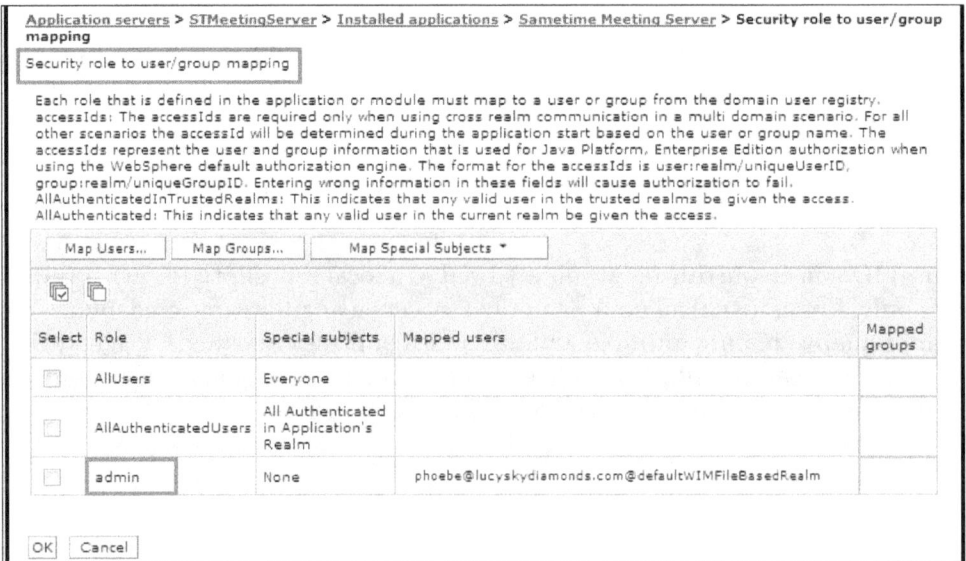

Each application will have its own security configuration and instructions for setting specific security roles.

WAS directory integration

WAS itself has no single directory for an application to use when setting up authentication. The access to an application is granted through any directories you configure WAS to use for authentication. All applications installed in the same cell and using the same Deployment Manager will use the same directories. There are four types of directory configuration in WAS:

- Local operation system registry
- LDAP server
- Federated repository
- Custom repositories

Local operating system registry uses the directory for the operating system on which WAS is installed. For example, if you install WAS on a Windows 2008 server, the local registry would be any users and groups defined locally in Windows on the install machine.

LDAP server is another type of directory configuration. Even though there is no built-in LDAP server under WAS, you can configure the WAS directory and authentication mechanism to point to an external LDAP server and utilize that server as your directory. Using LDAP is the most common method of directory configuration under WAS, and you can use any server that provides an LDAP interface such as Active Directory, eDirectory, or Domino. However, you can only select one LDAP server to use as your directory.

Federated repository is the configuration of multiple LDAP servers into a single realm. WAS will treat this federated repository as a single directory. This is the approach used by the IBM Sametime servers, and the initial LDAP server details you provide to the installer are automatically added to a federated repository for you. This allows you to go back to your WAS configuration at a later date and add additional LDAP directories to supplement your list of users and groups.

In a federated repository model, WAS sees the combined directories as one single directory. Because of this, it is critical that each user only appears once across all directories. If users appear in more than one LDAP directory, configuring multiple LDAP directories as a federated repository will present ongoing authentication and rights problems for these particular users. Similarly, if you use bind credentials to authenticate to an LDAP server, the name of those credentials must be unique for each LDAP server to which WAS binds. You also cannot isolate users in different directories from each other in this model. If you think of your federated repository as a single giant directory, then you will understand how WAS is working with it. Most Lotus WAS-based products use federated repositories as their directory option.

Custom repositories are designed to address the issue of WAS only being able to select one repository type to use. If you decide to use the Local System Registry option, then you cannot add an LDAP server. Similarly, if you choose **LDAP server**, you cannot add additional LDAP directories. A custom repository allows you to select multiple other repository types to create your single WAS directory. In a custom repository model, you can have authentication for both users from the local operating system registry as well as users from an LDAP server.

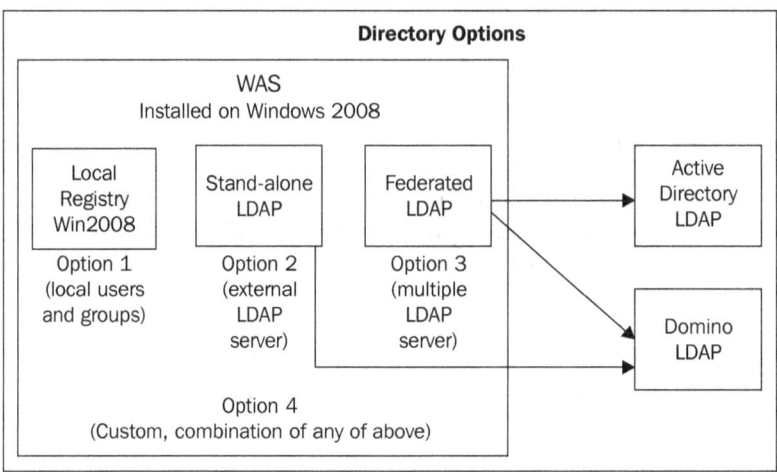

WebSphere deployments

When designing your Sametime infrastructure, you need to understand the deployment options available to you with WAS. Earlier we discussed the concepts of cells, nodes, and Deployment Managers, where a single Deployment Manager in a cell holds the configuration for all the servers in that cell. You may also have nodes which contain application servers and node agents that are responsible for the management of those servers. You should consider those concepts, as they can affect your infrastructure design. We will discuss some of these deployments in the following sections.

Single server deployment

In Sametime 8.5.2, you can install every application onto the same server. During each application installation, you will be prompted with the choice of adding that application to an existing cell or to create a new cell.

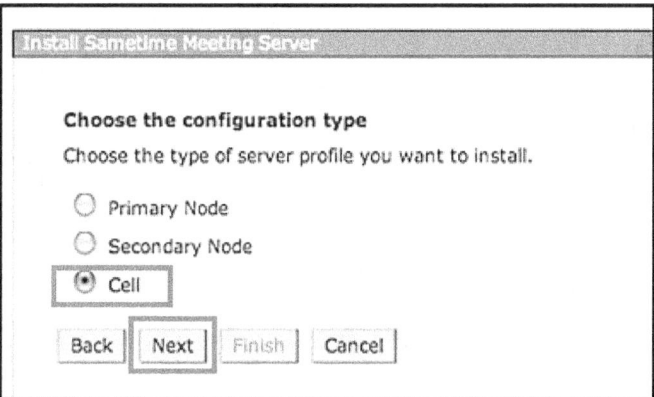

Installing separate applications in their own cell means each application has its own configuration and Deployment Manager, and each has to be managed separately through its own management interface. To clarify, if you install the Sametime Meeting Server in a separate cell from the Sametime Proxy Server, then each application will install its own administrative port. You will have two different WAS administration URLs to work with should you want to change the underlying configuration.

Prior to Sametime 8.5.2, you could only install each application into its own cell on the same WAS server. However, this has been resolved in IBM Sametime 8.5.2 and you can now install all applications into one cell. This single server approach makes administration much easier as all changes can be done from one URL and only one Deployment Manager server needs to be running.

The following is a diagram of an IBM Sametime 8.5.2 single server installation:

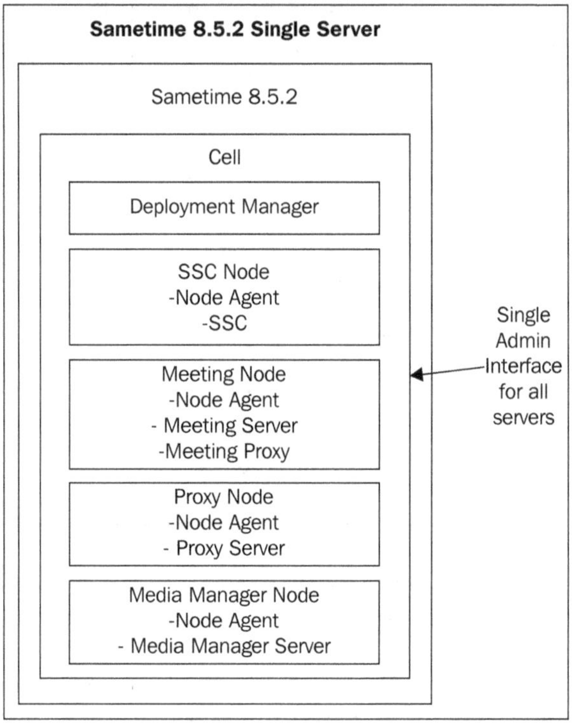

Multi-server deployment

A multi-server deployment assumes you want to install different IBM Sametime applications onto different machines. In this deployment you may want to give the Sametime Proxy, Sametime Meeting, and Sametime Media Manager applications their own resources on dedicated machines away from the SSC. As the first server installed on a new machine always creates its own cell, you would have four different machines (SSC, Proxy, Media Manager, and Meetings) running in their own isolated cell environments. You would also have four administration interfaces or URLs, one for each machine.

The following diagram shows the installation configuration in a multi-server deployment in which each server is independent from the other with its own Deployment Manager:

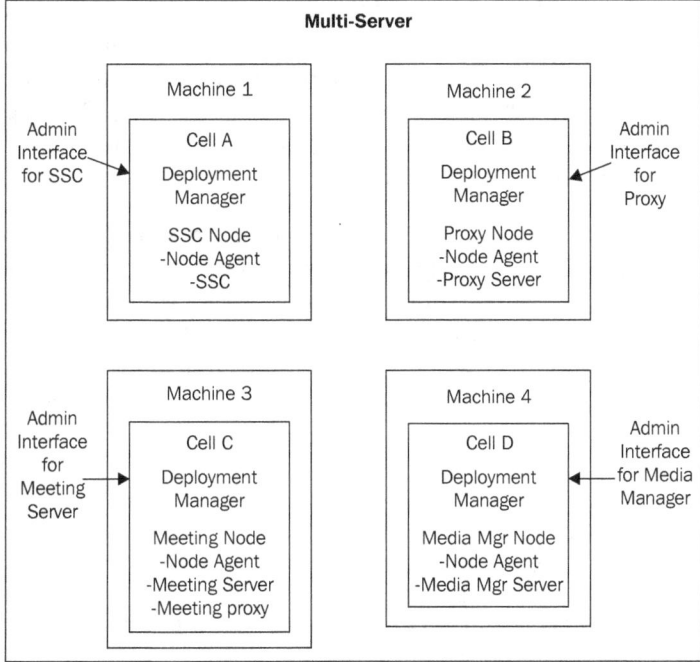

There is obviously some advantage of installing different application servers on their own hardware, but a more manageable way of handling this requirement is to build a cluster environment using Network deployment.

Network deployment and clustering

Installing an application as part of a network deployment tells WAS that, although the application will be installed on a remote machine, the management and configuration of the application will be handled and stored on the machine running your Deployment manager. In the case of IBM Sametime, that would be the machine running your SSC.

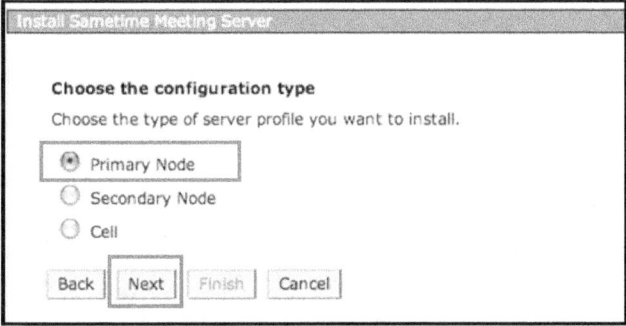

Every network deployment must have at least one primary node and can have multiple secondary nodes. However, these nodes are not available for management until they are added to a WAS cluster. The network deployment model installs only the application server on the remote server. The server running the Deployment Manager (in this example case, the SSC) is responsible for maintaining the configuration and managing the servers.

With IBM Sametime, you have the option of clustering the Sametime Proxy Server and Sametime Meeting Server during install. It is a limitation of WAS that only servers within the same cell are available for clustering. If you make the decision to install your first Meeting Server in its own cell (as with the preceding multi-server deployment example), then you will need to rebuild that server to be a primary node deployed from the SSC if you want to expand out to a Meeting Server cluster at a later date.

It is perfectly viable to build a Network deployment with only a single primary node. If there is a possibility that you may want multiple Sametime Meeting Servers or Sametime Proxy Servers in the future, then deploying them initially as primary nodes is a good solution.

WAS has two methods of clustering that are available, but they refer to decisions on where and how machines are located as opposed to any different approaches to configuration. A vertical cluster assumes multiple servers of the same type on a single machine, for example, a primary Meeting Server node plus multiple secondary Meeting Server nodes. This allows services to be provided from multiple servers, but leaves the machine itself as a single point of failure. A more common clustering method is a horizontal cluster, where a single node of each application is located on each machine. In other words, a single machine may contain the primary node of the Sametime Meeting Server and a primary node of the Sametime Proxy Server.

The following diagram shows the beginning of a horizontal network deployment where we have two nodes in place for the Sametime Meeting Server:

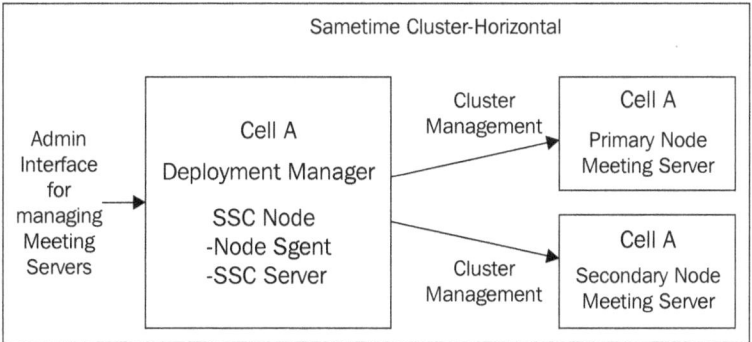

Even if you do not intend to expand beyond a single dedicated server per application, from an administrative perspective this is a better deployment scenario for IBM Sametime than a simple multi-server/multi-cell deployment.

Summary

In this chapter, you learned what WAS is and what it does in a Sametime environment. You learned the different concepts and terms used when referring to a WAS environment and deployment. You learned about the directory structure of WAS and what information is stored in each subdirectory in a Sametime environment. You learned how WAS security is implemented, as well as what directory options are possible. Finally, you learned about the different deployment configurations and the benefits associated with each one. In the next chapter, you will learn about the decisions you need to consider when planning for an installation of Sametime 8.5.2.

5

Executive Decisions: Preparing for your Sametime 8.5.2 Installation

In this chapter, those decisions that need to be made prior to a Sametime installation will be reviewed and discussed. As with any complex project requiring not only software installation but also planning for additional hardware, operating system, network, authentication, and database infrastructure, Sametime requires careful and deliberate planning. Regardless of whether you are implementing a clustered, multi-location, full-service deployment, or a basic Classic Meeting Server upgrade, taking the time to develop a project plan for your environment will save you effort and steps by the end of the project.

In this chapter you will learn:

- What decisions are required for your Sametime 8.5.2 installation
- What is needed for the growth and stability of a Sametime 8.5.2 environment
- How the Sametime software is obtained
- What are the software prerequisites
- What are the hardware requirements
- How to plan for the WAS environment
- Whether coexistence or migration is required
- How to plan for DB2
- How to plan for LDAP
- How to plan for network requirements

Decisions required for planning your Sametime environment

Many sites considering the deployment of Sametime 8.5.2 will also have some level of infrastructure already in place. Your site may be using an earlier version of Sametime for instant messaging but you now want to introduce meeting and web conferencing features. You may want to deploy Sametime Proxy Server to expand the client platform options available to your users. Regardless of your current environment, installing or upgrading to Sametime 8.5.2 will need to be done in a controlled manner to avoid any disruption to your users. Now is the time to put the effort into planning and preparation. We need to look at the following topics:

- Upgrade or new install
- Infrastructure design
- Pilot to production plan
- Operating system
- What features will be installed?
- Integration points with Quickr, Connections, Sametime Advanced, and Sametime Gateway
- Chat logging
- Use of Business Cards
- STLinks versus Sametime Proxy

Upgrade or new install

There are several options for installing and upgrading Sametime server components that allow you to use the existing infrastructure until the new one is ready to go into production. Whether or not you have a Sametime deployment already in place, much of your initial planning for Sametime 8.5.2 remains the same. In Sametime 8.5.2, many of the features are tied to the client versions currently in use. For example, the use of audio and video is managed differently depending upon client versions in 8.0.x, 8.5.1 and 8.5.2, and the versions are not cross-compatible. Therefore, considering how and when the clients will be deployed becomes a key milestone in your plan.

Fortunately, most internal Sametime and cross-component communication relies on fully qualified hostnames resolvable in DNS. Working with the networking team that manages internal or public DNS is a critical part of the planning process. This gives you the option of building under one hostname in test and switching out to a production hostname at a later date. It is also a viable option to upgrade or deploy in stages according to your own priorities, introducing new services and components to existing users without disrupting their daily work.

Infrastructure design

As part of our infrastructure design review, we will examine several types of configurations. With Sametime 8.5.2 you have a lot of flexibility as to how you design your Sametime architecture. We will examine the following:

- Use of Multiplexors for IM
- Multiple Proxy Servers
- Multiple Meeting Servers
- Multiple Media Manager components
- Bandwidth Manager
- Multiple TURN Servers

Use of Multiplexors for IM

The MUX is the Sametime service on a Community Server that handles authentication requests from the client to the Community Server where they are processed. In a standard server install, the MUX runs as one of the many Sametime Community Server services on the same physical server. However, you also have the option of running the MUX service as a stand-alone service on a separate physical server. This enables the Community Server to handle more concurrent client connections. Distributing MUXs in front of your Community Servers also gives you the option of placing local network MUXs for your centralized servers improving client performance and reducing network traffic.

Without a separate MUX in place, each client has its own network connection to the Community Server. This requires the server to maintain and manage each individual connection. With MUXs deployed separately, the client connections are to that service only, and the MUXs themselves maintain a single network connection to the Community Server. In this way, a single Community Server that could support 20,000 users would instead be able to support over 100,000 users concurrently.

When deploying a Sametime Community Server, you continue to have the option to do so in a cluster. Additionally, you can put a MUX in front of the Community Server cluster to distribute load. If you expand that to have multiple MUXs managed by a network load balancer, then it allows you to provide Instant Messaging services to hundreds of thousands of users using very little hardware.

The following is a simple MUX deployment diagram showing a three-server Sametime cluster managed by a single MUX. The clients only connect to the fully qualified hostname of the MUX itself and never to the Community Servers directly.

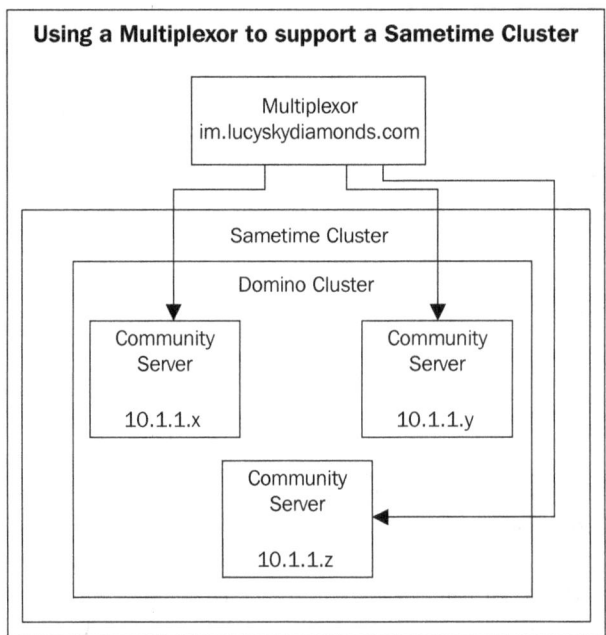

Things to consider before planning your MUX server deployment:

- Do you want to use a MUX purely for load balancing?
- Do you want multiple MUXs for failover, and if so, will you use round-robin DNS or a network load balancer to decide how to route users to each one?
- A MUX will direct users to each of its defined Community Servers in a simple manner, so if the MUX has three Community Servers defined, a user could end up being directed to any one of those at any point.

Multiple Proxy Servers

In a Sametime 8.5.2 deployment, it is possible to have two different configurations of Proxy Servers. You can build multiple separate instances of Proxy Servers, each with their own configuration and each connecting to a separate Community Server or MUX. You can also build clusters of Proxy Servers to help balance client connections.

In a multiple Proxy Server deployment, where you want different Community Servers managed, you could install and manage those servers either in their own individual cell or together in a single cell. The difference would be that the servers with their own cell would also have their own Deployment Manager and a dedicated administration interface. By installing multiple Proxy Servers you could provide location-based access to your Community Servers.

In the example that follows, there are two Proxy Servers providing services to users in the United States and the United Kingdom respectively. In the US, the Proxy Server connection is to an instant messaging cluster. Although in following diagram the two Proxy Servers have different fully qualified hostnames, it would be viable to have them configured to use the same hostname. They would then rely on regional DNS settings to determine the resolution of the hostname.

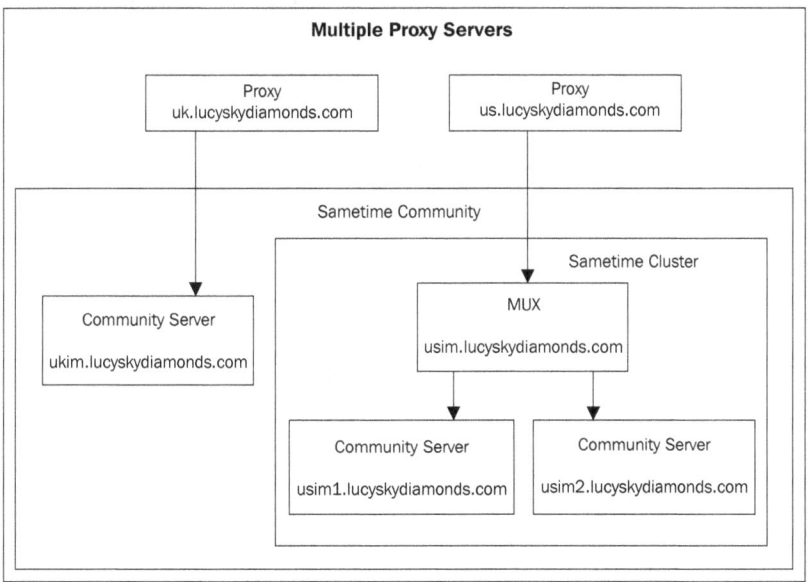

The Proxy Servers themselves can also be clustered. In that configuration, each Proxy Server would be configured identically. WAS clustering works on the basis of having a primary server definition and a series of secondary server definitions that have identical configurations. A Proxy Server cluster will provide load balancing and disaster recovery capabilities as well as simplified management.

The following are some decisions you should consider before planning your Proxy Server deployment:

- Is the Proxy Server going to be used purely for Sametime clients, or will it also be used for awareness in applications (replacing STLinks)?
- Will your users require a browser client and where are they based?
- Are there users external to your firewall that will require a browser client?
- Where are the Community Servers or MUXs located?
- Considering that a single Deployment Manager can only support a single Proxy Server cluster, will you deploy your Proxy Server cluster as part of the SSC or in its own cell with its own Deployment Manager?

Multiple Meeting Servers

In Sametime 8.5.2, it is possible to have both multiple Meeting Servers and multiple clustered Meeting Servers. In the first instance we would have different Meeting Servers, each with their own dedicated DB2 database and Meeting Server HTTP Proxy. Each Meeting Server would be unaware of the other and would host different meetings. A user wanting to attend a meeting would need to log onto the specific server hosting that meeting.

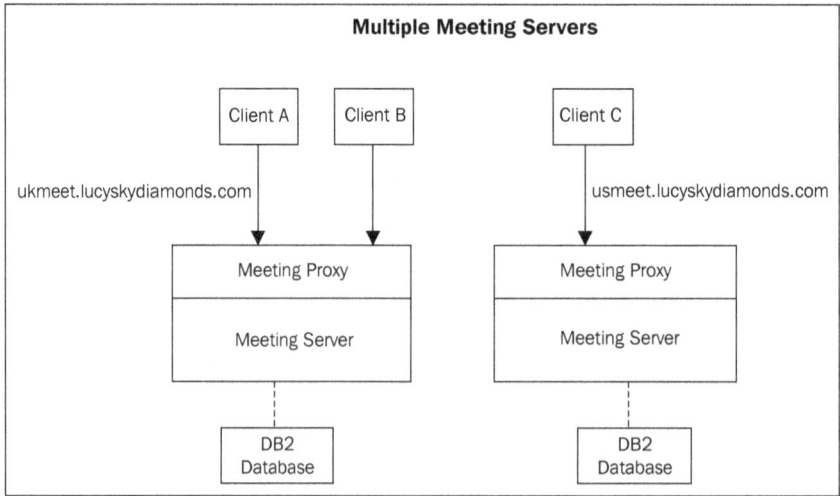

If your meetings are primarily among users in a particular location or region, this would be an effective way of giving that location their own dedicated Meeting Server.

Clustering of Meeting Servers is designed to support load balancing and failover requirements. In a Meeting Server cluster, multiple Meeting Servers configured as nodes within a single cluster share a single DB2 database, a single Meeting Server HTTP Proxy, and support any meetings created on any server.

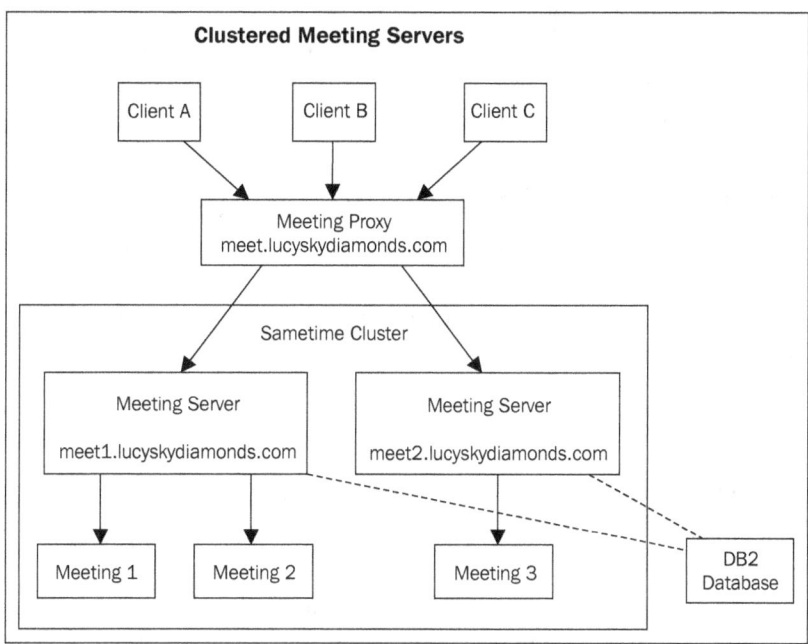

When a meeting is started, it is assigned a home node by the Deployment Manager in its cell. All attendees of that meeting are directed to that Meeting Server node. For load balancing, different meetings may be directed to different nodes. Users cannot attend the same meeting on different nodes and see each other, nor would the Sametime clients connect them in that manner. If a node fails over while users are in a meeting, then they will be prompted to reconnect to the meeting. That reconnection will silently happen on a different Meeting Server node. If your meetings are heavily attended or centralized, this would be an effective deployment scenario.

Decisions to consider before planning your Meeting Server deployment:

- Who will need to attend meetings?
- What is the network bandwidth between meeting attendees and the location of the Meeting Servers?
- When and where should you use multiple discrete Meeting Servers versus larger clusters?

- Will the users all need audio and video connections, and therefore need a Media Manager connection?

- As a Deployment Manager can only support a single cluster, will you be deploying Meeting Server clusters in their own cells and with their own deployment managers?

- Where will the Meeting Server HTTP Proxy servers be located? In a cluster, you can have multiple Meeting Proxy Servers installed separately from the Meeting Servers themselves.

Multiple Media Manager components

The Media Manager server consists of several different components. In the Sametime documentation, you will find many references to IBM only supporting one Media Manager within a SSC. While this is true, it is possible to break out the component parts into multiple servers and even cluster them for load balancing and high availability.

The Media Manager itself consists of three separate components:

- The SIP Proxy/Registrar is used for handling client connections and directing clients to an available Conference Manager. The SIP Proxy/Registrar can be clustered.

- The Conference Manager handles client connections within meetings and routes data between attendees. The Conference Manager can be clustered.

- The Packet Switcher is responsible for the routing of audio and video packets, as well as using voice-activated switching to manage client traffic. The Packet Switcher cannot be clustered and must be connected to a single Conference Manager or Conference Manager cluster.

In a small deployment or a pilot install, it is acceptable to install all the Media Manager components as one element within its own cell or as part of the SSC cell.

In the following diagram, all Media Manager components are installed and running as a single server instance under WAS. This installation, although suitable for a small environment, can never be expanded beyond this single server install as this install type (with all components) cannot be clustered.

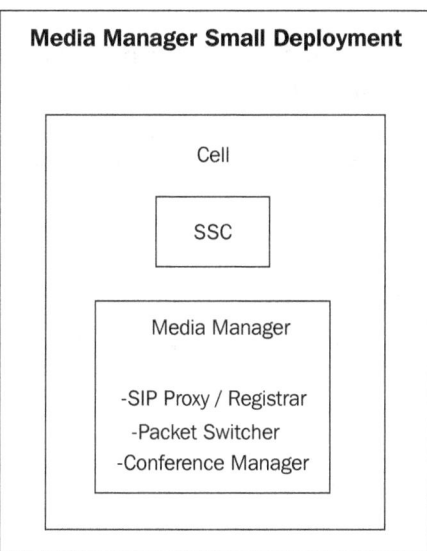

Media Manager Small Deployment

Cell

SSC

Media Manager

-SIP Proxy / Registrar
-Packet Switcher
-Conference Manager

Alternatively, in an enterprise deployment, you can select individual Media Manager components to install on separate physical or virtual servers. You can also have multiple instances of those components deployed. The SIP Proxy/Registrar and Conference Manager components can be installed either as separate multiple servers or as cluster groups. The installation order should be as follows:

- A SIP Proxy/Registrar requires a Community Server to already be installed, and it must be installed ahead of the Conference Manager and Packet Switcher. You can install multiple servers with the same configuration in a cluster or multiple servers pointing to different Community Servers as a stand-alone server.

- A Conference Manager requires both a Community Server and SIP Proxy/ Registrar to be assigned to it during install. Conference Managers in a cluster will all have the same configuration, or you can install multiple servers each with different configurations as stand-alone servers.

- A Packet Switcher must have a Conference Manager (or a Conference Manager cluster) to be assigned to it during install. It can only provide services to users working with that Conference Manager.

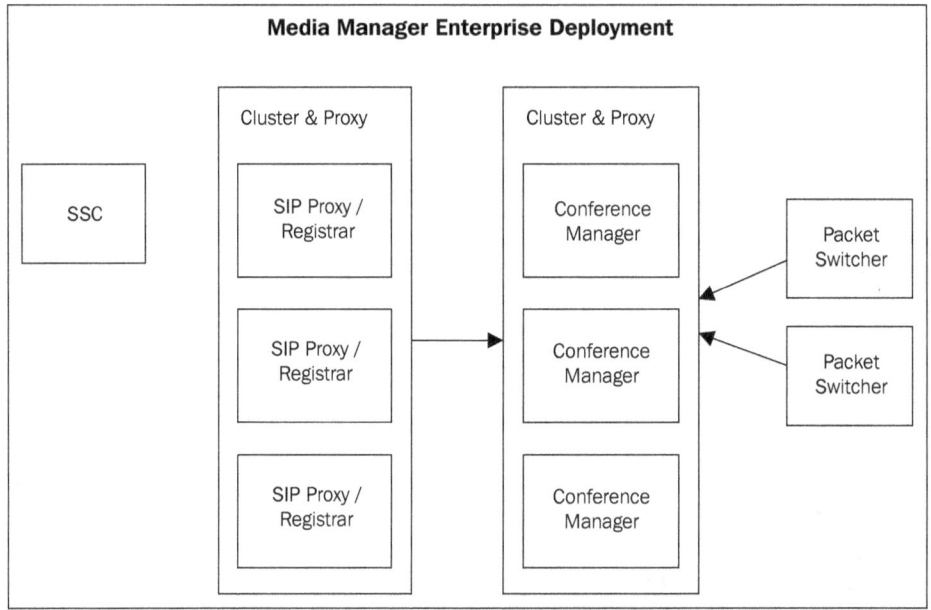

Additionally, in a WAS cluster there is a proxy server created that acts as the interface between the clients and the servers in the cluster. So in a clustered Conference Manager or SIP Proxy/Registrar deployment, there is also scope to deploy multiple distributed proxy servers to individually provide access. However, it is important to note that in a clustered environment the Proxy Server manages both client connections, and the load balancing between cluster members provides no additional advantage for users in different locations to always utilize specific cluster members. There is no requirement that you must cluster any of the elements or cluster them all equally.

The following are decisions to consider before planning your Media Manager server deployment:

- Where are the users requiring audio and video services located?
- What is the bandwidth between the clients and the intended location of the Packet Switcher?
- Is it possible that your initial deployment could grow in the future? If so, would you be prepared to rebuild your Media Manager deployment as separate servers at that point?

- You cannot make an existing server, such as a Conference Manager, which has already been deployed as a stand-alone primary node into a secondary node member of a cluster. However, you can deploy a single primary node and add additional secondary nodes into a cluster at a later date.

- Do you want everything centralized so you have a large central cluster of components all providing service to everyone, or do you want to provide stand-alone scaled services for different locations and user groups?

- The Conference Manager can only support two TCSPI adaptors: one for external audio and one for external video (which also includes audio). This applies to all Conference Managers in a cluster but can be different for stand-alone non-clustered Conference Managers.

Bandwidth Manager

The Bandwidth Manager is a new server component introduced in Sametime 8.5.2, which is designed to enable the Sametime administrator to finely control the audio and video service and quality of each individual call. The Bandwidth Manager is a WAS server install which runs either as a stand-alone or as a clustered service and connects to the SIP Proxy/Registrar component of a Media Manager server. Within the Bandwidth Manager, the Sametime Administrator can define call rate policies which are rules for local site calls, cross site calls, and users or groups that are calculated on the fly when a call is initiated. These call rate policies determine the resources assigned to a call including the quality of the audio codec and video frame rate and the ability to deny audio or video services completely, for example during peak load times.

When a user connects to the SIP Proxy/Registrar to start a call, the Bandwidth Manager reviews its call rate policies for that site, site connection, and user to determine what level of service to authorize for the new call.

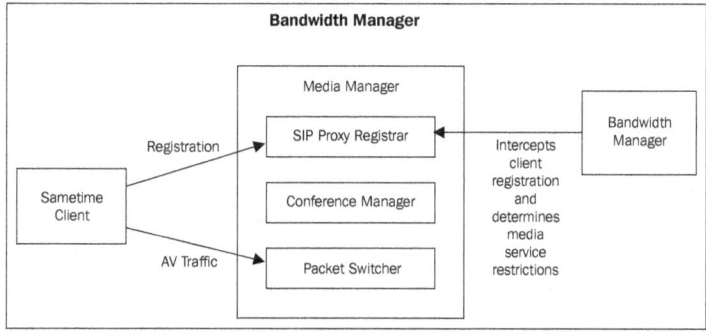

By deploying a Bandwidth Manager alongside your Media Manager Server, you are able to control the media traffic generated around your organization.

Multiple TURN Servers

There is an additional server in Sametime 8.5.2 which is not part of the Media Manager install. It complements those components when clients are not on the same network as the Media Manager components, if they are behind a firewall, or if they have multiple network cards or IP addresses. This is the TURN Server, a Java server program which handles NAT traversal issues and the routing of audio and video packets across networks.

The TURN Server does not require WAS to install or run, and it can be placed on multiple servers. However, in the configuration of the Conference Manager, you must specify if a TURN Server is used for audio and video traffic. You then provide the hostname for that server. TURN Servers must also be installed on the same network and subnet as the Media Manager components they are supporting, as well as being directly accessible by both internal and external clients using the same fully qualified hostname. Therefore, multiple TURN Servers would only be deployed to either support different Media Manager component clusters, or they would be identically configured and rely on round-robin DNS or network load balancing for high availability.

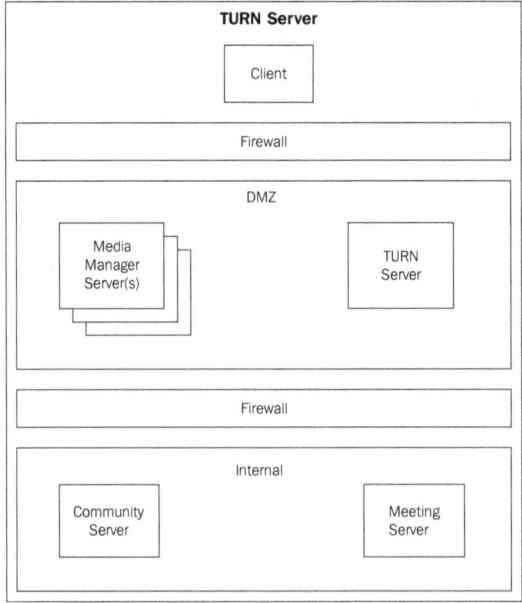

The following are decisions to consider before planning your TURN Server deployment:

- What networks are the Media Manager components on?
- What networks are the clients on?

- Can you deploy the TURN Server in a DMZ for both internal and external traffic?

- Adding additional TURN Servers to support a single Media Manager Server or cluster is easy after initial deployment.

- Enabling or disabling the use of a TURN Server from the Conference Manager (and thereby reverting to peer-to-peer traffic) is easy after initial deployment, assuming you have considered the network requirements in advance.

Pilot to production plan

Whether you already have a Sametime infrastructure in place or you want to install a new server set, you will want to begin by creating a pilot deployment. The goal of a pilot deployment is to establish that the services you are installing will meet the requirements of the business, as well as to assist you in defining demand. Many companies start with a pilot install and the pilot system becomes their production environment for better or worse. If there is any possibility your pilot deployment will be converted or expanded into a production environment rather than rebuilt, then you should consider the following:

- Your Sametime Community Servers will need to use LDAP for their directories. If you have existing Sametime servers that are currently using Domino Directories, then those servers will need to be converted to use LDAP and the buddy list and contact details changed to LDAP format. Using a Domino server as your LDAP server is a valid option but you cannot use the Domino server running your Sametime Community server for this purpose.

- Once a WAS server has been installed in its own cell or as a primary or secondary node, it cannot be changed from that state. It can only be rebuilt.

- Once you have installed a single Media Manager Server as a single instance (with all components on one physical or virtual machine), you cannot expand further without rebuilding.

- Everything in a Sametime environment is DNS-specific and tied to fully qualified hostnames. It is possible to change the DNS for an existing hostname and have that traffic redirected to a new server to move from pilot to production.

- It is simple to add additional Community Servers, MUXs, and non-clustered Proxy and Meeting Servers at a later date.

- Adding additional Proxy Servers, Meeting Servers, or Media Manager components in a clustered configuration requires that the initial pilot servers to be installed as primary nodes.

It is always recommended that your pilot install is separated from your production Sametime environment. This prevents early test systems from integrating with production systems before they are completely configured. Additionally, decisions made to deploy a temporary evaluation pilot do not then end up driving the best practice configuration for your production requirements.

Operating system

Although Sametime supports multiple operating systems, not all components support all operating systems. For instance, DB2 is not supported on all platforms and is a requirement for both the Meeting Server and SSC. However, it does not need to be installed on the same physical or virtual server as the Sametime servers that use it.

When selecting an operating system for your Sametime deployment, your decision should be guided by your existing infrastructure. Do you or the staff managing the servers have the skills to support and manage the operating system? Deploying an operating system that is largely unknown to you will limit your ability to troubleshoot or tune Sametime performance.

In general, all server components can be deployed on Windows 2003 and Windows 2008 including R2 32-bit and 64-bit, as well as Linux 32-bit and 64-bit. All the Sametime server components themselves are only 32-bit even if running on a 64-bit operating system. The Media Manager components are only supported on Linux and Windows platforms.

What features will be installed?

When initially designing your pilot or production environment, you need to take a step back and identify what the business goals are behind deploying Sametime 8.5.2. Identifying and prioritizing the objectives will help you decide which servers are needed and to what scale they should be deployed. The following objectives should be considered:

- For Instant Messaging, you will need to deploy a Community Server and if your company or organization requires browser client access, a Proxy Server. The Proxy Server is best installed alongside a Sametime Solutions Console, which itself requires DB2, although it can be installed and managed in isolation.

- For meetings, you will need to deploy a Sametime Community Server, SSC, DB2, and Meeting Server. This combination provides the new Meeting Server and meeting client but includes no audio or video services. Although it is possible to continue to have meetings using the Domino-based Classic Meeting Server, it is only recommended as a short term or transitional solution as it is a product that is no longer being developed or enhanced.

- For web-based meetings, you will need to deploy the Proxy Server as well as all the servers required for Sametime meetings, including Community Server, SSC, DB2, and Meeting Server. The Proxy Server provides features such as awareness and business cards in web-based meetings.

- If audio or video services are required, then you will need to deploy the Sametime Media Manager components to integrate with both the Community Server and Meeting Server elements. If you only want audio and video between instant messaging clients then you do not need the Meeting Server. However, if the goal is to offer web conferences in meetings, then you will need the Meeting Server as well as the Proxy Server.

Integration points with Quickr, Connections, Sametime Advanced, and Sametime Gateway

Sametime 8.5.2 is designed to be part of the IBM/Lotus collaborative toolset. When Sametime is integrated with products such as Quickr, Connections, Sametime Advanced, or Sametime Gateway, it enhances their features as well.

Lotus Quickr is a web-based project collaboration tool for teams and is available as both a Domino and WAS application. Although the implementation of Quickr for WAS and Domino differ, there are certain key collaboration concepts that apply. In a Quickr Place, you may have people working together on documents, sharing project plans, and assigning tasks. By integrating Sametime with Quickr, those people can be logged into the instant messaging environment, see each other online in the Team Place, and discuss the project in real time. They can also initiate a breakout real-time meeting to take place on the Sametime Meeting Server and store the meeting record or chat transcripts as part of the Quickr Project Place. Quickr supports **Single Sign-On (SSO)** between the Sametime Community Server and its own environment.

IBM Connections is an enterprise social networking solution that is designed to bring the right information to the people who need it. It does this by creating a secure environment to discover information, share ideas, and identify people with similar expertise or interests. Everyone in a Connections community has a profile which details personal information about them, including their job responsibilities, reporting structure, and career history. Integrating Sametime with Connections provides the ability to view online presence for participants in various Connections communities.

Users of Connections can begin an instant message chat with other Connections users as well as with other Sametime users. Sametime can be configured to use the Connections profiles as its business card information for users. This brings together a single directory of people and information and provides identities for those who only meet online. Sametime chat transcripts, meeting recordings, and meeting reports can all be added to Connections discussions, activities, and files.

IBM Sametime Advanced is a separate server product that also runs on a WAS platform. Sametime Advanced integrates using SSO with your existing Sametime Community Server and adds the features of persistent chats, instant sharing, and Skill Tap searches using real-time broadcast announcements, chats, and polling.

IBM Sametime Gateway is a WAS-based instant messaging server that provides a conduit between your secure internal instant messaging environment on Sametime and the public instant messaging environments of AOL and Google. By installing and configuring Sametime Gateway to connect to your existing Sametime Community Servers, your Sametime users can add external community users to their buddy lists, be seen online by those on external systems, and engage in Instant Messaging conversations.

Chat logging

One of the key requirements many companies have when deploying Sametime is ensuring that conversations that happen in real time are recorded and accessible for future use. Some organizations or companies may be required to store these chat transcripts due to legal or records retention requirements. The ability to save chat transcripts and meeting activity is often a prerequisite before servers may be placed into production. In Sametime, logging of chat activities and transcripts is managed by each individual server responsible for providing that service, and logs for each server are not stored centrally. Given different situations and server components, there are a number of chat logging options for you to configure, and these can vary for each service and server.

In the Sametime Meeting Server, the meeting rooms themselves can retain the history of each meeting including conversations that took place, files that were shared, and collaborative work that was completed. The Meeting Server can also record each meeting but cannot record the audio or video components.

The Sametime Community Server has its own chat logging service to record all instant messaging conversations. As this service runs on the Community Server, it is independent of whatever client is being used. The chat logging service only provides an interface to record conversations. To actually record conversations and save them in a readable way requires a custom application to be developed using the supplied chat API. Several effective chat logging applications are available as third-party add-ons that support current versions of Sametime. Refer to Appendix B for chat logging tools.

There is a client-side chat logging option that allows transcripts to be saved to client machines. As this is not an enforceable feature (client-side logging can be disabled by administrators but not enabled), it should be seen as a client usability feature and not an administration or management record of chat activity.

If you are considering deploying Sametime Advanced, then you will have the additional feature of persistent chat rooms. Persistent chat rooms are managed and maintained by the Sametime Advanced server itself and transcript logs in those rooms are automatically accessible on the server.

Use of business cards

Sametime Business Cards are a way of providing summary information about the person you are contacting on Sametime. This information includes their name, job title, phone number, and photo. In a world where many of us only meet online, being able to easily see who we are talking to and visualizing them enhances the experience of online meetings and conversations. If a person has a Business Card, then it will be visible to you in a chat window when interacting with that person.

The Business Card information is available to you when hovering over the person's name in meeting rooms, when viewing a contact list, or when looking at your e-mail inbox. Sametime Business Cards are another Sametime service that runs on the Domino-based Community Server. The configuration of Business Cards is maintained as part of the Sametime Community Server configuration and is applied to all users on a server. This allows Business Card configuration to be different for different servers.

Alternatively, if your organization uses IBM Connections, you can leverage the profiles within Connections as your Business Card details for users. This creates additional ways that people, who never meet, can learn about each other.

STLinks versus Sametime Proxy

STLinks is a Java applet provided with the Domino-based Community Server that enables online presence and instant messaging from within browser-based applications. STLinks is used extensively in the web-based iNotes mail client, and many customers also utilize it in their own applications.

STLinks uses an applet on the application or mail server which connects to the Sametime Community Server for services. Although STLinks is a stable product, the use of Java applets might be blocked as a security issue by various browsers and by a user's desktop operating system. In addition, the Java applet itself can significantly slow the load time of a web page and is memory intensive.

The Sametime Proxy Server's Ajax (Asynchronous JavaScript and XML) functions can be used instead of STLinks if Sametime Proxy has been deployed in your environment. The Ajax calls are JavaScript functions that do not significantly impact page load times or memory utilization. In addition, the Sametime Proxy services offer a much richer set of features than STLinks including rich text and multi-way chat.

As of Domino 8.5.2, the embedded Sametime awareness in the iNotes mail client still uses STLinks.

What is needed for growth and stability?

Suppose you are considering adding to your existing Sametime server architecture, deploying more features, or perhaps your current Sametime environment is experiencing some load-based issues due to the server sizing being too small. Or what if you now have a requirement for clustering or moving stand-alone servers to virtual machines? Either of these scenarios could occur or you could also be asked to add third-party software to your Sametime environment. We will now examine the following:

- Testing of existing tools and plugins
- Clustering
- Virtualization

Testing of existing tools and plugins

If your environment already has Sametime in place, then it is possible you already have systems on the Sametime server or clients that will need to be tested and validated against the new Sametime 8.5.2 environment. Many third-party tools are written using the published Sametime APIs and these have changed significantly in Sametime 8.5, and again in Sametime 8.5.1. Testing non-IBM products against new Sametime versions is good practice in planning any upgrade. The following areas are where third-party products may exist in your environment:

- Sametime Connect client or embedded client—plugin
- Sametime Community Server or other workstation—Sametime bot
- Sametime Community Server—chat logging
- Sametime Community Server—TCSPI adaptor

The TCSPI adaptor is no longer deployed on the Community Server. It now uses the Conference Manager component of the Media Manager. Installing a TCSPI adaptor on the Community Server is still supported for classic meetings and for Community Servers deployed without a Media Manager.

Clustering

The clustering of server components is designed to provide load balancing and failover functionality. **Load balancing** is a method for allowing server resources to be fulfilled based on load or requests to multiple identically configured servers. A process takes the request and directs it to any of the servers in a way that is transparent to the user. **Failover** is a method for redirecting service when a server that is in use stops responding. A process reconnects the users to another identically configured server. In failover cases, it is usual for the clients to receive some notification that they are moving to a new server and that recently entered data may be lost.

Many of the Sametime server components offer clustering features but each behaves differently. In some cases, multiple independent servers may be more appropriate than a single large cluster of servers.

When clustering with WAS, there are two models which reflect how the servers are deployed rather than their functionality. **Vertical clustering** entails deploying multiple instances of the same server on a single physical or virtual machine. This is primarily for load balancing purposes. Due to port conflicts, not all components can be vertically clustered. Vertical clustering makes the hardware a single point of failure for that server component.

Horizontal clustering involves servers in a cluster that are deployed across multiple physical or virtual machines, but where the horizontal cluster also sits alongside other server types. For example, with horizontal clustering, a Meeting Server node may share a machine with a Proxy Server node although they are in two entirely different clusters.

Both Domino and WAS servers will load balance users in a cluster, but each server type behaves differently:

- Community Server clustering primarily supports failover. Adding a MUX, round-robin DNS, or network load balancer in front of the Community Server can add support for load balancing and can make failover transparent to the user.

- Meeting Server clustering can be deployed under WAS, but the default configuration of having a single DB2 database makes that a single point of failure. In addition, all users must attend a meeting on the same server so meetings are load balanced by name, not by usage across servers. It is also not possible to select which server in a cluster you will connect to, so all servers should be collocated to ensure good performance. If a Meeting Server fails over, then the user will be informed through a dialog box message and redirected to another server to continue the meeting.

- Proxy Server clustering can also be deployed under WAS but the Proxy Server accesses a URL. The resolution of the hostname in that URL will determine which Proxy Server is assigned to the connecting user. In this way, it is possible to force regional DNS to resolve the same hostname to different Proxy Servers on different addresses, offering a degree of load balancing.

- The Media Manager itself cannot be clustered. However, if the component parts are separated, it is possible to cluster the SIP Proxy/Registrar, which handles user connections, and the Conference Manager, which handles data traffic to and from the clients. In a clustered environment, users are again randomly assigned to an available server in response to their requests.

The following are some decisions for you to consider before planning your use of clusters:

- The definition of a cluster is a group of identically configured servers behaving as a single server. This allows you to scale up for demand but does imply a certain degree of centralization in your infrastructure design. The alternative to a cluster is the deployment of multiple independent servers, each with their own configuration.

- Under WAS, all cluster servers must be in the same cell profile. When installing your first server, it should be defined as a primary node in either its own cell or a pre-existing cell such as with the SSC.

- Changing a single primary server into a cluster by adding secondary nodes at a later date is viable, as is building a cluster initially containing only one server.

- If you install multiple primary node instances of a server such as a Meeting Server, you will not be able to get them to behave as a cluster. A cluster is a single primary node which acts as the master record and a series of secondary nodes.

- Sametime only supports one cluster type per cell. This means one Proxy Server cluster, one Meeting Server cluster, one Conference Manager cluster, and so on. If your design includes multiple clusters of the same type, then these must be installed in their own cell.

- You cannot define which servers in a cluster a particular user connects to through any Sametime or WAS configuration setting.

Virtualization

Deploying Sametime servers in a virtual environment is fully supported as an infrastructure choice. Sametime runs well as a virtualized system; and as with any other virtual environment, there are some key things to consider when planning the virtual system configuration. You need to ensure that there are distinct allocated network resources and that the full system requirements are allocated to each virtual server and are available on the hardware. For instance, if your virtual environment has only two cores left unassigned and you attempt to assign four cores to a new Sametime server build, most virtual management software will attempt to move around resources between servers on demand. This may cause your virtual servers, including the Sametime servers, to behave erratically and therefore this type of deployment is not supported.

When scaling your virtual environment, make sure you have enough hardware resources, especially CPU, memory, and network cards to fully support the requirements of each Sametime server and the virtual environment itself. The installation of Sametime servers does lend itself to the use of virtualization. However, the use of virtual cluster technology such as VMotion should not be configured for load balancing, but only to provide cluster failover. The Sametime products cannot work with such products as VMotion in a load balancing-type scenario.

Obtaining Sametime software

Sametime software is usually downloaded from the IBM Passport Advantage site. You must have an IBM Passport Advantage account prior to downloading. Once you have logged into the Passport Advantage site, begin by looking for your authorized downloads, specifically those in the Lotus Software product family.

Click on the plus sign to expand the Lotus Software family list to find the IBM Sametime products. Each of the Sametime product lists can also be expanded, so that you only download those packages for the operating systems, languages, and features you plan to install.

Description		
☐ ⊞ IBM DB2 9.7 Lmtd Use for Sametime V8.5.2 Multiplatform Multilingual eAssembly (CRE9VML)		
	Size	8 files (7199mb)
	Date posted	01-Jun-2011
	🗗 Multi-product package terms	
☐ ⊞ IBM Domino V8.5.2 Language Pack for Sametime Standard V8.5.2 Multiplatform Multilingual eAssembly(CRE9UML)		
	Size	52 files (14209mb)
	Date posted	01-Jun-2011
	🗗 Multi-product package terms	
☐ ⊞ IBM Lotus Domino V8.5.2 for Sametime V8.5.2 Multiplatform Multilingual eAssembly (CRE9FML)		
	Size	31 files (22285mb)
	Date posted	01-Jun-2011
	🗗 Multi-product package terms	
☐ ⊞ IBM Sametime Gateway Server V8.5.2 Multiplatform Multilingual eAssembly (CRE9SML)		
	Size	2 files (692mb)
	Date posted	01-Jun-2011
☐ ⊞ IBM Sametime Standard V8.5.2 Multiplatform Multilingual eAssembly(CRE9WML)		
	Size	23 files (41835mb)
	Date posted	01-Jun-2011
☐ ⊞ IBM Sametime Standard V8.5.2 SDK Multiplatform English eAssembly(CRE9TML)		
	Size	1 files (45mb)
	Date posted	01-Jun-2011
☐ ⊞ WebSphere ND V7.0.0.15 Customized Installation Package Multiplatform for Sametime V8.5.2 Multilingual eAssembly(CRE9EML)		
	Size	12 files (8508mb)
	Date posted	01-Jun-2011
	🗗 Multi-product package terms	

When expanding the files in a Windows environment, use a short path name such as `c:\sametime`. Corruption may occur if long path names or deeply nested directories are used with the Windows extract utility. In some cases, the maximum path lengths for some Windows versions can be exceeded.

Sametime 8.5.2 software prerequisites

The following table provides an overview of the operating systems supported by Sametime 8.5.2 Standard and those components that will run on the specific operating systems:

Operating system	Sametime 8.5.2 Standard server component	Additional information
AIX **5.3 TL10 POWER System i/p 64-bit or 6.1 TL3 POWER System i/p 64-bit**	Classic Meeting Server; Community Server; Gateway Server; Meeting Server; Proxy Server; System Console Server	Requires 32-bit Domino
Linux **Red Hat Enterprise Linux (RHEL) 5.0 Update 4 Advanced Platform x86-32 or x86-64 or SUSE Linux Enterprise Server (SLES) 10.0 SP1 or 11.0, x86-32 or x86-64**	Classic Meeting Server; Community Server; Gateway Server; TURN Server; Bandwidth Manager Server; Media Manager Server; Meeting Server; Proxy Server; System Console Server	Requires 32-bit Domino
Solaris **10 SPARC 64-bit**	Classic Meeting Server; Community Server; Gateway Server; Meeting Server; Proxy Server; System Console Server	Requires 32-bit Domino

Operating system	Sametime 8.5.2 Standard server component	Additional information
SYSTEM i **i 5.4 IBM POWER 64-bit or i 6.1 IBM POWER 64-bit or i 7.1 IBM POWER 64-bit**	Classic Meeting Server; Community Server; Gateway Server; Meeting Server; Proxy Server; System Console Server	
SYSTEM z **(Sametime 8.5.1)**	Community Server; Meeting Server; Proxy Server; System Console Server (Sametime 8.5.1 components)	Requires 64-bit Domino Requires 64-bit Red Hat Enterprise Linux Server 5.0 (RHEL) Advanced Platform or SUSE Linux Enterprise Server (SLES) 10.0 SP1 System z
Windows 2003 SP1 / Windows 2003 R2 **Enterprise Edition x86-32 or Standard Edition x86-32**	Classic Meeting Server; Community Server; TURN Server; Bandwidth Manager Server; Gateway Server; Media Manager Server; Meeting Server; Proxy Server; System Console Server	For IPv6 support, both IPv4 and IPv6 stacks must be enabled
Windows 2003 / Windows 2003 R2 **Enterprise Edition x86-64 or Standard Edition x86-64**	Classic Meeting Server; Community Server; TURN Server; Bandwidth Manager Server; Gateway Server; Media Manager Server; Meeting Server; Proxy Server; System Console Server	For IPv6 support, both IPv4 and IPv6 stacks must be enabled

Operating system	Sametime 8.5.2 Standard server component	Additional information
Windows 2008 **Enterprise Edition x86-32 or Standard Edition x86-32**	Classic Meeting Server; Community Server; TURN Server; Bandwidth Manager Server; Gateway Server; Media Manager Server; Meeting Server; Proxy Server; System Console Server	
Windows 2008 / Windows 2008 R2 **Enterprise Edition x86-64 or Standard Edition x86-64**	Classic Meeting Server; Community Server; TURN Server; Bandwidth Manager Server; Gateway Server; Media Manager Server; Meeting Server; Proxy Server; System Console Server	Requires 32-bit Domino

As always, review the supporting documents that are included in the Sametime download package. They will refer any new requirements regarding software that may need to be installed prior to the installation of Sametime. Additional information about System i requirements can be found at the following website: `https://www-304.ibm.com/support/docview.wss?rs=203&uid=swg21092193`.

It is important to know that the software for the Sametime Bandwidth Manager and the Sametime TURN Server are part of the Sametime Media Server download and are not available as separate downloads themselves.

Sametime 8.5.2 hardware requirements

The following table summarizes the disk space requirements for the various Sametime 8.5.2 Standard server components. Note that these are only minimum recommendations; you should plan to allow for additional space for growth and any future server upgrades.

Operating system	Sametime 8.5.2 Standard server component	Disk space requirements
AIX	Classic Meeting Server	2 GB minimum
	Community Server	2 GB minimum
	Gateway Server; Meeting Server; Proxy Server; System Console	9 GB configurable space, plus 1 GB available in /tmp
Linux	Classic Meeting Server; Community Server	2 GB minimum
	TURN Server; Bandwidth Manager Server; Gateway Server; Media Manager Server; Meeting Server; Proxy Server; System Console Server	9 GB configurable space, plus 1 GB available in /tmp
Solaris	Classic Meeting Server; Community Server	2 GB minimum
	Gateway Server; Meeting Server; Proxy Server; System Console Server	9 GB configurable space, plus 1 GB available in /tmp
SYSTEM i	Classic Meeting Server; Community Server	2 GB minimum for each Sametime server; minimum of 4 disk drives (arms)
	Gateway Server; Meeting Server; Proxy Server; System Console Server	5 GB free space (3 GB minimum) with a minimum of 6 disk drives with a caching disk controller

Operating system	Sametime 8.5.2 Standard server component	Disk space requirements
SYSTEM z (Sametime 8.5.1)	Community Server	10 GB minimum
	Meeting Server	2.5 GB configurable space, plus 2 GB available in /home, and 1 GB available in /tmp
	Proxy Server	9 GB configurable space, plus 1 GB available in /tmp
	System Console Server	2.5 GB configurable space, plus 2 GB available in /home, and 1 GB available in /tmp
Windows	Classic Meeting Server; Community Server	2 GB minimum
	TURN Server; Bandwidth Manager Server; Gateway Server; Media Manager Server; Meeting Server; Proxy Server; System Console Server	8.5 GB configurable space, plus 1.5 GB available in %TEMP%

Refer to the following table for minimum memory recommendations. It may be easier to include additional memory in a new server purchase rather than justify additional memory later. So plan accordingly!

Operating system	Minimum memory (RAM) recommended
AIX Linux Solaris Windows	4 GB physical memory (RAM) minimum per server component
SYSTEM i	6 GB physical memory (RAM) minimum for Gateway, System Console Server, Meeting Server, and Proxy Server; 4 GB physical memory (RAM) minimum for Community Server and Classic Meeting Server plus 1 GB for each additional Sametime and Domino server

Planning for the WAS environment

As we have mentioned in previous chapters, WAS acts as the underlying architecture for many of the Sametime 8.5.2 server components. As part of your planning checklist, you need to consider what is required for WAS as well as Sametime:

- Determining where to install your WAS servers
- Planning for SSL requirements
- Planning for SSO requirements

Determining where to install your WAS servers

Many of the Sametime server components will live happily side-by-side on a shared server. It is even possible for all of the server components including the Domino Community Server and DB2 to be installed on a single server for a small or pilot deployment. Deciding which servers to install on a single piece of hardware and which servers to separate onto different hardware is a decision based on your choice of services and requirements for clustering.

The following are decisions to consider before planning your hardware configuration:

- Confirm that none of the server components have ports that may conflict with each other so they can all technically install on the same hardware.
- Clustered Proxy or Meeting Servers will use a HTTP WAS proxy to handle connecting traffic on port 80 or 443. Multiple proxy servers must be on separate hardware.
- Separating the Media Manager and Meeting Servers onto dedicated hardware leaves more room for future growth. If there is a possibility that your requirements for voice and video or meetings could grow significantly, then assigning them dedicated hardware at the outset would be a good idea.
- Clustering for load balancing can be done in a vertical deployment where multiple Meeting Servers are identically configured and managed as part of a cluster with all sharing the same hardware. Vertical clustering offers significant load balancing functionality and a common experience for all users, but has no capacity for hardware failover.

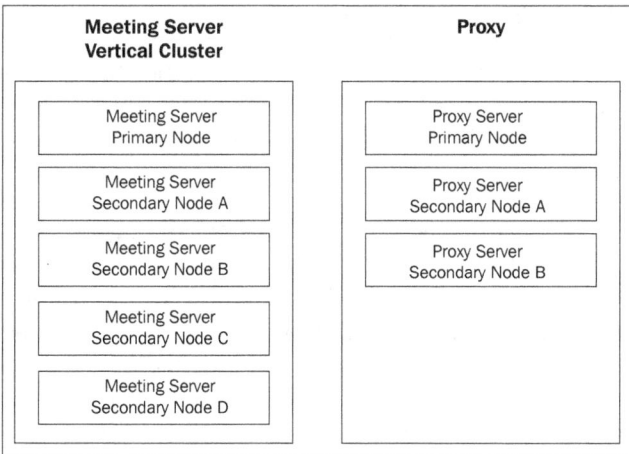

- Clustering can also be done horizontally with each server node in a cluster deployed on separate hardware. In this instance, you may want to maximize the use of the remaining hardware resources by also deploying another server node of a different type on the same hardware. Clustering horizontally requires more hardware but does provide additional capability for failover.

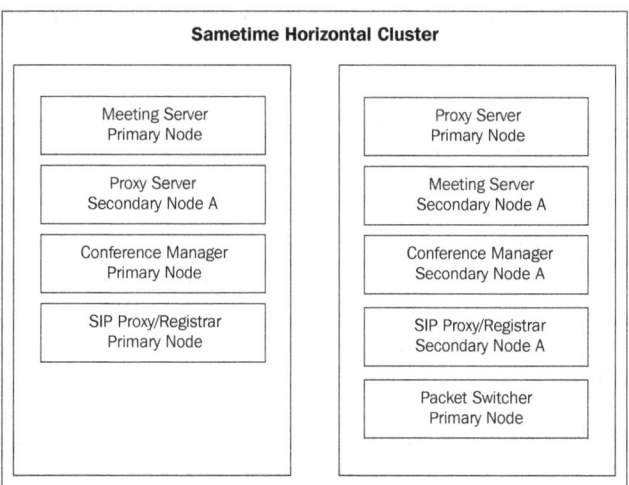

- Deploying multiple servers to provide services to users in a particular location does not prevent the installation of different server components on a single piece of hardware.

- If you are building a horizontal cluster, mixing primary and secondary nodes of different server types on the same hardware is a good approach to avoid having all the primary nodes on the same machine.

Planning for SSL requirements

SSL encrypts the traffic between servers and between the client and servers. Although there is a small networking performance penalty as a result of enabling SSL across all servers, the additional security benefits make this approach a best practice.

To enable SSL, you can acquire a **Certificate Authority (CA)** certificate for the Sametime Domino server from CA and put that in place on the Domino server. You can then export that certificate from Domino and import it into the WAS environment using the IBM keystore utility (**iKeyman**), which is free and readily available online. Once the certificate is imported into each WAS server, the servers themselves can be re-configured to encrypt the network traffic. If you already have an SSL certificate for your WAS environment, then you can export that SSL certificate, and import it into the Domino CA. This does not require iKeyman to be used.

Planning for SSO requirements

SSO for Sametime allows you to use the **Simple and Protected GSS-API Negotiation Mechanism (SPNEGO)** for authentication against WebSphere and Domino components. SPNEGO takes the user's identity when logged into a Windows desktop and issues a token against those credentials. Those credentials can then be read and authorized by the Sametime Community Server and the WAS-based Sametime server elements. In doing so, you can ensure that a user need only login to their Windows desktop to use Sametime with no further prompting for name or password.

The initial steps of configuring SPNEGO involve ensuring the Sametime Community Server is configured to use LDAP for authentication within the same **Active Directory (AD)** domain as the user is logging into. In addition, the Sametime servers should be part of the same AD domain as the users, or the user domains should be cross-certified within AD.

An account within the AD domain must be created to handle the authentication from Sametime and that account tied to a **Kerberos Service Principal Name (SPN)**. You then use that account to configure the SSC for SPNEGO and export a **Lightweight Third-Party Authentication (LTPA)** token that can be used by the other Sametime servers for SSO.

Coexistence or migration: What is required?

If a coexistence or migration deployment is under consideration in your company or organization, then these deployments may not require as much planning as you might undertake for a new install. However, you should not underestimate the importance of understanding how new Sametime servers will coexist or what effort might be required to migrate:

- Which servers can coexist with older versions?
- Understanding migration sequence.
- Dealing with older data—what will migrate and what won't.

Which servers can coexist with older versions?

There are some specific coexistence rules that you need to consider when attempting to integrate Sametime 8.5.2 components into an earlier Sametime infrastructure. Many of these refer to client behavior or versions as opposed to server elements.

Community Services

For Community services, the existing Domino-based Sametime servers of earlier supported versions will coexist with Sametime Community Server version 8.5.2. That means that the server can be added to an existing Sametime Community of earlier Sametime servers and users on all servers will be able to send instant messages to each other.

Keep in mind that adding a Sametime 8.5.2 Community Server into a cluster of older Sametime servers is not recommended. In addition, it is a prerequisite of Sametime 8.5.2 that LDAP be used instead of native Domino for the directory. For contact list consistency, users on a Sametime 8.5.2 server should only log into LDAP-enabled servers although they can talk to users on Domino Directory-configured Sametime servers.

Features such as rich text instant messaging, pasting from the clipboard, emoticons, and other features will be dependent upon the server and client version being used. If a user with a 6.5.x client logs into a Sametime 8.5.2 server, then they will not get rich text editing features in their client as these are an element of the Sametime 8.5.2 client.

Meeting Services

Sametime 8.5.2 continues to support the Classic Domino-based Sametime Meeting Server, which is used by earlier versions of Sametime and earlier Sametime clients. Although the Classic Meeting Server is not being enhanced by IBM, it continues to be fully supported by the Sametime 8.5.2 policies. These policies allow you to direct users to hold meetings on the Classic Meeting Server instead of the new Meeting Server. In addition, the 8.5.2 Notes mail templates are still designed to use the Classic Meeting Server by default.

To use the new Meeting Server for instant meetings directly from the Sametime client or to use the rich meeting client, the Sametime 8.5.2 client must be deployed. This can be either as a stand-alone product or by upgrading the embedded client version. Users who are on earlier versions of Sametime clients can only attend meetings on the new Sametime Meeting Server by using a browser to access the meeting directly. The browser meeting interface offers many, but not all, of the features of the rich client meeting interface.

Meetings created in the Classic Meeting Server cannot be transferred, migrated, or automatically recreated in the new Meeting Server. They must be left on the Classic Meeting Server. It is common during migration or coexistence for meetings to be held by some users on the Classic Meeting Server and by others on the new Meeting Server. The common browser interface is then used to allow both sets of meetings to be accessible to all users.

Proxy Server

The Sametime Proxy Server does not need to connect to a Sametime 8.5.2 Server, as it will work with any supported Sametime Community Server you have deployed. The Proxy Server offers a browser client interface to a Sametime Community Server and an optional replacement for the use of STLinks. Users on these earlier servers will be able to make use of the Proxy client. The caveat to this is that, like the other Sametime 8.5.2 components, deploying Proxy Server as part of the SSC requires the use of LDAP on the Community Server. To deploy Proxy Server against a Community Server, using only a Domino Directory for authentication requires both servers (Proxy and Community) to be deployed and managed outside of the SSC.

Audio and video

One issue to consider when integrating Community services is the change in behavior between Sametime 8.0.x and Sametime 8.5.2 clients. This is especially true with regard to audio and video functionality. The Sametime 8.5.2 client requires the presence of a Media Manager for client-based audio and video, but the Sametime 8.0.x client does not. For this reason, it is not possible for a user with a Sametime 8.5.2 client to participate in a native Sametime audio or video call with an earlier Sametime client. If the web plugin has been installed on the client machine, then it is possible for a user with an earlier Sametime client to participate in a web meeting on the new Meeting Server that does includes audio and video.

It is also possible for a user to run a Sametime 8.5.2 client against an older Community Server and a new Sametime Meeting Server. However, as SSO will not be configured, they will be prompted to supply credentials for both. In this model, the user could attend a Sametime 8.5.2 meeting including audio and video from their rich meeting client.

Understanding migration sequence

Deciding which components to upgrade and in what order is a key part of your planning process. It is often critical that existing services be disrupted as little as possible and that users are seen to be gaining features, not losing them.

The initial starting point is ensuring you have a LDAP infrastructure in place that can be used by Sametime 8.5.2. If your existing Sametime Community Servers are currently using Domino as their directory type, then those servers will need to be converted to use LDAP before they can be incorporated into the Sametime 8.5.x infrastructure. If the server is in a cluster, then all cluster mates must also be converted. Once you have a Sametime server of any supported version configured to use LDAP, you can continue to rollout the remaining Sametime 8.5.2 servers.

Adding the Sametime Meeting Server and Media Manager will not impact your existing environment, as their functionality only affects clients running the Sametime 8.5.2 stand-alone client or embedded client. Therefore, it is possible to install both the Meeting and Media Manager Servers in advance of upgrading your clients to Sametime 8.5.2 and have them in place as the client upgrades roll out. It is only once the Sametime 8.5.2 clients are in place that Sametime 8.5.2 meetings and Sametime 8.5.2 audio and video calls can be created directly by the users. For this reason, the work to rollout the Sametime 8.5.2 client should be a high priority in the planning process.

For users who have older stand-alone clients or who do not use the Notes embedded client, you can direct them to use the Sametime Proxy browser client instead. The Proxy Server does not impact the existing infrastructure at all and can be deployed against older supported Sametime Community Servers that are running LDAP. A Sametime Proxy Server can be added into the existing infrastructure at any time.

Dealing with older data—what will migrate and what won't

If Sametime has been in use in your company or organization prior to version 8.5.2, you may have users with extensive buddy lists or meetings that have been set up in a Domino-based environment. What will migrate if you upgrade? A significant detail in your design of an upgrade plan is to know that only buddy list and contact information will be migrated for a user during the upgrade of a Community Server.

The WAS-based Sametime environment cannot migrate data from the Domino-based environment for scheduled meetings that already appear in the Classic Meeting Server. The meetings have to be left on the Classic Meeting Server and new meetings created on the new Meeting Server. It is possible to continue to attend these classic scheduled meetings through a browser.

The choice of which server to use for meetings is controlled by Sametime policies and the client preferences. A client can configure their own preferences to always create and attend meetings on the new Meeting Server. Additionally, an administrator can create web redirection URLs in Domino that force users—attempting to access a meeting on the Classic Meeting Server—to be sent to the new Meeting Server, where they can recreate the meeting.

Planning for DB2

The use of a separate data store is a requirement for both the SSC and any Sametime Meeting Servers you are installing. The only supported database for Sametime is DB2 and there is a limited use license for DB2 9.5 and 9.7, which comes as part of the Sametime licensing entitlement. This allows you to install a customized version of DB2 for use with Sametime databases only.

Many companies also have their own DB2 infrastructure using enterprise licensing and, assuming it is a supported version, this pre-existing infrastructure can be leveraged for the Sametime databases. Your company or organization may have dedicated database staff as well. Consult them about storage requirements, database growth, and how to manage your backups and restore processes.

Understanding how many DB2 instances will be required

Each Meeting Server that doesn't exist in a cluster will require its own DB2 database but not necessarily its own DB2 instance. It is acceptable to have multiple DB2 databases for different Meeting Servers running in the same DB2 instance. This does create a bottleneck in your Meeting Server design and a potential single point of failure. Best practice would be to place the Meeting Server DB2 databases on a server on or near the Meeting Server itself for performance.

In a Sametime Meeting cluster, all Meeting nodes will use the same DB2 database. You can separately use DB2 Enterprise features such as database mirroring to ensure your data itself is distributed and can provide failover, but this isn't part of your Sametime licensing entitlement.

Planning for LDAP

Sametime 8.5.2 is completely dependent on using LDAP for authentication and for its directory. As we have indicated earlier in the chapter, you must use LDAP with Sametime 8.5.2. We will examine the following:

- Choosing an LDAP source
- Impact on existing Community Servers using Domino Directory
- Considerations when using LDAP

All the Sametime server components require the use of an LDAP directory defined in the SSC.

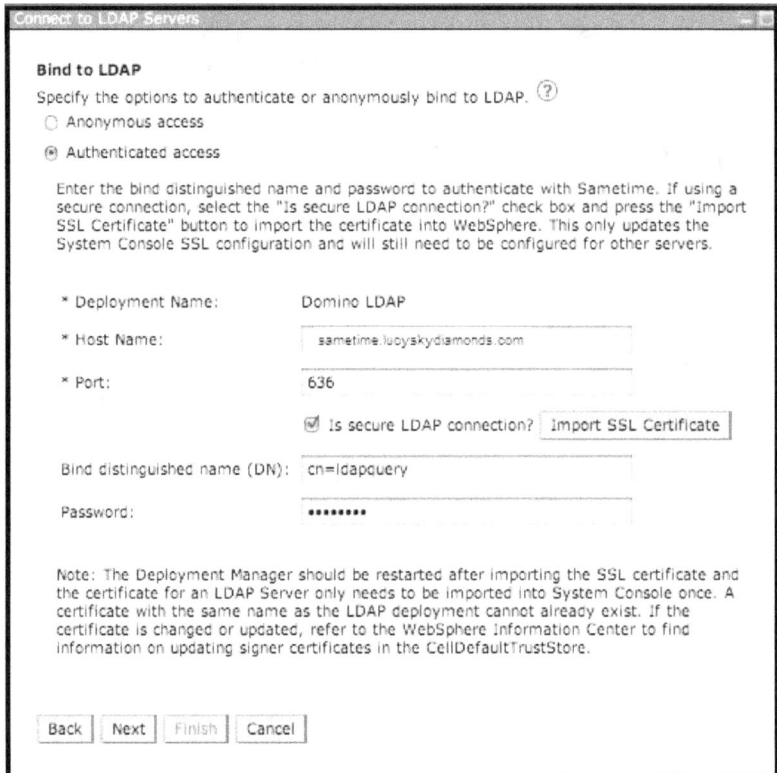

The following are decisions to consider when selecting your LDAP source:

- As the LDAP directory is core to everything Sametime does, select the best single source to use as your main directory.

- You can define multiple LDAP directories but Sametime will use them all. You cannot securely isolate users from each other without building another Sametime environment and SSC.

- All users must appear only once in the LDAP directory. If you have multiple LDAP directories in your environment, then the same rule applies. The unique key is usually the mail address but it may also be the UID.

- Any administration account you created when installing WAS should not be in a LDAP directory, as this would be seen as a duplicate account.

- LDAP lookups are continuous when using Sametime. The LDAP source should be easily accessible and not present any networking bottlenecks. Failure to access the directory, authenticate a user, or even timeouts will cause unexpected behavior for your users.

- LDAP traffic should always be authenticated, not anonymous, and secure. Credentials should not be looked up or passed across the network without being encrypted.

Impact on existing Community Servers using Domino directory

Existing Community Servers that use Domino as their directory cannot be integrated into a Sametime 8.5.2 SSC environment or use SSO to connect to a Meeting Server. They can reside alongside other Sametime servers and join a Community of other Sametime 8.5.2 servers so their users can participate in chats. They can also work with a stand-alone Sametime Proxy Server that is not itself part of a SSC.

When a Domino directory Sametime server is converted to LDAP, the administrator must also use the Domino utility to convert the buddy list and contact data stored in vpuserinfo.nsf. This utility changes the format of names stored from the Domino format of CN=Shaka Walters/O=DominionFuels to the LDAP format of CN=Shaka Walters,O=DominionFuels.

Planning for network requirements

When planning your Sametime environment, whether for a proof of concept installation, upgrade, or production environment, it is critical to include the network requirements in your plan. If a port is not available through your corporate or organization's firewall, or if bandwidth requirements are not considered, then any well-planned software installation can come to a complete halt. When ports or NATed networks are not properly configured, they can lead to very complex troubleshooting issues. The issues at first may seem to be software-related, when in fact they may simply be related to the correct port being open. It is important to spend some time on this planning phase. Especially in complex network environments with multiple firewalls or DMZs, consult with the network and Internet security teams in your organizations. Include them in the planning process so they are aware that you have specific port needs. Ask them to review your plan to avoid arguments later!

- Port requirements
- IPv6 versus IPv4
- Determining ports for WAS Sametime applications

Port requirements

The following tables include those ports that are required for the various Sametime components. Unless otherwise stated, they refer to TCP ports that should be open for traffic in and out of the firewall.

The table that follows includes those ports required by the Sametime components:

Sametime System Console ports	
Default port	Purpose
8700	Provides default browser access to the SSC.
8701	Provides HTTPS browser access to the SSC.
9080	Port used by the Sametime Community Server to access the SSC HTTP port.
9443	Port used by the Sametime Community Server to access the SSC HTTPS port.
50000	SSC database port used by installation manager utilities, post-registration utilities, and Sametime Meeting Server.
Sametime Community Server ports	
Default port	Purpose
80	The Sametime Community Server listens for the SSC on port 80.
Alternate HTTP port (8088)	If HTTP tunneling on port 80 is configured during the Sametime Community Server installation or afterward, the Domino HTTP server on which the Sametime Community Server is installed must listen for HTTP connections on a port other than port 80.
389	The Sametime Community Server connects to the LDAP server on port 389 if configured to connect to an LDAP Server.
443	The Domino HTTP server listens for HTTPS connections from the SSC on this port by default. This port is used only if you have set up the Domino HTTP server to use SSL for web browser connections.
1352	The Domino server on which Sametime Community Server is installed listens for Notes clients and Domino server connections on port 1352.
9092	Port 9092 is the Event Server port for the Sametime Community Server and is used for server connections between Sametime components.
9094	Port 9094 is the Token Server port on the Sametime Community Server and is used for server connections between Sametime components.

Sametime Community Service (CS) ports

Default port	Purpose
1516	Port 1516 is used by CS to listen for direct TCP/IP connections from the CS of other Sametime Community Servers. This port must be open for chat, awareness, and other CS data to pass between the servers.
1533	The CS listens for direct TCP/IP connections and HTTP-tunneled connections from the CS clients (such as Sametime Connect and Sametime Meeting Room clients) on this port.
80	If HTTP tunneling was configured on port 80 during the Sametime Community Server installation, the CS clients can make HTTP-tunneled connections to the CS multiplexer on port 80. But the CS multiplexor listens for HTTP-tunneled connections on both port 80 and 1533. The CS multiplexer simultaneously listens for direct TCP/IP connections on port 1533.
8082	When HTTP tunneling support is enabled, the CS clients can make HTTP-tunneled connections to the CS multiplexer on port 8082 by default. CS clients can make HTTP-tunneled connections on both ports 80 and 8082 by default. Port 8082 ensures backward compatibility with previous Sametime releases. In previous releases, Sametime clients made HTTP-tunneled connection to the CS only on port 8082.

Sametime Classic Meetings ports

Default port	Purpose
554	The Sametime Classic Recorded Meeting client attempts a direct RTSP TCP/IP connection to the Recorded Meeting Broadcast Services on the Sametime Community Server on port 554.
1533	Port 1533 is used by the Sametime Classic Meeting Room client when the user attends an instant or scheduled meeting through a web browser.
8081	The Meeting Room client uses port 8081 to connect with the Meeting Services on the Sametime Community Server.

Sametime Proxy Server port

Default port	Purpose
8880	The SSC accesses the Deployment Manager Simple Object Access Protocol (SOAP) port. This is used for server-to-server communication and the port may vary depending on how WAS was configured.

Sametime Media Manager Server ports

Default port	Purpose
9080	Port 9080 is an HTTP port used for the management of audio/video calls. In a cluster, HTTP ports are proxied through a WebSphere Proxy Server.
42000-43000	Sametime Media Manager Packet Switcher routes audio data through a range of ports starting with 42000 to 43000. It uses values as needed in increments of two. If encryption is enabled (SRTP), the numbers to be used will be odd numbers.
46000-47000	Sametime Media Manager Packet Switcher routes video data through a range of ports starting with 46000 to 47000. It uses values as needed increments of two. If encryption is enabled (SRTP), then the range starts with an odd port number.
5060 and 5061	The Conference Manager and Packet Switcher are SIP applications, and therefore use WebSphere SIP container ports.
8880	Port 8880 is used for server-to-server communication. The SSC accesses the Deployment Manager SOAP port.

Sametime Meeting Server ports

Default port	Purpose
443	In a single node environment using HTTPS that bypasses the WAS proxy, the Sametime Meeting Server listens for data from the Sametime Meeting Room client over this connection.
9080	Port 9080 is used in a single node or multiple node environment when Sametime Meeting Server listens for data from the Sametime Meeting Room client over this connection when HTTP bypasses the WAS proxy.
9443	In a multiple node environment using HTTPS, the Sametime Meeting Server listens for data from the Sametime Meeting Room client that is passed through the WAS proxy.
8880	Port 8880 is used for server-to-server communication. The SSC accesses the Deployment Manager SOAP port.

Sametime TURN Server ports

Default port	Purpose
3478	UDP Port for basic STUN/TURN handling. This port should be open for internal and external access.
49152-65535	UDP Ports for dynamic packet allocation. These ports should be available for internal client access.

Sametime Bandwidth Manager Server ports	
Default port	Purpose
9060	Admin host port for Bandwidth Manager.
5060	SIP port used by Bandwidth Manager.
9080	Default HTTP port.
Sametime Packet Switcher (MCU) ports (Internal Use)	
Default port	Purpose
39000	UDP audio port for the MCU in single port mode.
40000	UDP video port for the MCU in single port mode.
42000-43000	UDP audio ports for the MCU in multi-port mode.
46000-47000	UDP video ports for the MCU in multi-port mode.

IPv6 versus IPv4 addressing

If your organization is using IPv6 addresses versus the older IPv4 addresses, then you will need to consider the impact on your Sametime 8.5.2 deployment. IPv6 addressing helps to reduce the need for NATed networks. Beginning with release 8.0.2, Sametime servers and clients began supporting the use of IPv6 address. However, there are some limitations:

- Sametime System Console: If you are installing the SSC on a system that supports both IPv4 and IPv6, then the addresses associated with the SSC must be mapped to the same hostname.

- Sametime Gateway: The ST Gateway must be installed with a special parameter to enable IPv6. This cannot be changed after you deploy the Gateway.

- Media Manager: Media Manager does not support IPv6 in Sametime 8.5.2.

- Sametime Connect Client: If your environment only supports IPv6 addressing, clients prior to Sametime Connect 8.0.2 will generate error messages. In an IPv4 and IPv6 environment they will connect, provided those servers are configured to listen for both addressing formats.

- Sametime Advanced: Sametime Advanced does not yet support IPv6 addressing.

Determining ports for **WAS** Sametime applications

You can determine the ports used by WAS by logging into the SSC. For each of the WAS-based Sametime servers (Sametime Meeting Server, Sametime Media Manager, and Sametime Proxy Server) you can click on `Servers/Server Types/WebSphere Application servers/STMeetingServer` or `STMediaServer` or `STProxyServer/Port` to see the port associated with the port-specific keyword. For example, the following ports are listed for the `STProxyServer`:

Communications

Ports

Port Name	Port	Details
BOOTSTRAP_ADDRESS	9810	
SOAP_CONNECTOR_ADDRESS	8880	
ORB_LISTENER_ADDRESS	9100	
SAS_SSL_SERVERAUTH_LISTENER_ADDRESS	9401	
CSIV2_SSL_SERVERAUTH_LISTENER_ADDRESS	9403	
CSIV2_SSL_MUTUALAUTH_LISTENER_ADDRESS	9402	
WC_adminhost	9060	
WC_defaulthost	9080	
DCS_UNICAST_ADDRESS	9353	
WC_adminhost_secure	9043	
WC_defaulthost_secure	9443	
SIP_DEFAULTHOST	5060	
SIP_DEFAULTHOST_SECURE	5061	
SIB_ENDPOINT_ADDRESS	7276	
SIB_ENDPOINT_SECURE_ADDRESS	7286	
SIB_MQ_ENDPOINT_ADDRESS	5558	
SIB_MQ_ENDPOINT_SECURE_ADDRESS	5578	
IPC_CONNECTOR_ADDRESS	9633	

Summary

In this chapter, you learned about the decisions you need to consider when planning for an installation of Sametime 8.5.2. You learned about the essential choices for growth and stability of the platform, as well as how certain hardware and software choices will interact. You also learned how to plan for each part of the Sametime environment, such as WAS, LDAP, and DB2, and how those elements should be configured for current and future flexibility. In the next chapter, you will step through an actual Sametime install process. After each section, you will also learn about how to test each newly installed component.

6
Ready, Set, Install: Installing Sametime 8.5.2

As an administrator, the time has now arrived for you to begin your Sametime installation. In this chapter, we will step through a basic Sametime 8.5.2 server installation. After each server component is installed, we will review the steps for testing the success of the implementation.

Regardless of whether you are installing a pilot or production environment, many of the steps and installation options remain the same:

- Alistair wants to install a Sametime Community Server on Sametime 8.5.2 and have it managed by a Sametime Solutions Console so he can add other Sametime components at a later date.

- Marcus is building a new Sametime 8.5.2 pilot environment to evaluate the demand for Sametime in his company. He needs to install all the components on as little hardware as possible.

- Tania would like to install just a Sametime 8.5.2 Domino Community Server. But she would like a better understanding of how to prepare her environment should she want to add components later.

In this chapter, you will learn the following:

- How to complete a pilot installation of Sametime server components
- The proper installation order for each Sametime server component
- Which installation choices can be changed later and which choices are permanent without reinstalling the environment
- What steps you can take to test your installation to confirm each step has successfully completed

Downloading Sametime 8.5.2 software

Sametime software is usually downloaded from the IBM Passport Advantage site. You must have an IBM Passport Advantage account prior to downloading. Once you have logged into the Passport Advantage site, begin by looking for your authorized downloads, specifically those in the Lotus Software product family.

Click on the plus sign to expand the Lotus Software family list to find the Lotus Sametime products. Each of the Sametime product lists can also be expanded, so that you only download those packages for the operating systems, languages, and features you plan to install. The Sametime installers are downloaded as zip files for the Windows environment.

Understanding the Sametime server install

As the Sametime 8.5.2 environment is rather complex, it is important to understand that the installation needs to follow a step-by-step process in terms of installing the components in the proper order. We suggest the following components to be installed:

- Install IBM DB2 and create a DB2 database for the Sametime System Console
- Install the Sametime System Console
- Install or configure an existing LDAP server
- Install a Sametime Community Server
- Install a Sametime Proxy Server
- Install a Sametime Media Server
- Create a DB2 database for the Sametime Meeting Server
- Install the Sametime Meeting Server
- Install the Bandwidth Manager Server
- Install the TURN Server

The most important aspects of this install are correctly installing DB2, SSC (and WAS environment), and LDAP. We will also include information about installing a Bandwidth Manager and a TURN Server. These may be optional servers in your environment.

In our example that follows, we will be creating a Sametime environment which includes these components. The following are server names we are using:

- **SSC Server**: `baltic.lucyskydiamonds.com`
- **DB2 Server**: `databases.lucyskydiamonds.com`

- **Sametime Community Server**: `marianas.lucyskydiamonds.com`
- **LDAP Server**: `directories.lucyskydiamonds.com`
- **Sametime Multiplexor Server**: `stmux.lucyskydiamonds.com`
- **Meeting Server**: `meetings.lucyskydiamonds.com`
- **Media Server**: `baltic.lucyskydiamonds.com`
- **Proxy Server**: `proxy.lucyskydiamonds.com`
- **Bandwidth Server**: `swan.lucyskydiamonds.com`
- **TURN Server**: `baltic.lucyskydiamonds.com`

 Remember to have your fully qualified hostnames configured prior to beginning the installation, as you will need these DNS entries to be active in order to validate your installation.

Installing DB2

To begin your Sametime installation, you need to prepare your environment for the SSC. This becomes the central administration interface for all the components you are about to install. The SSC uses a DB2 database to store configuration and security information, so the first step is to install a DB2 server. DB2 v9.5 and v9.7 are both supported, and IBM supplies a Sametime-specific limited-use DB2 license as part of the Sametime downloads. You can also use an existing DB2 server environment if you have one in your organization.

To install DB2, you first need to unzip the Sametime-specific DB2 software and, from the top level directory, run the `launchpad` script. If this is the first IBM product to be installed on this server, then the installer will initially install IBM Installation Manager. This is a program that handles the installation and de-installation of any subsequent Sametime software. Once the Installation Manager completes, the installer launches the DB2 installation process.

- During the install you will be prompted for the DB2 install directory which will be under a `\IBM` subdirectory. If using Windows, then you should place the `\IBM` directory and the rest of the DB2 path directly at the root of one of your disks. Never install any of the Sametime components (including DB2) under `\Program Files`. Some operating systems and software have issues with paths that include spaces, and the directory structure has many nested levels which may cause path length issues in your operating system.

- The installer will also ask you to provide DB2 credentials. The account you create here is used to create and manage the DB2 databases that you will use for the SSC and Meeting Server, and it will be stored as a local operating system account.

 It is important to ensure the password you specify for the DB2 admin account during install, is actually valid for the security policy on your server operating system.

- The server must be configured to use a fully qualified hostname such as databases.lucyskydiamonds.com, which must also be resolvable both from itself and from any other server hardware you will be using.

Once DB2 is successfully installed, it should be listening on port 50000, and a local operating system account should exist for your DB2 administrator.

Installing the Sametime System Console

Once the DB2 server software installation is complete, you need to create a database to store the SSC information. Unzipping the SSC installer will produce a directory structure under \SametimeSystemConsole which includes the subdirectory \Databases. This subdirectory contains your database scripts. You should log in to your DB2 server using your DB2 administrator account to run these scripts.

The script createSCDB is run from a command prompt and creates the SSC database. The entire command string is CreateSCDB STSC db2admin where STSC is the name you want to call the SSC database and db2admin is the account you created to administer the DB2 server.

Once the database is created, you need to login again to the server where the SSC is to be installed using your initial installation account. Run the launchpad script from the root directory of the unzipped SSC installer. The installation menu for the SSC is very similar to that of all the other Sametime components and it is completed through the graphical interface.

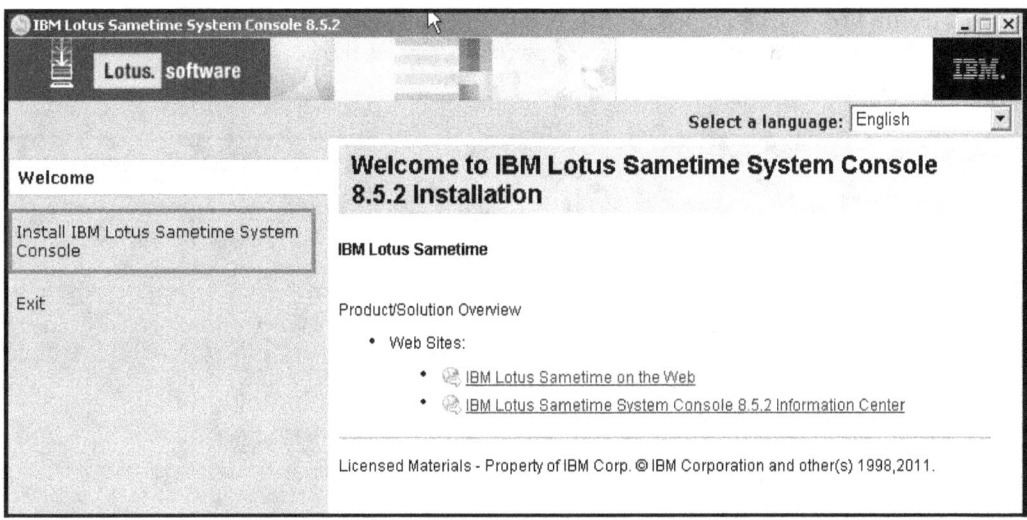

Each installation is managed by IBM's Installation Manager, which installs itself if it is not already present. The Installation Manager interface can also be used for uninstalling and updating the programs it managed during the install. Click on **Install** to begin the install process as shown in the following screenshot:

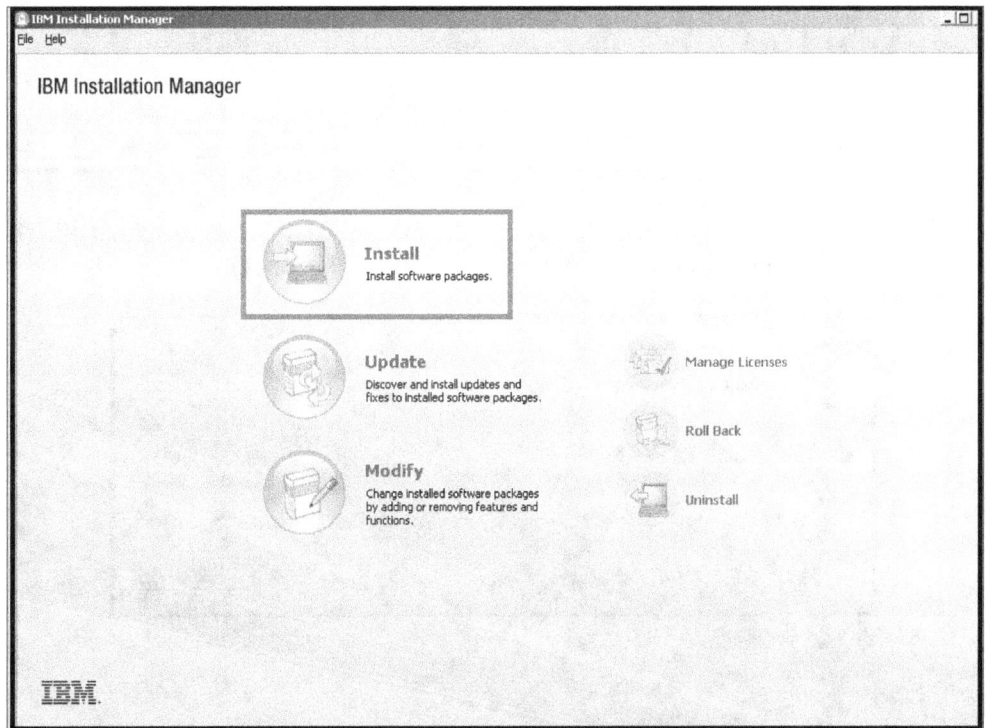

At this point, you select the installation package you wish to install. You are going to install the Sametime System Console package. Select that option and click on **Next** to begin.

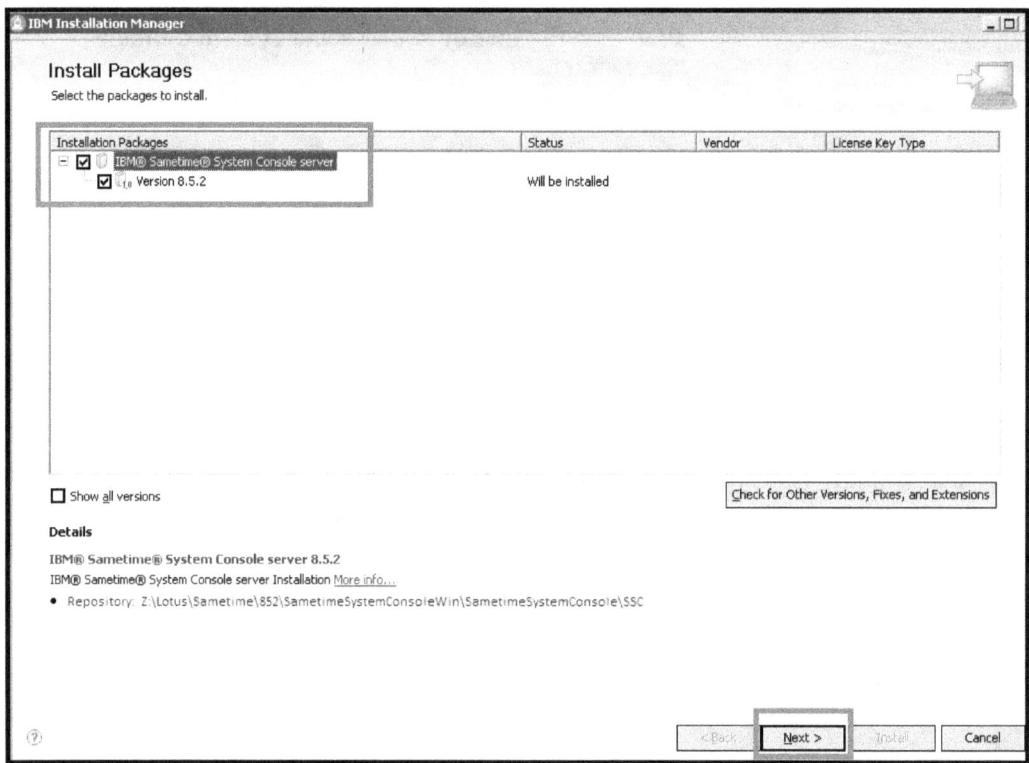

During the installation process, a **Progress Information** dialog box is displayed. This allows you to cancel the install at any time by clicking on **Cancel**.

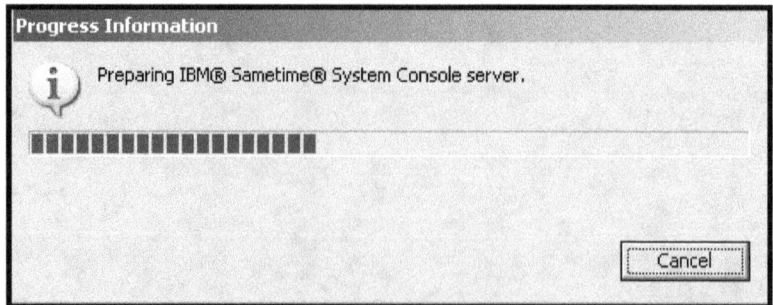

You are prompted to accept the licensing terms. Select the option **I accept the terms in the license agreements** and click on **Next**.

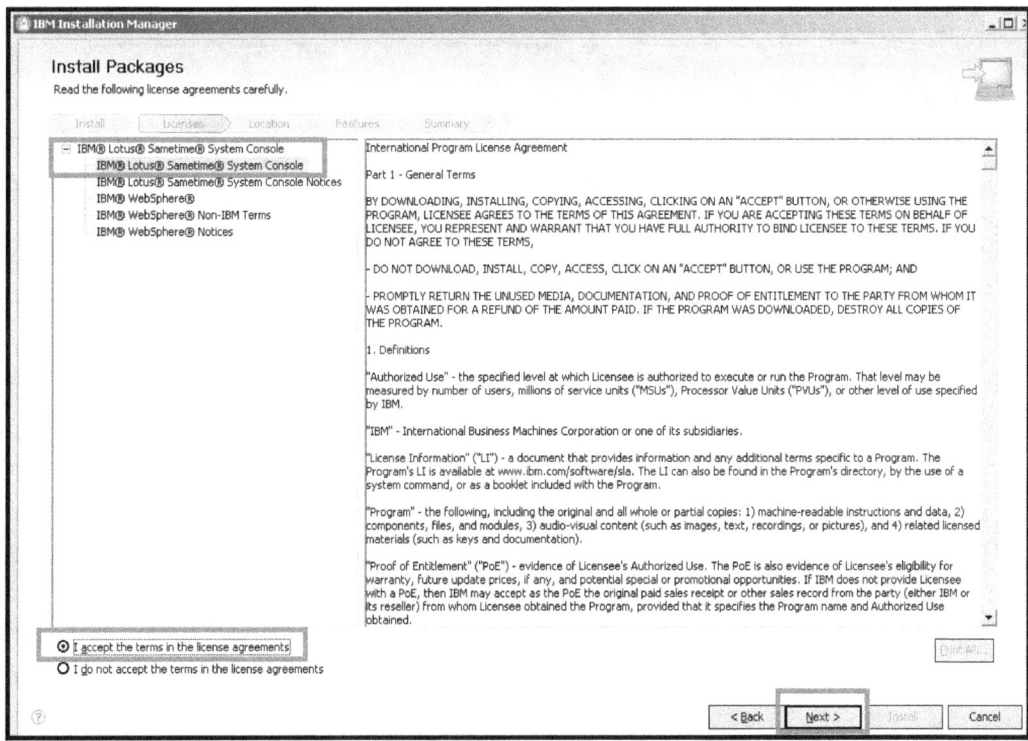

Each product installed by the Installation Manager must be part of a package group. A package group is usually represented by a single product, so if this is the first WAS product to be installed on the server, you will be creating a new package group. Additional WAS products installed on this server will, in most circumstances, use this group.

You will want your installation directory to be as close to the root of the install drive as possible. The Installation Manager may propose an IBM directory under \Program Files or \Program Files (x86), but we recommend you to adjust this to put IBM as the top level directory. Some operating systems and software have issues with paths that include spaces, and the WAS directory structure has many nested levels which may cause path length issues in your operating system.

In our example, we select **Create a new package group**. At this point you can also make a change in the directory for the software installation. Once you confirm all the settings on this page, click on **Next**.

The install screen confirms the disk space needed for the install and how much disk space is available. You would want to ensure that you have plenty of free disk space, more than required for the install so that you do not experience performance issues. Once you confirm this information, click on **Next**.

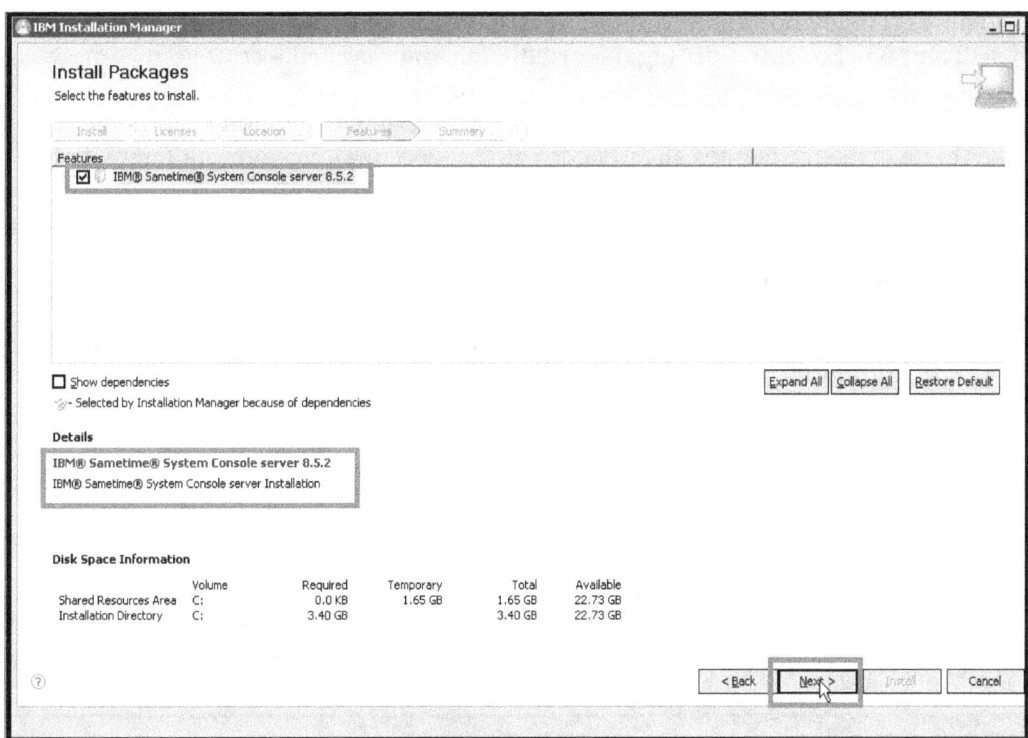

At this point, you need to provide the specifics for your WAS and SSC environment—cell, node, and sever names. The WAS installation page prompts you to complete the name of each cell, as well as the name of the node you are installing.

 Each WAS server must exist in a cell, although a cell can contain multiple server nodes.

As this is the first WAS server you are installing on this server, the Sametime installer wants to create a new cell for it. By default, it takes the name of the server for the cell and the node. Hence, the cell server `baltic` that hosts the SSC server is suggested as **balticSSCCell** and the server node for the SSC itself is suggested as **balticSSCNode**.

You can call the cell and node anything you choose, but we recommend you keep the default options presented during the install unless you have a reason not to do so.

 IBM recommends that the WAS server name should be no longer than eight characters.

The fully qualified hostname you use during the install will be tied to the server install and will be critical during the installation and maintenance of your Sametime environment. It should be resolvable in DNS from the server you are installing on and any other server or client in your environment. As we mentioned earlier, you want to have the hostnames already configured in your DNS environment prior to installation. In our example, we are using **baltic.lucyskydiamonds.com.**

Finally, you need to specify the install credentials that will be used to create and administer the SSC server instance. The values you enter here will initially be the only ones that allow you to manage your Sametime environment and build other components. The account that is created is stored inside the WAS environment; it cannot be accessed outside of WAS and it is required to start and stop the server after your installation is completed. In this example, we are using the default account name of **wasadmin**. Every Sametime server component you install will ask for credentials in this way.

We recommend strongly that you use the same name and password combination for each server in your environment to make maintenance easier. This account can not be allowed to exist in your LDAP directory and is only used to log in to the SSC.

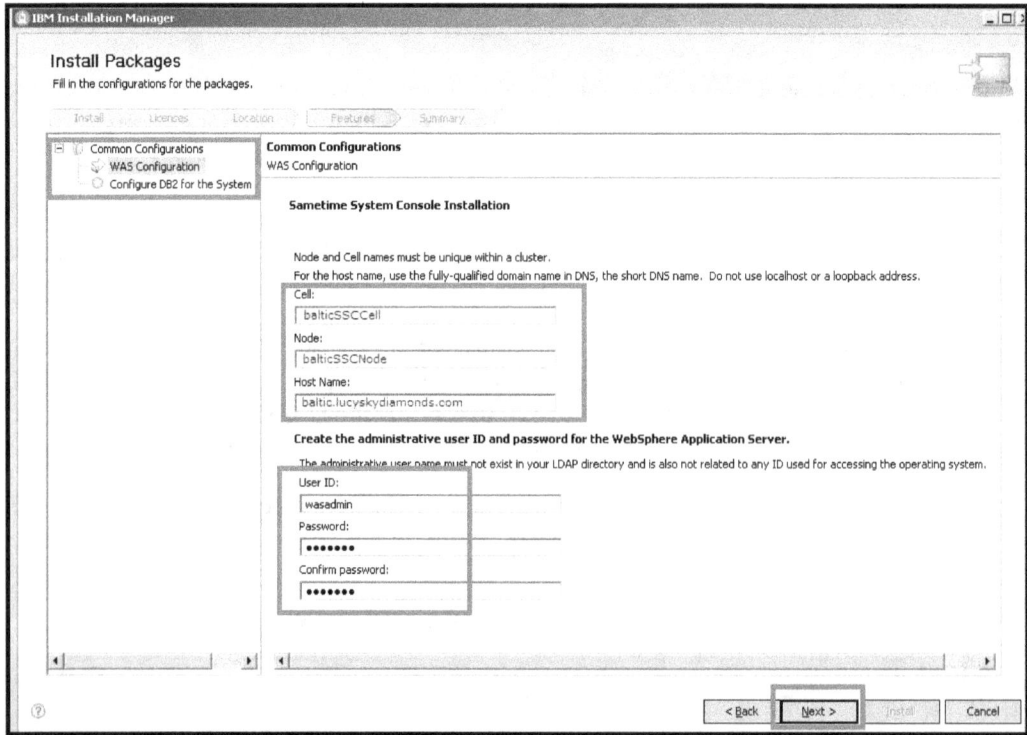

When the WAS configuration page is completed, select **Next** and move to the page where you tell the installer about the DB2 database you created to be used by the SSC.

The DB2 installation page asks for the hostname of the DB2 server, where you created the STSC database in the earlier install step. You are prompted for:

- DB2 server hostname (our example is **databases.lucyskydiamonds.com**)
- DB2 port—defaults to **50000**
- DB2 database name (our example is **STSC**)
- DB2 credentials (our example is **db2admin**)

Once completed, click on **Validated** and the installer will attempt to connect to your DB2 database using those details. If the connection cannot be validated, then you cannot complete the install. At this point your DB2 server must be running; it must be listening on the port you specify; it must be resolvable using the hostname you provided, and the STSC database must be created.

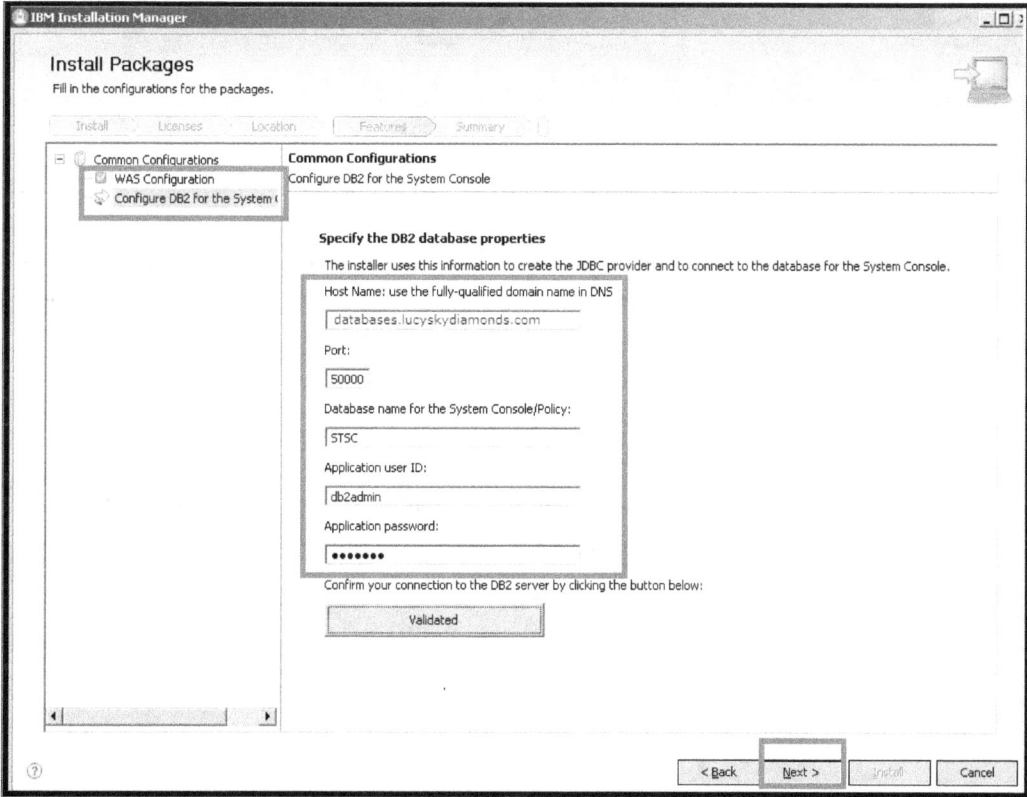

Once the validation works, click on **Install**. At this point the Installation Manager will install and configure WAS, followed by the installation of the SSC server component.

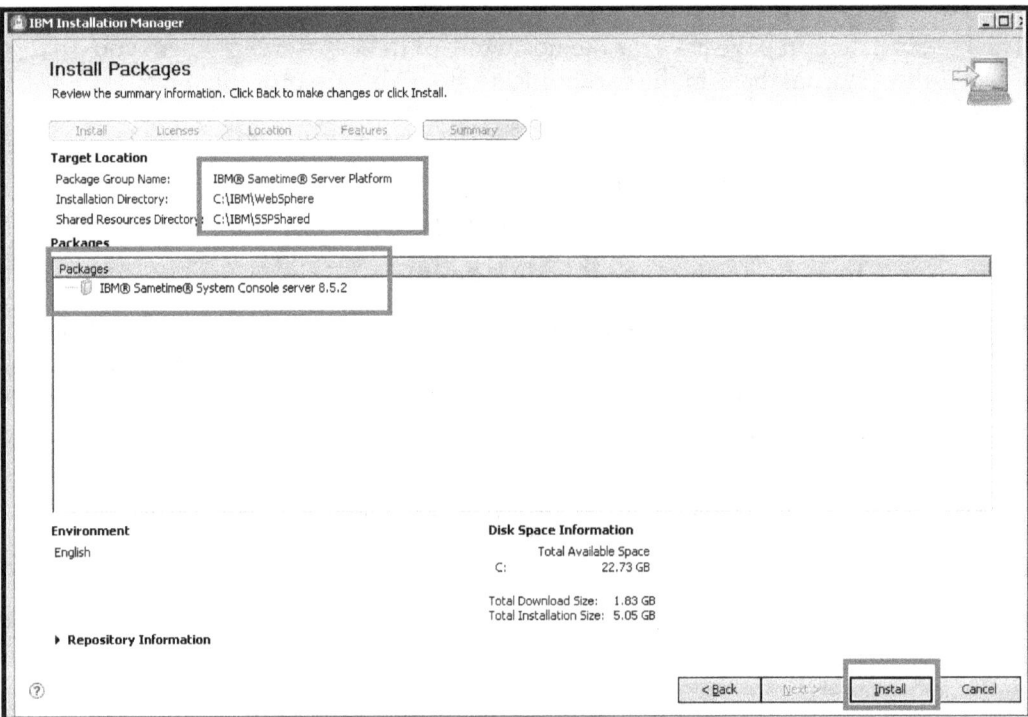

The install itself may take anywhere from a few minutes to over an hour depending on the performance of your hardware and disks. The most important thing is to not give up! The installation log files can be viewed at any time to see if progress is still going on. These can be found at:

- c:\Documents and Settings\All Users\Application Data\IBM\ Installation Manager\logs (Windows)

- c:\programdata\ibm\installation manager\logs (Windows 2008)

- /var/ibm/installationmanager/logs (AIX, Linux, and Solaris)

A progress bar updates at the bottom of the installation dialog to give you a visual indication of where the installer is in the process.

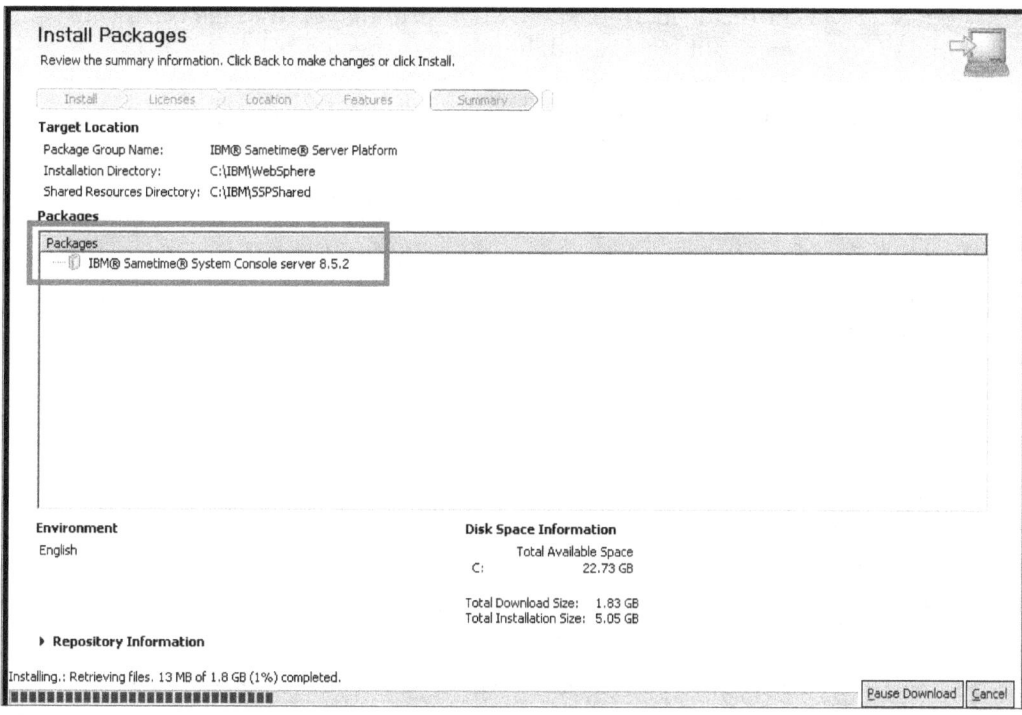

Confirming the SSC installation

Once the installation of the SSC is complete, you should find that the SSC Deployment Manager, node agent, and STConsoleServer are all present and started on the Windows' **Services** screen.

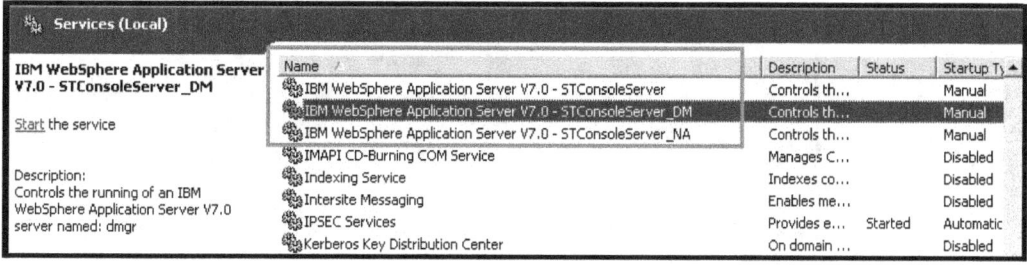

To test if the SSC is installed correctly, use a browser and open the following URL: `https://<hostname>:8701/ibm/console/`.

You may receive a certificate alert for the URL informing you that the certificate inside the WAS server is not recognized, but this is expected behavior. No configuration for SSL has been set up at this point. If you fail to get a login screen and instead receive a browser timeout error, then it is likely your SSC server is not started correctly.

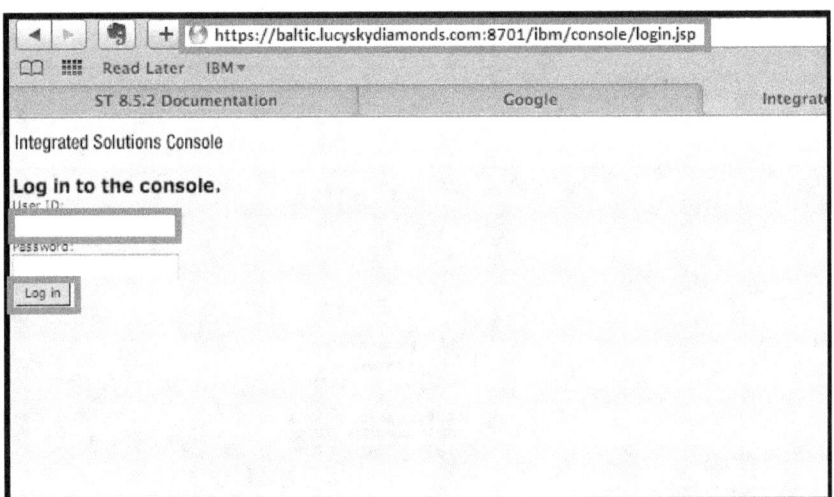

When you receive a login screen, you should enter the name and password credentials you used during install. Remember, in our example we used **wasadmin**. This launches the administrative console which is the **WAS Integrated Solutions Console (ISC)**. It now has an added menu section for the Sametime Solutions Console.

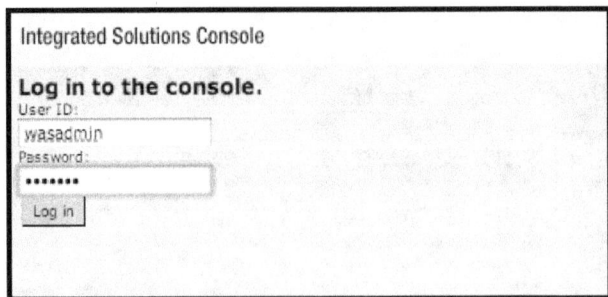

If you can login and can see the SSC menu section in the ISC, then you have confirmed that SSC is installed and running correctly.

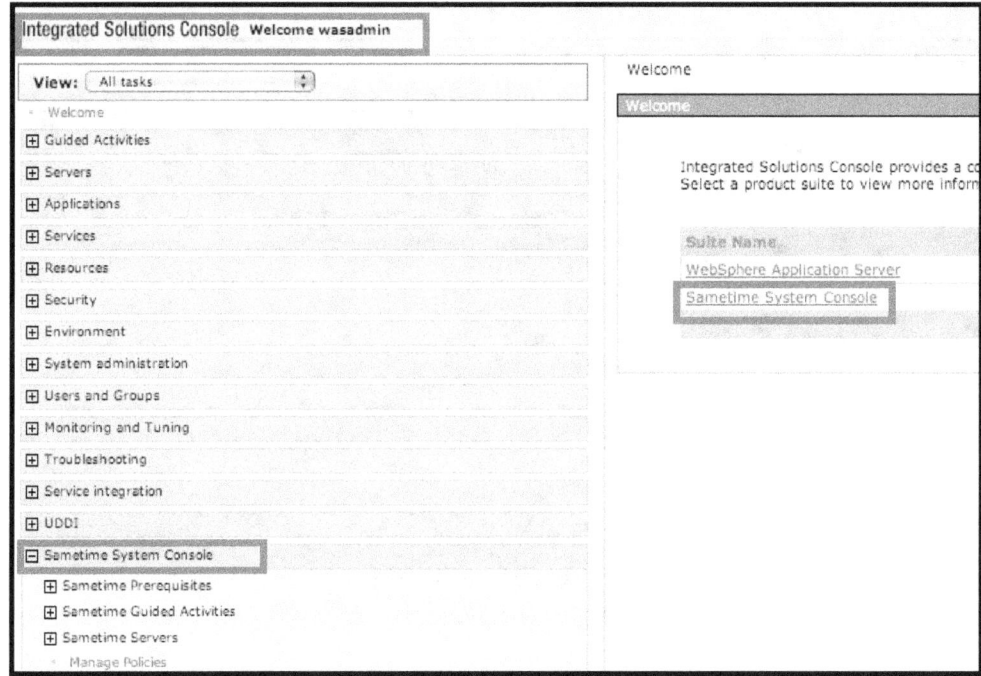

Configuring LDAP

From the SSC menu you now move to the Sametime prerequisites. You already have your SSC database which is in place, and your next step is to set up the LDAP server details for your directory and authentication. The LDAP server(s) configured here are used by all of the Sametime server components.

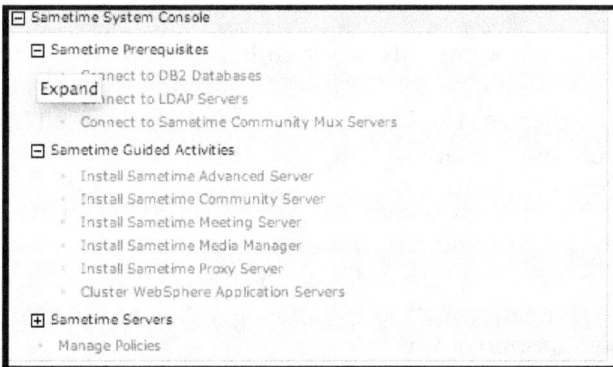

The LDAP **Deployment name** you use is purely for maintenance and administrative purposes. It is not visible to any user and selecting a meaningful name can be very useful for administration.

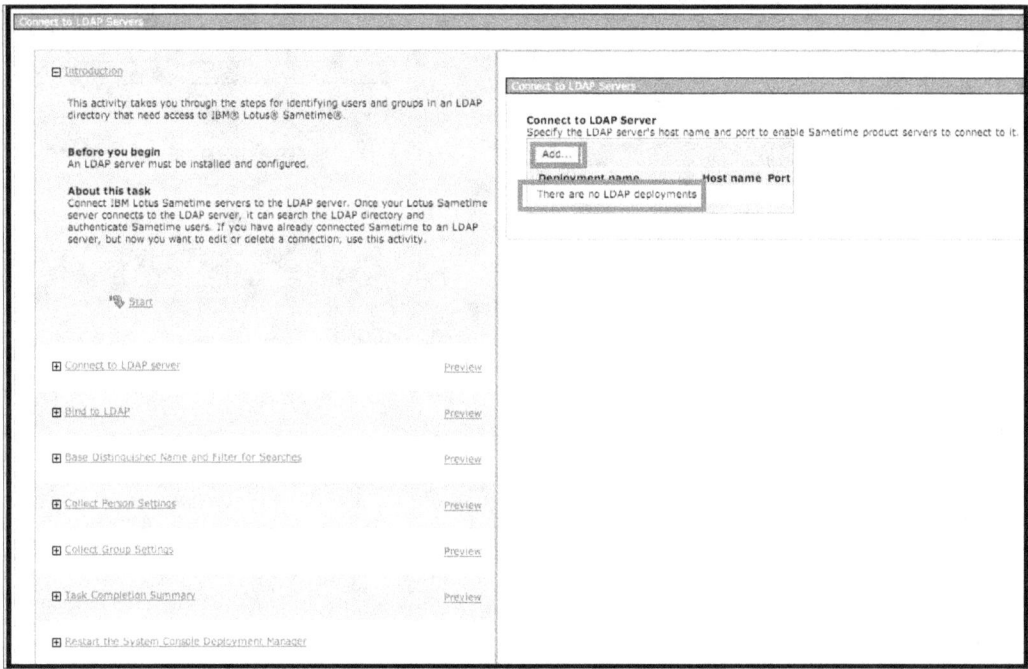

The required fields are the hostname of the LDAP server and the port on which the LDAP server is available. Although you can use the unencrypted LDAP port 389 and anonymous access to connect to your directory, this is extremely insecure. Your LDAP administrator should be able to provide you with credentials that give you ready access to the directory and that you can use to bind to the LDAP store. They should also be able to enable SSL on their LDAP server so you can connect using the secure port 636.

LDAP is critical to all Sametime activity for authentication and for user lookups. Your LDAP server performance and network connection is essential for a successful Sametime server installation. The LDAP server should be accessible on a LAN connection to any of your Sametime component servers.

When you click on **Next**, the installer will attempt to connect to the LDAP server by the hostname using the port and credentials you specified. Any failure to connect will prevent you from moving forward with the installation, as the LDAP server must be active as you set up Sametime. In our example, we are using the hostname **directories.lucyskydiamonds.com**.

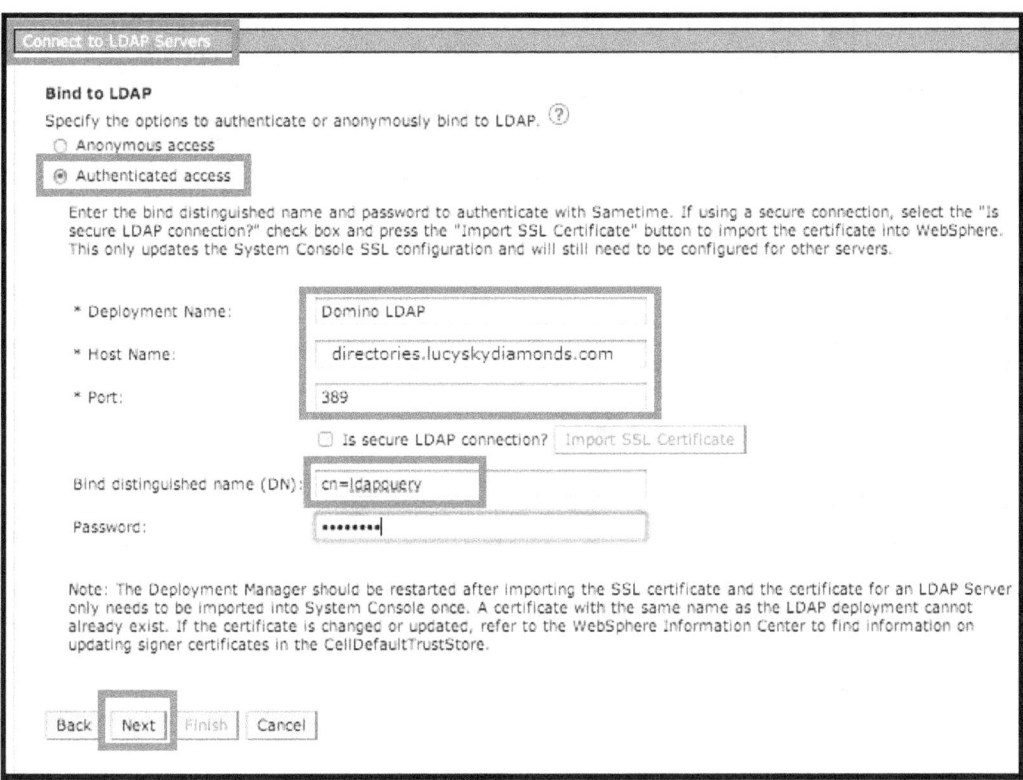

The **LDAP base entry** field is used to define the scope of users who will be authenticating from LDAP. In many LDAP environments, the complete directory contains more users and elements that you want to provide to Sametime. The base entry provides a base distinguished name (DN) to limit the scope of the directory lookups.

 You should make sure this is as specific as possible, as a base DN that incorporates too many LDAP attributes may cause performance issues for authentication or lookup processes.

In a Domino environment, there is rarely a base DN as many Domino entries are non-hierarchical yet still need to use Sametime. For Domino LDAP servers you would usually leave this field empty.

After you have completed your changes, you will be prompted to restart the SSC Deployment Manager for your changes to take effect.

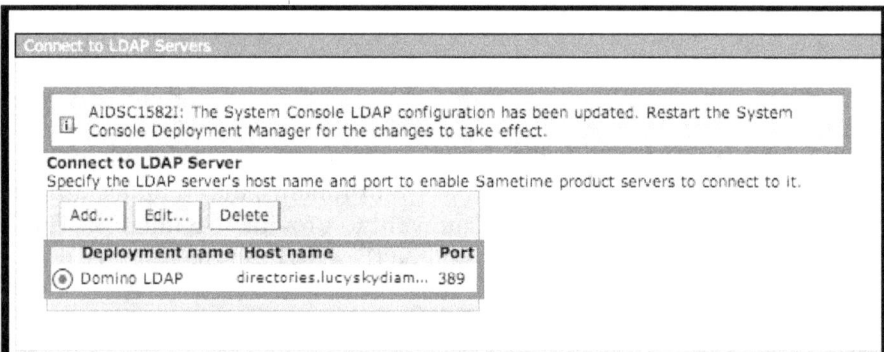

Confirming the LDAP connectivity

Once the LDAP server is set up, you can confirm connectivity by performing a search from within the SSC menu. Under the **Users and Groups** menu you can choose to manage users, and you should be able to successfully search for LDAP entries. In the following screenshot, you are searching by **Last name** for **davis** which matches any last name with that string in the LDAP directory.

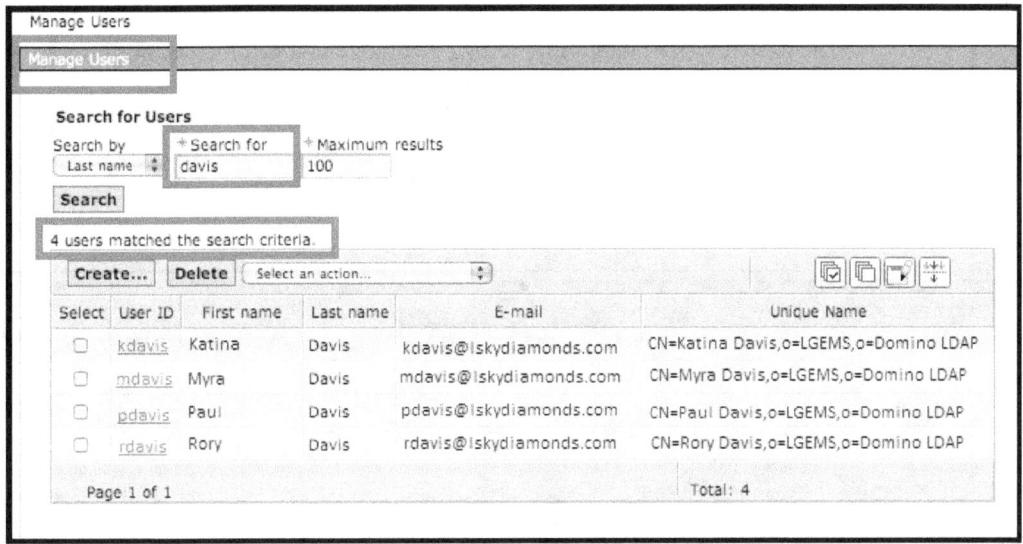

Installing a Sametime Community Server

The Sametime Community Server is based on a Domino server rather than a WAS server, but when installed in the overall Sametime environment, it can be managed by the SSC. This gives you a single administrative interface for managing all Sametime server components.

To build a new Sametime Community Server, you must first install a Domino server running HTTP, which will act as the host for the Sametime Community Server. Once installed, you can return to the SSC and configure a Community Server Deployment Plan under **Sametime System Console | Guided Activities**.

The Deployment Plan is configured with the fully qualified hostname for the host where the Domino server is running and where the Community Server is to be installed. You must also provide credentials that the SSC can use to remotely manage the Sametime environment once it is installed in Domino.

 The user ID associated with these credentials must be an account in the Domino directory that has Sametime admin roles and rights to all the Domino-based Sametime databases such as **stconf.nsf**, **stconfig.nsf**, and **stcenter.nsf**. The Deployment Plan will attempt to connect to the Domino server and log in using the credentials you provide before continuing.

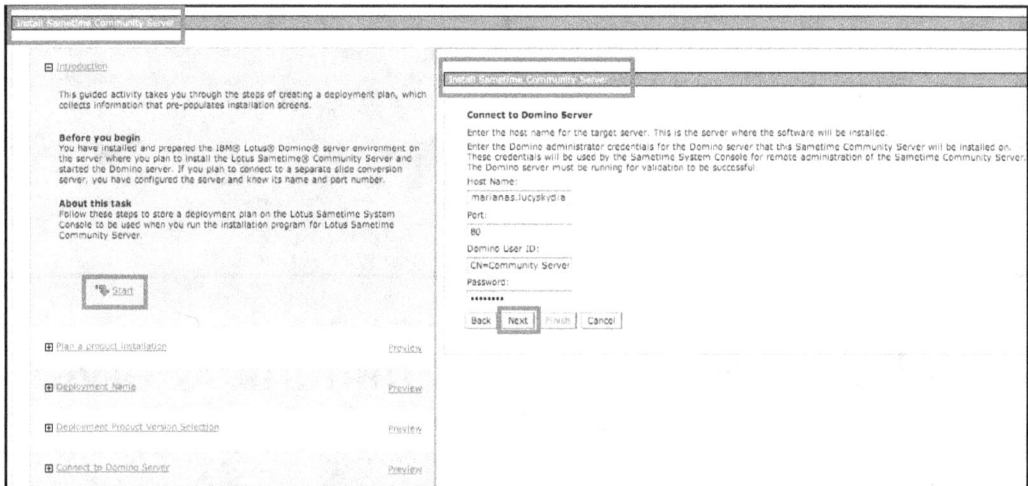

As with a stand-alone Domino Community Server install, you can choose to separate the slide conversion activity utilized in meetings to another server to offload this resource-intensive service. This setting can also be changed at any time after installation. Once you decide which setting to use, click on **Next**.

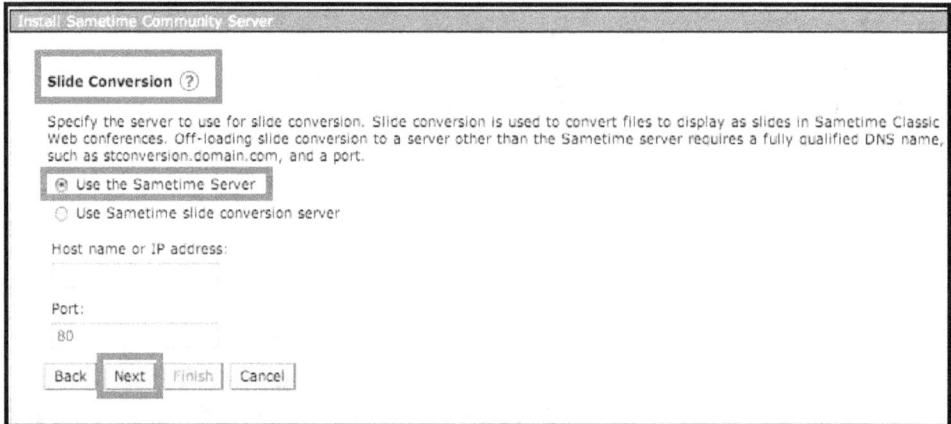

Sametime Community Server 8.5.2, unlike earlier versions of Sametime, must use LDAP as its directory, so your Deployment Plan must be directed to an LDAP directory for Domino to use when authenticating Instant Messaging clients. The list of choices provided here will be restricted to those you have already configured. In our example, our LDAP server is **directories.lucyskydiamonds.com**.

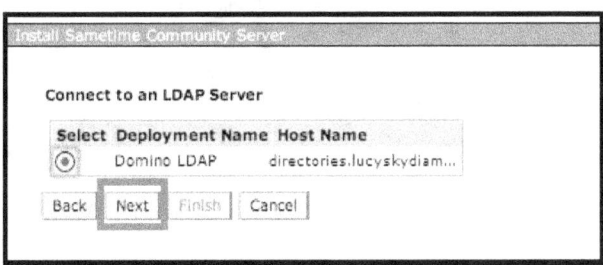

Sametime tunneling enables Instant Messaging clients to connect using port 80 instead of port 1533. Tunneled connections have the advantage of being more accessible through firewalls and networks but do not perform as well as direct connections. After you make your selection, click on **Next**.

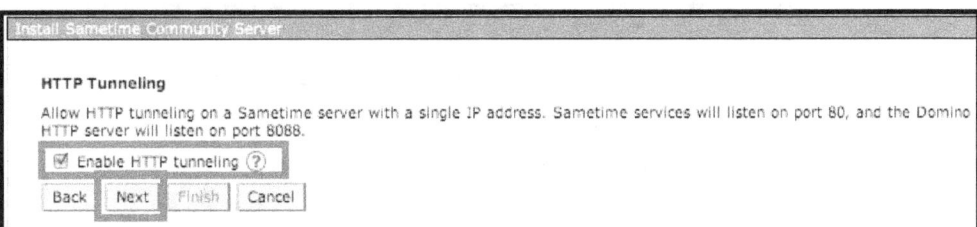

The final confirmation screen summarizes all the choices made during the build of the Deployment Plan and then displays the plan as **Ready to Install**. Click on **Next** to proceed.

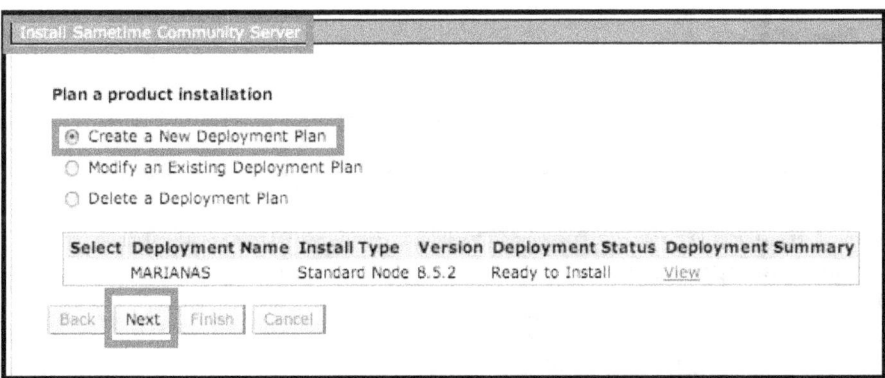

At this point, you can launch the Sametime installer on the Domino server where you plan to install the Community Server. In the Windows environment, the installer is **setupwin32.exe**. The Domino server must be shut down during this step.

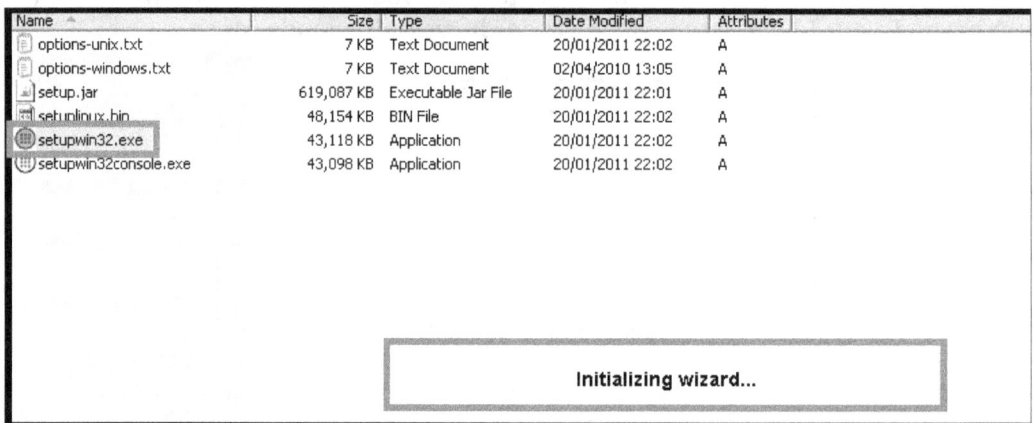

The installer launches the Sametime server installer. Click on **Next**.

If the server ID used by the Domino server has a password associated with it, then you will need to supply that password during the installation process to enable it to continue.

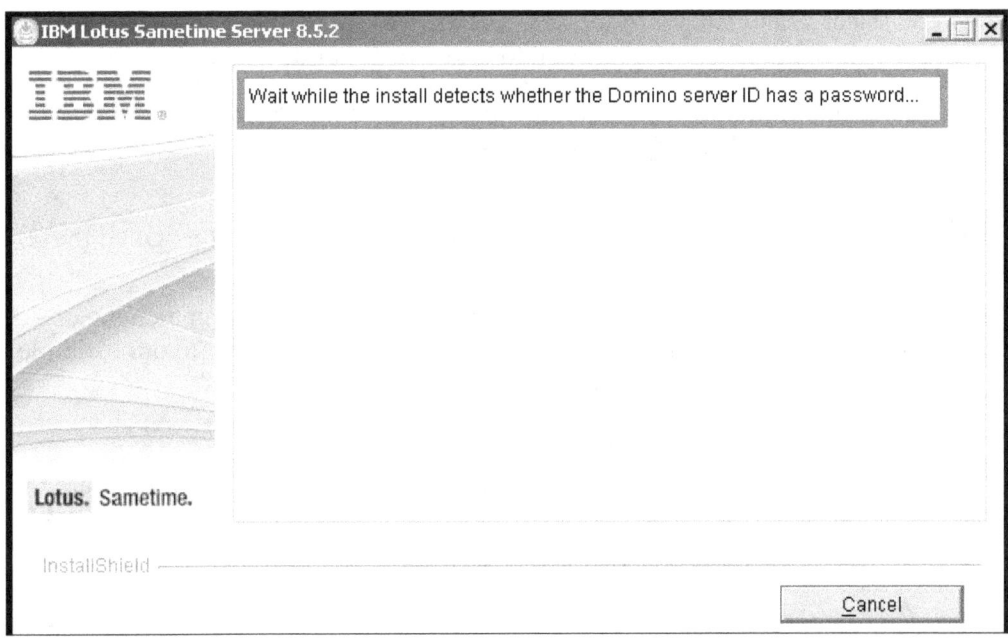

The installer will be very familiar to Sametime administrators from earlier versions of the Community Server with one exception. The following dialog box asks if the SSC is to be used to configure and manage this install. If you select **No**, the install will continue as a stand-alone Domino-based install and will not be connected to any of the other Sametime components installed under the SSC.

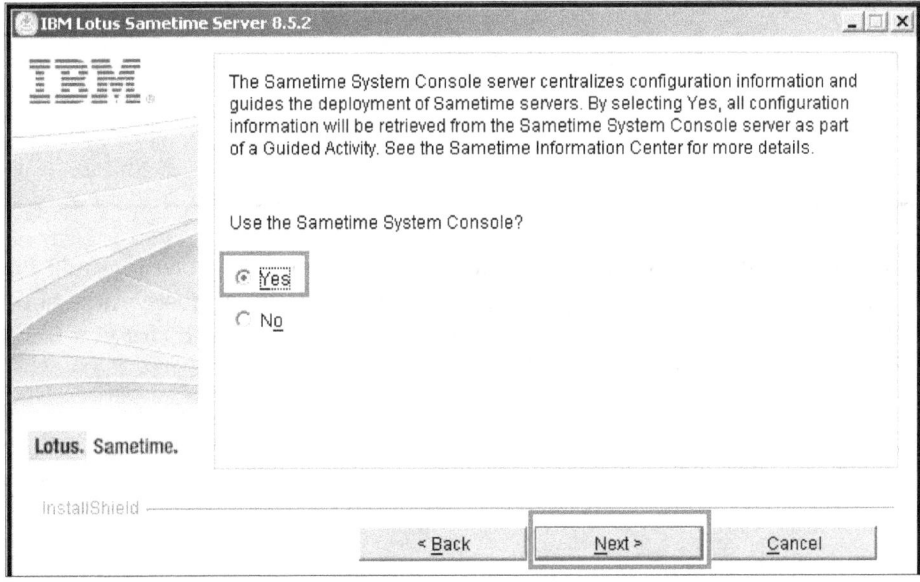

When you select **Yes** to tell the installer to use the SSC for installation instructions, you must provide details for the location to find the SSC and how to access it:

- Hostname is the fully qualified hostname where the SSC can be found (in our example: **baltic.lucyskydiamonds.com**)

- The default SSC port is **9443**

- The login credentials are those you provided when you first installed the SSC (in our example: **wasadmin**)

- The fully qualified hostname for this Sametime Server must match the one used in the Deployment Plan you configured for this install (in our example: **marianas.lucyskydiamond.com**)

Once you have confirmed these values, click on **Next** to continue.

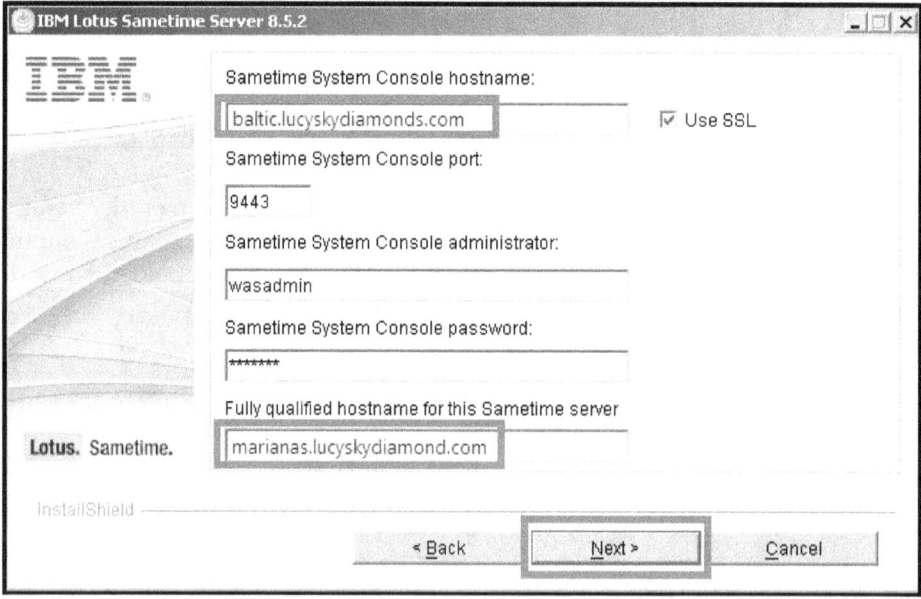

When the installer connects successfully to the SSC, it looks for a Deployment Plan for this server type—a Community Server on the fully qualified hostname where it is installed. It returns a list of any matching Deployment Plans it finds for you to select from. Choose the correct entry and click on **Next** to continue.

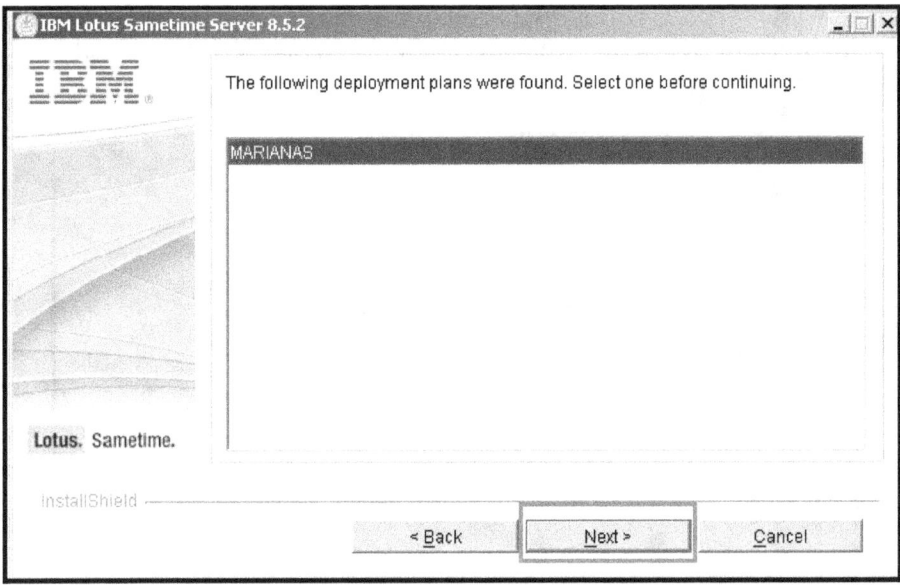

Once you have selected your Deployment Plan there are no more questions to complete, as all other information has already been completed and stored in the plan. The following summary screen dialog is displayed. Click on **Install** and the Sametime server will proceed.

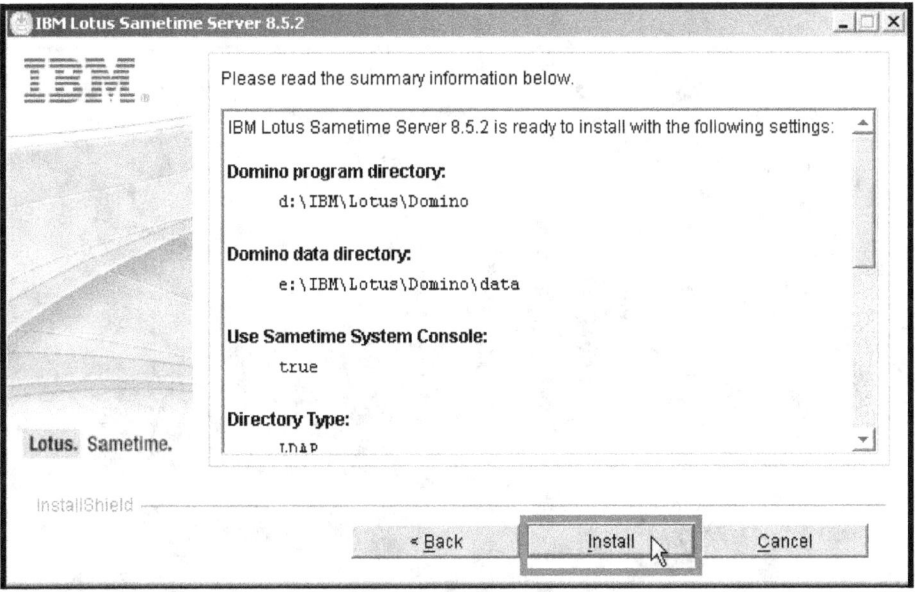

The Sametime server code will be extracted to the install location during this step. A progress indicator will be displayed to indicate the percentage that has been completed.

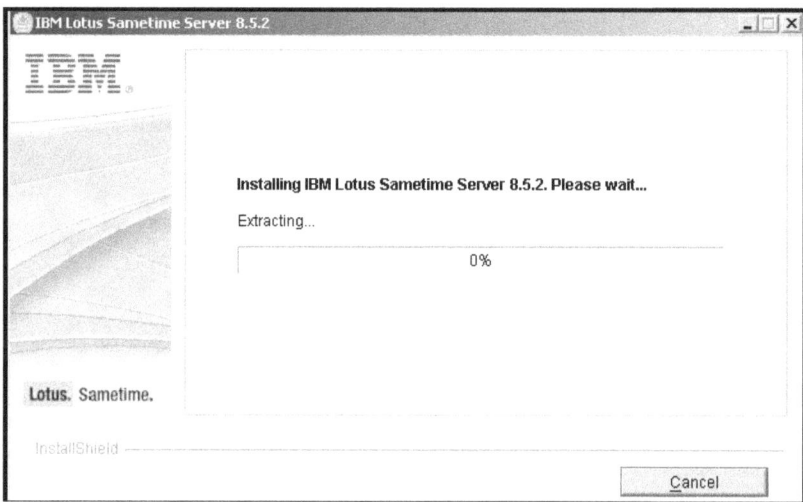

As with other Domino server components, the completed Sametime Community Server install runs as an add-in task under the Domino Console. The following screenshot shows a Domino Console running and, once HTTP is loaded, the Sametime Community Server services are called:

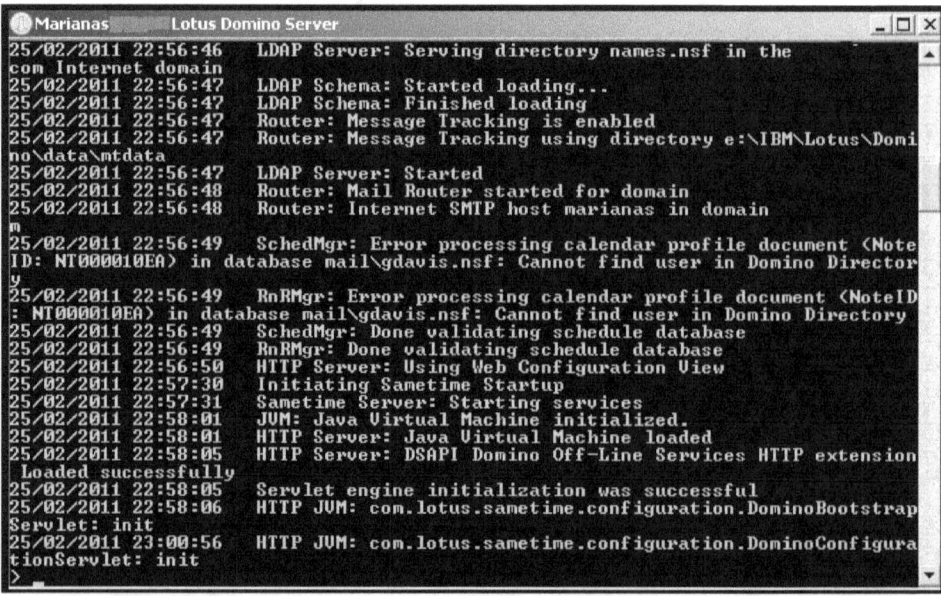

From the Windows' **Services** panel, you can see all the running Sametime Community Server services such as business cards, presence awareness, and user storage. These services should always be set to **Manual** as they are called by Domino itself and are not run outside of Domino.

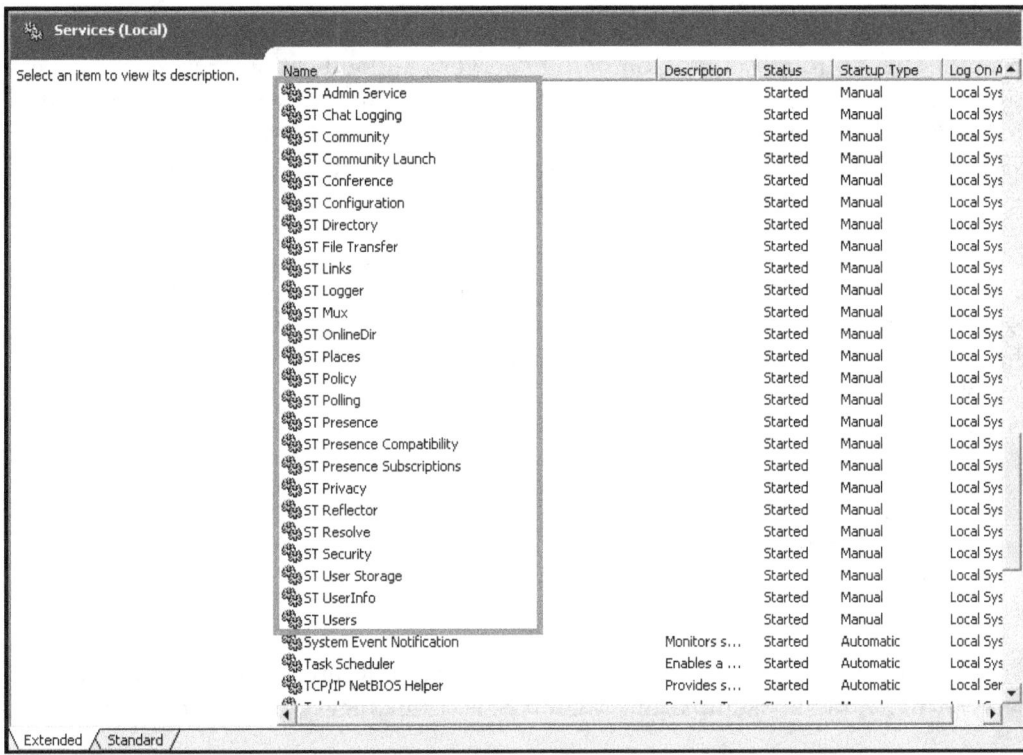

Upgrading an existing server

Sametime 8.5.2 must use LDAP as its directory store, so the first task to upgrade an existing server to Sametime 8.5.2 is to ensure you are using an LDAP directory instead of the Domino Directory. If you are using Domino Directory authentication for Sametime, you would want to convert the Sametime server to use LDAP (which itself can be a Domino Directory on another server). This is a fairly simple process and there is a server command that can convert all the buddy lists from Domino to LDAP format once it is complete.

To upgrade an existing Sametime Community Server to Sametime 8.5.2 and connect the upgraded server to the SSC, you use the same instructions as if you were installing a new server. You create a Deployment Plan and install Sametime Community Server 8.5.2 on the Domino server.

Once this is complete, the SSC will be managing your Domino server and all settings and policies are done from within that administration interface.

Adding multiplexors

The MUXs act as a gateway for Community Server traffic, passing login requests from the client through to the Community Server's authentication process. It can be installed on separate hardware from the Sametime Community Server. You would do this to reduce demand on the servers themselves and improve the number of concurrent connected users that can be supported on a single server. You can also use MUXs to support failover for Community Services in a clustered environment.

The MUX installer is found in the MUX directory on the unzipped Sametime Community Server. When you copy that installer to a separate workstation and run it, you get a Sametime MUX service and a `sametime.ini` file that instructs the MUX how to connect to the Community Servers. The following code is a sample `sametime.ini` from a MUX that connects to a cluster of three Sametime Community Servers:

```
# Sametime.ini Configuration
[Config]
VPMX_CAPACITY=80000
[Connectivity]
VPS_HOST=10.9.2.8,10.9.2.41,192.168.0.100
```

Once a MUX is in place, you can tell the SSC about it so it can be used for Community Server activity. In our example, our MUX host is **stmux.lucyskydiamonds.com**.

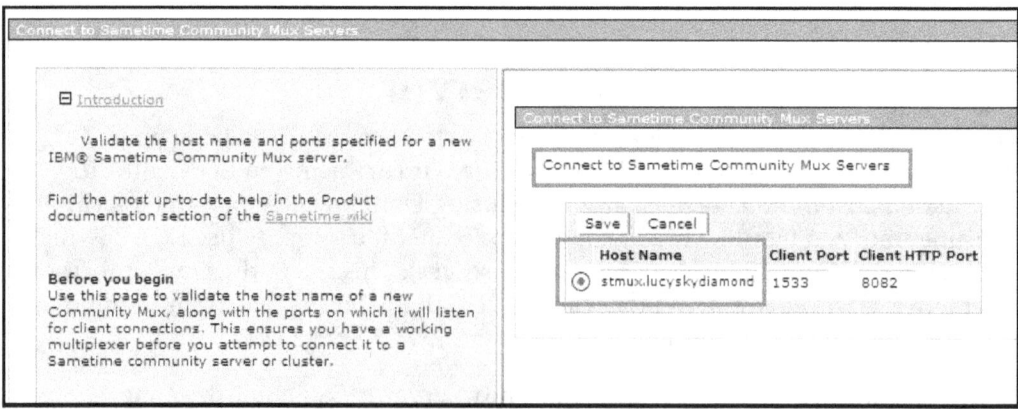

Confirming Community awareness

After your new Sametime Community Server is installed or upgraded, you should be able to:

- Sign-on using your Instant Messaging client and initiate conversations with people on your server and with other servers in your community
- View whether your contacts are online or offline in your Instant Messaging client

Installing a Sametime Proxy Server

The next Sametime server to be installed is the Proxy Server. A Proxy Server is required if you want browser-based clients or a lightweight alternative to STLinks, otherwise a Proxy Server install is optional.

As with all other Sametime server components installed from the SSC, the Proxy Server install starts with the build of a Deployment Plan for Proxy Server which provides details for the later install. In our example, our Proxy Server hostname is **proxy.lucyskydiamonds.com**.

After entering the Deployment Name, click on **Next**.

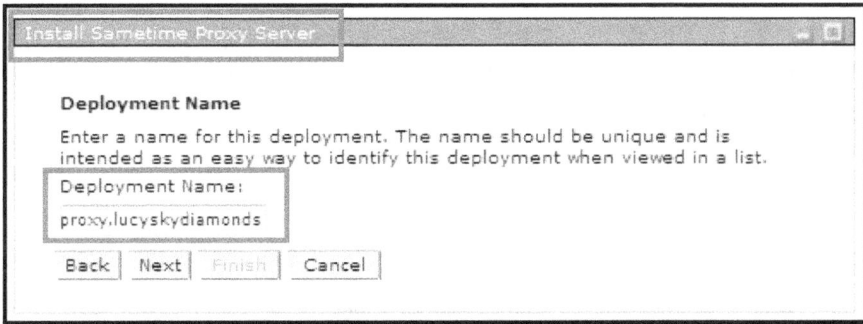

The dialog box to select the version of the Proxy Server will be displayed. Click on
Next to continue.

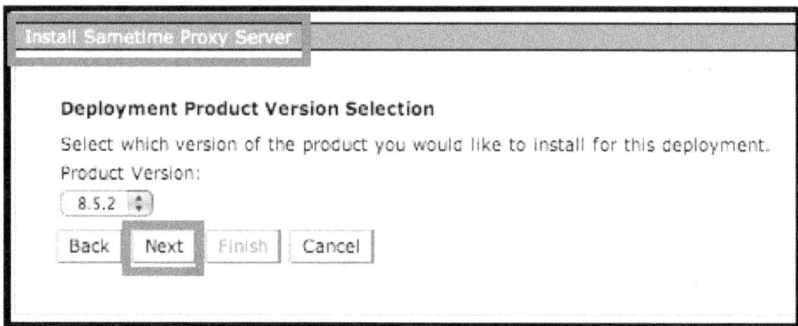

The Proxy Server is a WAS-based component so the installer needs to be told how
to configure its WAS instance. Installing a server in its own cell gives it its own
Deployment Manager and Management Interface outside of the SSC. In most cases,
you would install the Proxy Server as either a primary node that is managed by the
SSC or a secondary node in a cluster with an existing primary node.

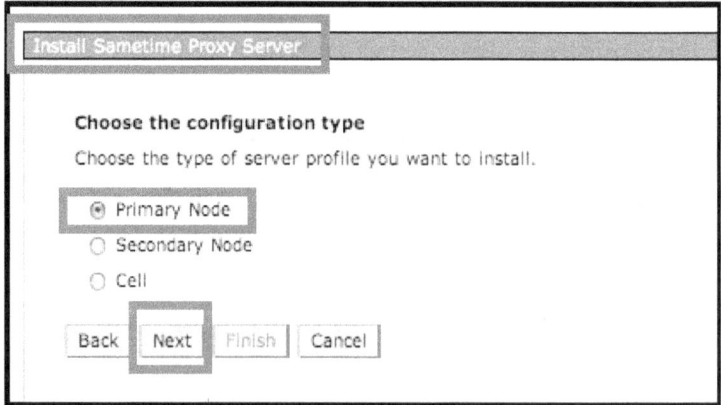

As you have chosen **Primary Node** on the previous screen, the Deployment Plan
knows that the Proxy Server will not have its own cell and instead needs to be added
into the Deployment Manager process of a pre-existing cell. In this instance, where
you are installing all WAS components on the same server, there is only one cell,
which is the one you created for the SSC, so you are prompted to select that.

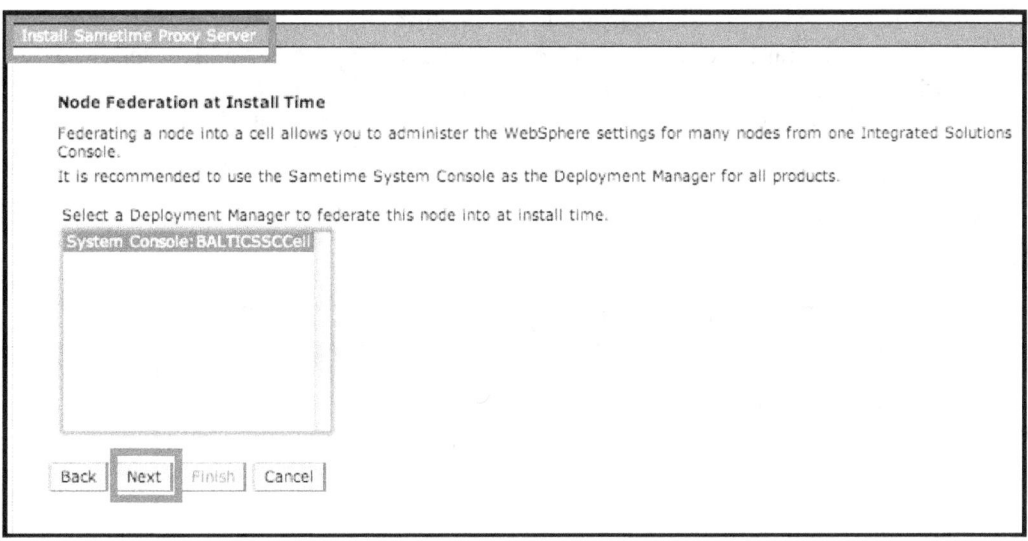

The next screen is where you specify the fully qualified hostname where the Proxy Server is to be installed, as well as the WAS credentials that will be used to create and manage the server. The credentials you specify here will be the ones used to start, stop, and maintain the server outside of the SSC and are not stored anywhere outside of the WAS environment itself.

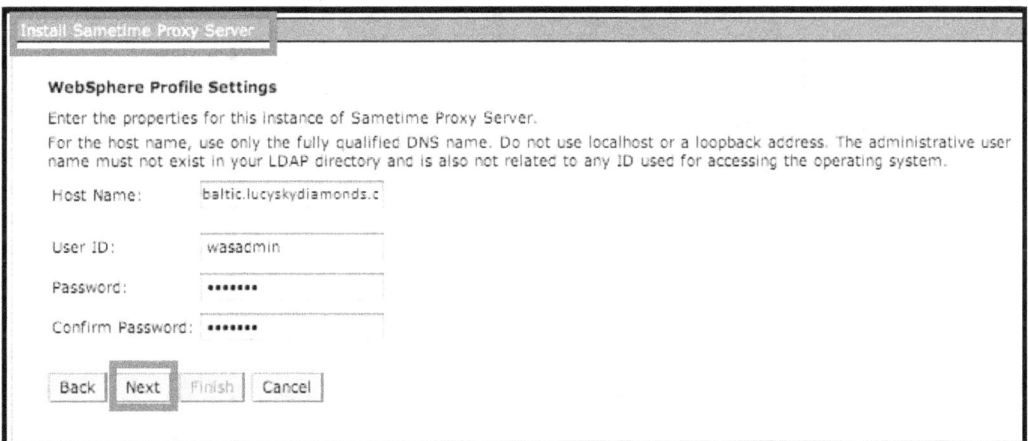

The Proxy Server is simply an interface to an existing Community Server. It does not provide any Instant Messaging services itself. It only presents a browser client front-end to the Sametime Community Server services. The relationship between a Proxy Server and a Community Server is one-to-one. You cannot have a single Proxy Server connecting to different Community Servers. On the following screen of your Deployment Plan, you specify which Community Server the Proxy Server will be working with. In the example, you only have one Community Server setup in the SSC and so there is only one to choose from.

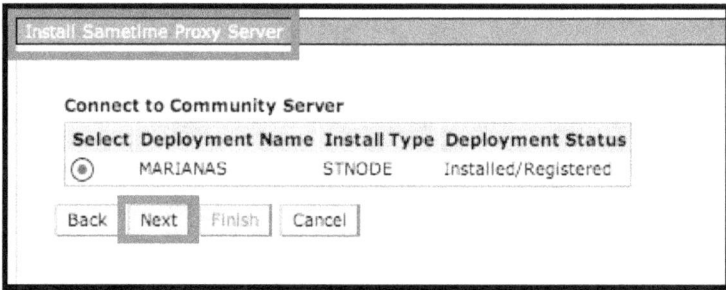

As all settings are now completed, the summary dialog box appears which allows you to see what is going to be installed and where the install will occur. Click on **Finish** to continue.

Once the Deployment Plan is completed, your Proxy Server shows as **Ready to Install**. Click on **Next** to continue to the actual installation of the software.

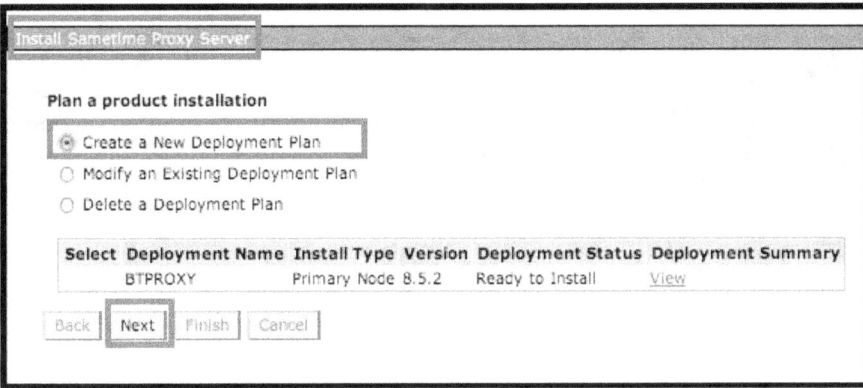

The Proxy Server executable has a `launchpad` script in the unzipped root directory under **SametimeProxyServer**. You use this script to start the software install. The SSC must be up and running during this install phase.

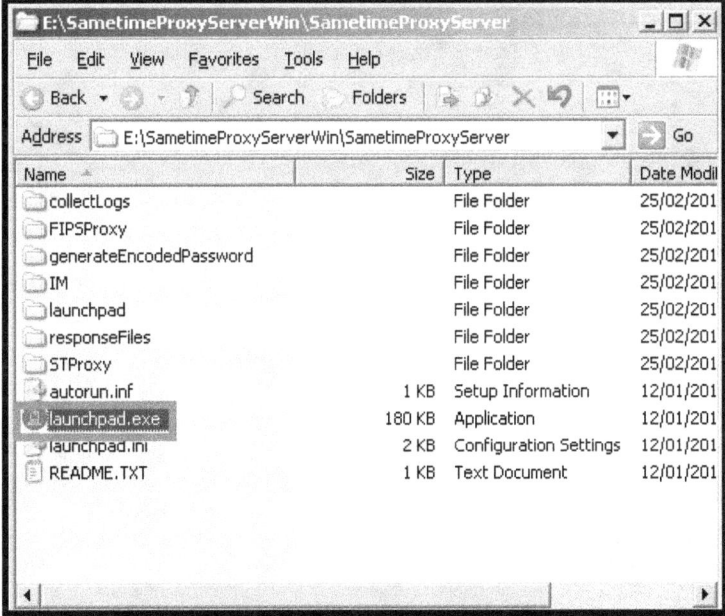

Launchpad.exe starts the Installation Manager which then takes over the install. The install screens should be familiar to you if you have installed any other Sametime WAS components.

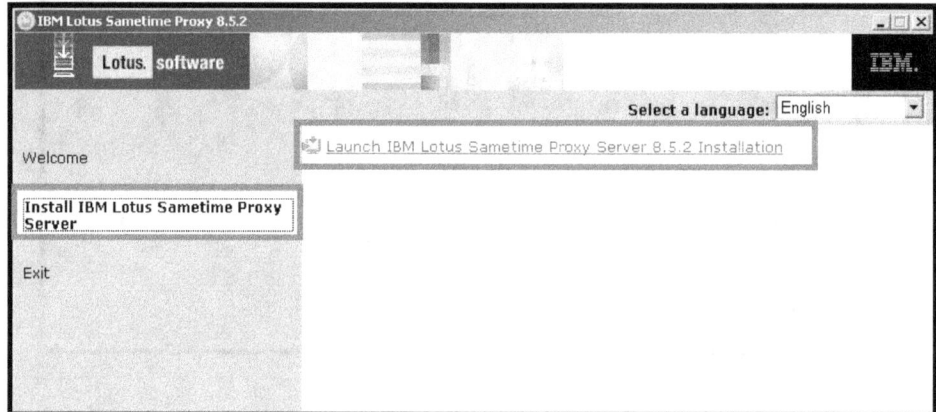

You see that the package being installed is the Sametime Proxy Server. Click on **Next** to continue.

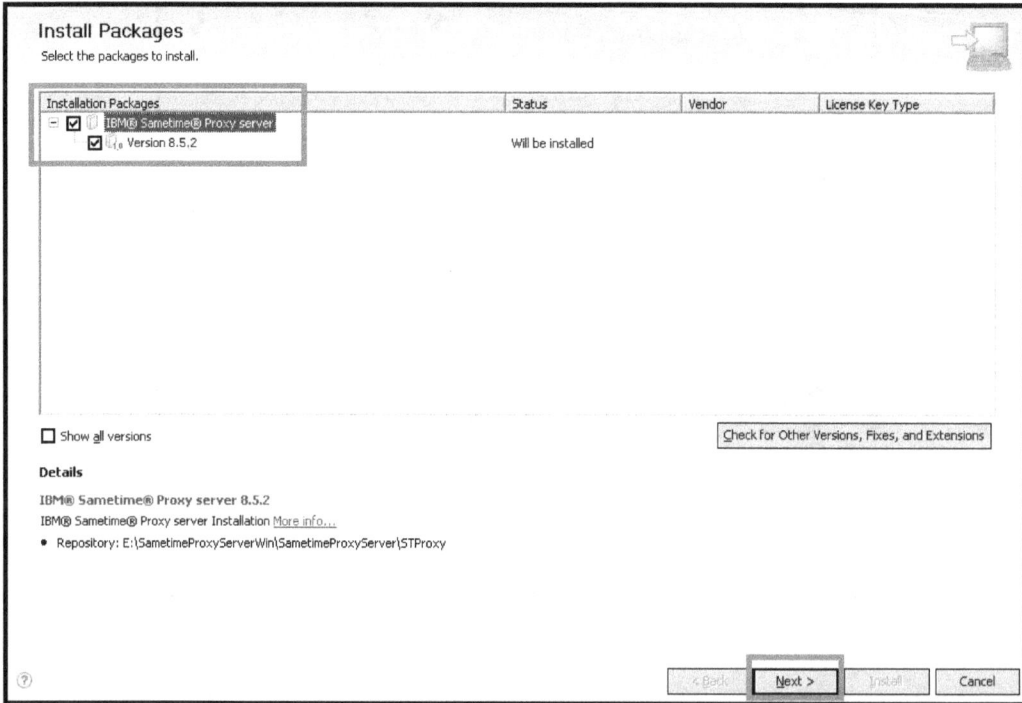

In our example, the Proxy Server is being installed on hardware where existing WAS servers are already in place. As a package group was created when the SSC was installed, we can also use this package group to install additional Sametime WAS components. By using the same package, the same directory structure is used for this server install as with earlier servers on this machine. This makes ongoing management and file backup easier. There are no security or performance advantages to using a separate installation package. Click on **Next** to proceed.

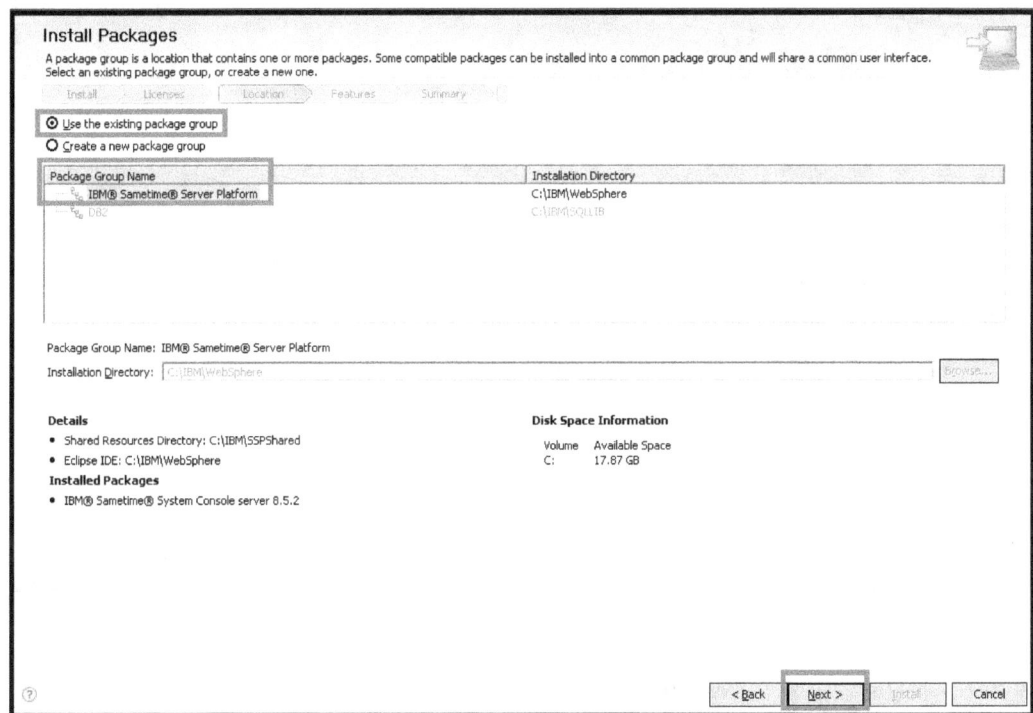

On the next screen you have the option to use the SSC for the install, in which case the Installation Manager attempts to find a Deployment Plan to match this server and fully qualified hostname. It is possible to install the Proxy Server without the SSC and as a stand-alone WAS product by deselecting the **Use Lotus Sametime System Console** to **install** option.

At this point, the installer also confirms the disk space available and disk space required to complete the install. You should always ensure there is plenty of free space after the install if you want to avoid performance issues.

Now you proceed with the install by using the SSC to complete the work. Click on **Next** to proceed.

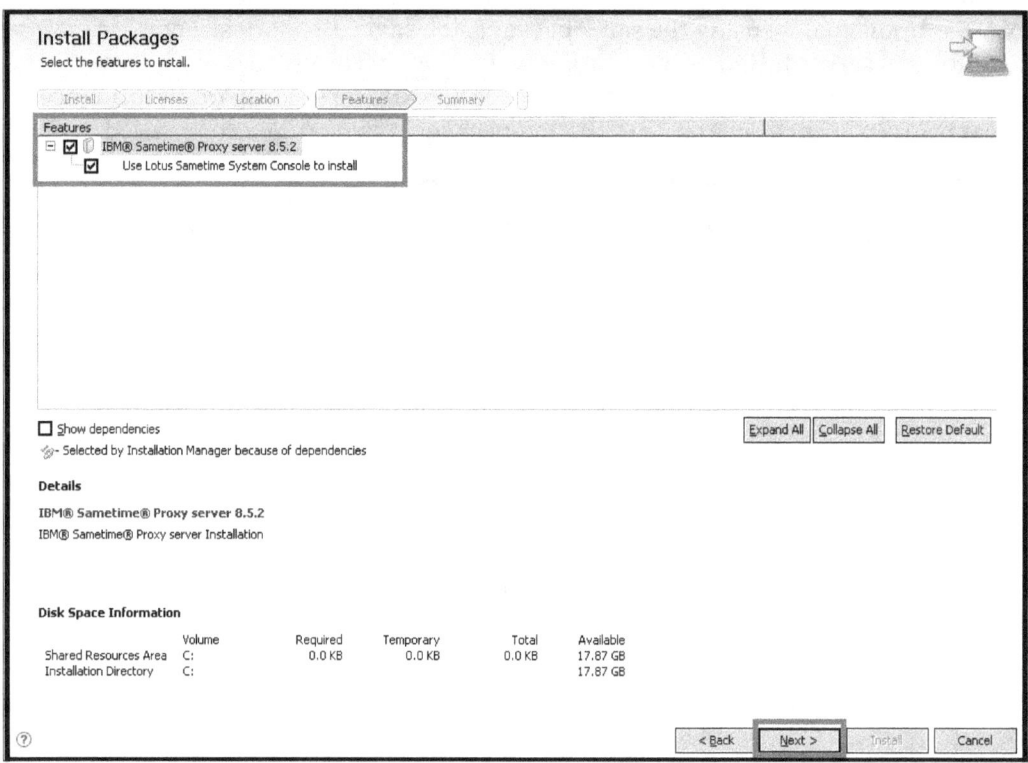

As you chose to use the SSC, you now need to tell the installer where it can be found, on what port, and the fully qualified hostname of the server you are currently installing on. This is how the installer logs into the SSC and finds a Deployment Plan that matches this product and the fully qualified hostname given.

First you complete the fully qualified hostname of the SSC and provide the login credentials. These are the login credentials you use for the SSC, not the ones you selected in the Proxy Server Deployment Plan. You are logging into the SSC and it is those credentials that will be used. Once you provide the credentials, click on **Validate** at the bottom of the page. The button should switch to **Validated** if the installer is able to log into the SSC. Until this switches to **Validated** you cannot choose **Next** and continue on with the installation.

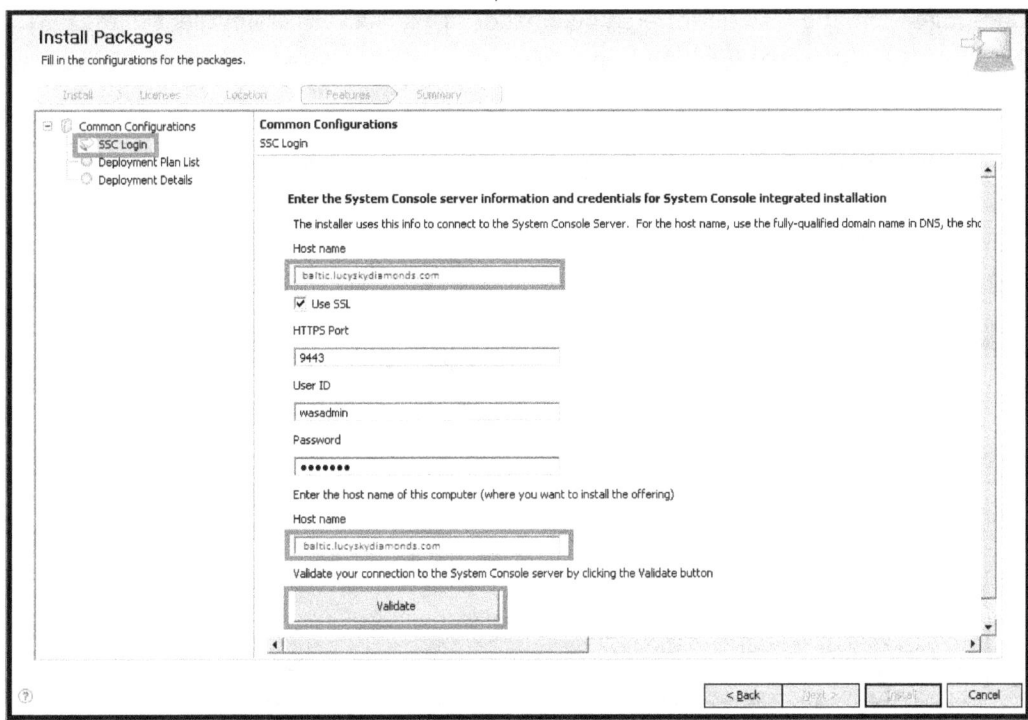

If the installer screen says that it is unable to find the SSC then you will want to verify that:

- The hostname used by the SSC is resolvable from this new server being installed

- The hostname used by the SSC is accessible through ICMP (ping traffic) from this new server being installed

- The port you are using to access the SSC from the installing server is open on the SSC server

Once logged in, the installer offers you a list of Proxy Server Deployment Plans that have this fully qualified hostname as the server location. In most circumstances, and unless you are building a vertical cluster, you would only have one Deployment Plan of each type for each fully qualified hostname.

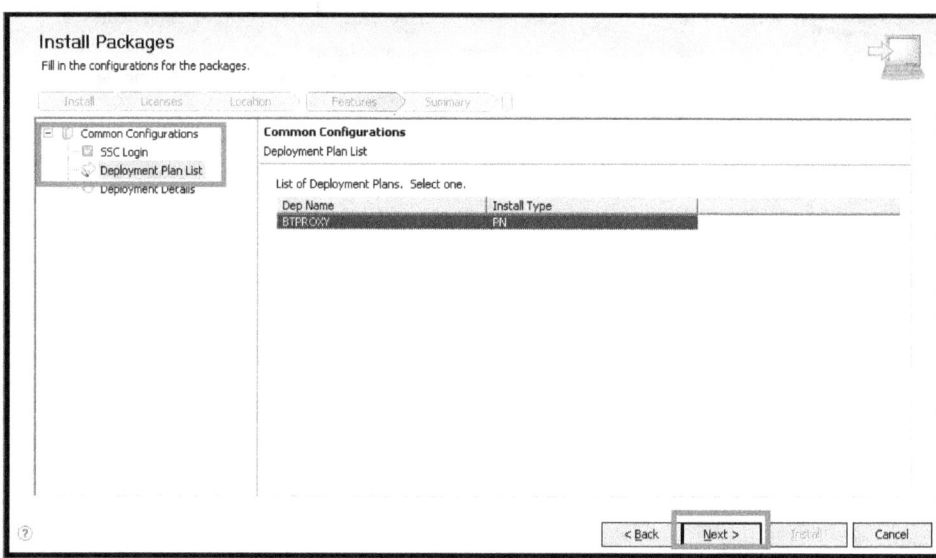

The following screenshot is the summary screen for the installation which is about to begin. At this point, it is worth taking a screenshot for reference purposes, as this screen shows you the Deployment Plan which includes the WAS profile. Click on **Next** to continue.

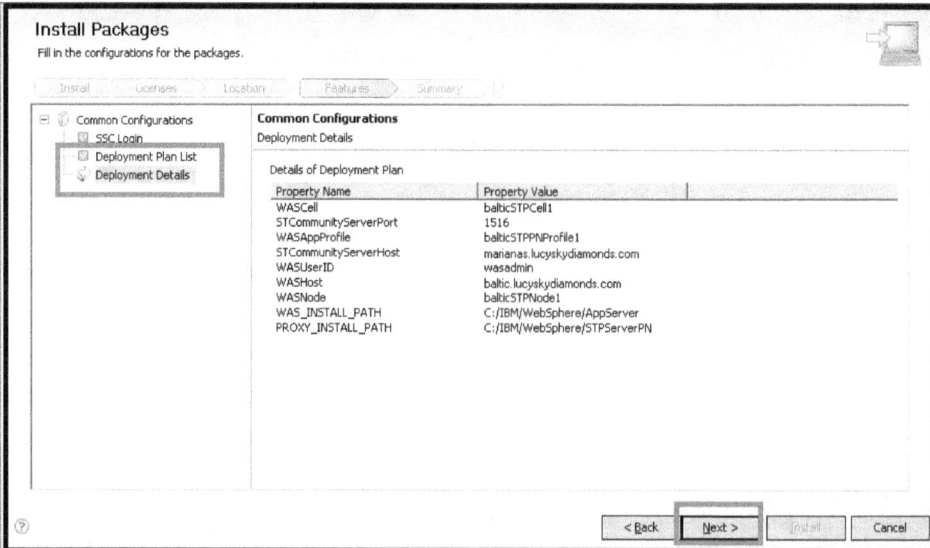

The install itself may take anywhere from a few minutes to over an hour depending upon the performance of your server hardware and disk infrastructure. It is important to let the installation run to completion even though it may seem to be stalled. There are installation log files you can view at any time to see if progress is still being made. These can be found at:

- `c:\Documents and Settings\All Users\Application Data\IBM\ Installation Manager\logs` (Windows)

- `c:\programdata\ibm\installation manager\logs` (Windows 2008)

- `/var/ibm/installationmanager/logs` (AIX, Linux, and Solaris)

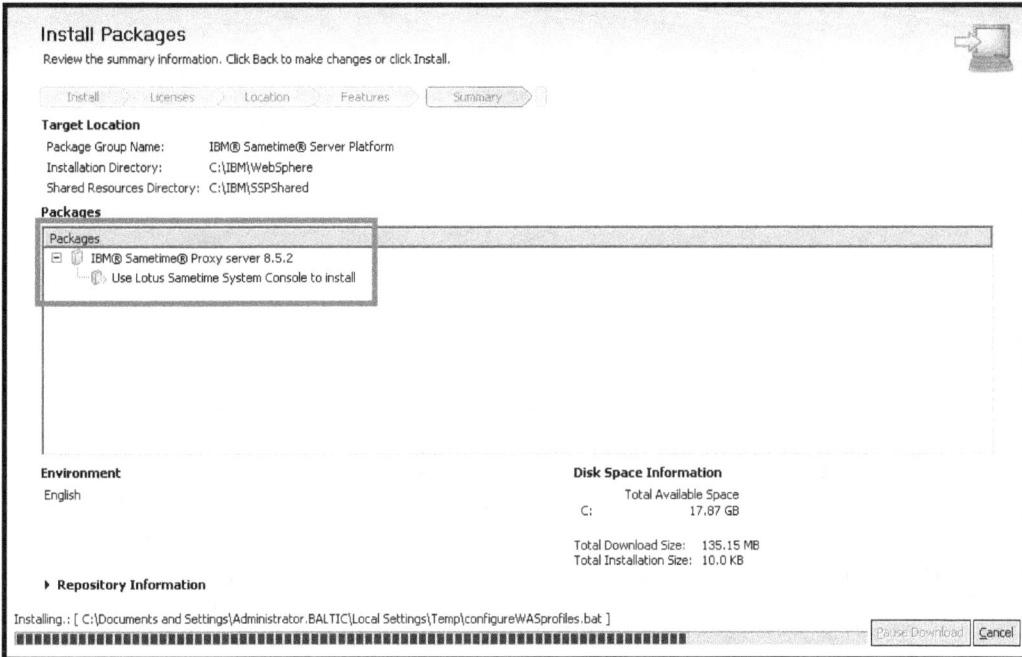

Adding Proxy Server trusted IP to Community Servers

Once the Proxy Server is installed, you have one more step to complete before you can test the server. By default, the Sametime Community Server will not allow another server to connect to it and participate as a community member. Unfortunately, this is exactly what the Proxy Server wants to do. You have to first tell the Community Server that the Proxy Server is trusted and can be allowed to interact directly with its services. To do this, you need to go back to the SSC administration console and modify the Community Server settings.

The SSC shows a list of Community Servers that it manages, with each one named according to its Deployment Plan. Select the name of the Deployment Plan for the Community Server to begin modifying the server configuration options.

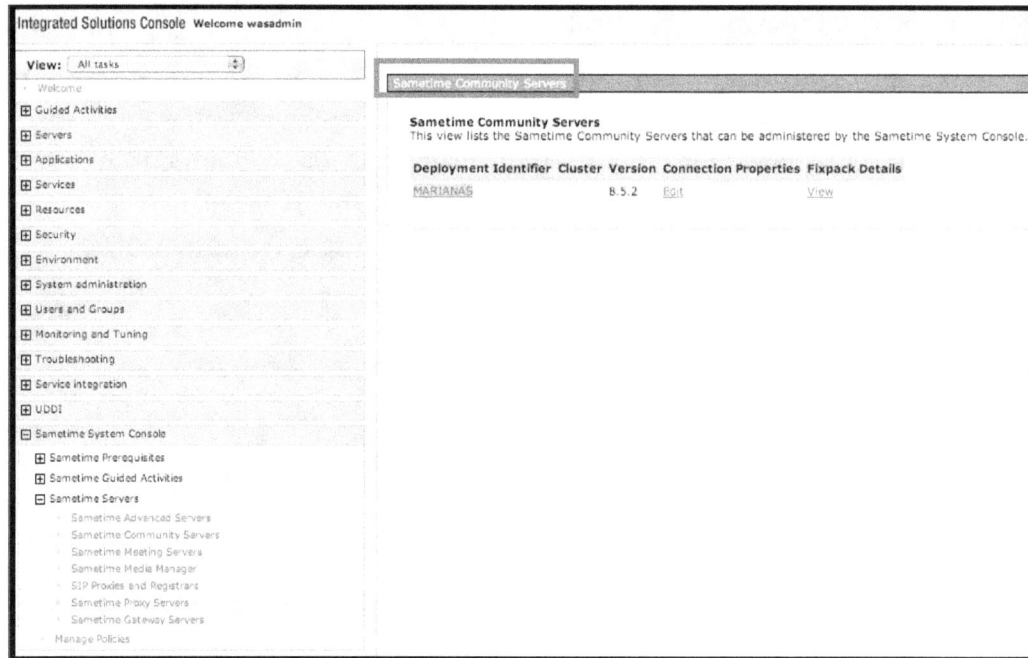

At the bottom of the server configuration option list is a table entitled **Trusted Servers**. The IP address of the Proxy Server needs to be added to the list of Trusted Servers. Once added and saved, you may have to wait up to an hour for the Community Server to pick up the update from the SSC. Another option is to restart the Community Server in order for the changes take effect immediately.

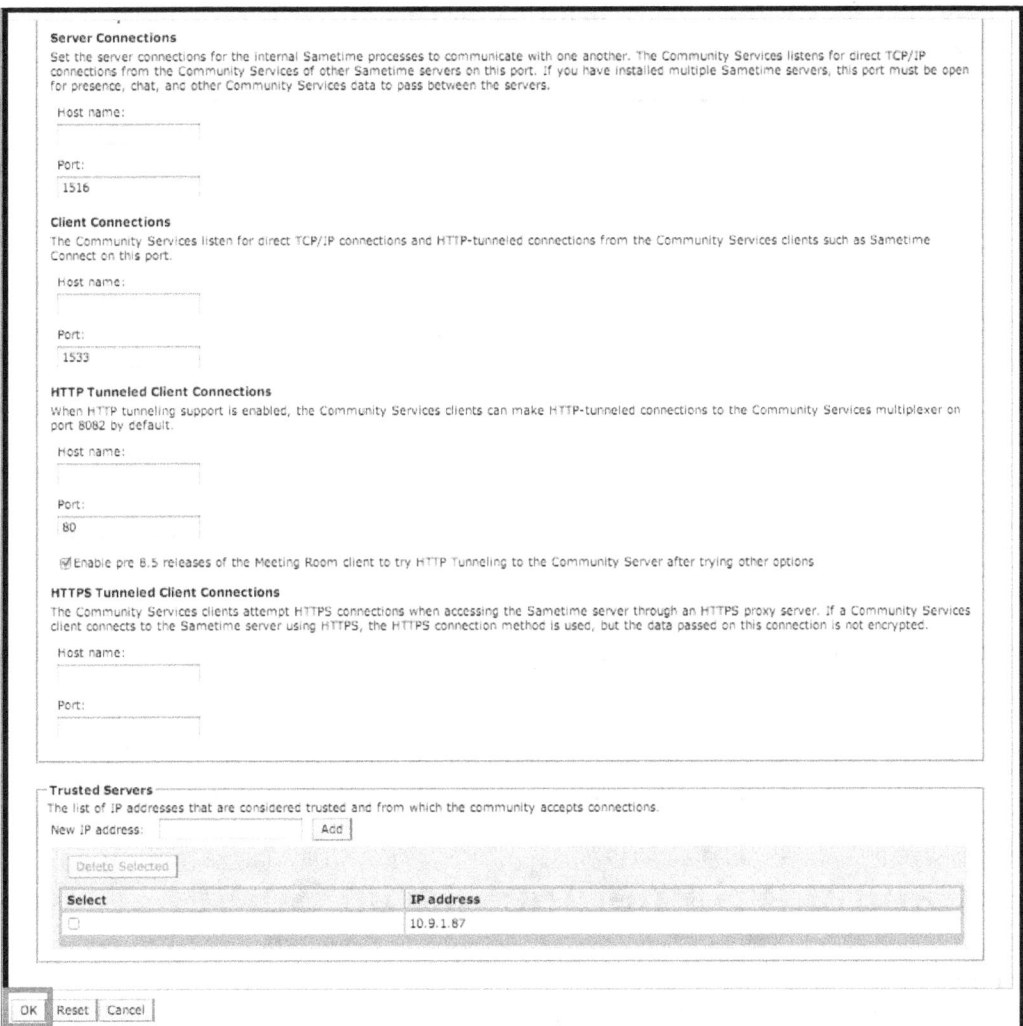

Server Connections

Set the server connections for the internal Sametime processes to communicate with one another. The Community Services listens for direct TCP/IP connections from the Community Services of other Sametime servers on this port. If you have installed multiple Sametime servers, this port must be open for presence, chat, and other Community Services data to pass between the servers.

Host name:

Port:

1516

Client Connections

The Community Services listen for direct TCP/IP connections and HTTP-tunneled connections from the Community Services clients such as Sametime Connect on this port.

Host name:

Port:

1533

HTTP Tunneled Client Connections

When HTTP tunneling support is enabled, the Community Services clients can make HTTP-tunneled connections to the Community Services multiplexer on port 8082 by default.

Host name:

Port:

80

☑ Enable pre 8.5 releases of the Meeting Room client to try HTTP Tunneling to the Community Server after trying other options

HTTPS Tunneled Client Connections

The Community Services clients attempt HTTPS connections when accessing the Sametime server through an HTTPS proxy server. If a Community Services client connects to the Sametime server using HTTPS, the HTTPS connection method is used, but the data passed on this connection is not encrypted.

Host name:

Port:

Trusted Servers

The list of IP addresses that are considered trusted and from which the community accepts connections.

New IP address: [   ] [Add]

[Delete Selected]

Select	IP address
☐	10.9.1.87

[OK] [Reset] [Cancel]

Testing for a successful Proxy Server installation

Once the Proxy Server is installed, you can confirm it is present as a Windows service and browse to its default login screen: `http://<hostname>:<defaulthostport>/stwebclient/index.jsp`.

The default host port can be found in the SSC by reviewing the Proxy Server configuration itself. In the example, the port is 9084:

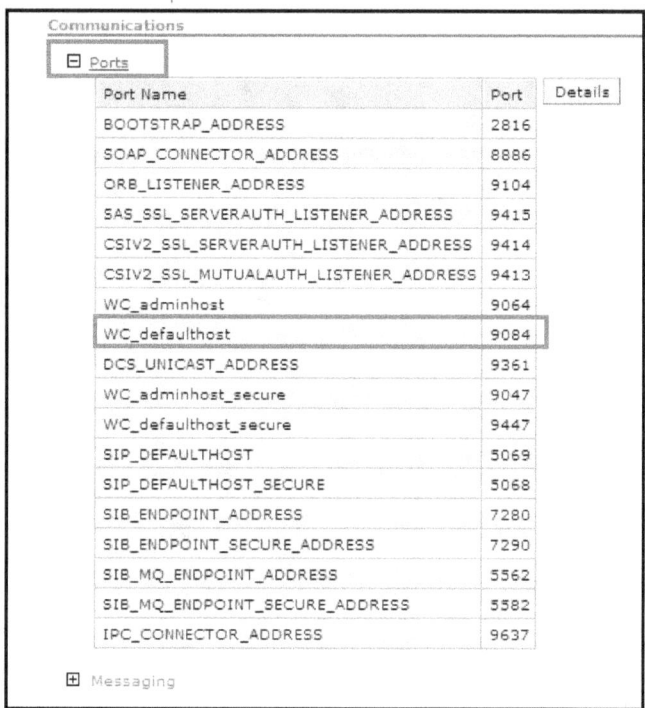

Installing a Sametime Media Server

The Media Server is a WAS-based server component that handles audio and video services both within Instant Messaging clients and in meetings. It is required if you want to use audio or video services, but you can choose not to install it if audio and video functionality is not a requirement.

If you do choose to install the Media Server, then you must first have installed a Community Server as a minimum prerequisite. The Media Server must also be installed as part of the SSC, so the first step is to build a Deployment Plan to define the Media Server install itself.

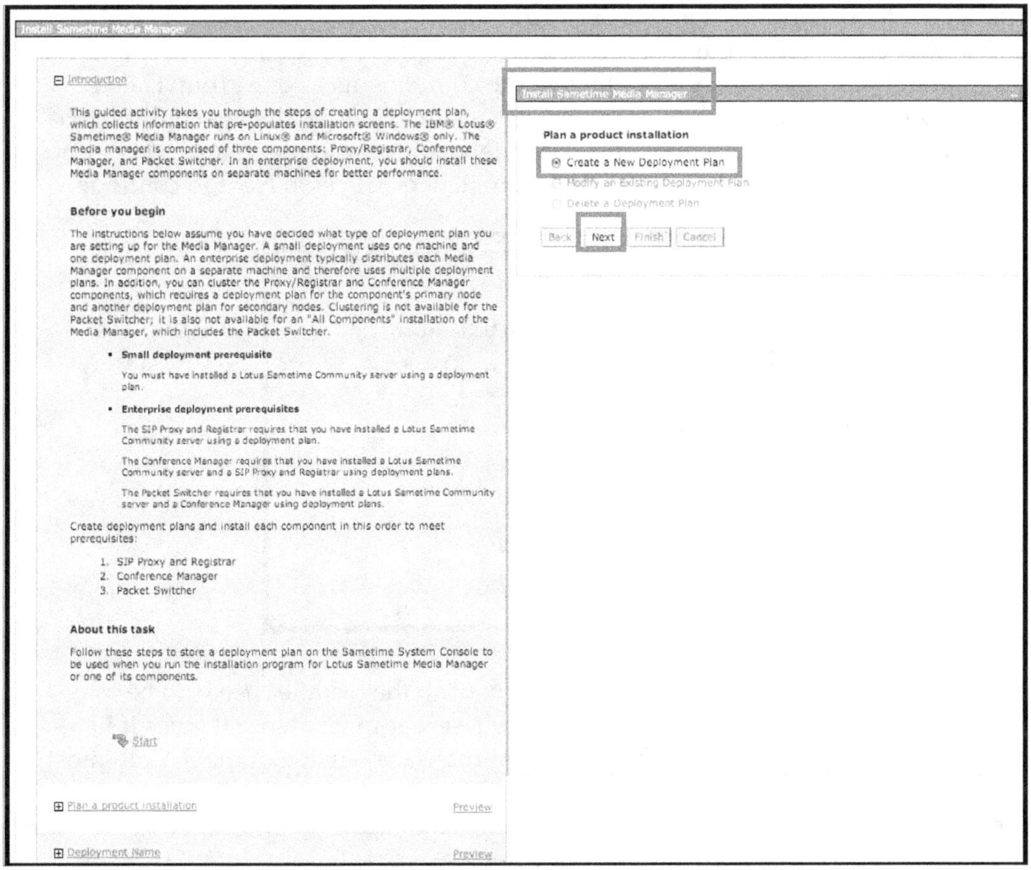

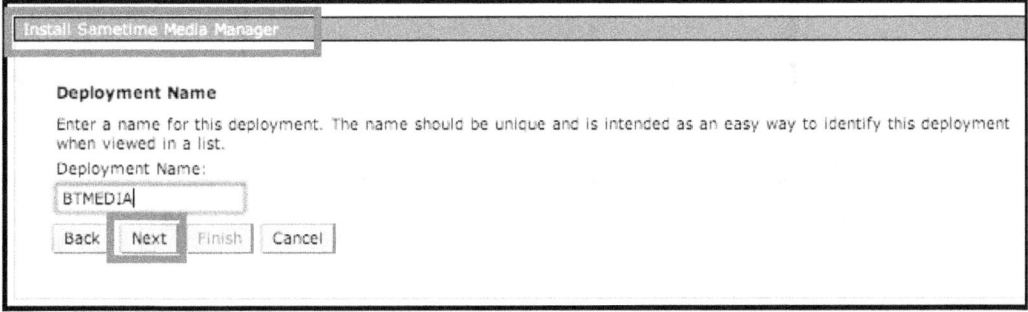

The name of the Deployment Plan determines how this server appears in the SSC in the future. It can have whatever name you choose, but it should be descriptive as it will aid your administration and maintenance efforts going forward. Click on **Next** to proceed.

The Media Manager itself consists of several different server components that can be installed separately on different machines to improve scalability and availability. In the pilot example, you are installing all the components as one group called **Media Manager**. Each SSC can only support a single Media Manager, although if you choose to install the components separately, you can create a single cluster of Conference Managers and multiple Packet Switchers. Click on **Next** to continue.

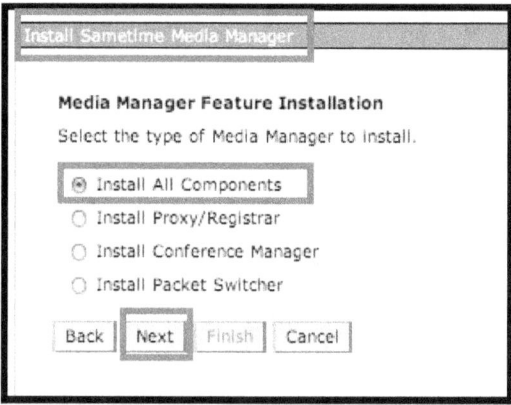

The Media Manager is a WAS-based component so the installer needs to be told how to configure its WAS instance. Installing a server in its own cell gives it its own Deployment Manager and Management Interface outside of the SSC. In most cases you would install the Media Manager, Conference Manager, Packet Switch, or Proxy/Registrar as either a primary node that is managed by the SSC or a secondary node in a cluster with an existing primary node.

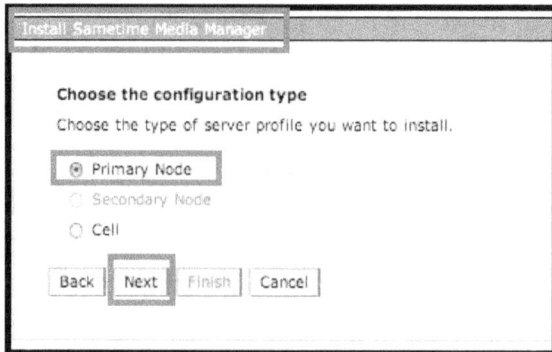

As you chose **Primary Node** on the previous screen, the Deployment Plan knows that the Media Manager will not have its own cell and instead needs to be added into the deployment manager process of a pre-existing cell. In this instance, where you are installing all WAS components on the same server, there is only one cell which is the one you created for the SSC, so you are prompted to select that cell. Click on **Next** to continue.

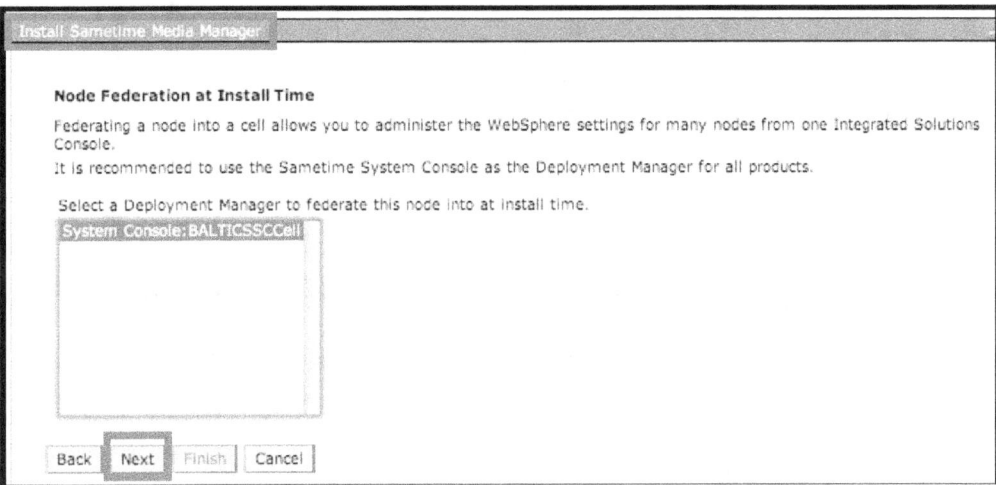

You now need to tell the Deployment Manager the details of the Media Manager WAS install, including the fully qualified hostname where you intend to install it and the administration credentials you wish to create to manage it. In the configuration where the Media Manager is part of the SSC cell, the credentials for the SSC are used to login and manage the Media Manager options. You may need the Media Manager credentials themselves if you need to work outside of the SSC.

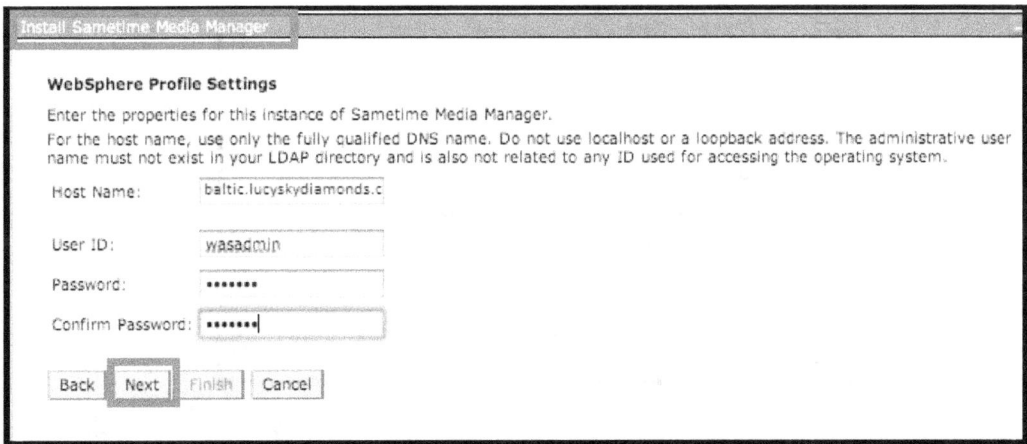

Finally, as with the Proxy Server, the Media Manager itself needs a Community Server with which to connect and provide services. The Media Manager and Community Server relationship is one-to-one, so you cannot have a single Media Manager supporting multiple Community Servers unless they are in a cluster and behind a MUX.

Once this is completed, the **Deployment Summary** will be displayed. As with the install of previous components, take a look at the summary and confirm that everything is correct. Click on **Finish** to proceed.

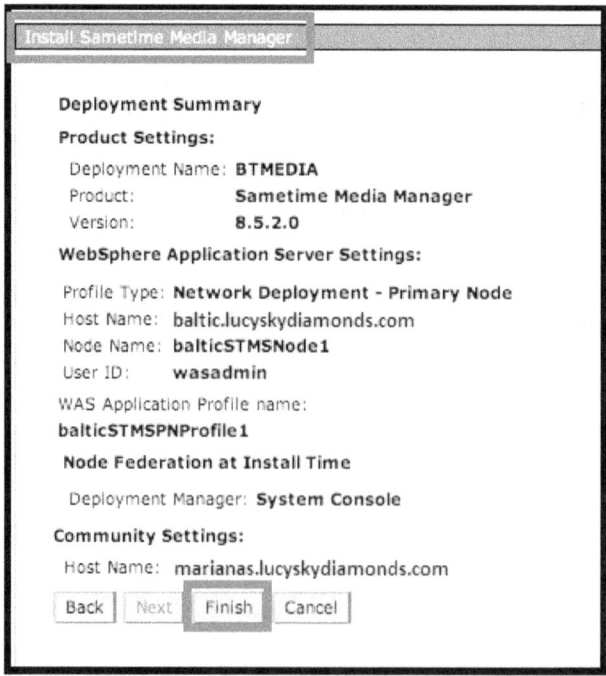

Now you can continue with the install of the software itself. On the server where you want to install Media Manager, extract the zip file. In the root of the extracted folder there is a `launchpad` script to run. The `launchpad` loads Installation Manager to manage the install. Choose the installation package and click on **Next**.

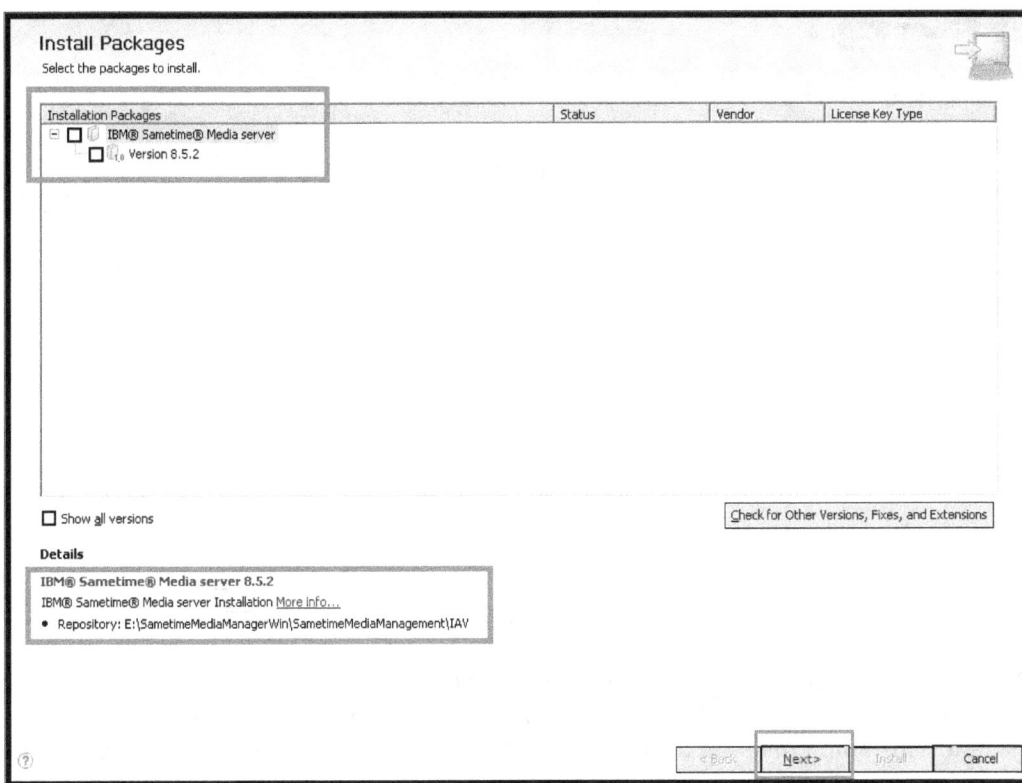

This Media Manager Server is being installed on hardware where existing WAS servers are already in place, in this case the SSC and the Proxy Server. The Installation Manager created a new package group for the SSC. As that package group exists, we can use it for additional Sametime WAS components. By using the same package, the same directory structure will be used for this server install as with earlier servers on this machine, making ongoing management and file backup easier. There are no security or performance advantages to using a separate installation package.

Click on **Next** to continue.

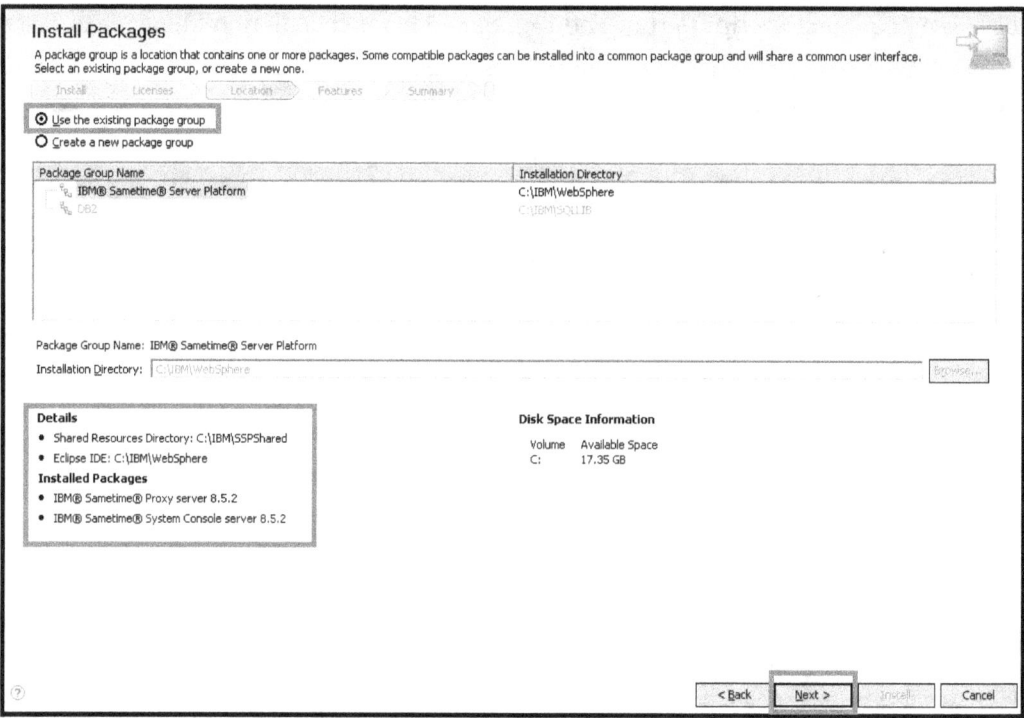

As you are using the SSC, you need to tell the Media Manager installer where it can be found, on what port, and what the fully qualified hostname of the server you are currently installing on is set to. This is how the installer will log into the SSC and find a Deployment Plan that matches this product and the fully qualified hostname.

First you complete the fully qualified hostname of the SSC and provide login credentials. These are the login credentials you use for the SSC, not the ones you selected in the Media Manager Deployment Plan. You are logging into the SSC here and it is those credentials you need. After providing the credentials, click on **Validate** at the bottom of the screen. The button should switch to **Validated** if the installer is able to log into the SSC. Until this switches to **Validated** you cannot click on **Next** and continue on with the install.

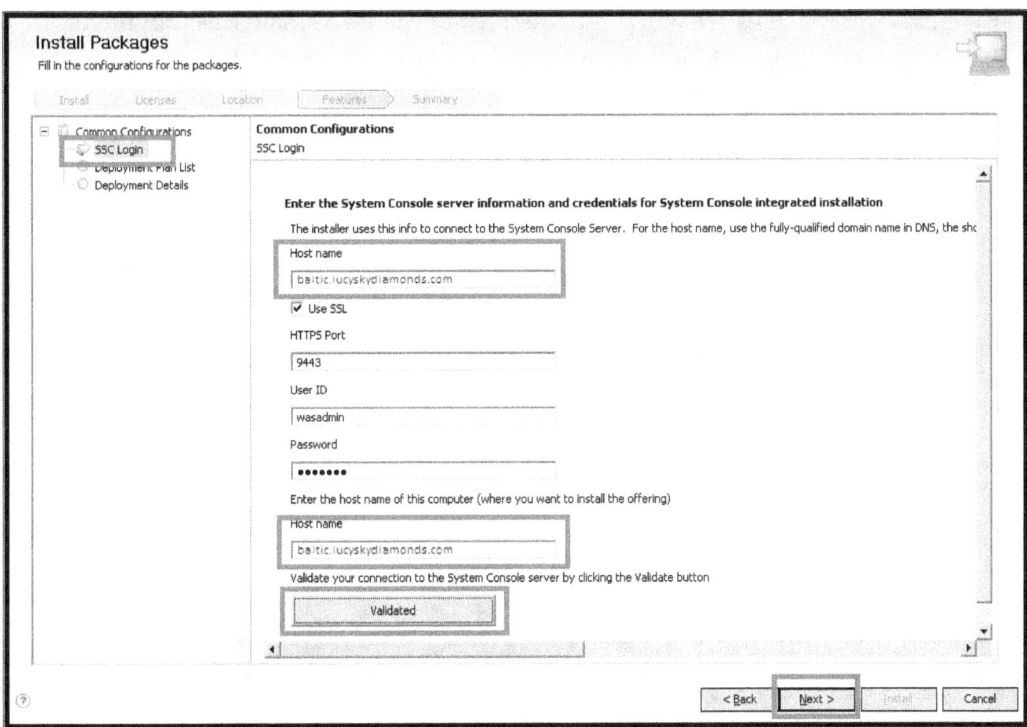

If the installer screen says that it is unable to find the SSC then you will want to verify that:

- The hostname used by the SSC is resolvable from this new server being installed

- The hostname used by the SSC is accessible through ICMP (ping traffic) from this new server being installed

- The port you are using to access the SSC from the installing server is open on the SSC server

Once logged in, the installer will offer you a list of Media Manager Deployment Plans that have this fully qualified hostname as the server location. In most circumstances, you would only have one Deployment Plan of each type for each fully qualified hostname.

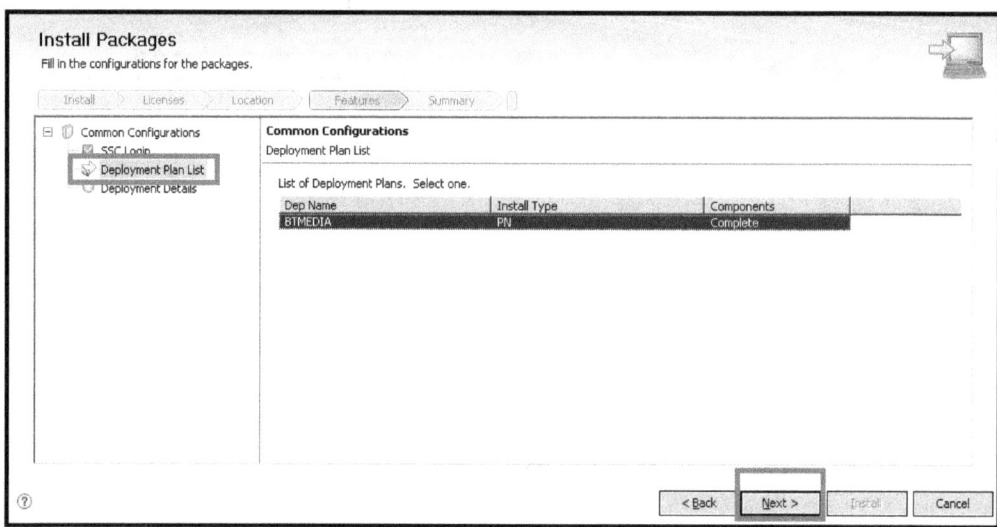

The following is the summary screen for the installation which is about to begin. At this point, it is worth taking a screenshot for reference purposes, as this screen shows you the Deployment Plan which includes the WAS profile. Click on **Next** to continue.

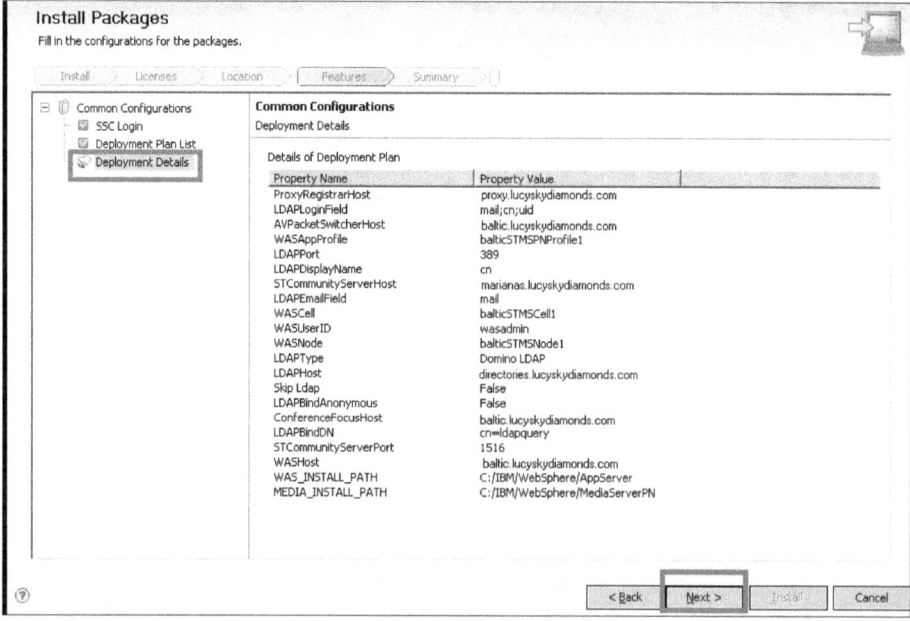

Confirm that the Deployment Package information is correct and click on **Install** to begin the installation of the server.

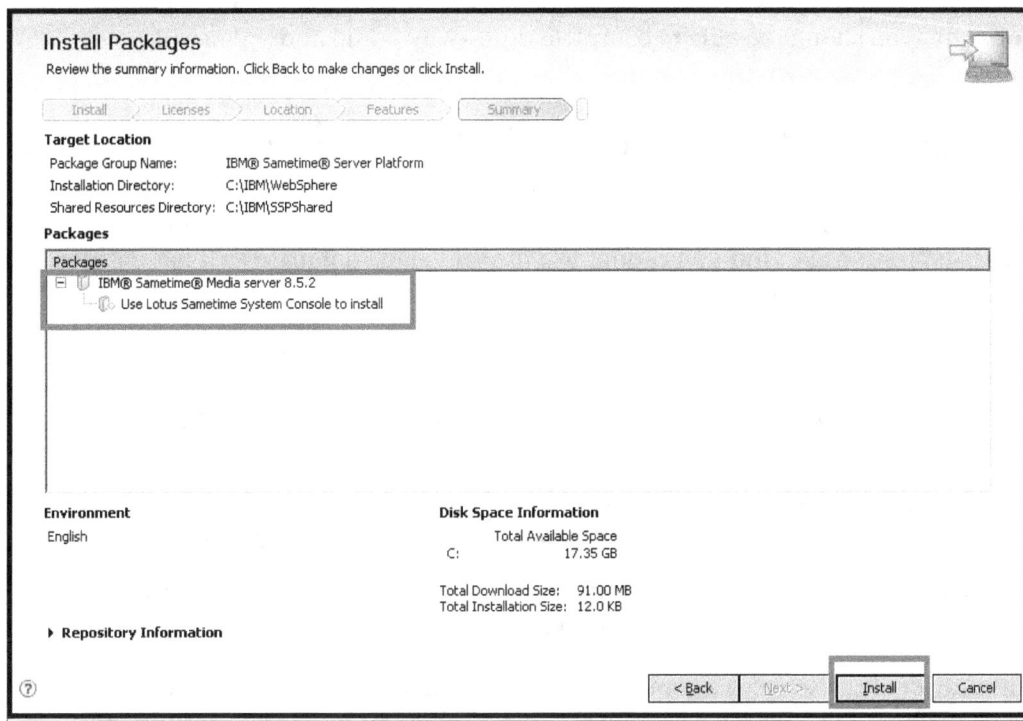

When the software installation has completed successfully, you will see a dialog box that tells you the package has installed. Click on **Finish** to proceed.

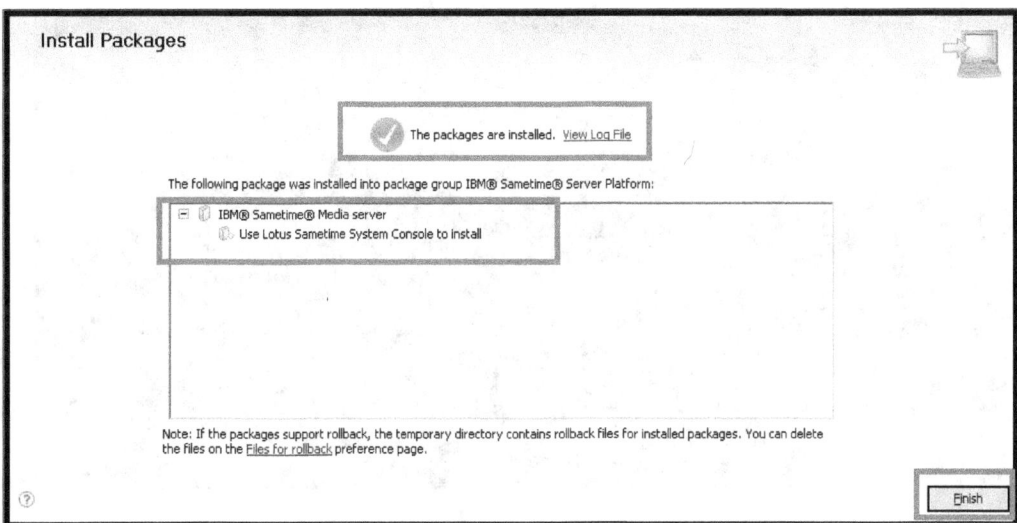

Once the Media Manager is installed, you should see it listed as a service on a Windows server. Also, you can confirm the successful installation by signing into your Sametime 8.5.2 Instant Messaging client. If Media Manager is installed correctly, you should be able to complete multi-way audio and video calls.

Installing a Meeting Server DB2 database

The Sametime Meeting Server is another Sametime server component that requires a DB2 database to store its meeting information. You can use the same DB2 server that was used for the SSC, but you cannot use the same DB2 database as it has a different format than that required by the Meeting Server.

In the unzipped install files for the Meeting Server there will be a Databases directory, in which will be a CreateMeetingDB script. That script is used to create the Meeting database. Each Meeting Server must have its own Meeting database.

Log in to your DB2 server using your DB2 administrator account to run any of the database scripts. The script createMeetingDB runs from a command prompt and creates a meeting server database: **CreateMeetingDB STMS db2admin**

STMS is the name you want to call the Meeting Server database and **db2admin** is the account you created to administer the DB2 server.

The output of the script is a command window that can take up to 30 seconds to run and should finish with a **The QUIT command completed successfully** entry as shown in the following screenshot:

```
CREATE INDEX MTG.UI_ML_I ON MTG.USER_INFO(MAIL_LOWER)
DB20000I  The SQL command completed successfully.

CREATE INDEX MTG.R_CD_I ON MTG.ROOM(CREATED_DATE)
DB20000I  The SQL command completed successfully.

CREATE TABLE POLICY.TEMPLATE ( POLICY_ID VARCHAR(128) NOT NULL, POLICY_LABEL VAR
CHAR(128) NOT NULL, POLICY_WEIGHT VARCHAR(128), POLICY_PRODUCT VARCHAR(128), POL
ICY_TYPE VARCHAR(128), POLICY_XML LONG VARCHAR, PRIMARY KEY(POLICY_ID) )
DB20000I  The SQL command completed successfully.

CREATE TABLE POLICY.ASSIGNMENT ( POLICY_ID VARCHAR(128) NOT NULL, POLICY_PRODUCT
 VARCHAR(128) NOT NULL, USER_ID VARCHAR(128) NOT NULL, IS_GROUP SMALLINT NOT NUL
L, FOREIGN KEY(POLICY_ID) REFERENCES POLICY.TEMPLATE(POLICY_ID) )
DB20000I  The SQL command completed successfully.

DISCONNECT STMS
DB20000I  The SQL DISCONNECT command completed successfully.

QUIT
DB20000I  The QUIT command completed successfully.

E:\SametimeMeetingServerWin\SametimeMeetingServer\DatabaseScripts\MeetingServer>
```

Once the database is created you need to tell the SSC about it so it is available to use when building a Meeting Server Deployment Plan. Log in to the SSC and select **Connect to DB2 Databases** under the **Sametime System Console — Prerequisites** menu.

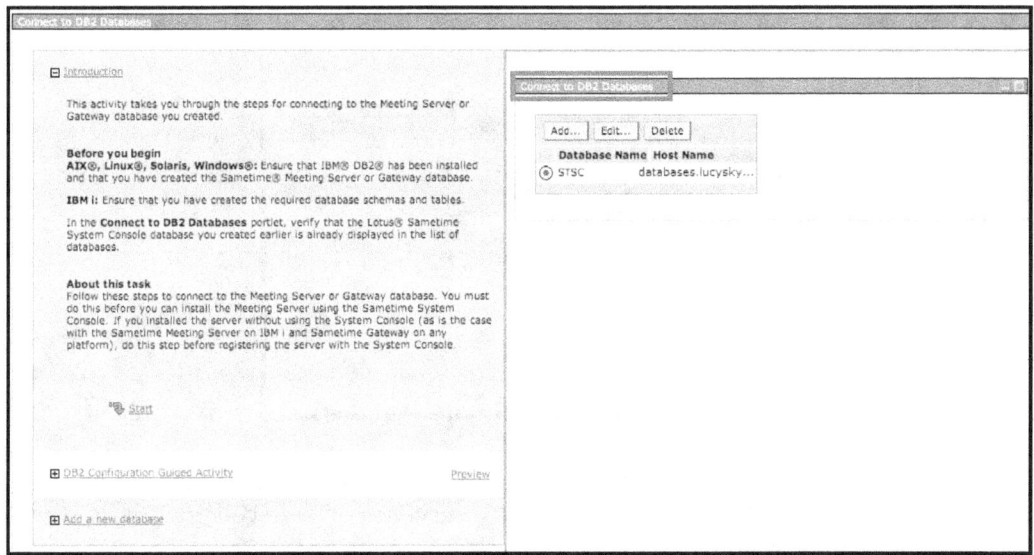

You would want to add your newly created database. Click on **Add** and then complete the details telling the SSC where to find the DB2 database. This includes the fully qualified hostname of the DB2 server, the credentials of the DB2 administration account, and the name of the newly created database. The **Add Database** wizard will confirm that it can connect to the DB2 server, find the Meeting Server database, and that it has the correct database design for a Meeting Server. Click on **Finish** to complete the configuration.

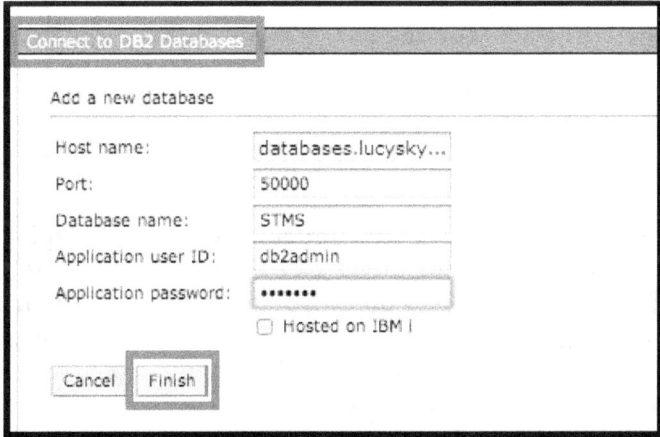

Installing a Sametime Meeting Server

The Sametime Meeting Server is only required if you want to use the new meeting center for meetings, otherwise this is an optional installation. Once the Meeting Server database is added to the SSC, you can continue to build a Deployment Plan to add your new Meeting Server. As you have done previously, create a new Deployment Plan and click on **Next**.

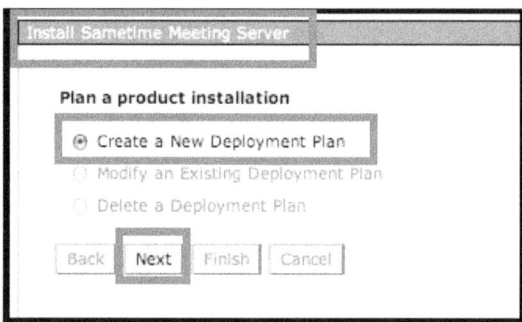

The Meeting Server is a WAS-based component so the installer needs to be told how to configure its WAS instance. Installing a server in its own cell gives it its own Deployment Manager and Management Interface outside of the SSC. In most cases, you would install your Meeting Servers as either primary nodes managed by the SSC or as a secondary node in a cluster with an existing primary node.

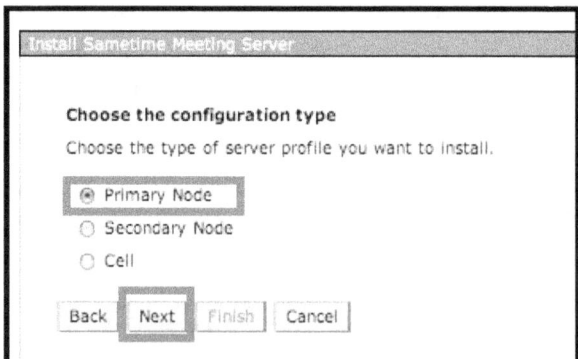

As you have chosen **Primary Node** on the previous screen, the Deployment Plan knows that this Meeting Server will not have its own cell and instead needs to be added into the Deployment Manager process of a pre-existing cell. In this instance where you are installing all WAS components on the same server, there is only one cell, which is the one you created for the SSC. You are prompted to select that option, and then click on **Next** to continue.

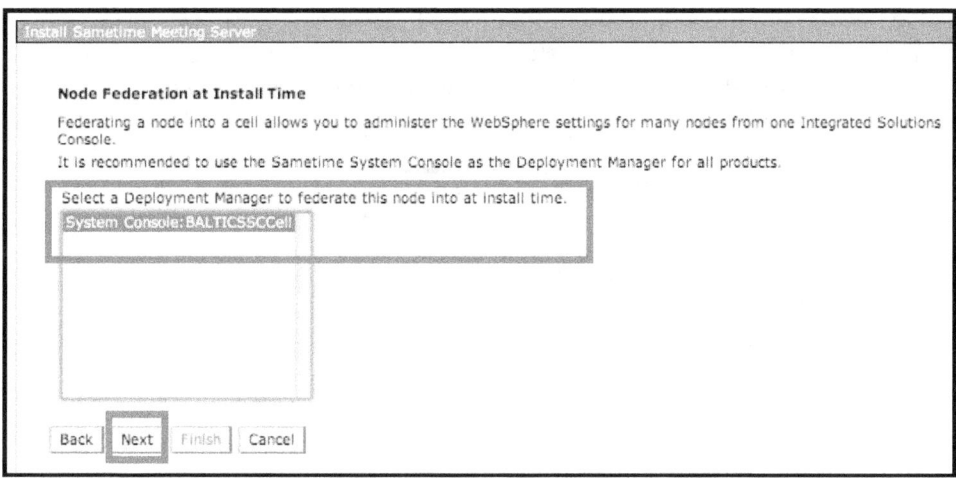

Next you have to define where the Meeting Server will be installed by fully qualified hostname and what credentials you want to use for the installation. These credentials will only be used when managing the Meeting Server outside of the SSC environment.

You also need to tell the Deployment Plan which database to use for storing the meeting information owned by this Meeting Server. Here you select the database you just created and added to the SSC. Be sure to choose the **STMS** database as this DB2 database is specifically structured for the Meeting Server. Click on **Next** to continue.

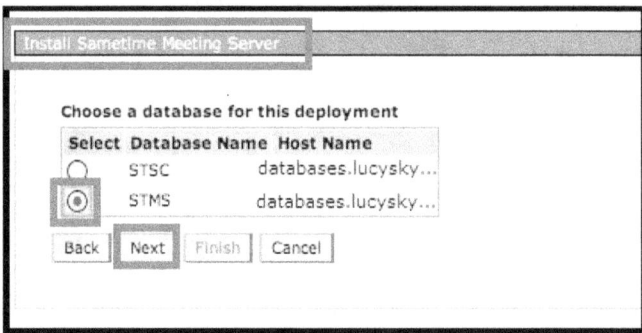

Once the Deployment Plan is complete, it shows as **Ready to Install** and you can proceed with the installation of the software.

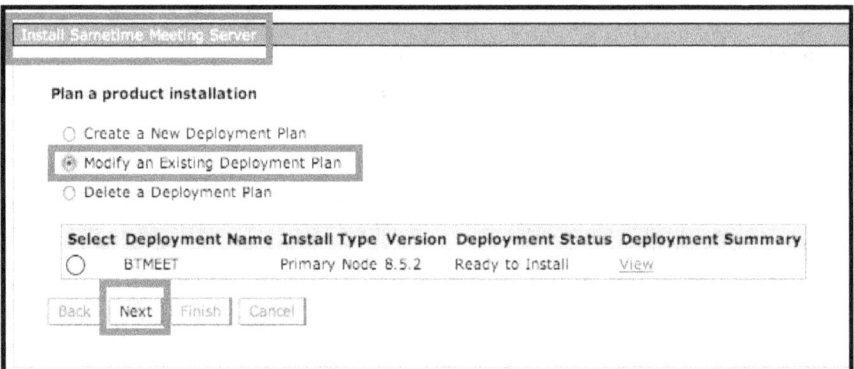

In the root directory for the unzipped Sametime Meeting Server install files, you have the `launchpad` script which starts the Meeting Server install using Installation Manager.

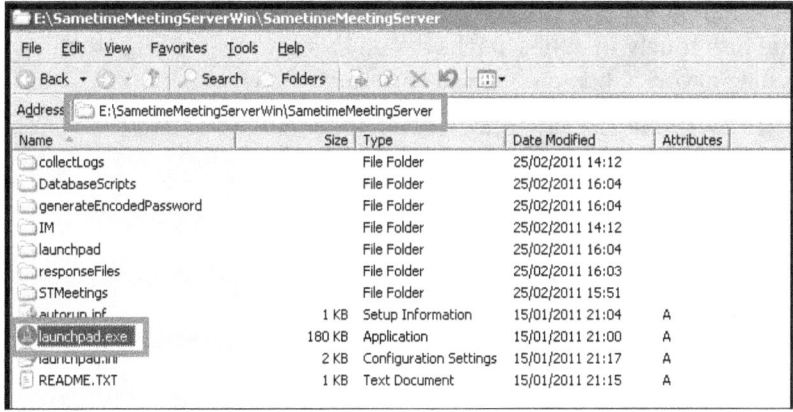

This Meeting Server is being installed on hardware where existing WAS servers are already in place. In this case, the existing WAS instance is the SSC. The Installation Manager created a new package group for the SSC but now that it exists you can use it to install additional Sametime WAS components. By using the same package, the same directory structure will be used for this server install as with earlier servers on this machine, making ongoing management and file backup easier. There are no security or performance advantages to using a separate installation package. Click on **Next** to continue.

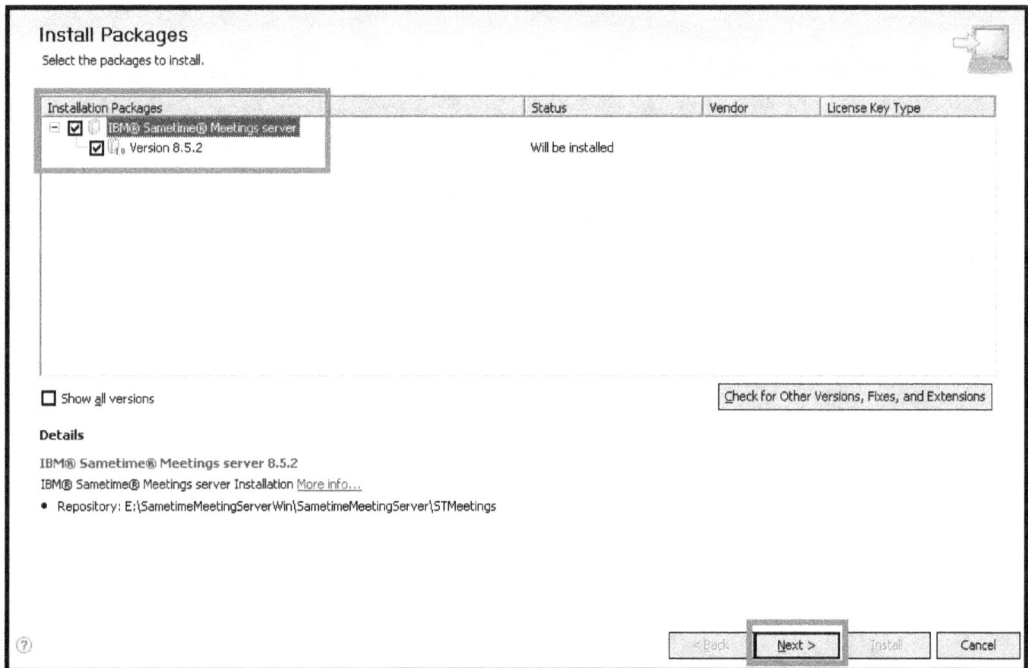

In the installation panel, you can see that the Installation Manager already has a record of the previously installed packages on this server (the SSC, the Proxy Server, and the Media Server). Click on **Next** to continue.

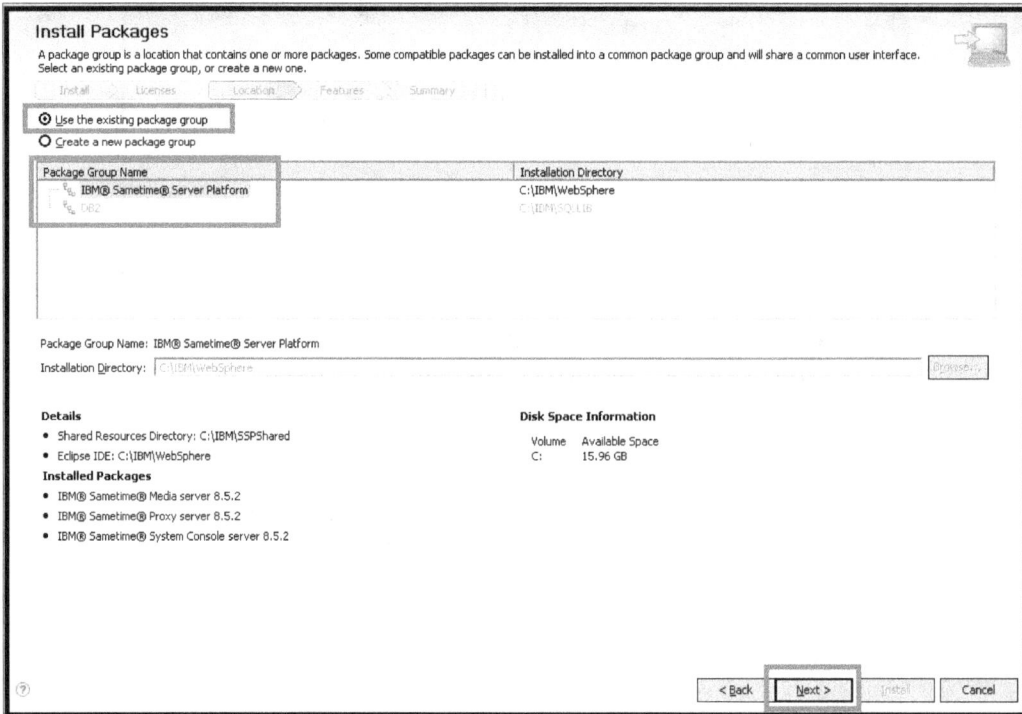

On the next screen you have the option to use the SSC for the install, in which case the Installation Manager will attempt to find a Deployment Plan to match this server and fully qualified hostname. It is possible to install the Meeting Server without the SSC and as a stand-alone WAS product by deselecting the **Use Lotus Sametime System Console to install** option.

This screen also confirms the disk space available and disk space required to complete the install. You should always ensure there is plenty of free space after the install if you want to avoid performance issues. Click on **Next** to proceed with the installation.

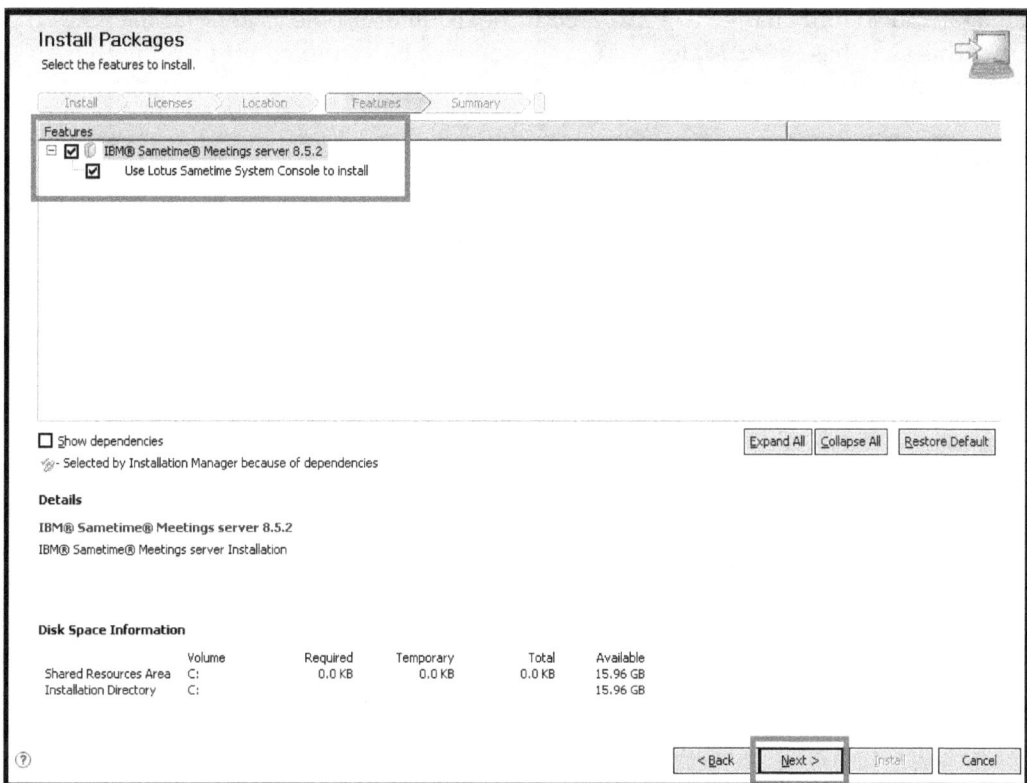

As you chose to install the Meeting Server as part of the SSC and using a Deployment Plan, you now need to tell the installer where the SSC can be found, what port it uses, and the fully qualified hostname of the server you are currently installing on. This is how the installer will log into the SSC and find a Deployment Plan that matches this product and the fully qualified hostname.

First, you complete the fully qualified hostname of the SSC and provide login credentials. These are the login credentials you use for the SSC, and not the ones you selected in the Meeting Server Deployment Plan. You are logging into the SSC and it is those credentials you need. Click on **Validate** at the bottom of the screen.

That button should change to **Validated** if the installer is able to log into the SSC. Until this switches to **Validated** you cannot choose **Next** and continue on with the install process.

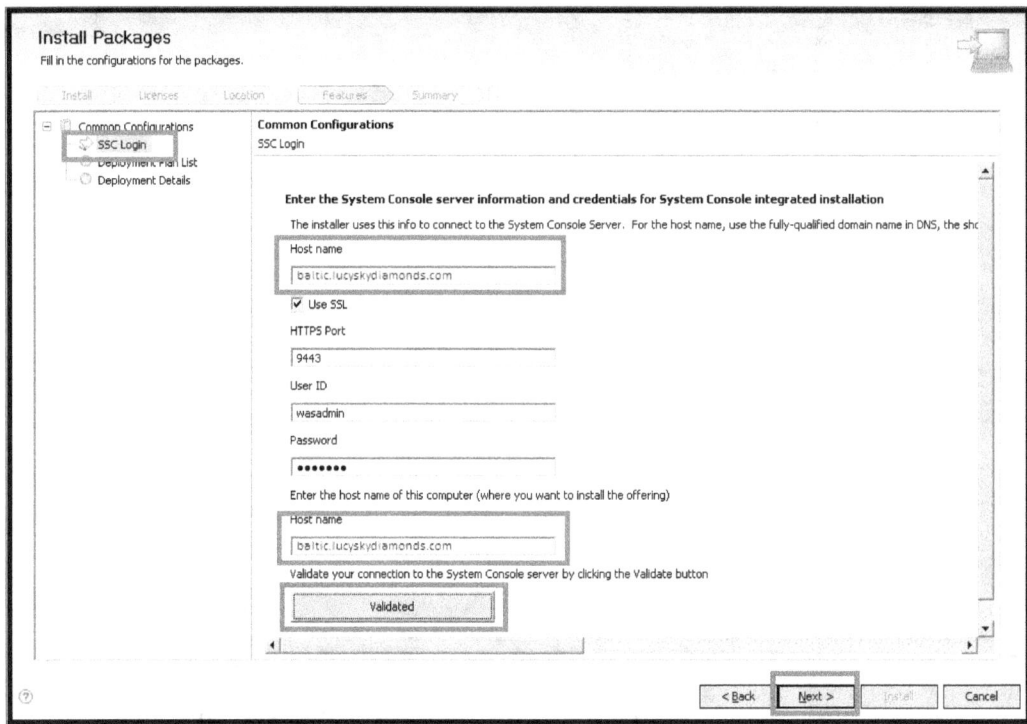

If the installer screen says that it is unable to find the SSC, then you will want to verify that:

- The hostname used by the SSC is resolvable from this new server being installed
- The hostname used by the SSC is accessible through ICMP (ping traffic) from this new server being installed
- The port you are using to access the SSC from the installing server is open on the SSC server

Once logged in, the installer offers you a list of Meeting Server Deployment Plans that have this fully qualified hostname as the server location. In most circumstances, and unless you are building a vertical cluster, you would only have one Deployment Plan of each type for each fully qualified hostname.

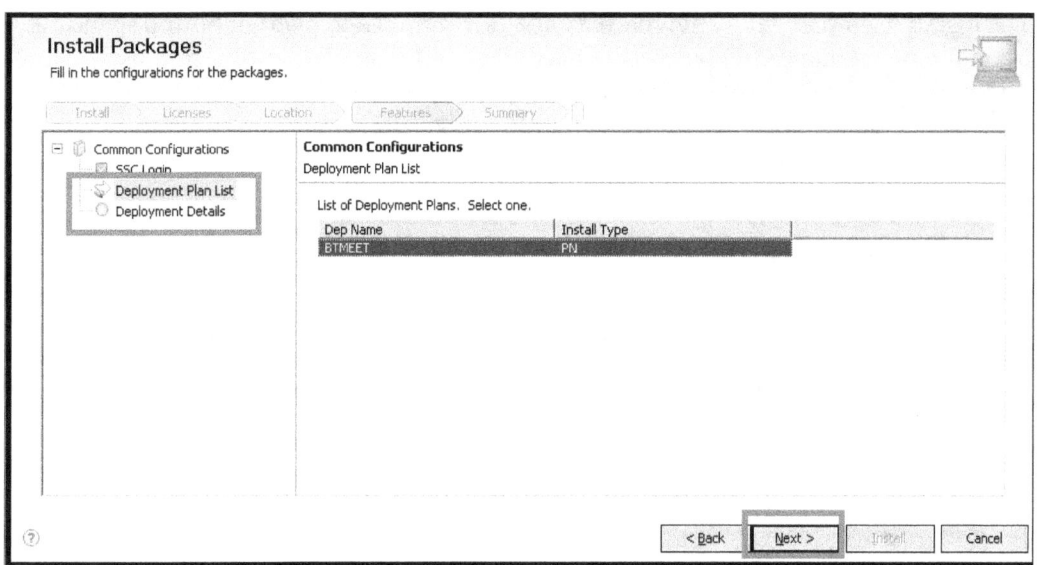

The following is the summary screen for the installation which is about to begin. At this point, it is worth taking a screenshot for reference purposes, as this screen shows you the Deployment Plan which includes the WAS profile. Click on **Next** to continue.

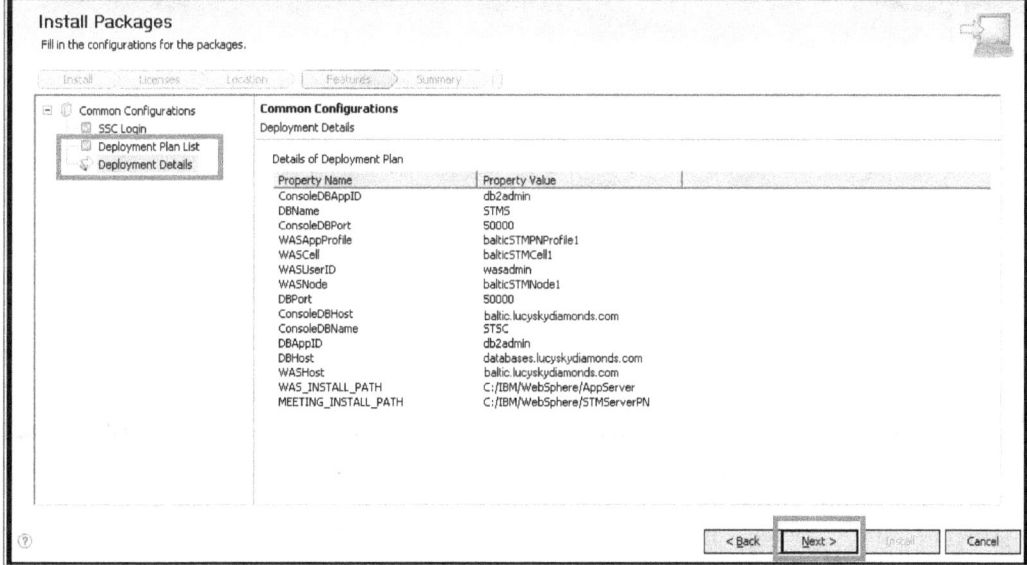

The install itself may take anywhere from a few minutes to over an hour depending upon the performance of your server hardware and disk configuration. Most importantly, be patient and let the installation run to completion. There are installation log files you can view at any time to see if progress is still being made. These can be found at:

- `c:\Documents and Settings\All Users\Application Data\IBM\ Installation Manager\logs` (**Windows**)

- `c:\programdata\ibm\installation manager\logs` (Windows 2008)

- `/var/ibm/installationmanager/logs` (AIX, Linux, and Solaris)

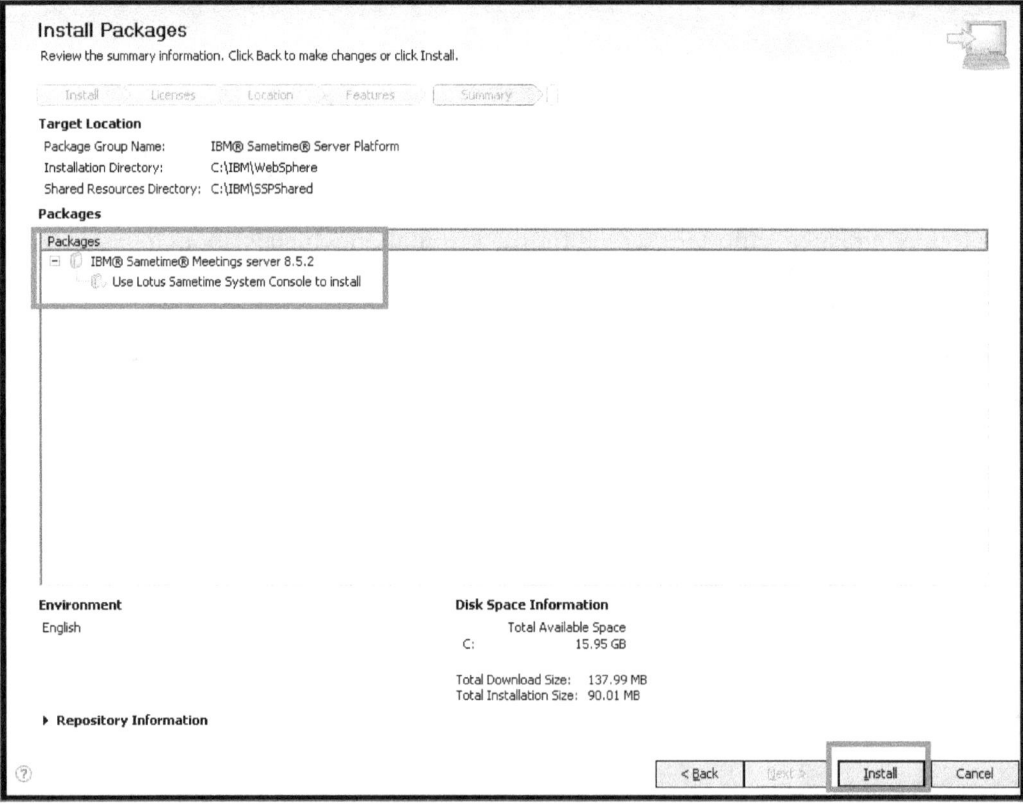

When the software installation has successfully completed, you will see a dialog box that tells you the package has installed. Click on **Finish** to proceed.

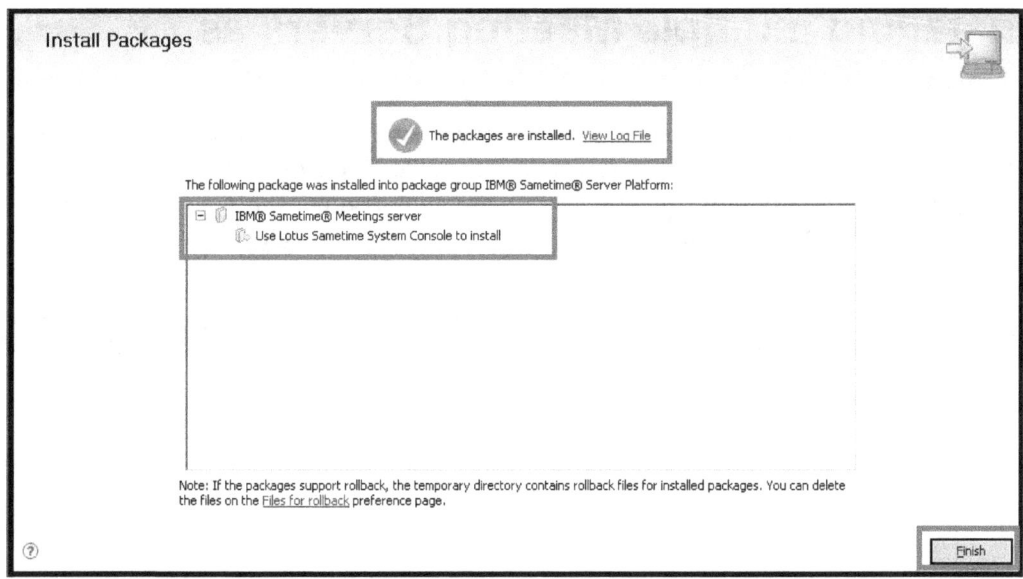

Testing for a successful Meeting Server installation

Once the Meeting Server is installed, you should be able to see it in Windows as an installed and running service. You should also be able to browse to it and login using your LDAP credentials and the URLs: `http://<hostname>/stmeetings` or `https://<hostname>/stmeetings`.

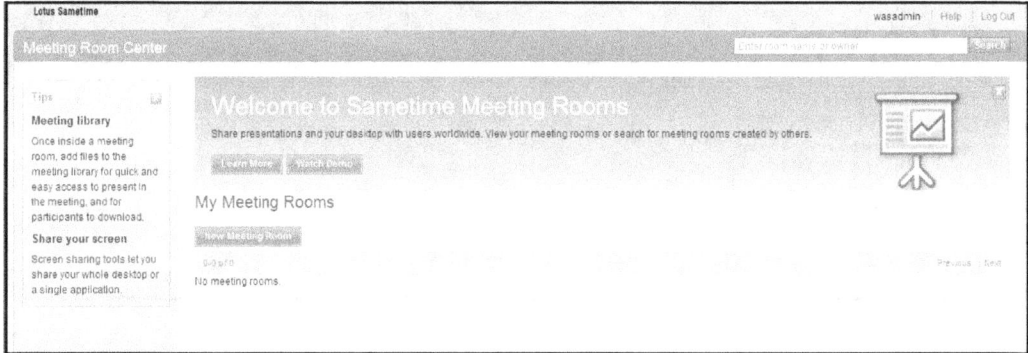

Installing multiple Meeting Servers as a cluster

If you are building a Meeting Server cluster, then you have additional steps before your standard install of a primary or secondary node is complete. You might only consider this if you are building your production environment rather than a pilot or test environment. In the SSC, there is a guided activity to help you build your Meeting or Proxy Server cluster. Click on **Next** to continue.

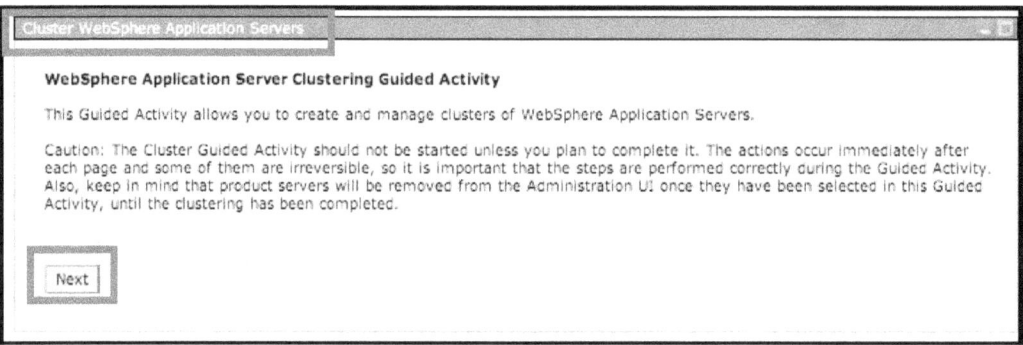

A cluster must consist of servers of the same type (such as Meeting Servers or Proxy Servers) and can be a single server cluster should you want to start an environment that can accommodate a later expansion. In our example we are selecting **Sametime Meeting Server**. Click on **Next** to continue.

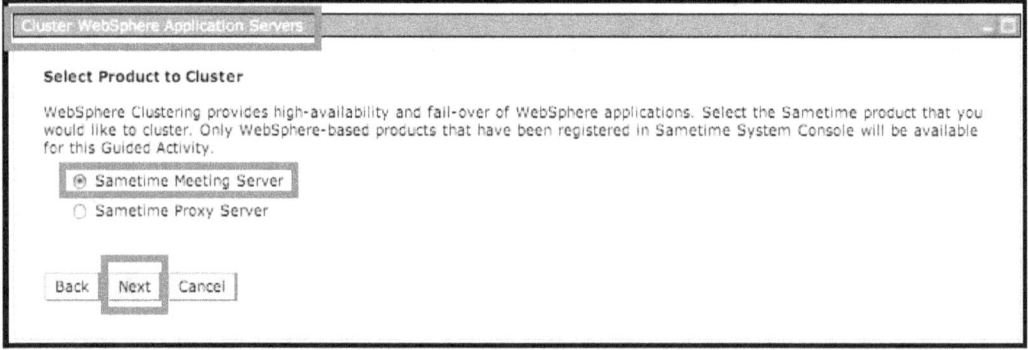

Your cluster name can be anything you choose, but it should be unique within the SSC. The cluster name is not seen by anyone other than Sametime administrators. After completing the settings in this dialog box, click on **Next** to continue.

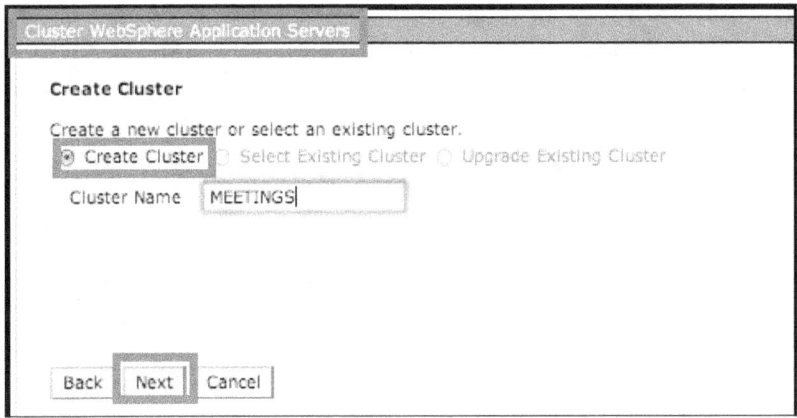

You also have to tell WAS which cell and therefore which Deployment Manager will be responsible for this cluster. The Deployment Manager will retain and synchronize the configuration for all servers in the cluster so they remain identical. In this instance, you only have one cell on this server as you have installed everything into the one cell. Click on **Next** to continue.

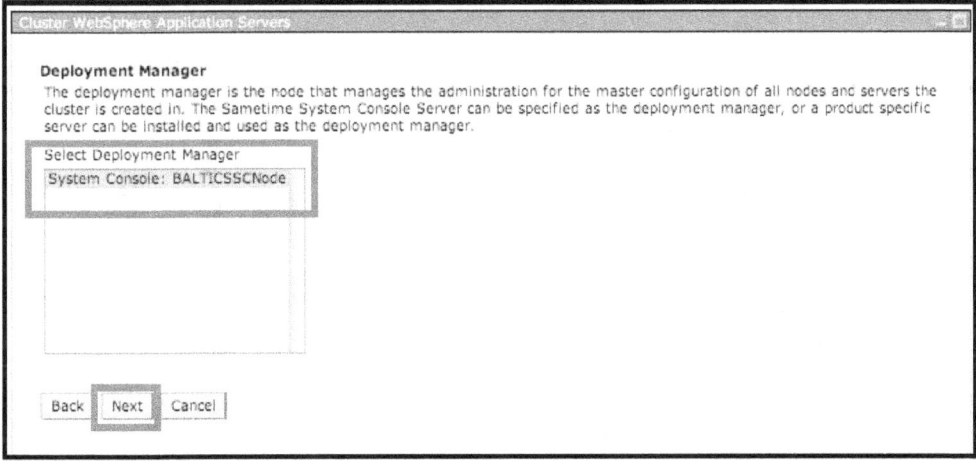

Each cluster can have only one primary node but as many secondary nodes as necessary. The primary node holds the configuration for the Meeting Server and is used as a master record by the Deployment Manager. Click on **Create cluster** to continue.

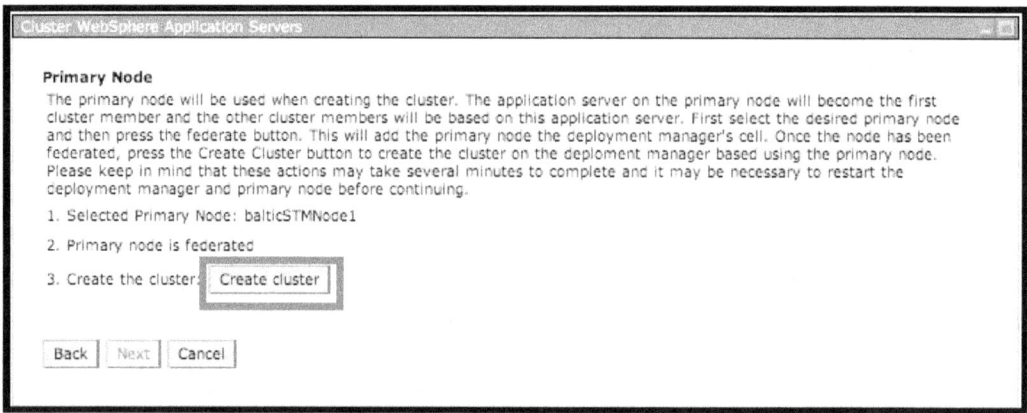

Once the cluster is created, the cluster setup will offer a list of primary nodes in that cell that are of that server type. In this case, you need a primary meeting node. Click on **Next** to continue.

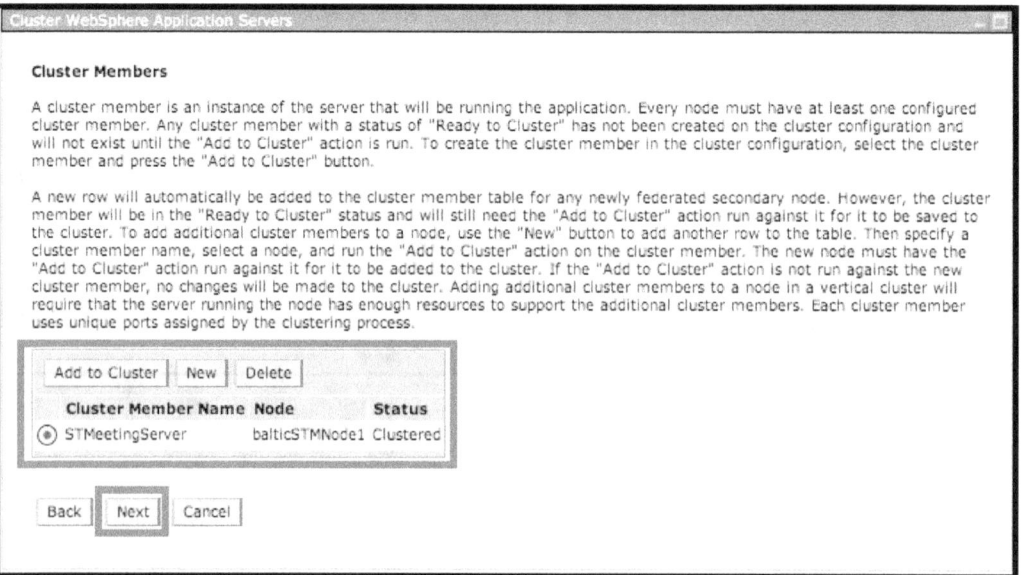

Configuring the WAS proxy server

If you installed the Meeting Server cluster using a stand-alone Deployment Manager, you must deploy a WebSphere proxy server to operate with the cluster. If the cluster uses the SSC as its Deployment Manager, then the WebSphere proxy server is automatically deployed on the console but it still needs to be configured. The WAS proxy server acts as the HTTP interface for your cluster environment. From the ISC choose **Servers | Server Types | WebSphere proxy servers**. Click on **New** to add a new WAS proxy server.

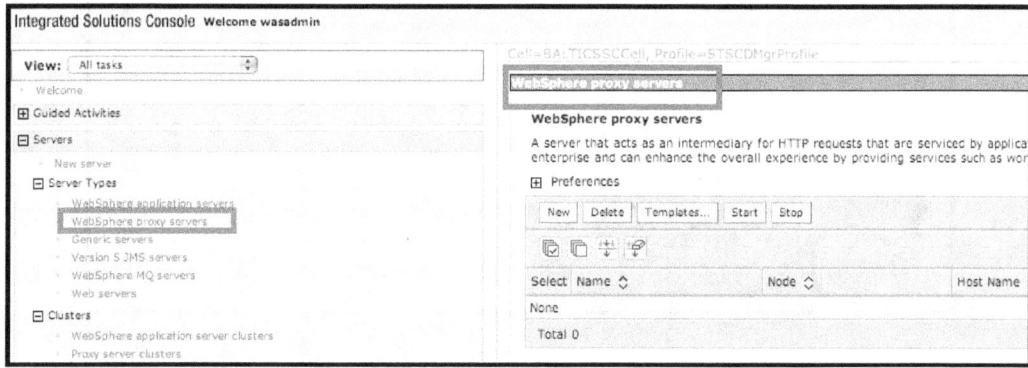

You first need to select a node to use for your WAS proxy server. In our example, we are selecting **balticSTMNode1**, which is the node agent for our Meeting Server. We are creating a server name for our WAS proxy of **meet_proxy**. Once this is completed, click on **Next** to continue.

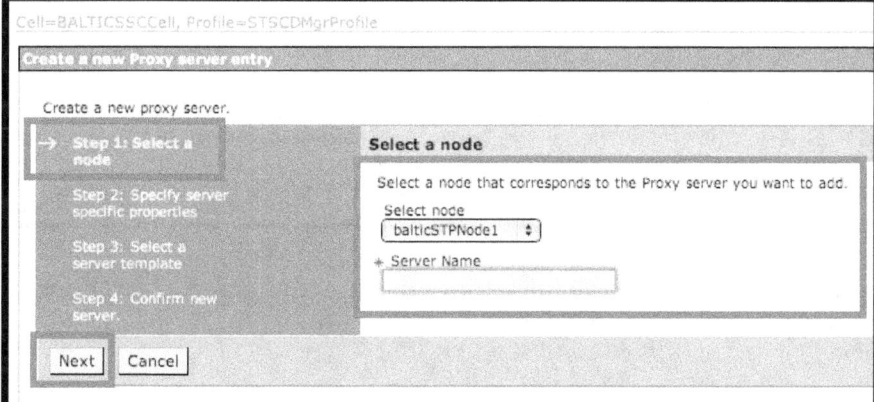

The next step involves configuring the server protocol properties. Select **HTTP** and **Generate unique ports**. This confirms that you are setting up a WAS proxy to support HTTP connectivity, and WAS should generate unique ports for the proxy so that they do not conflict with any existing ports on the server. For a Meeting Server proxy, you should make sure the SIP protocol is not selected. Click on **Next** to continue.

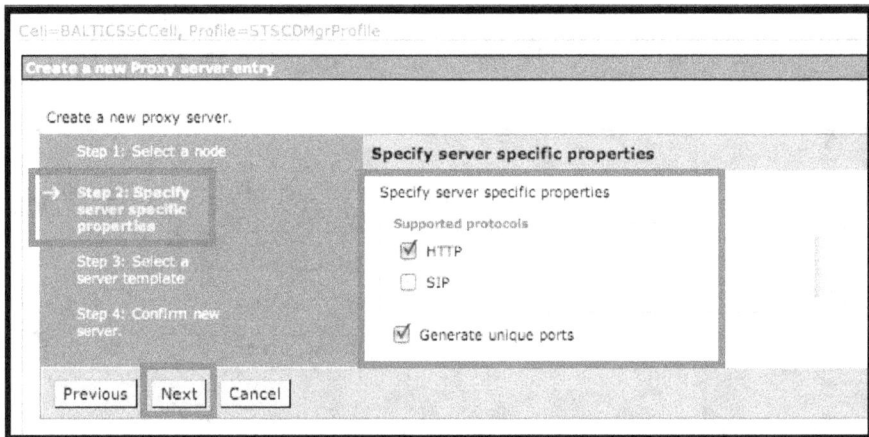

Select a template for the proxy server. In this case, use the default template named **proxy_server_foundation**. Click on **Next** to continue.

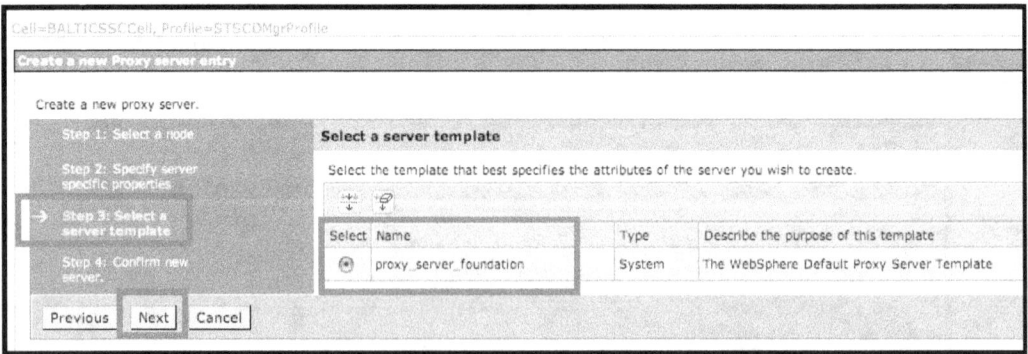

The next dialog box confirms all the settings that are configured so far. If they are correct, then click on **Finish** to continue.

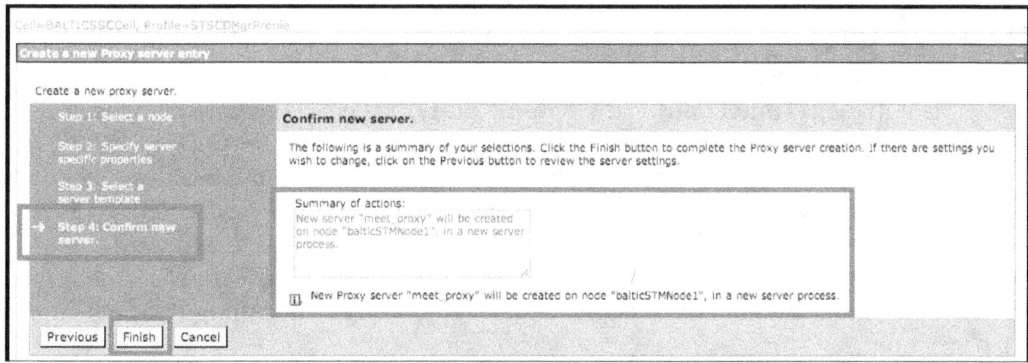

Once the new WAS proxy server is configured, you will see it included in the WAS proxy server list. However, note that the server status is not started. Before you can start the WAS proxy, you must restart the Meeting Server node agent and that will then allow you to start the WAS proxy server successfully.

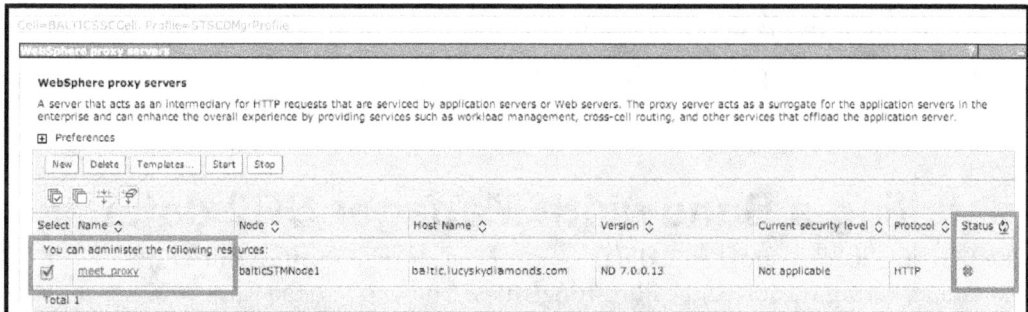

After starting the WAS proxy server, a message will be displayed to indicate that it has started successfully.

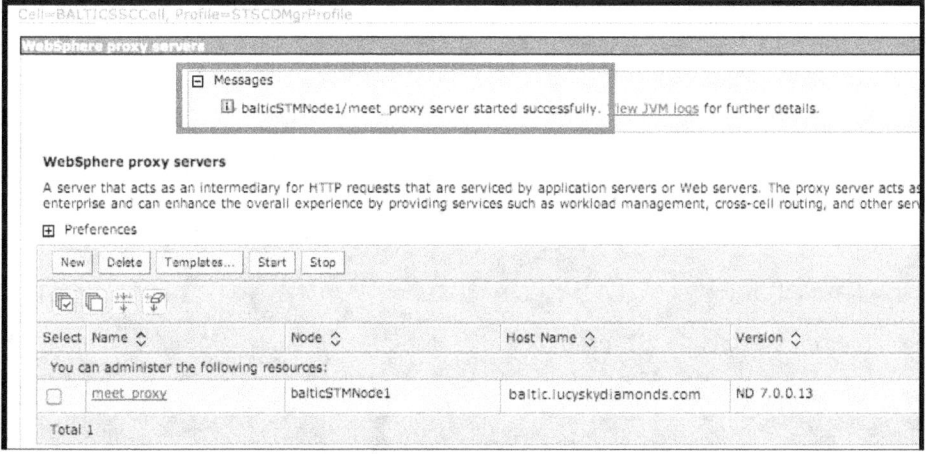

Installing a Bandwidth Manager Server

The Bandwidth Manager Server is installed as an accompaniment to the Media Server as it manages and controls the volume of traffic being generated by audio and video chats and meetings. It also requires a DB2 database and must be installed independently of the SSC and preferably in its own cell. The install files for the Bandwidth Manager are not available for independent download but are part of the Media Server download. Once the Media Server install files are extracted, the Bandwidth Manager files are found in a subdirectory called `BandwidthManager`. This subdirectory must be manually copied to the server you are installing Bandwidth Manager onto.

The Bandwidth Manager install is very different to the earlier server installs we have discussed, as there is no GUI installer for you to use. It includes the following steps:

- Creation of a new DB2 database
- Copying of install files to the new server
- Manual editing of `db2.properties` file
- Manual editing of `websphere.connections.properties` files
- Manual running of a `.jar` file to complete the install

Installing a Bandwidth Manager DB2 database

The first step is to create a DB2 database to act as storage for the Bandwidth Manager's configuration and call routing rules. You can use the same DB2 server as you have used for other Sametime server components such as the Meeting Server and the SSC, but you must create a new and dedicated DB2 database.

To do this, you go into the **Control Center** for DB2 and choose **Create Database** shown in the following screenshot:

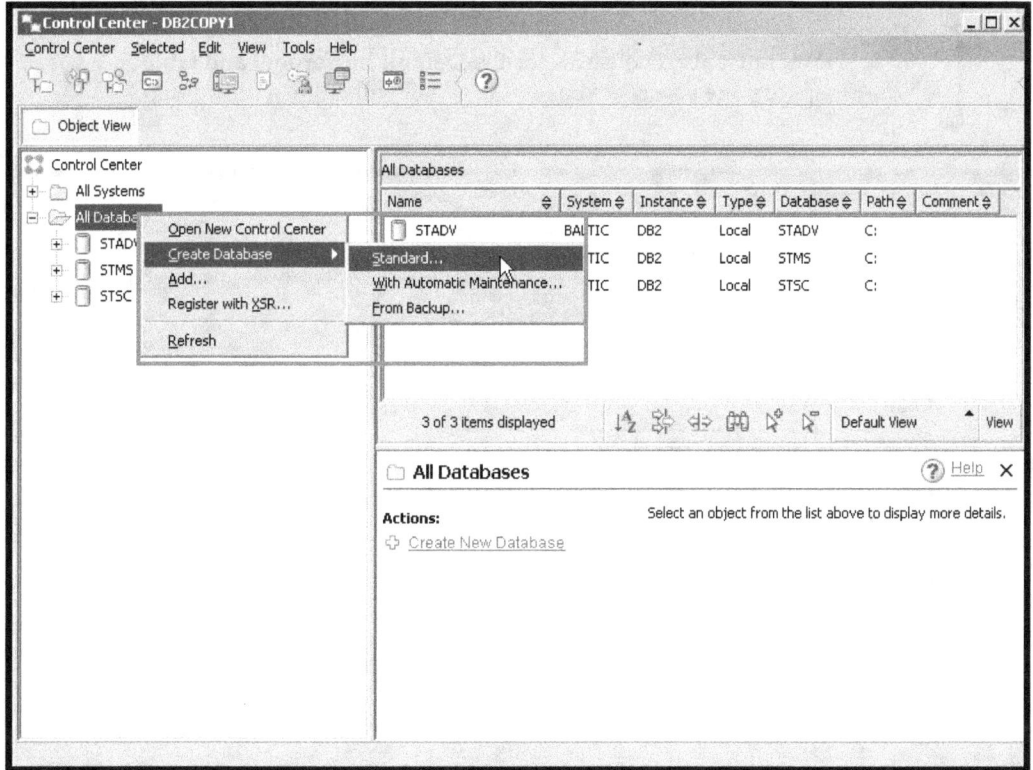

On the **Create Database** screen, you have the opportunity to name your database. In our example, we have called the database **BWM** (for Bandwidth Manager). The database location can be anywhere in DB2, but in this instance we have chosen to place it alongside our other existing databases to make backups easier.

You must also choose **8K** for the **Default bufferpool and table space page size** checkbox or the install will fail in a future step.

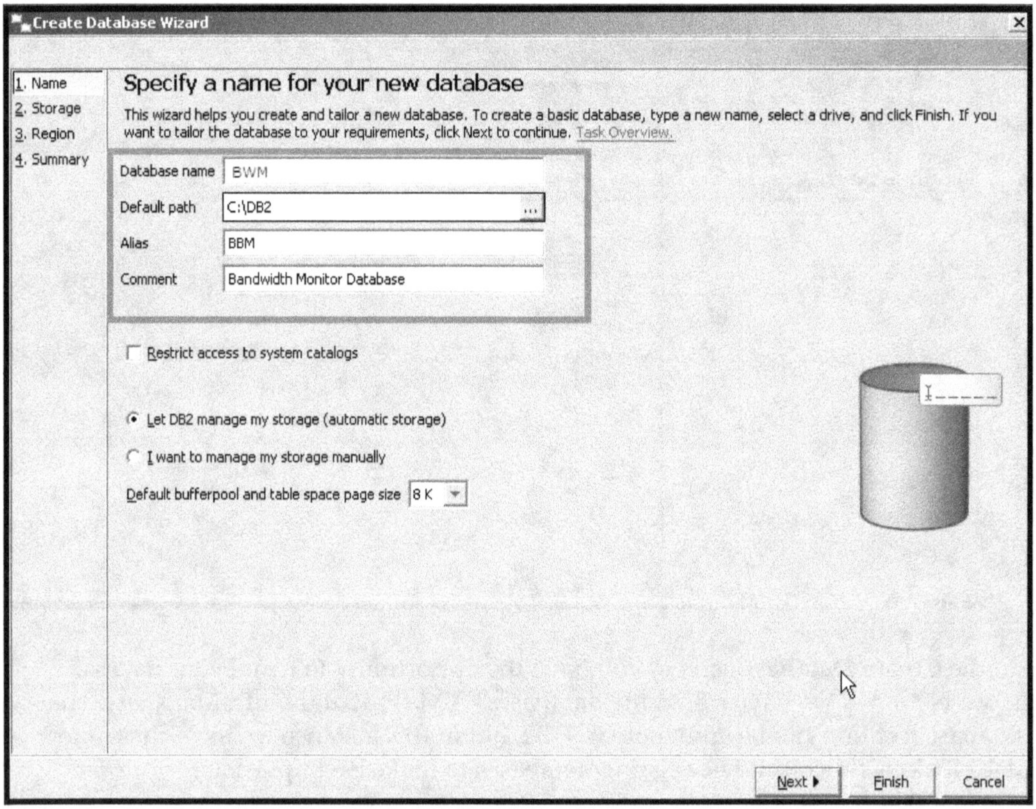

Create Database Wizard ✕

1. Name
2. Storage
3. Region
4. Summary

Specify a name for your new database

This wizard helps you create and tailor a new database. To create a basic database, type a new name, select a drive, and click Finish. If you want to tailor the database to your requirements, click Next to continue. Task Overview.

Database name	BWM
Default path	C:\DB2 ...
Alias	BBM
Comment	Bandwidth Monitor Database

☐ Restrict access to system catalogs

● Let DB2 manage my storage (automatic storage)

○ I want to manage my storage manually

Default bufferpool and table space page size 8 K ▼

Next ▶   Finish   Cancel

Click on **Next** and select the checkbox **Use the database path as the storage** path on the **Storage** dialog screen.

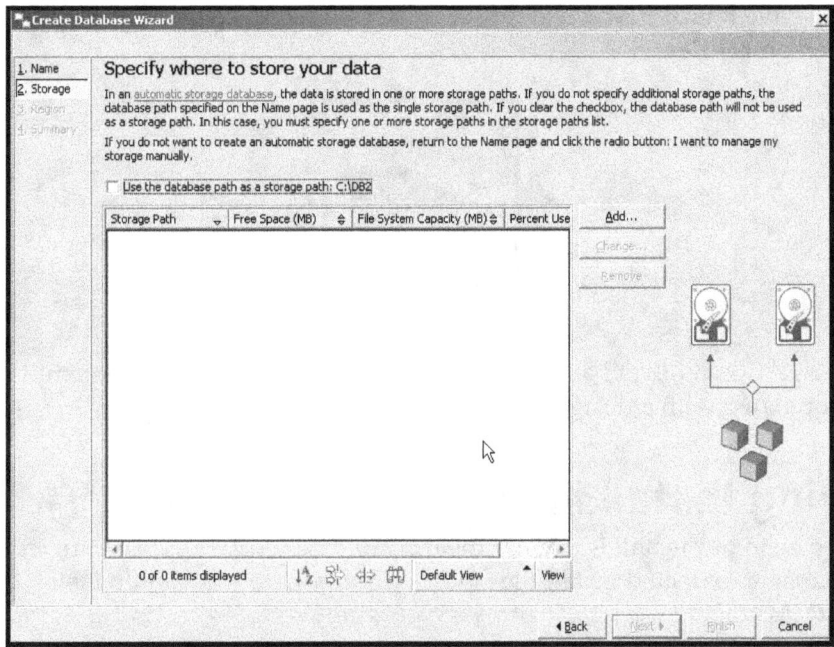

Finally, click on **Next** and ensure the **Code set** is using **UTF-8** and the **Collating Sequence** is set to **UCA400_NO**. This is necessary for the installation to successfully complete.

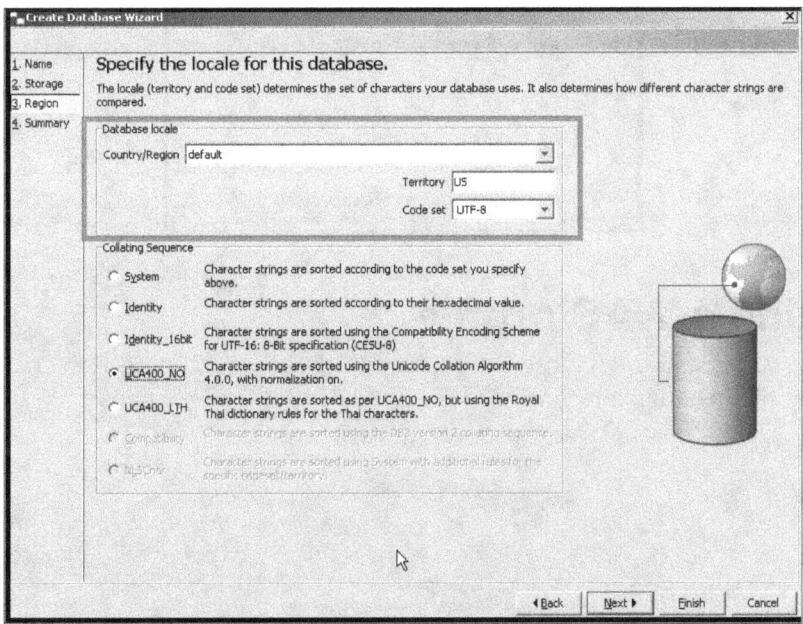

When you have finished, you should see another database created and available in your DB2 **Control Center**.

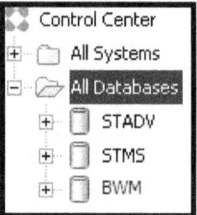

This database does not yet have any schema set and is merely a blank template that will be populated with a design later during the install process.

Copying install files

The next step in our install is to copy the directory `BandwidthManager` from the Media Manager extracted install files to the server where we want to install the Bandwidth Manager.

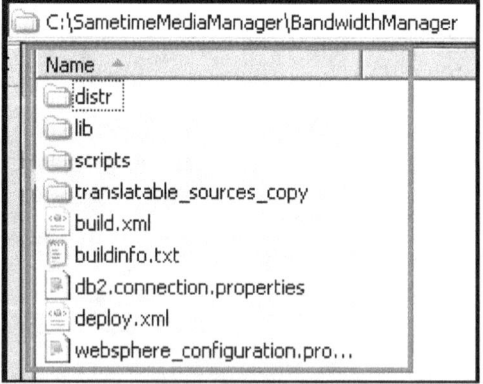

Creating a WAS profile

Before you can install the Bandwidth Manager Server, you first need to create a WAS profile that the installer can configure the Bandwidth Manager to use.

The server you intend to use for Bandwidth Manager must already have WAS 7.0.0.15 or higher installed on it.

With WAS already installed, you will also have a **Profile Management Tool** available to you. You start by running the Profile Management Tool to create a blank profile.

As the Bandwidth Manager cannot be installed into the SSC cell, you will have to choose to create a cell profile dedicated to it alone. A cell profile will create both a Deployment Manager and a node for the Bandwidth Manager to be installed against.

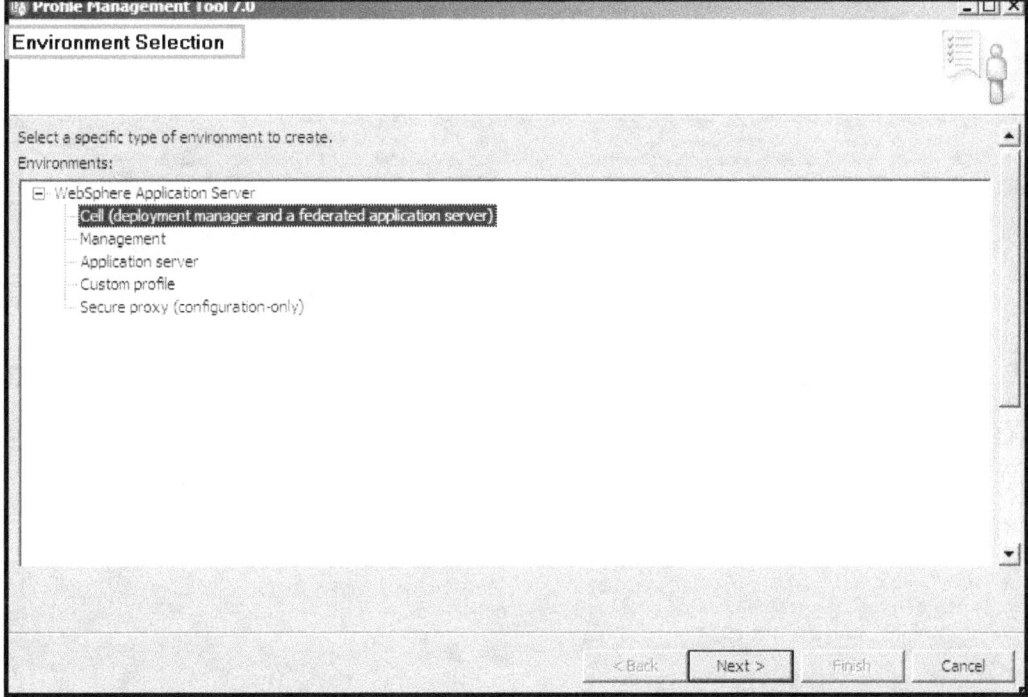

Choose **Advanced profile creation** which will allow you to name your own cell, profile, and node rather than have default names assigned.

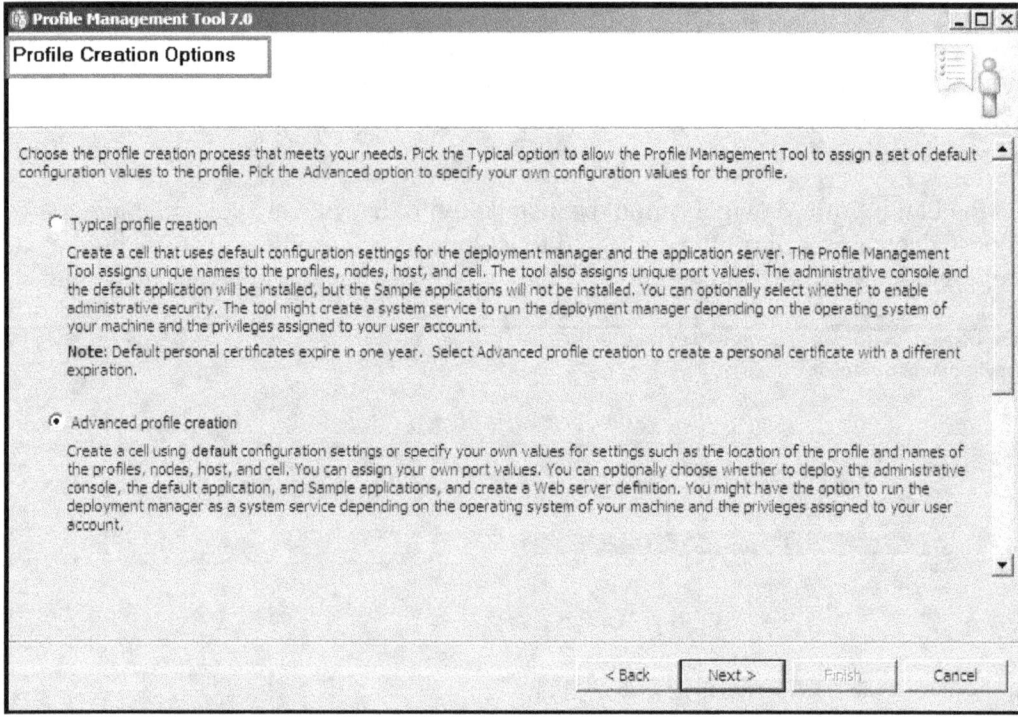

On the **Profile Name and Location** dialog box, you should choose a name for your profile that is short and meaningful. Make sure you note down the settings you put here as you will need them later during the install.

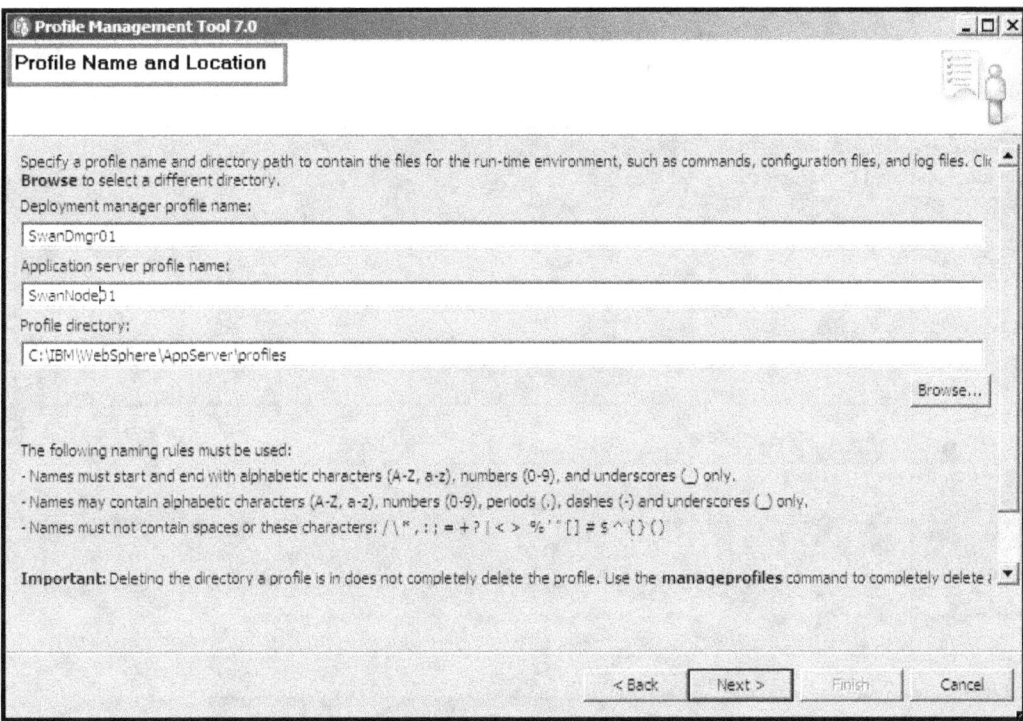

On the node, host, and cell names make sure the hostname you choose is resolvable both on this server and from the other Sametime servers.

 The node and cell names are case-sensitive in the install process, so you should continue to choose short meaningful names and note the names you have set.

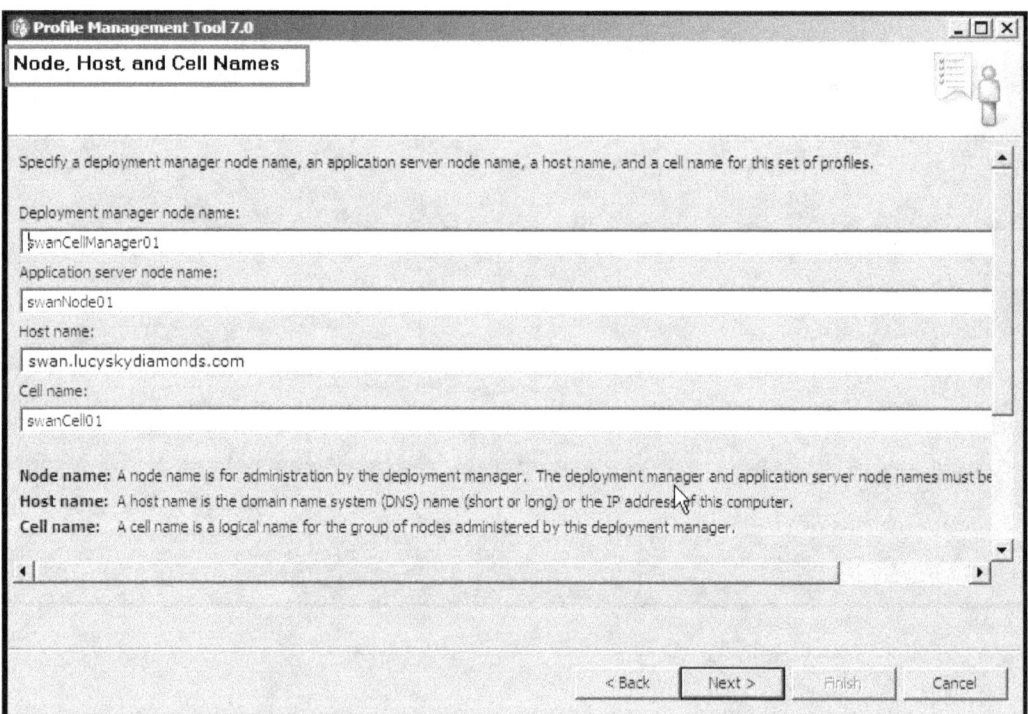

To complete this profile creation process, you will be presented with a list of ports that are being assigned to the newly created server instance. You will need to make a note of the ports assigned to the following services:

- WAS Host (default 9061)
- WAS SIP (default 5060)
- WAS HTTP (default 9080)

Once the profiles are created you would want to start both servers.

Running the Bandwidth Manager installer

The installer itself is a program that will have been created in the new profile directory for the node you just built. When running the file you must be in a command window and in the BandwidthManager folder. The batch file used for the install is called ws_ant and must be called using its full file name and path as: C:\ BandwidthManager>c:\ibm\websphere\appserver\profiles\SwanNode01\bin\ ws_ant -Dinstall.db=true.

 To monitor the log during the install, you can output the messages being written on the screen to a text file for later review. You do this by appending >installog.txt to the ws_ant install command line.

Once the install completes successfully, you will have a new menu item for Sametime servers when logging into the ISC on https://<hostame>:9043/ibm/console.

Installing a TURN Server

The TURN Server is used as a reflector service for audio and video traffic generated by the Media Manager and destined for clients on a different network. If you want to enable audio or video chats or meetings outside your organization or across sites, you will need a TURN Server.

The install files for the TURN Server are not available as an independent download but are part of the Sametime Media Manager download. Once the Media Manager files are extracted into a directory, the TURN Server files are found in a subdirectory called TURN. There is no install process for the TURN Server itself but the files must be copied to a server, modified, and run from that location. The TURN Server files comprise a batch file, which runs the program (**run.bat** for Windows or **run.sh** for Unix), as well as a properties file that defines the TURN Server customizable settings (**TurnServer.properties**) as shown in the following screenshot:

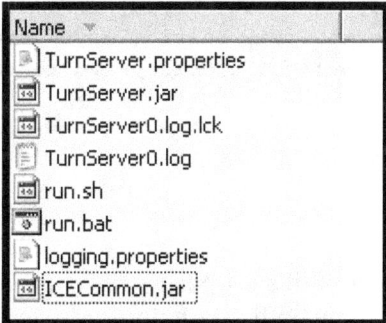

The IBM JVM

The TURN Server requires the IBM JVM to be able to run. The JVM exists as part of any WebSphere, Lotus Notes, or Lotus Domino install. If you do not have WAS, Lotus Notes, or Lotus Domino installed on your TURN Server already, you will need to install one of those applications first.

The file java.exe can usually be found in the `<programdirectory>/java/bin` directory (for WAS) or `<programdirectory>/jvm/bin` (for Notes and Domino). Do not attempt to use anything other than one of the stated IBM JVMs.

Editing the TURN batch file

The next step in our install is to edit the file run.bat or run.sh depending on your platform. This file contains only a single command line and you need to modify that line to ensure that the path to the Java executable is correct. In the following example, we are calling the JVM from an existing WAS install on the server, so it is located in c:\ibm\websphere\appserver\java\bin\java.exe.

This would make the full, modified command in run.bat or run.sh read:

c:\ibm\websphere\appserver\java\bin\java.exe -Djava.util.logging.config. file=logging.properties -cp TurnServer.jar;ICECommon.jar com.ibm.turn.server. TurnServer

Editing the TURNServer.properties file

The TURNServer.properties file allows you to set custom hostnames and ports that the TURN Server will use when reflecting the Media Manager traffic. This is an optional step. In the following example, UDP is disabled, the IPv6 ports are commented out, and we have set a custom public hostname for the TURN Server activity:

```
#optional properties
turn.local.hostname.ipv4=baltic.lucyskydiamonds.com
turn.allocation.hostname.ipv4= baltic.lucyskydiamonds.com
turn.public.hostname.ipv4= baltic.lucyskydiamonds.com
#turn.local.hostname.ipv6=
#turn.allocation.hostname.ipv6=
#turn.public.hostname.ipv6=
tcp.turn.port=3478
#udp.turn.port=3478
```

It is not necessary for you to edit this properties file at all but the hostname of the TURN Server must be resolvable both internally and externally.

Configuring the Media Manager to use the TURN Server

Once you have the TURN Server configured, you will need to tell the Media Manager to use it as a reflector for sending Media traffic to clients. There are two configuration steps to complete this work.

Modifying the stavconfig.xml file

The `stavconfig.xml` file can be found both in the Media Manager profile and in the Deployment Manager profile for the Media Manager cell. The file you want to edit is the one in the Deployment Manager profile. This profile holds the configuration for the servers in its cell, so this is where configuration changes are made.

The `stavconfig.xml` file can be found in: `<deploymentmanager>/config/cells/deploymentcell/nodes/medianode/servers/STMediaServer`

An example of this would be:

`C:\IBM\WebSphere\AppServer\profiles\STSCDMgrProfile\config\cells\balticSSCCell\nodes\balticSTMSNode1\servers\STMediaServer`

Edit the `stavconfig.xml` file with any text editor and modify the following line: `name="NATTraversalEnabled" value="false"` to `name="NATTraversalEnabled" value="true"`.

Modifying the Media Server configuration

Next, we need to login to the SSC and modify the Media Server configuration to tell it where the TURN Server is. Log into the SSC and modify the Sametime Media Manager Server configuration.

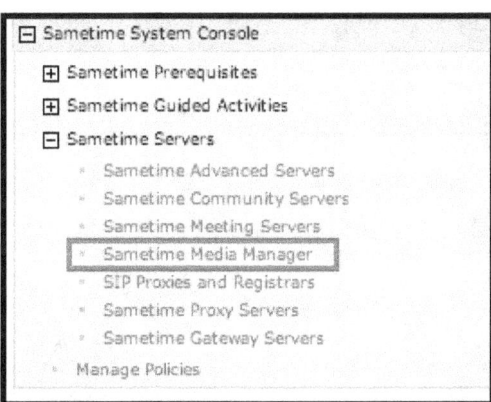

Modify the **NAT Traversal** section of the Media Manager configuration to add the fully qualified hostname of your new TURN Server and to specify if the Media Manager Server traffic should use UDP or TCP. If you enter a hostname for both the UDP and TCP server, the TCP server settings will be ignored.

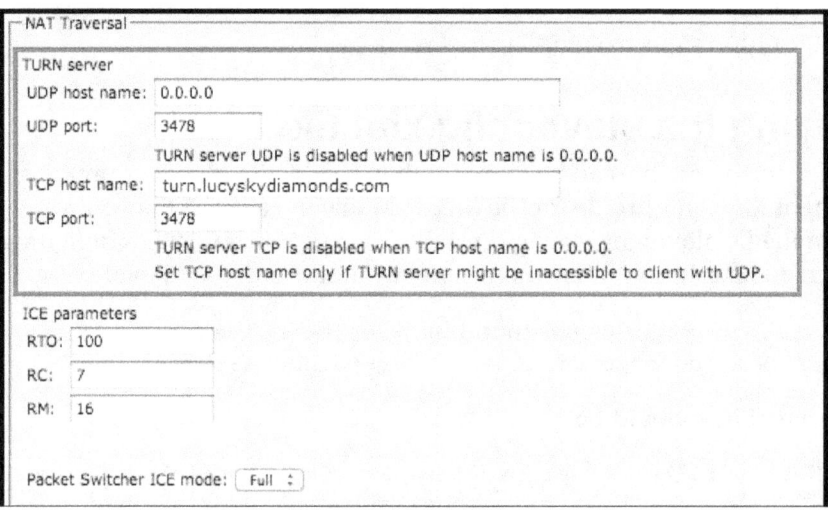

Now that your Media Manager configuration is complete, you must perform a full resynchronization of all nodes from within the SSC and restart the Media Manager Server.

Choose **Nodes** from within **System administration** in the SSC.

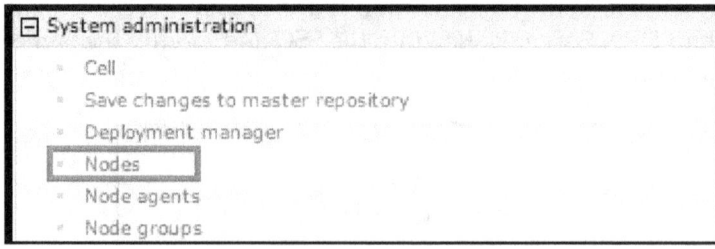

Select all the nodes and choose **Full Resynchronize** as shown in the following screenshot:

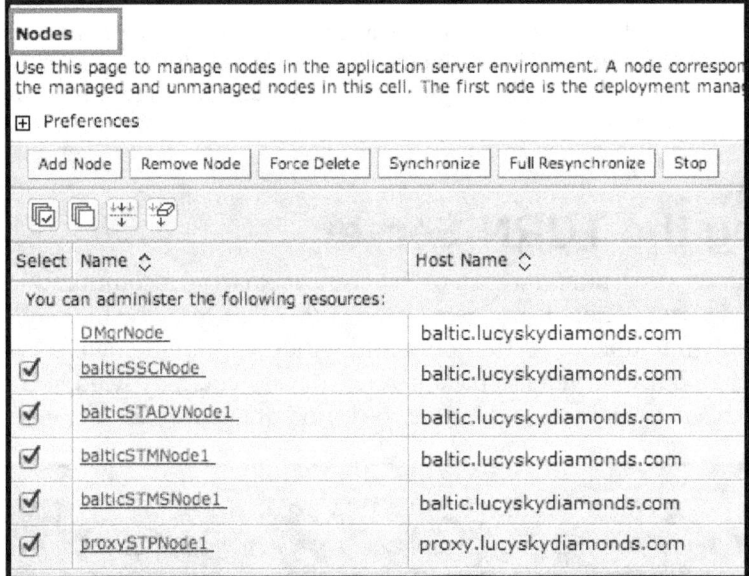

TURN Server ports

The TURN Server performing a reflector service of all Media Manager Server traffic requires several ports to be open to both internal and external clients. The following are some key ports that are required:

Internal port for client connections:

- 3478 STUN/TURN traffic, either UDP or TCP (if selected)
- 49152-65535 UDP for dynamically assigned packet relay
- 39000, 40000, 42000-43000, and 46000-47000 — all UDP

Firewall ports:

- 3478 STUN/TURN traffic, either UDP or TCP (if selected)
- SIP_ProxyRegHOST (default 5080)
- SIP_ProxyReg_SECUREn (default 5081)

These ports can be found by reviewing the Media Manager Server's listed ports from within the SSC.

 The TURN Server must be installed on the same network as the Media Manager Server and in the same subnet. If you decide to install the TURN Server in a DMZ, the Media Manager Server must be installed in the DMZ as well.

Running the TURN Server

The TURN Server program (run.bat or run.sh) is run from a command window on the designated server. There is no install procedure other than the file modifications we have already mentioned. As the command window is an interactive session, if you want to run the TURN Server as a background process you may need to utilize a third party tool such as FireDaemon, which can be found at http://www.firedaemon.com.

```
C:\WINDOWS\system32\cmd.exe                                              _ □ X
[02/08/2011 18:34:22:895] 0000 MessageHandler      I No MessageHandelerKeyCallback
defined
[02/08/2011 18:34:22:911] 0000 Agent               I socket factory com.ibm.network
.agent.nio.NioAgent version 8.5.2.15
[02/08/2011 18:34:22:911] 0000 NioAgent            I Creating 32 NIO Selectors
[02/08/2011 18:34:23:098] 0000 TurnServer          I
Properties File = TurnServer.properties Found
Creating UDP IPv4 Server, listening on : turn.lucyskydiamonds.com/10.10.10:3478
No IPv4 UDP Redirect server defined
Creating TCP IPv4 Server, listening on : turn.lucyskydiamonds.com/10.10.10:3478
No IPv4 TCP Redirect server defined
No IPv6 UDP server defined
No IPv6 UDP Redirect server defined
No IPv6 TCP server defined
No IPv6 TCP Redirect server defined
IPv4 Allocations on: turn.lucyskydiamonds.com/10.10.10 Public address: baltic.lucyskydi
monds.com/10.10.11
No IPv6 Allocations defined.
Enabling TCP No Delay (Disable Nagle's algorithm).
UDP Send service port buffer size = 33 KB
UDP Receive service port buffer size = 33 KB.
UDP Send allocated ports buffer size = 33 KB
UDP Receive allocated ports buffer size = 33 KB.
[02/08/2011 21:01:24:176] 0001 SecurityUtils       I Not working with SSLite
```

To confirm if the TURN Server is configured correctly, attempt to login to the Community Server from outside your local network and initiate an audio or video call. The audio and video options should also be available in the client's Sametime Connect preferences and not grayed out. It is important to note that audio and video settings are only available in the Sametime Connect client if the client has an enabled camera and microphone.

Adding web conferencing to browser-based meetings

Web conferencing for meetings attended through a browser is only available if an additional configuration step is completed. The audio and video from within a browser is generated by the Media Manager Server, but delivered by the Sametime Proxy Server. To enable web-based media traffic, you must deploy the new plugins that are part of the Sametime Media Manager download.

Installing the audio and video files

Once the Media Manager software has been extracted, the plugins can be found in a folder called `WebAVBrowserInstalls`. Copy these files to any HTTP server or to your Sametime Proxy Server. If you are copying them to your Sametime Proxy Server, then they must be copied into the folder: `<profilename>installedapps\<cellname>\SametimeProxy.ear\stproxyservlet.war\`.

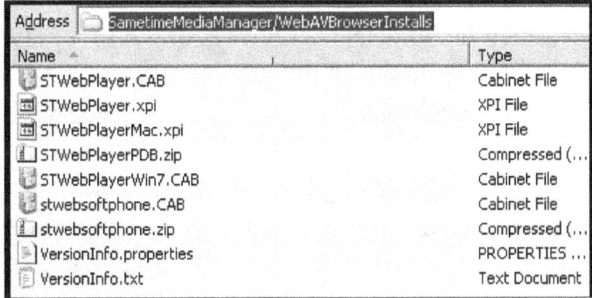

Configuring the Sametime Proxy Server

As you are setting up browser-based services, the Sametime Proxy Server must be configured. From within the SSC you need to modify the configuration of the Sametime Proxy Servers.

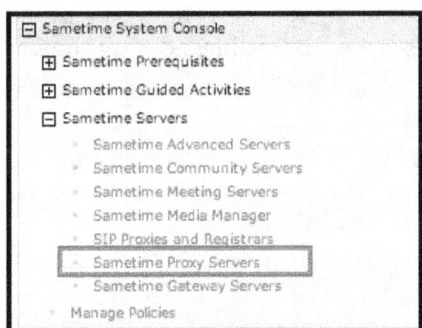

The **Web A/V Settings** section of the configuration is where you need to enter the details of the audio and video plugin. The URL is the location of the files you copied from WebAVBrowserInstalls. In the following screenshot, the block highlighted is the Sametime Proxy Server:

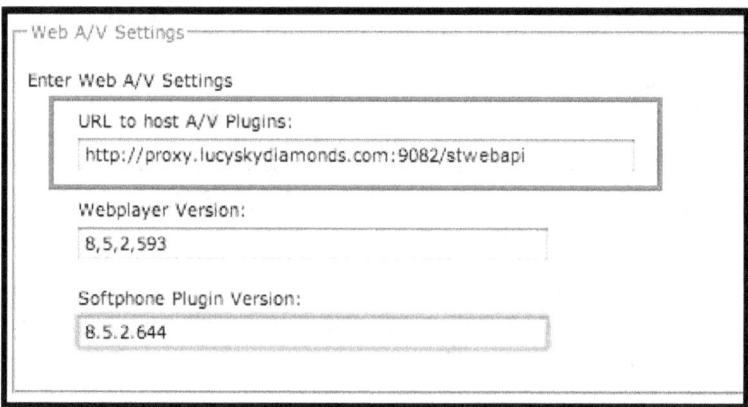

In addition, you must include the version numbers of the Webplayer and Softphone components. These can both be found in the file VersionInfo.txt. Note the use of commas in the Webplayer version number. Once this configuration is complete, the Sametime Proxy Server should not need restarting.

Once the configuration for web-based audio and video is complete, clients attending meetings using a browser such as Firefox or Internet Explorer for the first time should be automatically prompted to install the new audio-video plugin. Once installed, the browser-based client can participate in audio and video calls.

As audio and video in a browser is delivered through the Sametime Proxy Server, the client must be able to resolve the fully qualified hostname of the proxy server.

Troubleshooting the installation

We have included a number of log locations for you—in the event that you should need to review them—to assist with troubleshooting the installation.

 In order to prevent network issues during the install, confirm that your network team has the list of required ports and they have made them available to your server and firewall configurations.

Any host names should be configured in your domain name server so that they are ready to use as soon as your servers are ready for testing. Testing after each component install helps to confirm your configuration is correct at each stage of the install process.

Installation log files

Installation log files can be found in the following locations:

- Windows:

  `C:\Documents and Settings\All Users\Application Data\IBM\ Installation Manager\logs`

- Windows 2008:

  `C:\ProgramData\IBM\Installation Manager\logs`

- AIX/Linux/Solaris:

  `/var/ibm/InstallationManager/logs`

- WAS-based application log files are created on the server's file system for each server's instance:

  `WebSphere_install_directory\profiles\program-profile\logs\*`

- IBM i:

  `/QIBM/UserData/LOTUS/stii/logs`

Sametime System Console log files

Lotus Sametime System Console log files can be found in the following locations:

- Windows:

  `C:\...\ibm\WebSphere\AppServer\profiles\STSCDMgrProfile\logs`

  `C:\...\ibm\WebSphere\AppServer\profiles\STSCAppProfile\logs`

- AIX/Linux/Solaris:

  `/opt/IBM/WebSphere/AppServer/profiles/STSCDMgrProfile/logs`

  `/opt/IBM/WebSphere/AppServer/profiles/STSCAppProfile/logs`

- IBM i:

  /QIBM/UserData/WebSphere/AppServer/V7/SametimeWAS/profiles/
  STSCDMgrProfile/logs

  /QIBM/UserData/WebSphere/AppServer/V7/SametimeWAS/profiles/
  STSCAppProfile/logs

Sametime Proxy Server log files

Lotus Sametime Proxy Server log files can be found in the following locations:

- Windows:

  C:\...\IBM\WebSphere\AppServer\profiles\<servername>STPPNProfi
  le1\logs

- AIX/Linux/Solaris:

  /opt/IBM/WebSphere/AppServer/profiles/<servername>STPPNProfi
  le1/logs

- IBM i:

  /QIBM/UserData/WebSphere/AppServer/V7/SametimeWAS/profiles/<ser
  vername>STPPNProfile1/logs

Meeting Server log files

Lotus Sametime Meeting Server log files can be found in the following locations:

- Windows:

  C:\...\IBM\WebSphere\AppServer\profiles\<servername>STMPNProfi
  le1\logs

- AIX/Linux/Solaris:

  /opt/IBM/WebSphere/AppServer/profiles/<servername>STMPNProfile/
  logs

- IBM i:

  /QIBM/UserData/WebSphere/AppServer/V7/SametimeWAS/profiles/<ser
  vername>STMPNProfile1/logs

Media Manager log files

Lotus Sametime Media Manager log files can be found in the following locations:

- Windows:

  `C:\...\IBM\WebSphere\AppServer\profiles\<servername>STMSPNProfi le1\logs`

- Linux:

  `/opt/IBM/WebSphere/AppServer/profiles/<servername>STMSPNProfi le1/logs`

Bandwidth Manager log files

Lotus Sametime Bandwidth Manager log files can be found in the following locations:

- Windows:

  `C:\...\IBM\WebSphere\AppServer\profiles\<servername><profilena me>\logs`

- Linux:

  `/opt/IBM/WebSphere/AppServer/profiles/<servername><profilena me>/logs`

Community Server log files

The Lotus Sametime Community Server has a series of configuration and log files for problem determination. You can run a script that automatically collects these logs.

- Windows:

  From the Domino program directory, run the `stdiagzip.bat` file.
  For example:

  `C:\...\ibm\Lotus\Domino\stdiagzip.bat`

- AIX/Linux/Solaris:

  `/local/notesdata> sh stdiagzip.sh`

  A zip file generated by the `stdiagzip` script is created in the `data_dir/Trace` directory.

- IBM i:

  `call QSAMETIME/STDIAGZIP servername`

  A zip file generated by the `stdiagzip` program is created in the `data_dir/trace` directory.

Summary

In this chapter, you have gone through a full Sametime 8.5.2 install complete with DB2, LDAP, and Sametime server console installation. You have learned how to confirm if each step is completed properly so that the install can continue. You also learned where you can look for log files to watch the installation progress and troubleshoot any potential installation problems. In the next chapter, you will learn about the options for configuring your Sametime environment for authentication with LDAP, federated repositories, and SSO.

7
Collaborate Securely: Setting up Authentication and Securing your Sametime Environment

Now that you have your Sametime environment installed, you need to make sure you and your users can authenticate to Sametime and that you do so in a secure manner. We will describe how you can configure authentication for your Sametime systems. To do this, you need to identify a directory source that each of the Sametime server components can use. You also want to ensure that all the network traffic to and from your servers is also encrypted.

In this chapter, you'll learn the following:

- How WAS and Sametime use directories for authentication
- What is LDAP and why it is used with Sametime
- How to migrate from Domino Directory to Domino LDAP
- How to configure either Domino or Active Directory as a directory source
- What are federated repositories
- Using SSO for Sametime and other Domino and WAS servers
- Configuring SSL for all server communications

Understanding WAS authentication

By itself, WAS has no single directory for an application to use when setting up authentication. The access to an application is granted through the directories you configure WAS to use for authentication. All applications installed in the same cell and that use the same Deployment Manager will use the same directories. There are four types of directory configurations in WAS:

- Local operating system registry
- LDAP server
- Federated repository
- Custom repositories

A local operating system registry uses the directory for the operating system where WAS is installed. For example, if you install WAS on a Windows 2008 server, the local registry would be any users and groups defined locally in Windows on the install machine.

LDAP server is another type of directory configuration. Even though there is no built-in LDAP server under WAS, you can configure the WAS directory and authentication mechanism to point to an external LDAP server. WAS then uses that server as your directory. Configuring WAS to use an LDAP server is the most common method of directory configuration under WAS. You can use any server that provides an LDAP interface such as Active Directory, eDirectory, or Domino. However, you can only select one LDAP server to use as your directory.

A federated repository is the configuration of multiple LDAP servers into a single realm. WAS treats this federated repository as a single directory. This is the approach used by the Lotus Sametime servers. The initial LDAP server details you provide to the installer are automatically added to a federated repository. This allows you to go back to your WAS configuration at a later date and add additional LDAP directories to supplement your list of users and groups.

In a federated repository model, WAS views the combined directories as a single directory. Because of this, it is critical that each user only appears once across all directories. For those users who may have entries in more than one LDAP directory, configuring multiple LDAP directories as a federated repository will present ongoing authentication and rights problems. If you use bind credentials to authenticate to an LDAP server, then the name of those credentials must also be unique for each LDAP server to which WAS binds. You cannot isolate users in different directories from each other in this model. If you think of your federated repository as a single large directory, you will understand how WAS works with the contents. Most Lotus WAS-based products, including Sametime, use federated repositories as their directory option.

Custom repositories are designed to address the issue of WAS being able to select only one repository type to use. If you decide to use the local operating system registry option, then you cannot add an LDAP server. Similarly, if you choose to use an LDAP server, then you cannot add additional LDAP directories. A custom repository allows you to select multiple repository types to create your single WAS directory. In a custom repository model, you can have authentication for both users from the local operating system registry as well as users from an LDAP server.

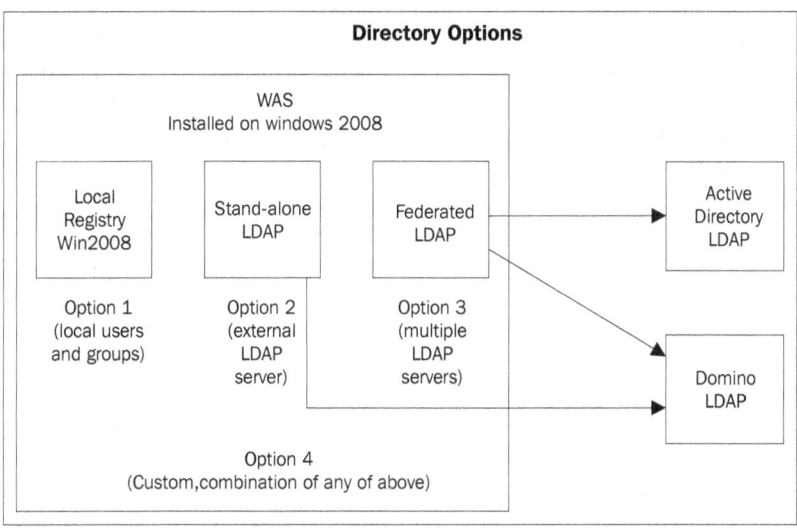

LDAP and its use

LDAP is an Internet standard protocol used for accessing directories. Software packages that include some sort of directory from vendors like IBM, Microsoft, Novell, and Oracle usually allow you to use LDAP for access. By adopting LDAP as a standard, it is possible for Sametime to authenticate users contained in any LDAP-compliant directory such as Domino, Active Directory, or eDirectory. These servers all expose their own proprietary directory formats through LDAP, enabling them to be accessed and utilized by LDAP clients and authentication mechanisms.

The structure of LDAP is defined by its entries and attributes. Entries represent a single object such as a person. Attributes represent object values such as first name, last name, or mail address. On a Domino server, an entry would be a document and an attribute would be a field. The entire structure of each entry and its attributes within an LDAP directory is called the LDAP schema. Although every LDAP server speaks the same language, they all have different schemas. It is important to understand the schema of the server you use for LDAP to ensure that you select the right attributes for use as login credentials.

In our Sametime model, the use of LDAP allows you to select any LDAP-compliant directory for holding your user information, and the authentication mechanism within Sametime will be able to work with it directly. In this way, you can easily integrate a Sametime environment into an existing enterprise infrastructure.

Connecting to LDAP

Creating an LDAP connection from within the SSC is the first task you do when configuring Sametime. You need to establish the details of which directory each Sametime component uses before you can complete the deployment plan for your installation. The Community Server, Meeting Server, and Media Manager all need to know which LDAP server you are using before they can be installed. The LDAP setup is reasonably simple.

The required fields are the hostname and port of the LDAP server. Although you can use the unencrypted LDAP port 389 and anonymous access to connect to your directory, this is extremely insecure. Your LDAP administrator should be able to provide you with credentials that give you read access to the directory and that you can use to bind to the LDAP store. They should also be able to enable SSL on their LDAP server so you can connect using the secure port 636.

The **LDAP base entry** field is used to define the scope of users who are authenticating from LDAP. In many LDAP environments, the complete directory contains more users and elements that you want to provide to Sametime. The base entry provides a base distinguished name (DN) to limit the scope of the directory lookups. You should make sure this is as specific as possible, as a base DN that incorporates too many LDAP attributes may cause performance issues for authentication or lookup processes. It may be useful to assign an attribute in your LDAP schema specifically to store a value for Sametime users and then filter by that attribute.

Once the LDAP server is set up, you can confirm connectivity by performing a search from within the SSC menu. Under the **Users and Groups** menu, you can choose to manage users and you should be able to successfully search for LDAP entries. In the following screenshot, you are searching by **Last name** for **davis** which matches any last name with that string in the LDAP directory. If you have multiple LDAP servers federated in WAS, then this search will encompass all of them. It is critical in a Sametime environment that the identity of each user such as the mail address or UID is unique. If multiple matches are found when a user attempts to login, then they will receive an inconsistent experience.

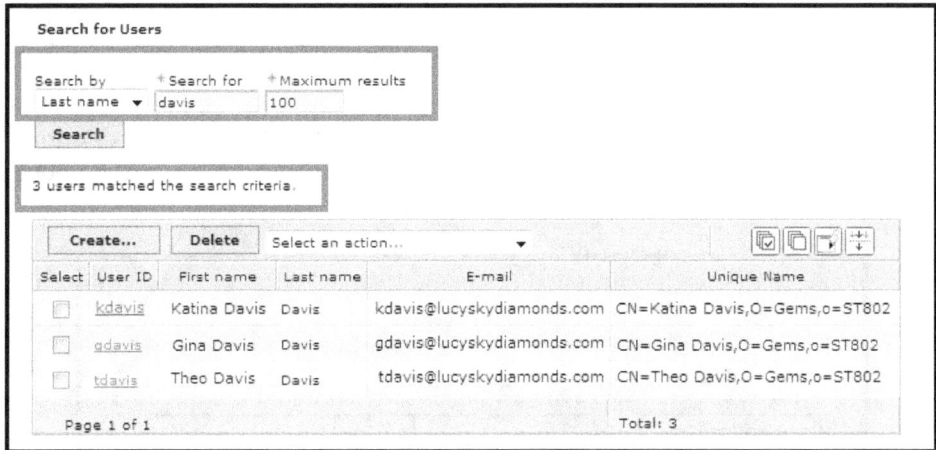

Migrating from Domino Directory to LDAP

In a pre-8.5.2 Sametime model, you had the option of using Domino or LDAP as the authentication directory source. In Sametime 8.5.2, you must use LDAP if you want to build a complete Sametime 8.5.2 environment through the SSC. If you already have a Domino server in place using the Domino Directory for authentication, then you will need to reconfigure that server for LDAP and convert your existing Sametime buddy lists to LDAP format. However, you can continue to use Domino in your domain as your LDAP server. You will retain the same users and data as you had previously, although they will be in the LDAP name format and schema.

Keep in mind that Sametime is very demanding of LDAP resources. You cannot use your Community Server as your LDAP server, and you should consider having a dedicated LDAP server for this purpose.

Converting Sametime with Domino Directory to LDAP

The following are the general steps required to reconfigure a Sametime server set up to use Domino Directory, to one set up to use LDAP:

1. Shut down Sametime on the Domino server by typing **tell staddin quit** on the server console.

2. Create a Directory Assistance database if you do not already have one, and add it to your server document.

3. Create an LDAP entry in your Directory Assistance database to point to your LDAP server source. During the installation of a new Community Server through the SSC, this work is completed for you.

   If you want to use another Domino server for LDAP, so you can continue to use the Domino Directory contents, your Directory Assistance document will use its hostname and Domino credentials. For example:

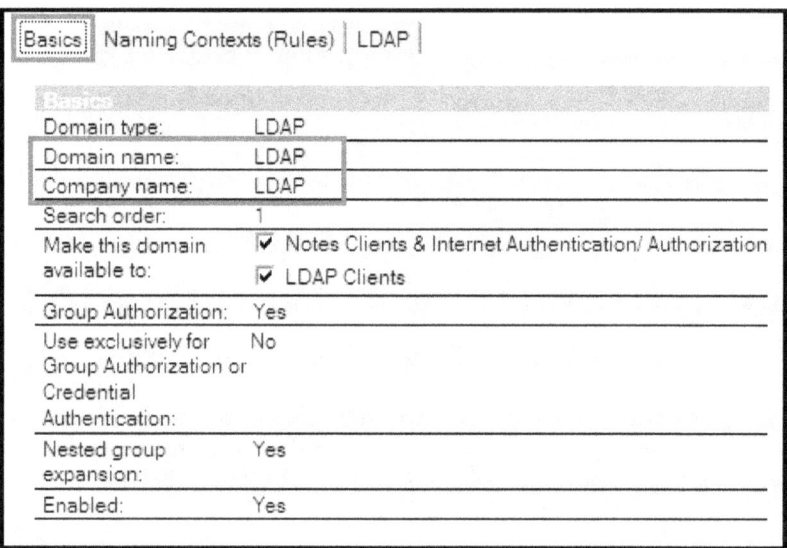

4. Within the **Naming Contexts (Rules)** tab, the document must be **Enabled** and **Trusted for Credentials** in order for authentication to take place.

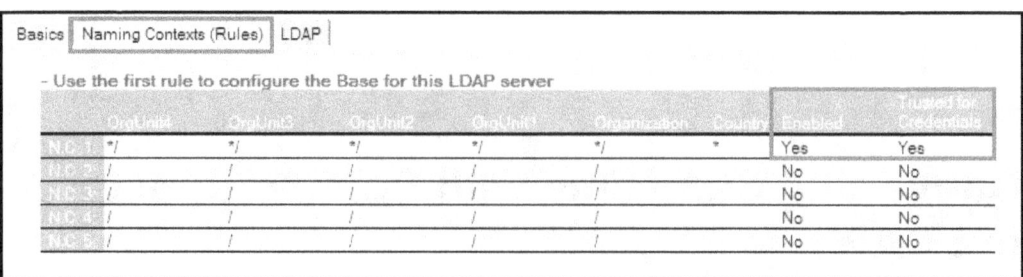

5. Within the LDAP tab, enter the hostname of the LDAP server. Include the username and password of the user who will be binding to the server to verify the credentials of each user. It is a good idea to click on the **Verify** buttons to confirm that the values you enter here are correct.

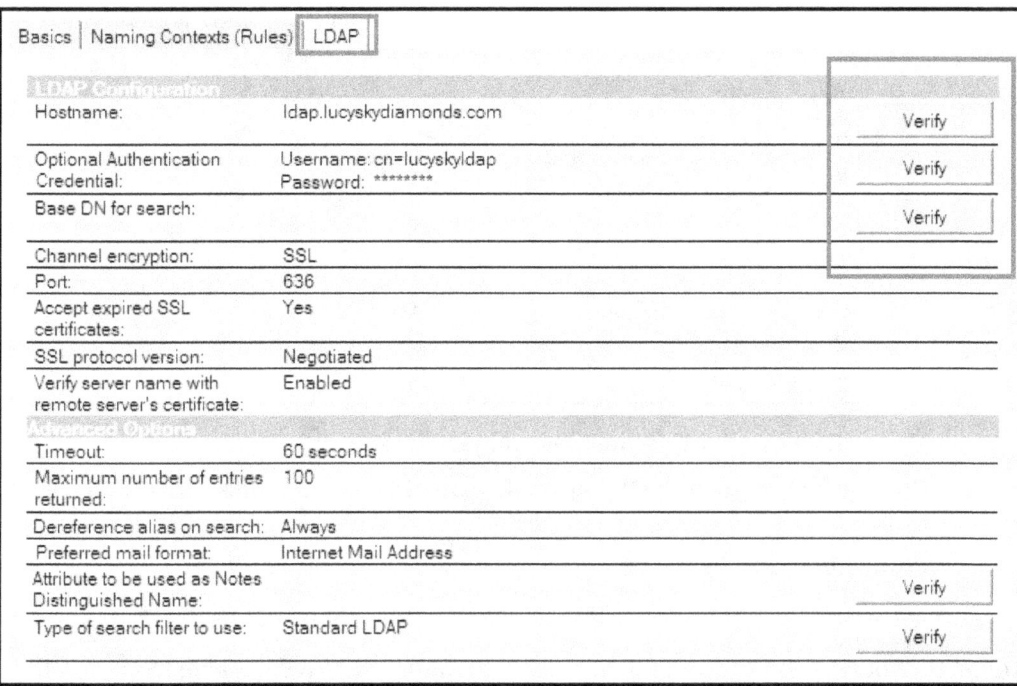

6. Open `stconfig.nsf` on the Sametime Community Server and select **Create | LDAP Server** to create a new LDAP server document. Complete that document and save it.

7. From your Sametime program directory under Domino, make a new copy or backup of the following files:

From	To
STAuthentication.dll	STAuthentication.dllbkup
STGroups.dll	STGroups.dllbkup
STBrowse.dll	STBrowse.dllbkup
STResolve.dll	STResolve.dllbkup
StDirectoryList.sym	StDirectoryList.symbkup

8. From either the Domino Directory or the directory `<DominoInstall>\`
`Directory BB\LDAP`, copy and/or rename the following files:

From	To
STAuthenticationLdap.dll	STAuthentication.dll
STGroupsLdap.dll	STGroups.dll
STBrowseLdap.dll	STBrowse.dll
STResolveLdap.dll	STResolve.dll
StDirectoryListLDAP.sym	StDirectoryList.sym
STLdap.dll	STLdap.dll
STLdap.ini	STLdap.ini

You will be overwriting the files you just backed up.

9. Run the Sametime `NameChange` task against `vpuserinfo` to convert all names
from Domino format to LDAP format. For instance:

From: `CN=Carlos Fandango/OU=US/O=LucySkyDiamonds`

To: `CN=Carlos Fandango, OU=US, O=LucySkyDiamonds`

If you do not perform the `NameChange` task, then the users will be able to log in but
their buddy lists will be empty.

Sample deployment scenarios

As you can see, there are a number of different ways you can implement your
LDAP directory and authentication in Sametime 8.5.2. To help clarify the previous
information, we will go over a few typical scenarios you might use in your
environment.

Domino Directory as LDAP

The simplest and most common deployment scenario is to use a Domino Directory
for authentication through an LDAP interface provided by the Domino server
running the LDAP server task.

As an existing Sametime administrator using Domino for your Sametime directory,
you may now want to extend the Sametime install to include other WAS-based
Sametime 8.5.2 components such as the Meeting Server or Media Manager. Before
you can do this, you must first change your Community Server to use LDAP instead
of the Domino Directory for authentication as previously discussed. You will need
to configure a server in your Domino domain to run LDAP in order to make its
directory LDAP-accessible.

To enable LDAP in your Domino environment, you must start with the global configuration document in Domino. That document sets the default for all servers. Only the default configuration document will display the LDAP tab, and there can only be one such document in each Domino domain.

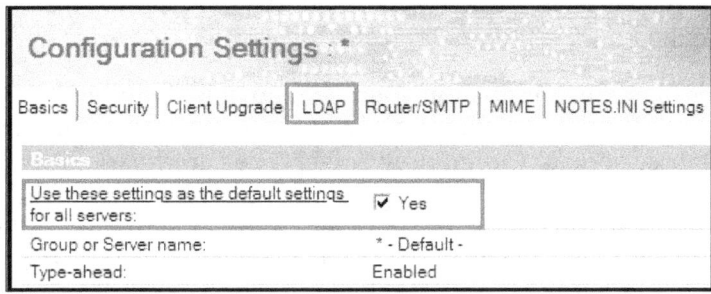

Once this document is complete, you can run the LDAP task on any Domino server, which makes its directory accessible through LDAP queries. To do this, simply type **load ldap** on the Domino server console. The Sametime Community Server makes significant demands of an LDAP server, especially an LDAP server managing a large directory or with nested groups used in Buddy Lists. Planning the assignment of LDAP resources is a major component of your Sametime design process.

When installing each of the WAS-based Sametime server components, the Guided Activities require you to configure an LDAP server. That is where you would tell WAS about the Domino LDAP server, which it would then use for the subsequent component configuration.

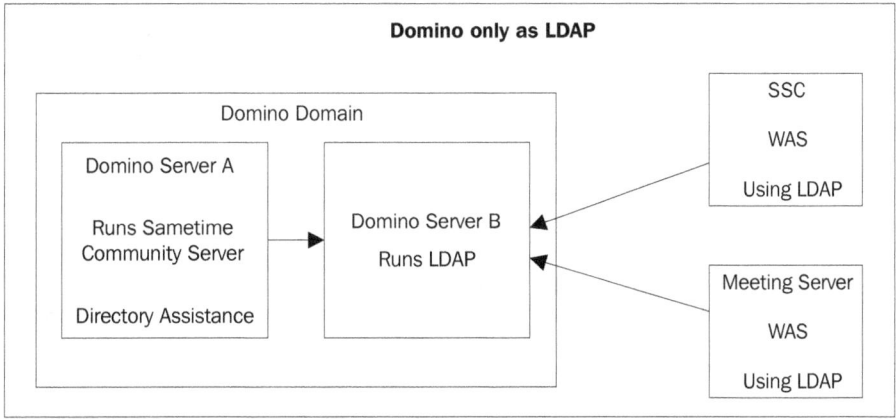

Domino Directory as LDAP with Active Directory

A more advanced deployment scenario is to extend your authentication of Domino users to also include non-Domino Active Directory (AD) users so that they can use Sametime with their own Windows logins.

You will need to configure a server in your Domino domain to run LDAP, making its directory accessible to LDAP queries. You will also need to create a Directory Assistance database on your Community Server. The Directory Assistance database will have two entries for LDAP. These entries are the Domino server designated as the LDAP source, as well as the AD domain controller entry that will be used to validate users. When setting up the WAS components such as the SSC, you create a single LDAP server pointing at the Domino LDAP host during install. You then federate additional LDAP servers into the environment after install. In this way, both the Domino Directory and the AD users are able to authenticate.

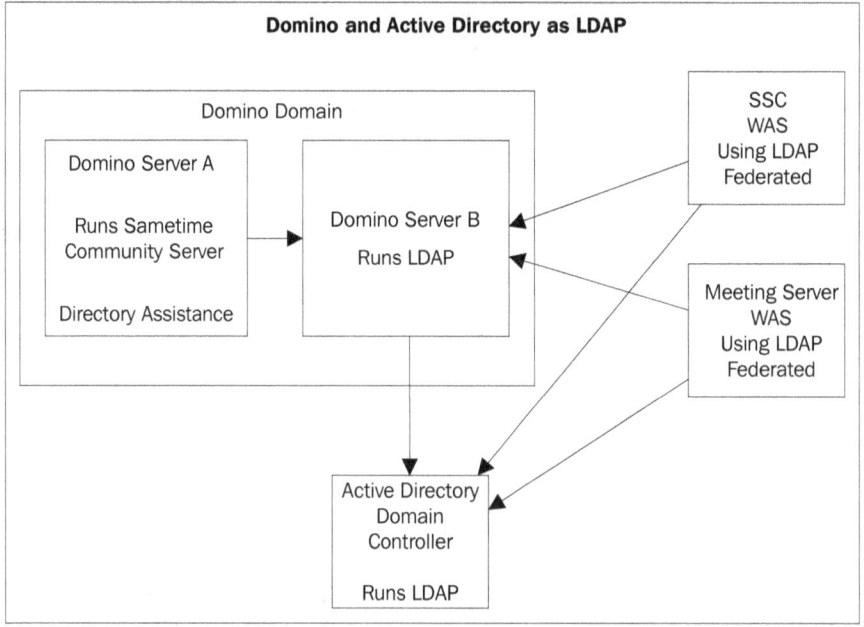

Understanding federated repositories

The Sametime prerequisites require you to identify at least one LDAP server for use with the server components. But in some cases, you may want multiple LDAP servers to be used for authentication. In the federated repository option, several different LDAP directories, each containing separate lists of users, would behave as a single directory from a Sametime perspective. Sametime would authenticate all users regardless of which directory they are in and give them the same status. It is critical that users do not appear in more than one directory with the same identity, as this could cause authentication issues.

It is important to note that this is not the same as having multiple LDAP servers representing the same directory and providing redundancy for each other. You cannot configure redundancy with multiple LDAP servers within Sametime, as Sametime expects each LDAP server to be unique. You would have to use a network load balancer and a single DNS hostname registered as an LDAP server in Sametime to accomplish that.

To configure more than one LDAP server in WAS, you normally would have to go into the WAS configuration menus and set up additional federated repositories. With Sametime, you do not need to do that. Simply registering a new Sametime server under Guided Activities automatically adds that as a new federated repository under Sametime. After you have installed your LDAP server, you may want to change some of the configuration options such as the bind credentials or port. To do this, you need to go into the WAS configuration itself. As directories are about authentication, you find all your federated repository information under the menu option **Global security**.

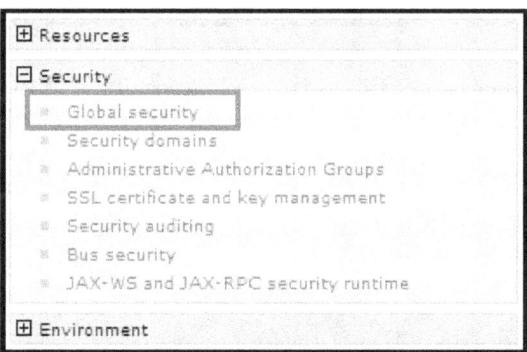

In the **Global security** menu, you have the option to configure your federated repositories. These are all the LDAP servers you have set up under the Guided Activities in the SSC.

A key point to remember is that this is truly global security and applies to every server installed under this Deployment Manager. In your install, where all servers are managed by the SSC's Deployment Manager, all servers use the same federated repository. There is no way to separate groups of users in different LDAP servers from each other. If you define multiple LDAP directories, then the authentication group is the sum of all those directories.

By selecting the options of a particular LDAP resource, you are able to change settings such as the hostname, port, bind credentials, and the attributes used for authentication. Changes made here require a restart of the servers that belong to this particular Deployment Manager.

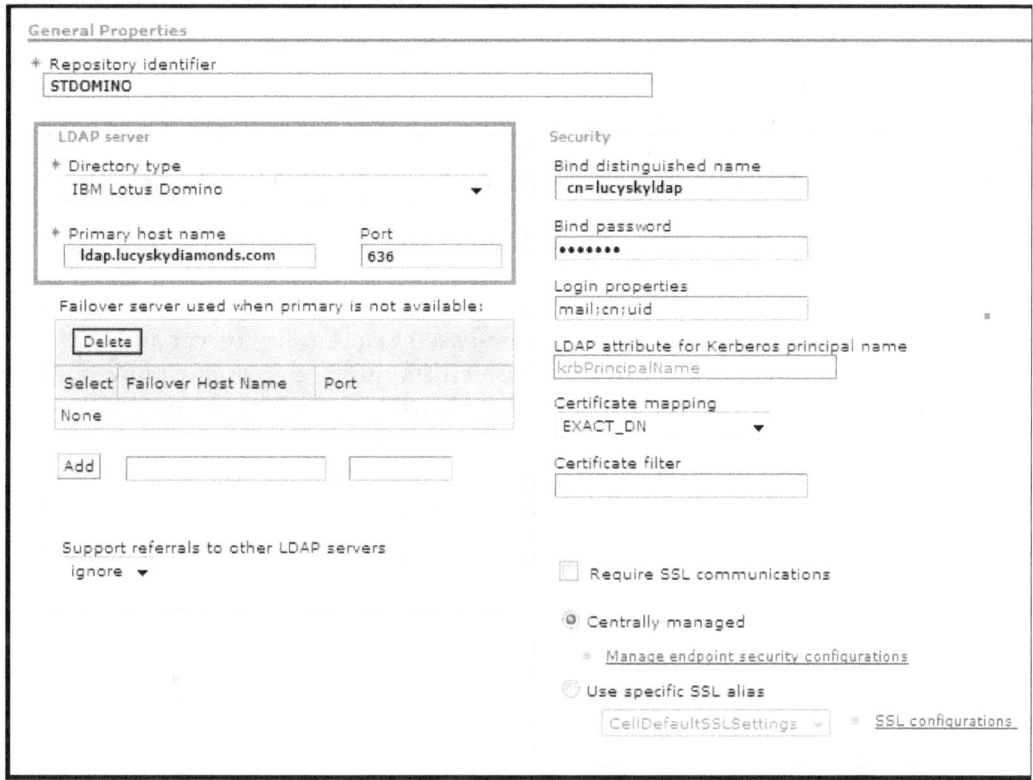

Using Single Sign-On for Sametime and other Domino and WAS servers

Single Sign-On (SSO) is a feature that allows users not to be prompted to re-enter credentials as they move around from server to server in your environment. SSO is dependent upon a shared domain between servers, and this is something you need to consider when building your Sametime environment. For instance, a Community Server at http://im.mrkitebenefit.com will never be able to provide SSO to a Meeting Server at http://meet.lucyskydiamonds.com.

SSO works by having the first server you log into create an LTPAtoken and storing that in your browser. The token contains credentials that are then passed to subsequent servers you use. These servers trust the token-generating server and accept the LTPAtoken as verification that your credentials are valid so you will not be prompted for further credentials during your time logged into the server.

There are several aspects to SSO in your Sametime environment, and not all of them behave in a manner to which you may be accustomed to seeing SSO work. The first aspect is that of the authentication that passes from your Community Server to your Meeting Server when using a Sametime client. You do not want users to be prompted to log in again when going into a meeting. With SSO, you log into the Community Server and a token is created. It is then passed to the other browser-based components such as the Meeting Server. This avoids the need for the user to login again.

In an SSO configuration between the Domino-based Community Server and the WAS-based Meeting Server, the Domino-based Community Server must have a Web SSO Configuration document specified that contains the keys from your WAS-based Meeting Server. The Sametime Community Server installation actually creates an SSO document for you in the Domino Directory and embeds the Domino server keys in it. It also sets the server document in Domino to use that token.

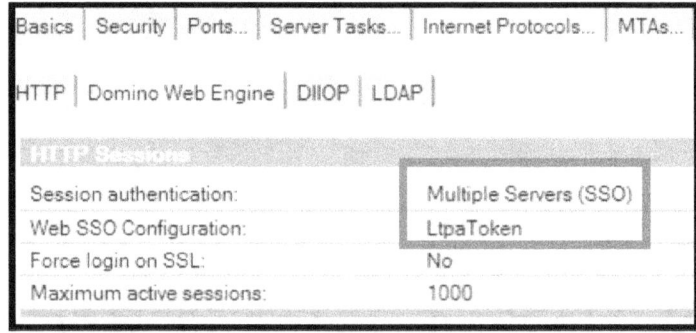

If you want SSO functionality between the Community Server and the Meeting Server, you need to remove the Domino keys from the SSO document and replace them with WAS keys generated from the Meeting Server.

Generating keys from the Meeting Server

Log into the ISC for the Meeting Server. If you have installed your Meeting Servers in a different cell to the SSC, then you need to log into that specific cell and not the SSC itself in order to generate the correct keys. Choose **Security | Global Security** to get to the LTPA management screen as shown in the following screenshot:

- If this is the first time you have exported any keys, you first need to select **Generate Keys** to have WAS generate a set of keys you can export.

- The password you enter on this screen is only used for the file you are about to export. You will be prompted for it when you import it into Domino.

- The file you create when you export the keys is only used to import the keys into the Domino SSO document. After that is done, the file can be deleted.

- The file name and location you specify on the following screen for export is relative to the Meeting Server install, not to your local client.

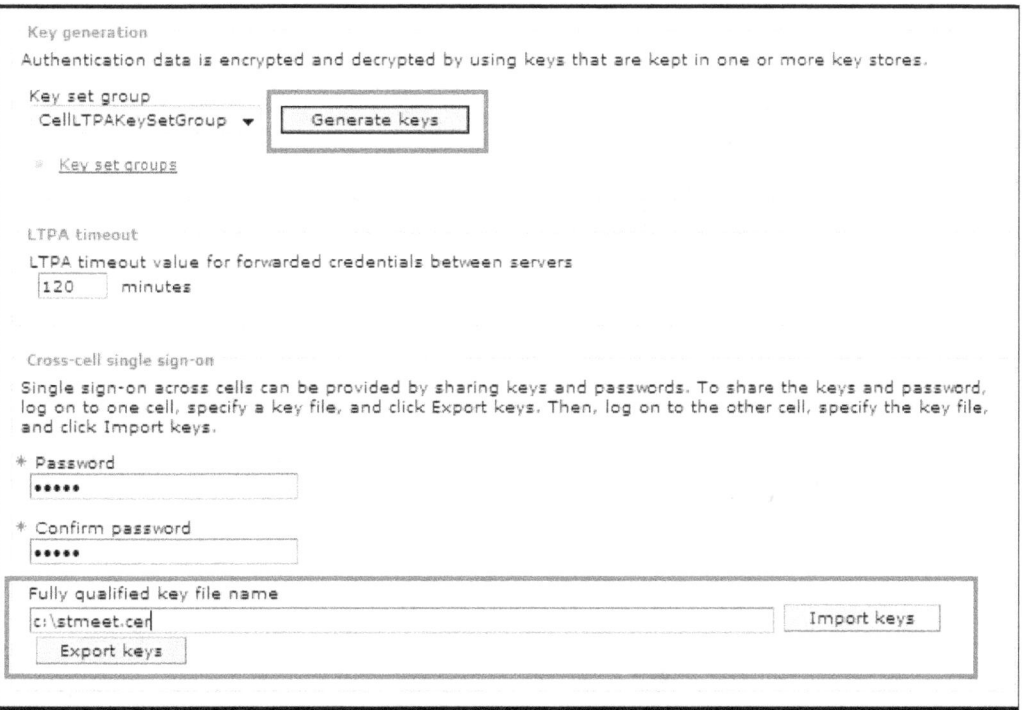

- Once you have the exported key file, you need to import it into the Web SSO document in Domino.

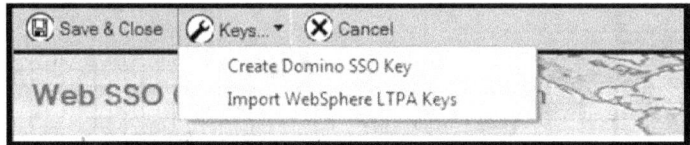

The following screenshot is what the SSO document should look like when the import is completed.

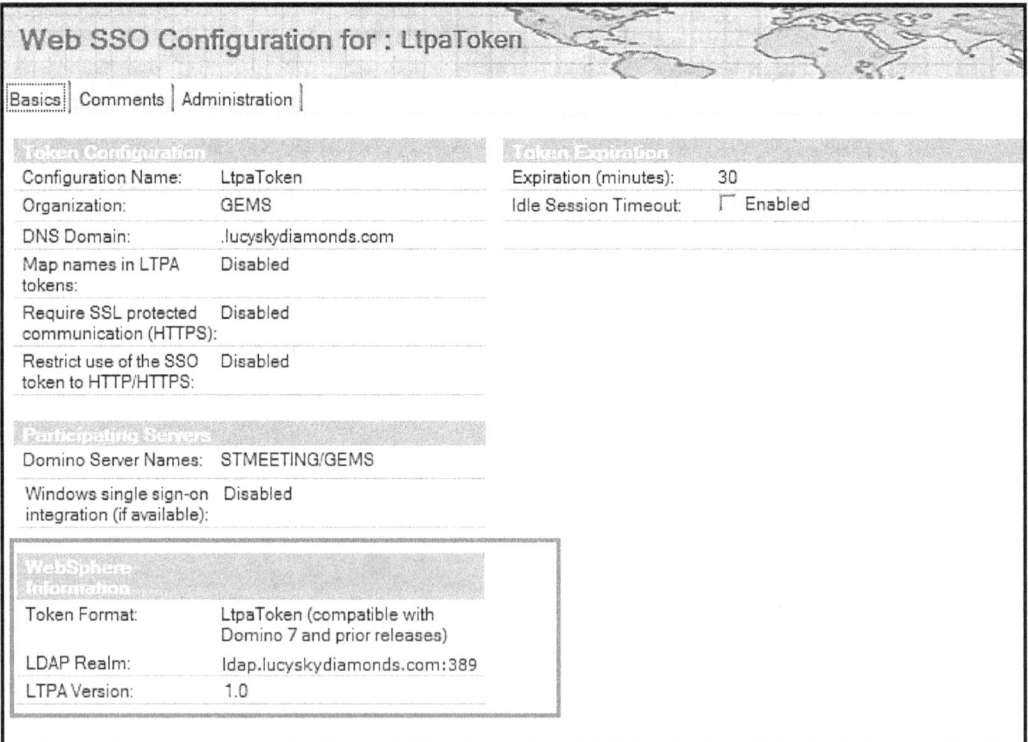

Both the Sametime Community Server and the Sametime Meeting Server will need to be restarted for the configuration to take effect.

Configuring authentication for clients using SPNEGO

Sametime clients can use SPNEGO to log into Sametime. This is another method for SSO using SPNEGO tokens. WAS must be configured to allow SSO. Steps include:

- Configuring WAS to connect to AD
- Enable the WAS SPNEGO feature
- Create the secure URL that will be used by the Sametime client
- Enable SSO for Domino and WAS

To begin, you would connect WAS to AD as an LDAP server as we have described earlier.

You would then need to enable the SPNEGO feature in WAS. To do this, select **Security | Global security**. From **Authentication**, expand **Web and SIP Security**, and then click on **SPNEGO Web authentication**.

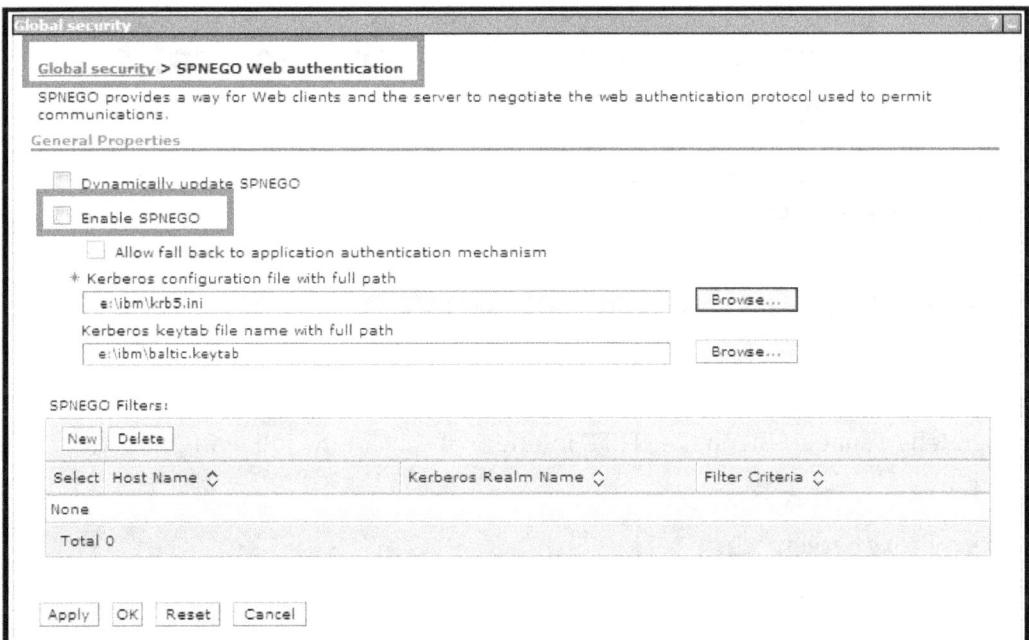

Enter the hostname of the Meeting Server in the **Host Name** field and the AD realm in the **Kerberos Realm Name**. Click on the option for **Trim Kerberos realm from principal name:** and click on **Apply**. Navigate back to the **SPNEGO Web authentication** page. Click on the **Dynamically update SPNEGO** and **Enable SPNEGO** options. Enter the full path in the dialog box to both the Kerberos configuration file `krb5.ini` and the Kerberos keytab file `keytab.ini`. For example, `c:\ibm\krb5.ini` and `c:\ibm\baltic.keytab`. The Kerberos keytab file contains one or more Kerberos service principal names and keys. The default keytab file is `krb5.keytab`. The keytab file is created using the `kpass` utility on your AD server. It is beyond the scope of this chapter to describe how to create it.

After the WAS configuration for SPNEGO SSO is completed, the Domino server must import the WAS LTPA key to allow SSO between WAS and Sametime as we have discussed earlier.

For additional detail regarding WAS, Sametime, and SPNEGO, refer to the following IBM document: `ftp://ftp.software.ibm.com/software/lotus/info/training/WAS_SPNEGO_ST.pdf`.

Understanding WAS SSL configuration

SSL is the technology used to encrypt traffic sent between a client and a server. Additionally, a server's SSL keys identifies that server uniquely and confirms to the user that the server they are talking to is the server they requested. In the next sections, we will discuss how SSL is configured for WAS.

Configuring SSL for all server communications

WAS-based Sametime 8.5.2 components are installed with an IBM certificate that is generated to enable SSL on the HTTP interface of each of the following servers:

- Meeting Server
- Proxy Server
- Media Manager
- SSC

As the certificate that is generated and installed with Sametime 8.5.2 is self-signed by IBM, browsers will throw an alert on accessing the page as that is not a valid public authority. You can ignore this message if you choose to, and your traffic will still be encrypted. If you want to use SSL for your servers and not have your users prompted with unrecognized certificate alerts, then you will need to generate your own SSL key from a recognized public authority and import it into each host server.

Where are SSL certificates managed

The SSL certificates are all managed within the SSC under the **Security** section of the ISC — **SSL certificates and key management | Manage endpoint security configurations**.

The following screenshot shows all the certificates generated and installed by default during installation, including those for all the cells and nodes:

SSL certificate and key management > **Manage endpoint security configurations**

Displays Secure Sockets Layer (SSL) configurations for selected scopes, such as a cell, node, server, or cluster.

Local Topology

- Inbound
  - balticSSCCell(CellDefaultSSLSettings)
    - nodes
      - DMgrNode
      - balticSSCNode(NodeDefaultSSLSettings)
      - balticSTMNode1(NodeDefaultSSLSettings)
      - balticSTMSNode1(NodeDefaultSSLSettings)
      - balticSTADVNode1(NodeDefaultSSLSettings)
      - proxySTPNode1(NodeDefaultSSLSettings)
      - clusters
    - nodegroups
      - DefaultNodeGroup
      meeting service bus
      rtc4web cluster service bus
      MQTT Bus
      rtc4web node service bus
      orgcollab service bus
- Outbound
  - balticSSCCell(CellDefaultSSLSettings)
    - nodes
      - DMgrNode
      - balticSSCNode(NodeDefaultSSLSettings)
      - balticSTMNode1(NodeDefaultSSLSettings)
      - balticSTMSNode1(NodeDefaultSSLSettings)
      - balticSTADVNode1(NodeDefaultSSLSettings)
      - proxySTPNode1(NodeDefaultSSLSettings)
      - clusters

If we want to change the SSL certificate used for a particular server, then we can drill down into that server configuration from here and select **Manage Certificates**. From this screen, we can import new CA certificates for the server(s).

Click on **Security | SSL certificate and key management | SSL configurations | CellDefaultSSLSettings | Key stores and certificates | CellDefaultTrustStore | Signer certificates**. Select the alias named **root**, and click on **Extract**. Enter the name of the `.cer` file, and select `Base64` as the type for storing the process server signer certificate.

Next click on **Security | SSL certificate and key management | SSL configurations | CellDefaultSSLSettings | Key stores and certificates | CellDefaultTrustStore | Signer certificates** and click on **Add**. Enter an alias for the new certificate. Enter the file name where you stored the new certificate. Click on **Apply**.

To view the personal certificates for the node, select **SSL certificate and key management | Management endpoint security configurations | nodename | Personal certificates**. In the following example, the default certificate generated during the install process is being used.

Click on **Receive from a certificate authority**. This will take you to the following screen. Enter the SSL certificate file name you have obtained from your CA provider.

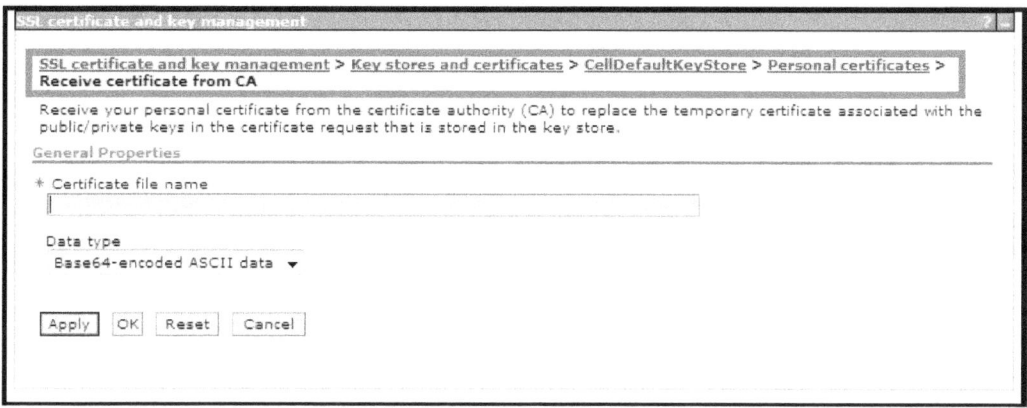

Security update

IBM have recently identified a security flaw in the Sametime Community Server that has led to them recommending you to use SSL to secure your environment. See the following technote— http://www.ibm.com/support/docview. wss?uid=swg21569452. It is important to note that you should always use LDAP credentials that have minimal (read) access to your directory and are not used anywhere else.

Summary

In this chapter, you learned about the different options for authenticating your Sametime users. You learned about how LDAP and federated repositories work, and how to configure those in Sametime. You learned about how SSO works, and the steps you need to take to configure your Sametime servers to use that option. You also learned how to install and configure SSL. In the next chapter, you will learn how to configure and implement the Sametime Business Cards feature.

8
Making it Personal: Using Sametime Business Card

As a Sametime administrator you want your company to get the maximum benefit from the features available to them. Business Card brings a level of personal engagement to online communications. This allows someone to not only easily see a person's contact details, but also to view a thumbnail photograph of them. The photo can be useful in so many ways—you or your users may never have met their Sametime contact in person, there may be multiple matches on the individual's name, or perhaps they only know the person by sight. Including a photo helps to personalize the chat so the conversation is occurring with more than just an awareness icon or a name. As many of our daily online contacts are people we rarely meet in person, the Business Card tool is invaluable in solidifying these remote relationships. The following are examples of scenarios where an organization might use the Business Card feature:

- Carroll Morgan is signed onto Sametime and a colleague he doesn't know opens a chat window to him. The Business Card allows him to easily learn who his colleague is and even what he looks like without having to ask.

- Cara Stine sees that some users in her inbox have icons showing when they are online. She notices that by hovering over the icon, a Business Card appears that tells her the person's contact details and phone number so she can respond immediately.

- Yasar Latef is attending a meeting at a new office next week. He quickly views the Business Cards for everyone attending the meeting by hovering over their names in the Sametime buddy list. By doing so, he can acquaint himself with their pictures and roles.

In this chapter, you will learn the following:

- What is a Business Card and how it is designed
- How to configure Sametime Business Cards using your Domino Directory
- How to configure Sametime Business Cards using LDAP directories
- Best practices for working with photos in Business Cards
- Integrating IBM Connections profiles as Sametime Business Cards
- Creating custom Business Cards

Sametime Business Card

A Sametime Business Card provides a Sametime user with a common interface for contact information, similar to a paper business card. A standard Business Card includes the user's name, job title, company, e-mail address, telephone number, address, and photo. In addition, your Business Card always shows location information from your Sametime location status.

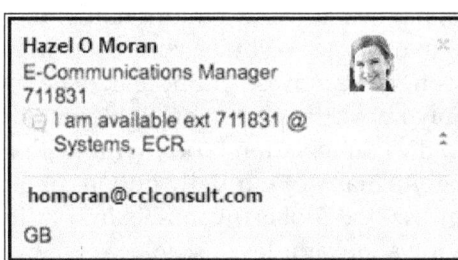

One thing to note is that even though the fields are labeled as address, company, and so on, you can store anything you wish in those fields. For example, you could store department information in the address field if that makes more sense for your environment.

The data in these fields are not held within Sametime itself or in any other Sametime data store. They are pulled in real time from an alternative data source which could be:

- Domino database(s)
- LDAP server
- IBM Connections profile

The Sametime Business Card is managed by the **UserInfo** service and servlet on the Sametime Community Server. When installing the Community Server a `userinfoconfig.xml` file is created on the server's file system. This file holds the configuration of the Business Cards.

Configuring Business Cards

Business Cards are configured in the administration interface of your Sametime Community Server. If the server is managed by the SSC, then that is where you will also configure your Business Cards. If you have configured a SSC to manage your Sametime Community Server, then you *must* use the SSC to configure your Business Cards. To do this, you log in to the SSC and choose Sametime Community Servers from the menu.

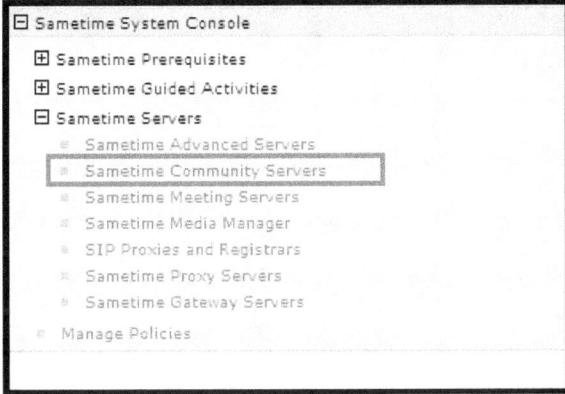

Once you have selected the server you want to modify, you can move to the Business Cards tab to make your changes.

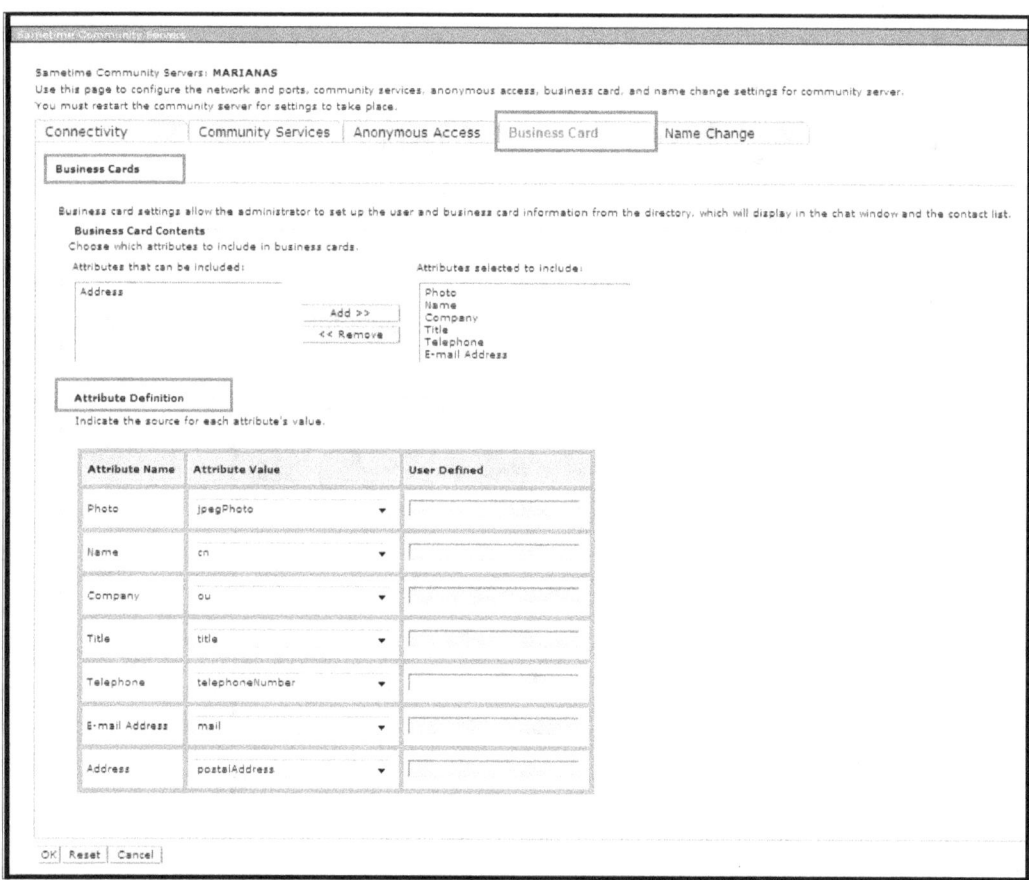

However, if you have installed a stand-alone Sametime Community Server that is not managed by a SSC, then the Business Card configuration is done directly in Sametime Administrator, which is a browser interface provided by the Domino server. After installing any Sametime Community Server, an administration interface is accessible from a browser on `http://<hostname>.stcenter.nsf?opendatabase`, where `stcenter.nsf` is set as the home page of the Domino HTTP task. In this way, `http://st.lucyskydiamonds.com/stcenter.nsf?opendatabase` would be the home page of the Sametime installation.

To use Sametime Administrator once you are logged in, access the Administrator screen.

Once logged into Sametime Administrator, the menu for configuring Business Cards against an LDAP directory is very similar to the one that is provided for configuring Business Cards against a Domino Directory. Domino Directory settings determine which LDAP server is used for the Business Card UserInfo servlet. This is the LDAP server specified for Directory Assistance in Sametime, and it becomes the source for the Business Card lookup and data.

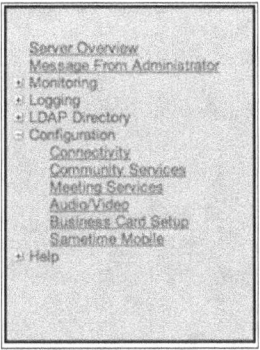

To begin, you need to tell Sametime which LDAP attributes you want to match to each Business Card attribute. As the attributes themselves are not labeled on the Business Card when it is displayed, you can substitute any LDAP attribute that makes sense for your organization.

The following diagram shows the Business Card attribute on the left and the LDAP attribute from the LDAP source on the right. It is critical at this stage to understand your LDAP schema, which attributes are used, and the values that are stored in order to ensure your Business Card displays the desired information.

If a selected attribute is invalid or empty, the Business Card attribute value will also be empty. No error is generated when displaying the Business Card. In addition, if you want to store and retrieve photographs from your LDAP source, then the attribute used must be one that allows the storage of binary images.

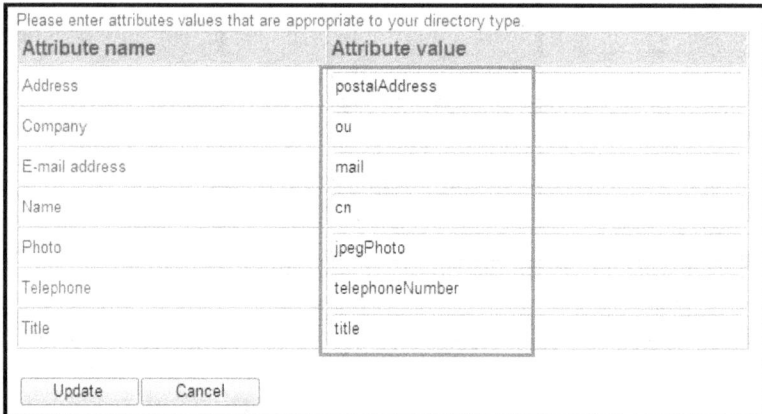

Once you map the LDAP attributes to the Business Card attributes, you can select which of these attributes you want to display on the Business Card.

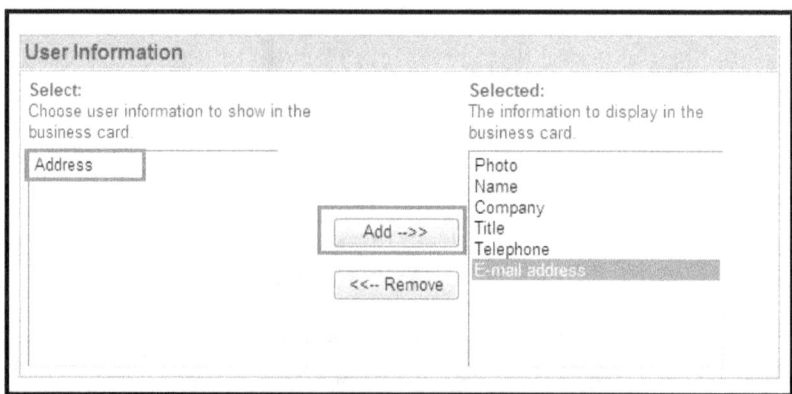

Choosing not to display an attribute will not leave a blank line on the Business Card, nor will having no photo value assigned leave any blank space. As shown in the following screenshot, our Business Card example has only a telephone number assigned:

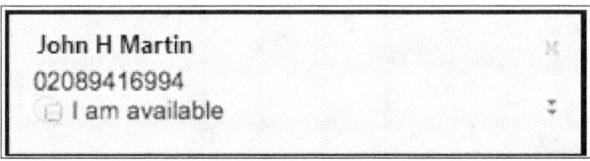

In many LDAP environments, a separate third-party LDAP tool is required to create the binary attribute store for the photo and to populate the LDAP repository with the image. You will need to work with your LDAP administrator to establish which attribute should be used and how the photo image will be supplied to LDAP.

It is important to note that when Business Cards are supplied by the Sametime Proxy Server, such as for browser clients, mobile clients, or in web meetings, the photo image is expected to be a URL that can be retrieved by the HTTP task. If the photo image is stored in an LDAP attribute, then the Sametime Proxy Server cannot access or display it and its clients will not be able to see any photos.

Using IBM Connections Business Cards for Sametime

If your company has deployed IBM Connections, then you already have a significant amount of personal information stored in your Connections profiles for each user. This also includes everything you would often want to display in a Business Card. Rather than duplicating data, so it is stored in both Connections and retrieved from LDAP for Sametime, you can instead have the Sametime client use the Connections data for the Business Card information.

The IBM Connections Business Card contains links to all of the Connections features and services, making Sametime and Connections appear as a single integrated application.

Depending upon the Sametime client type being used, there are three methods for ensuring Connections Business Cards are selected as a primary source.

Sametime Proxy Server

The Sametime Proxy Server is responsible for retrieving the Business Card information from the Connections server for browser-based clients and in web-based meetings. Business Cards bind using the e-mail address of the user in Connections. For this reason, you must have the e-mail address in LDAP available on the Business Card. The Sametime Proxy Server keys on that and retrieves the remaining information from Connections.

To configure Connections as your Business Card data source when using the Sametime Proxy Server, you need to log in to its management console which you would usually do through the SSC on `https://<hostname>:8701/ibm/console`. Select the Sametime Proxy Server bound to your Community Server under **Sametime System Console | Servers**.

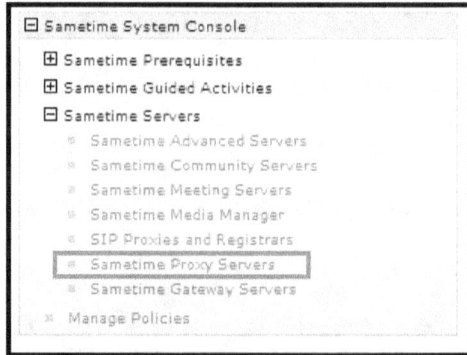

In the Sametime Proxy Server configuration settings, there is a section for Business Cards where you can select your Business Card server source. The default is set to use the Sametime Proxy Server itself.

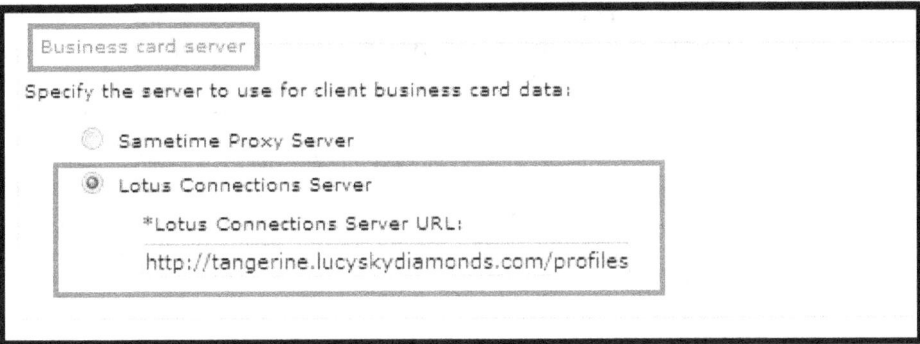

Embedded Sametime client

If you are using Sametime embedded within the Lotus Notes client, the client itself determines which Business Card to use, the selection order being:

1. Connections Business Card if a Connections server is defined in that client's preferences.
2. Sametime Business Card as defined in the Sametime Community Server configuration and the `userinfoservlet.xml` file.
3. Recent contacts information held within the local Notes client's `names.nsf`.

This selection order can be modified or restricted by changing the client's `plugin_customization.ini` file as detailed in the following URL: `http://www.lotus.com/ldd/dominowiki.nsf/dx/Defining_business_card_data_retrieval`.

Stand-alone Sametime client

The stand-alone Sametime client is designed to use the Business Card defined in the Sametime Community Server configuration and saved in `userinfoservlet.xml`. To configure a stand-alone client to use a Connections Business Card instead, you must install the IBM Connections Plug-in for IBM Sametime to each client. The plugin is available for download on the Greenhouse site at `https://greenhouse.lotus.com/catalog`.

Creating custom Business Cards

Although the visual layout of the Sametime Business Cards cannot be changed, the attributes, values, and data source can be changed. In a standard Sametime server installation, the Business Card attribute values are populated from the values stored in the LDAP or Domino Directory used for authentication. In some cases, you may not want to maintain user contact information and photos in your actual Domino Directory. You may have a pre-existing Domino application that already has that information, and you would prefer to access the data from that source. As the Business Card information is held in the `userinfoconfig.xml` file stored on the Sametime Community Server, you can edit that file to make modifications to the standard configuration. Editing the `userinfoconfig.xml` file allows you to make the following customizations:

- Use a custom application
- Use multiple attributes for a single value
- Populate the Business Card from dual repositories

A standard `userinfoconfig.xml` file configured for LDAP contains the details of your LDAP directory server as well as the attributes and values. If you update the Business Card details through the SSC and the Community Server configuration, then this XML file is updated at the same time. The UserInfo service and servlet reference the `userinfoconfig.xml` file directly and populate the Business Card according to those settings.

```xml
<UserInformation>
<Resources>
<Storage type="LDAP">
<StorageDetails HostName="tanger.lucyskydiamonds.com" Port="636" Username="bindldap" Password="" SslEnabled="false"
 SslPort="636" BaseDN="" Scope="2" SearchFilter="(&amp;(objectclass=organizationalPerson)(|(cn=%s)(givenname=%s)
(sn=%s)(mail=%s)))" />
<!-- Add another StorageDetails tag to support another ldap server.  The listing order implies the searching order -->
<!--Scope: 0=OBJECT_SCOPE 1=ONELEVEL_SCOPE 2=SUBTREE_SCOPE -->
<SslProperties KeyStorePath="" KeyStorePassword="" />
<Details>
<Detail Id="MailAddress" FieldName="mail" Type="text/plain" />
<Detail Id="Name" FieldName="name" Type="text/plain" />
<Detail Id="Title" FieldName="title" Type="text/plain" />
<Detail Id="Location" FieldName="postalAddress" Type="text/plain" />
<Detail Id="Telephone" FieldName="phone" Type="text/plain" />
<Detail Id="Company" FieldName="ou" Type="text/plain" />
<Detail Id="Photo" FieldName=jpgphoto Type="image/jpeg" />
</Details>
</Storage>
</Resources>
<ParamSets>
<Set SetId="0" params="MailAddress,Name,Title,Location,Telephone,Photo,Company"/>
<Set SetId="1" params="MailAddress,Name,Title,Location,Telephone,Photo,Company"/>
</ParamSets>
<BlackBoxConfiguration>
<BlackBox type="LDAP" name="com.ibm.sametime.userinfo.userinfobb.UserInfoLdapBB" MaxInstances="5" />
</BlackBoxConfiguration>
</UserInformation>
```

Using a custom application

If you use Lotus Notes in your organization, then you may have an application that stores your user data. Even if you do not have an application for storing user data, you may want to create one rather than use and maintain user information inside your Domino Directory. Attempting to maintain user information in your Domino Directory can have the following negative effects:

- It requires you to grant access to the Domino Directory to users who want to maintain their information. The Domino Directory is not an end-user application and its interface can be confusing.

- Permitting users to access the Domino Directory allows them to view other configuration details and settings such as server and configuration documents that they do not have a need to see.

- The Domino Directory itself is critical to server performance. When additional views or columns are added, additional update cycles are required for indexing. In addition, storing rich text data such as photos in each Person document can also add to the server load and increase replication traffic around your network if there are either frequent photo or Person document updates.

As an alternative, you can use a custom application for populating your Business Cards regardless of whether you use LDAP or Domino Directory for authentication. You continue to authenticate against your configured directory, but the Business Card information will come from the application you specify in the `userinfoconfig.xml` file.

In the original `userinfoconfig.xml` example configured for LDAP, the **Storage Type** parameter is set to **LDAP**, but it can also be set to **Notes** to point to the Domino Directory or to **Notes_Custom_db** to use a custom Notes application. To configure a Notes application to populate Business Cards, you need to ensure it takes only the values you want from the LDAP directory, and then specifies the remaining values to come from the application. This involves setting the configuration in the SSC and Sametime Community Server, along with manually modifying the `userinfoconfig.xml` file.

In the following example, the Business Card is populated with the user's e-mail address from the LDAP directory. The remaining user information such as address, telephone, and photo are populated from the Notes application. To ensure the value is not pulled from the LDAP directory, you must set the **Attribute Value** in the Community Server configuration to **User Defined** and leave the **User Defined** fields blank.

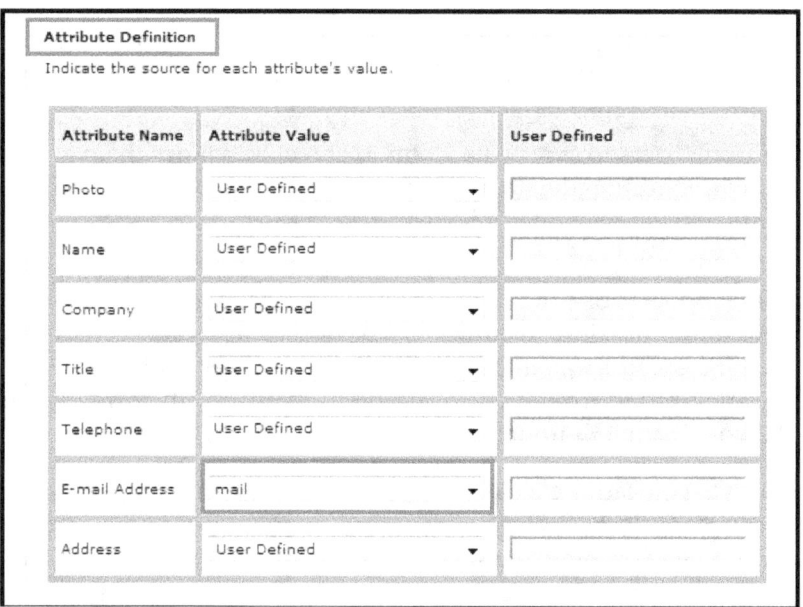

When you save this configuration, the `userinfoconfig.xml` file is updated to match your settings, but it contains blank entries for each of the **User Defined** values you left blank.

```
<UserInformation>
<Resources>
<Storage type="LDAP">
<Details>
<Detail Id="MailAddress" FieldName="mail" Type="text/plain" />
</Details>
</Storage>
<Storage type="NOTES_CUSTOM_DB"> <StorageDetails DbName="companybook.nsf" View="byemail" />
<Details>
<Detail Id="Telephone" FieldName="phone" Type="text/plain" />
<Detail Id="Title" FieldName="title" Type="text/plain" />
<Detail Id="Company" FieldName="coname" Type="text/plain" />
<Detail Id="Location" FieldName="Location" Type="text/plain" />
<Detail Id="Name" FieldName="PersonName" Type="text/plain" />
<Detail Id="MailAddress" FieldName="internetmail" Type="text/plain" />
<Detail Id="Photo" FieldName=jpgphoto" Type="image/jpeg" />
</Details>
</Storage>
</Resources>
```

To create a connection between the authentication directory and the custom Notes application, you must have a **Detail Id** that the two data sources have in common. You must also have a view in your application sorted by the field mapped to that **Detail Id**. In the following example, you are using the **Detail Id** called **MailAddress** for that common field. In the LDAP directory, that **Detail Id** maps to the **mail** field. In the Notes application, it maps to the **internetmail** field.

```
<Storage type="LDAP">
<CommonField CommonFieldName="mailaddress" />
<Details>
<Detail Id="MailAddress" FieldName="mail" Type="text/plain" />
</Details>
</Storage>
<Storage type="NOTES_CUSTOM_DB"> <StorageDetails DbName="companybook.nsf" View="byemail" />
<Details>
<Detail Id="Telephone" FieldName="phone" Type="text/plain" />
<Detail Id="Title" FieldName="title" Type="text/plain" />
<Detail Id="Company" FieldName="coname" Type="text/plain" />
<Detail Id="Location" FieldName="Location" Type="text/plain" />
<Detail Id="Name" FieldName="PersonName" Type="text/plain" />
<Detail Id="MailAddress" FieldName="internetmail" Type="text/plain" />
<Detail Id="Photo" FieldName=jpgphoto" Type="image/jpeg" />
</Details>
</Storage>
</Resources>
```

There is one other value you must add to your `userinfoconfig.xml` file, and that is the **BlackBoxConfiguration** node. This setting tells Sametime which library to use to process the instructions. There will be one entry for **BlackBox** for your primary directory (either Domino or LDAP), and you will need to add another **BlackBox** entry for your custom application.

```
<BlackBoxConfiguration>
<BlackBox type="LDAP" name="com.ibm.sametime.userinfo.userinfobb.UserInfoLdapBB" MaxInstances="5" />
<BlackBox type="NOTES_CUSTOM_DB" name="com.ibm.sametime.userinfo.userinfobb.UserInfoNotesCustomBB"
MaxInstances="4" />
</BlackBoxConfiguration>
```

Using multiple attributes for a single value

Another option for configuring the Business Cards is to have more than one value assigned to a single attribute. For instance, you may want to concatenate multiple values from your LDAP or Domino Directory to create a single attribute for items such as the user name or company. You may also want to display more information than the Business Card has fields to display. You cannot accomplish this in the native Sametime Administration console, but you can do it by modifying the `userinfoconfig.xml` file once again.

The standard entry for mapping a field to an attribute has the name of the value, followed by the attribute or field to map, and finally the data type. In the following example, you are mapping the attribute co from your LDAP directory to the company value.

<Detail Id="company" FieldName="co" Type="text/plain" />

If we wanted to construct the company value from multiple attributes, you can enter multiple attributes separated by a comma. For instance, you might want to have the company name followed by a dash and then the user's telephone extension. Following are some examples of how you can concatenate multiple values within a single Business Card attribute.

Your LDAP directory contains first name, middle initial, and last name attributes which you want to merge together to form the name to be used on the Business Card. You use the name value and supply it the FieldName values of firstname, mi, and lastname, with each value separated by a comma. In this way, the entry **<Detail Id="name" FieldName="firstname,mi,lastname" Type="text/plain"/>** would display as Marcus L Nouvelle if the person's firstname=Marcus, mi=L, and lastname=Nouvelle.

There is also an optional DisplaySeparator parameter which constructs the attribute but uses the separator you specify to join each value.

In the next example, the LDAP directory has co and ext attributes which you want to use to construct a display for the company attribute. To do this, you enter multiple values separated by commas for the attribute you want, but you add the DisplaySeparator parameter at the end of the line to specify that you want the values separated by a dash. For example, the entry **<Detail Id="company" FieldName="co,ext" Type="text/plain" DisplaySeparator="-" />** would display as Kite Benefits – 65096 if the person's co=Kite Benefits and ext=65096.

Dual repositories

It is also possible to set up multiple directories to use in constructing a Business Card. You can set up to two directories, but they must be of differing types. Valid examples would be:

- Domino Directory and LDAP directory
- Domino Directory and custom Notes application
- LDAP directory and Domino Directory
- LDAP directory and custom Notes application

In each instance, only the first repository is used for authentication, and it is your primary authentication source for Sametime. Both repositories can be used to populate the `userinfoconfig.xml` file and decide the format of the Business Cards. When modifying the `userinfoconfig.xml` file to add your second repository, it must be listed after the primary repository, which is also your authentication directory.

Domino Directory and LDAP directory

In this scenario, the Domino Directory is your primary authentication directory and you want to use an LDAP server to help populate the Business Cards. You do not want to use LDAP for authentication, so you do not need to configure it as a directory under Domino.

To accomplish this, modify the SSC and Community Server Business Card settings to use the values from Domino you want to apply. Define the LDAP repository fields as **User Defined** and leave the **User Defined** fields blank.

In the following example, only the e-mail address and photo image data are coming from the Domino Directory. The remaining attributes are left empty as you will supply those values in the `userinfoconfig.xml` file.

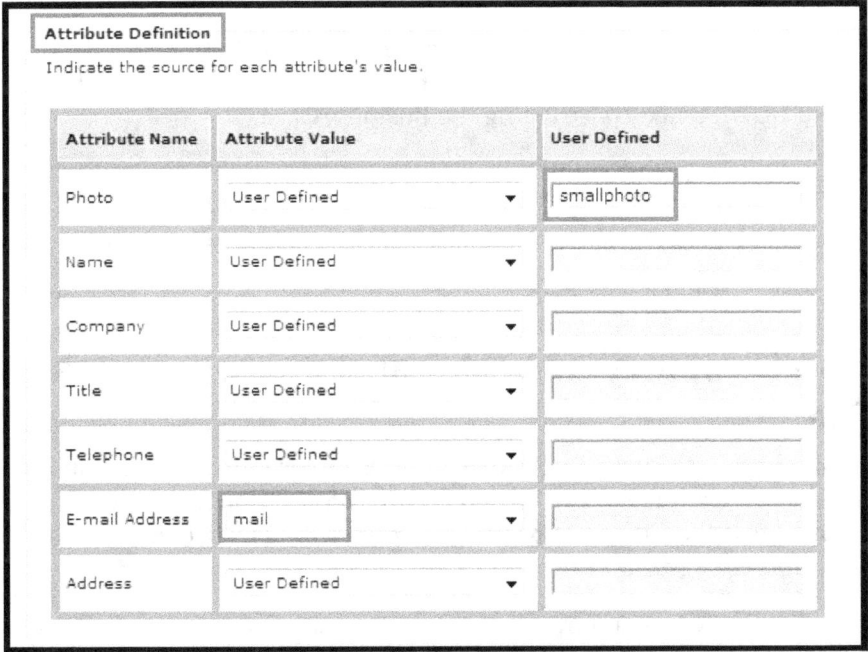

Having saved this configuration, you can now modify the userinfoconfig.xml file to have the Domino storage section only contain references to **smallphoto** and **mail**. The LDAP storage section will contain references to the remaining values as well as the **CommonField** (in this case, the **mail** value).You will have to delete the empty mappings that will be present under the Domino storage for the attributes that have no assigned values in Domino.

```
<Storage type="NOTES">
<CommonField CommonFieldName="mailAddress" />
<Details>
<Detail Id="MailAddress" FieldName="mail" Type="text/plain" />
<Detail Id="Photo" FieldName="smallphoto" Type="image/jpeg" />
</Details>
</Storage>

<Storage type="LDAP"> <StorageDetails HostName="tangerine.lucyskydiamonds.com" Port="636" Username="bindldap"
 Password="" SslEnabled="false" SslPort="636" BaseDN="" Scope="1"
 SearchFilter="(&amp;(objectclass=organizationalPerson)(|cn=%s)(givenname=%s)(sn=%s)(mail=%s)))" />
<Details>
<Detail Id="Telephone" FieldName="phone" Type="text/plain" />
<Detail Id="Title" FieldName="title" Type="text/plain" />
<Detail Id="Company" FieldName="coname" Type="text/plain" />
<Detail Id="Address" FieldName="Location" Type="text/plain" />
<Detail Id="Name" FieldName="PersonName" Type="text/plain" />
<Detail Id="MailAddress" FieldName="internetmail" Type="text/plain" />
</Details>
</Storage>
```

You also need to add a **BlackBoxConfiguration** line at the bottom of your userinfoconfig.xml file to tell the UserInfo servlet to use libraries for both Domino and LDAP when constructing the Business Card.

```
<BlackBoxConfiguration>
<BlackBox type="NOTES" name="com.ibm.sametime.userinfo.userinfobb.UserInfoNotesBB" MaxInstances="4" />
<BlackBox type="LDAP" name="com.ibm.sametime.userinfo.userinfobb.UserInfoLdapBB" MaxInstances="5" />
</BlackBoxConfiguration>
```

Domino Directory or LDAP and custom Notes application

In this configuration scenario, you are using Domino or LDAP as the primary directory but you want to supply Business Card information from another application. This is the **Custom Application** configuration reviewed earlier. The changes for this configuration are:

1. Modify the SSC—Community Server configuration to ensure no attributes you want supplied from your custom application are mapped.

2. Modify the `userinfoconfig.xml` file to add a new storage section for your custom application.

```
<Storage type="NOTES_CUSTOM_DB"> <StorageDetails Dbname="companybook.nsf" View="byemail" />
<Details>
<Details>
<Detail Id="Telephone" FieldName="phone" Type="text/plain" />
<Detail Id="Title" FieldName="title" Type="text/plain" />
<Detail Id="Company" FieldName="coname" Type="text/plain" />
<Detail Id="Address" FieldName="Location" Type="text/plain" />
<Detail Id="Name" FieldName="PersonName" Type="text/plain" />
<Detail Id="MailAddress" FieldName="internetmail" Type="text/plain" />
<Detail Id="Photo" FieldName=jpgphoto" Type="image/jpeg" />
</Details>
</Storage>
```

3. Modify the `userinfoconfig.xml` file to add a **CommonField** parameter which identifies a key that exists in both repositories:

   <CommonField CommonFieldName="MailAddress" />

4. Modify the **BlackBoxConfiguration** section to add an entry for **Notes_Custom_db**.

```
<BlackBoxConfiguration>
<BlackBox type="NOTES" name="com.ibm.sametime.userinfo.userinfobb.UserInfoNotesBB" MaxInstances="4" />
<BlackBox type="NOTES_CUSTOM_DB" name="com.ibm.sametime.userinfo.userinfobb.UserInfoNotesCustomBB"
MaxInstances="4" />
</BlackBoxConfiguration>
```

LDAP and Domino Directory

If an LDAP repository is your primary authentication source, then you may still want to take advantage of a Domino database to store Business Card information and provide data for the layout of the cards. In a pure LDAP configuration, Sametime does not know about the Domino Directory or how to access it. The first thing you need to do is create a Directory Assistance database and document for your Domino environment. The steps are given as follows:

1. Create a Directory Assistance database on the Sametime server using the Directory Assistance template (`da.ntf`) if the `da.nsf` database does not already exist.

2. Highlight the Sametime server document and choose **Actions | Set Directory Assistance Information**, giving the resulting dialog box the name of the database you created in the first step.

3. Create a new storage database on the Sametime server based on the Domino Directory template (`pubnames.ntf`) or use the `names.nsf` database that is already on the server.

4. Create a Directory Assistance document in the Directory Assistance database for a Notes domain.

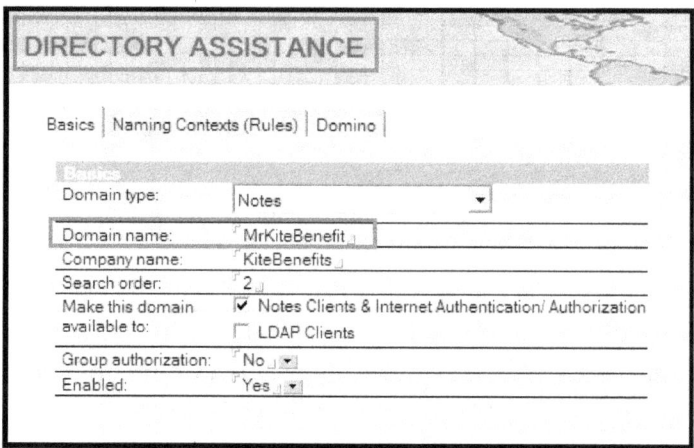

5. Make sure that the domain is not trusted for credentials. You only want to use this for Business Card information, not for authentication.

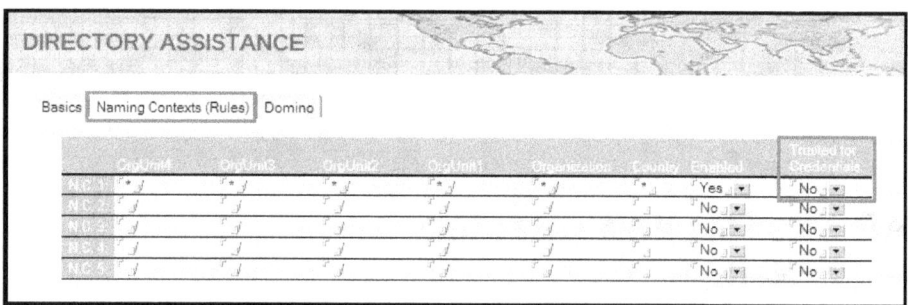

6. Finally, you specify the name of the database created in the earlier steps.

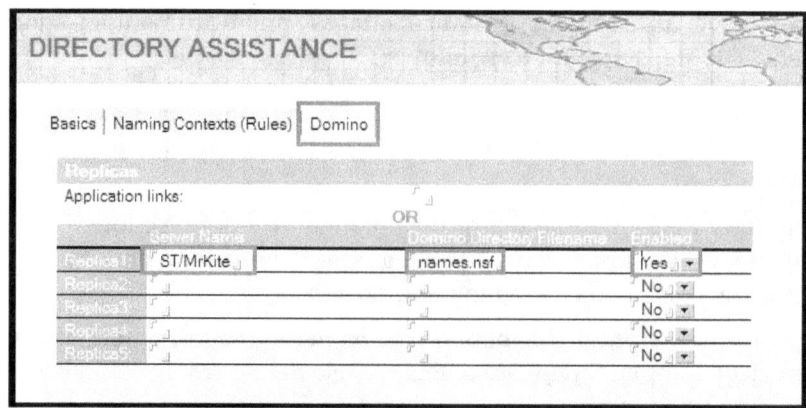

7. After completing the Directory Assistance configuration, you will need to restart the Domino server.

8. Modify the **SSC | Community Server** configuration to ensure no attributes you want supplied from your custom application are mapped.

9. Modify the `userinfoconfig.xml` file to add a new storage section for Domino.

```
</Storage>
<Storage type="NOTES">
<Details>
<Detail Id="Telephone" FieldName="phone" Type="text/plain" />
<Detail Id="Title" FieldName="title" Type="text/plain" />
<Detail Id="Company" FieldName="coname" Type="text/plain" />
<Detail Id="Location" FieldName="Location" Type="text/plain" />
<Detail Id="Name" FieldName="PersonName" Type="text/plain" />
<Detail Id="MailAddress" FieldName="internetmail" Type="text/plain" />
</Details>
</Storage>
```

10. Modify the `userinfoconfig.xml` file to add a `CommonField` parameter which identifies a key that exists in both repositories:

    <CommonField CommonFieldName="MailAddress" />

11. Modify the **BlackBoxConfiguration** section to add an entry for Notes.

```
<BlackBoxConfiguration>
<BlackBox type="LDAP" name="com.ibm.sametime.userinfo.userinfobb.UserInfoLdapBB" MaxInstances="5" />
<BlackBox type="NOTES" name="com.ibm.sametime.userinfo.userinfobb.UserInfoNotesBB" MaxInstances="4" />
</BlackBoxConfiguration>
```

Using and storing photos

The use of photos adds significant value to the Sametime Business Cards. Although it can take some additional configuration (especially with an LDAP environment), it should be considered a key part of your Sametime deployment.

The easiest method for deployment is to use a custom Notes application with a form that can store both a photo of the user and a field to use as your key to join dual repositories.

 The advantage of using a Notes application is that no change needs to be made to your LDAP schema and no third-party tool needs to be used to upload photos.

If you are using a Domino Directory or Domino LDAP for authentication, you may be considering adding the photos to the Domino names.nsf database. For most Sametime deployments, that is not recommended for performance reasons.

It is important to note that the image you see on the Business Card has been compressed to be thumbnail-sized, but is not necessarily stored in that format. If you move your mouse over the picture of the person on their Business Card, then the full-size photo is retrieved from the storage repository and attempts to display on your client. If the original photos stored in the repository are large, then the attempt to stream the entire image by the UserInfo servlet will cause the servlet to start failing and eventually it will crash.

For this reason any photo storage should be designed to ensure the uploaded image is not more than 64 KB in size regardless of the height and width. This is easy to accomplish with a Notes application, as you can use the thumbnail option for a Rich Text Lite field. That option is specifically designed to upload and display images in situations such as this. Whatever storage repository you decide to use for your photos, it is critical that you ensure image sizes are handled correctly before deploying.

Troubleshooting Business Cards

As Business Cards are so visible, this feature is usually the first thing people notice if they stop working. Understanding how to find and resolve a Business Card problem is critical to a successful deployment. The Business Cards are managed by the UserInfo servlet and service on the Community Server, so in most cases problems with Business Cards are usually isolated to just the display of Business Cards. Issues with the feature do not tend to impact other services such as chat or meetings, but as with any system issue, especially in large environments, it is prudent to resolve any issues with Business Cards first.

The first thing to consider when troubleshooting a Business Cards issue is that the UserInfo servlet on a server provides the same service to everyone.

- If no Business Cards are displayed or they appear incomplete or incorrect, it is usually a server-side issue
- If one user has a problem seeing Business Cards correctly but everyone else on that server is fine, it is usually a client-side issue
- If Business Cards appear to work for most people but one or more specific Business Cards are broken for everyone, then it is usually a data issue with that specific Business Card

To test if the UserInfo servlet is working at all, you can construct a URL to enter into a browser that requests the servlet to print a Business Card for a specified user to the browser window. The URL format is `http://<sthostname>/servlet/UserIn foServlet?operation=3&setid=1&UserId=<USERID>`, where `<sthostname>` is the fully qualified hostname of your Community Server and `<USERID>` is the name of the Business Card user.

> When constructing the URL, do not include any spaces. If the name has a space in it such as "Fernando Reyos", then you need to substitute the value `%20` for every space in the URL. In that case, you would enter the `<USERID>` as `Fernando%20Reyos`.

The query should return the Business Card for that user so that you can validate if the data is correct. If the data does not match what is seen on the client logged into that same server, then it is a client-side problem. If the query returns **Unknown** as a result, then it has not found a match for the `<USERID>` you entered in the URL.

If the query returns an error instead of results, then the UserInfo servlet is not running correctly on that server. Everyone connected to that server will be affected.

If you have ongoing problems with the Business Card service (such as those caused by overly large photos), you may want to turn on advanced debugging on the server. To do this, follow the steps:

1. Find the file `DebugLevel.class.5` in the location `<dominodatadir>\domino\html\sametime\stlinks\debug\.`

2. Copy the file to the Domino program directory and rename it to `DebugLevel.class.`

3. Restart Sametime.

4. This will create log files in the `\Trace` directory under the Domino program directory. The log files related to the **UserInfo** service will be named with a string that begins with `userinfo` and include a date and time stamp.

5. The log files that are created are quite verbose, so it is not recommended to leave the debugging turned on for an extended period of time. You should also delete the log files after you review them.

In most cases, Business Card performance is usually a result of photo-size problems or client-side caching, but much of the awareness relies upon the presence of a mail address in the Business Card itself. If you do not include the mail attribute on your Business Card design, you may have unpredictable behavior in matching names to the correct Business Card.

Business Cards and the Sametime clients

Once Business Cards have been configured for your Sametime environment, your users can select whether or not they want to see the Business Cards in their Sametime client. To begin seeing the Business Card information in a chat window, a user needs to make some changes to their Sametime settings. For the Embedded Client, go to **File | Preferences | Sametime | Chat Window** and select **Display chat partner's business card in the chat window** option.

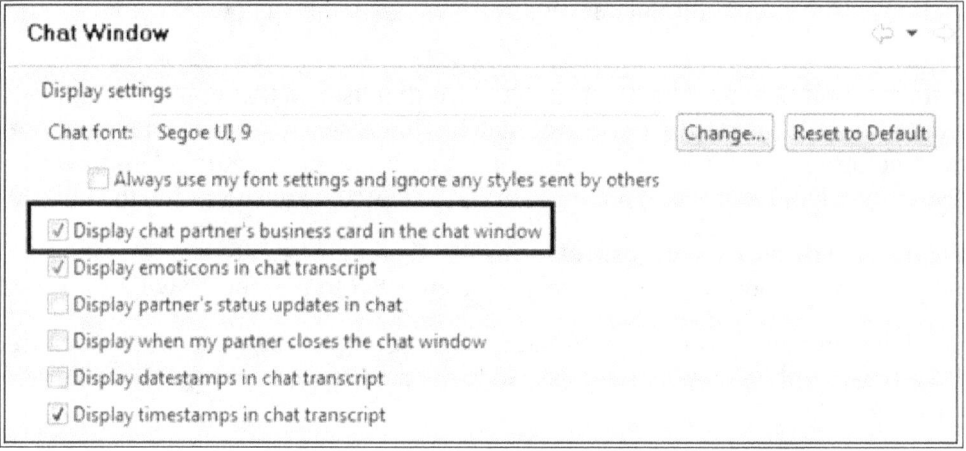

Another option is to see the Business Card info when a user moves their mouse or hovers over a contact's name. This setting needs to be selected as well. From the Embedded Client, go to **File | Preferences | Sametime | Contact List** and select the **Show business card when hovering over a contact's name** option.

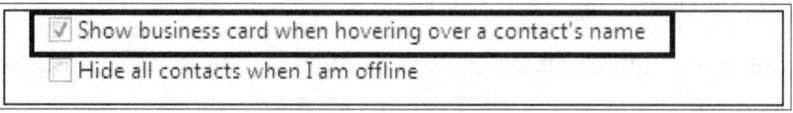

You can also enable the ability to hover over Business Card information in the Sametime Connect Client. Select **View | Show | Hover Business Cards** to enable this function.

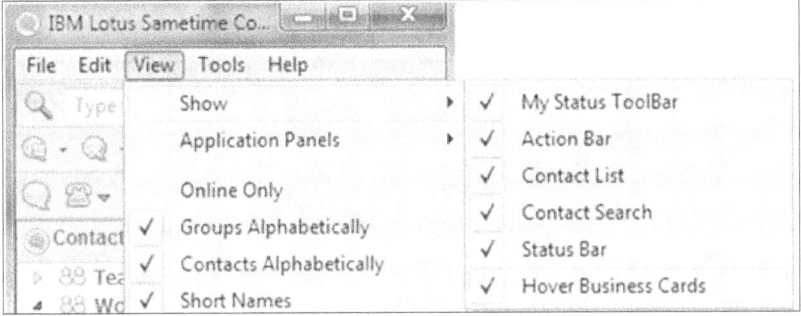

Summary

In this chapter, you learned about Business Cards and how they are useful in a Sametime environment. You learned how to configure the data that is seen in a Business Card, as well as how to select where that data comes from. You learned how to customize the output for the Business Card, and how to troubleshoot issues you may see when using Business Cards. You learned how important photos are for Business Cards, and how best to configure that information to prevent performance issues. Finally, you learned how to configure the Sametime clients to use the Sametime Business Card information. In the next chapter, you will be introduced to Sametime Advanced and Sametime Gateway and learn how to prepare to connect either system to your Sametime 8.5.2 environment.

9

Extending the Sametime Environment: Connecting to Sametime Advanced and Sametime Gateway

At this point perhaps you have installed Sametime 8.5.2. Two add-on products, Sametime Advanced and Sametime Gateway, allow you to provide more features and functionality for your users and your organization while still maintaining a secure and stable environment. In this chapter, an overview will be provided for connecting your Sametime 8.5.2 environment to Sametime Advanced and Sametime Gateway servers. The following are the examples of deployment scenarios:

- Giselle is interested in extending Sametime chat to other networks. She has read that she can connect her Sametime Community to Google Talk and AOL by adding a Sametime Gateway to her Sametime environment.

- Raoul's users want to be able to set up persistent chat rooms that they can use for ongoing project discussions, allowing people who were not online during the chat to review the transcripts later.

- Jerome is working as a part of a worldwide project team involving many members from different disciplines. He needs to be able to find the right people who can quickly answer his questions. Using Broadcast Communities with Sametime Advanced, he can contact anyone signed up in his project community for information.

- The marketing department at Erica's company would like to be able to poll their users for product feedback. Using Sametime Advanced, users can sign up to receive poll questions through Sametime, and Marketing can see the answers consolidated in real time.

- Li Zao is planning a large Sametime network across multiple nodes and countries. He would like to include the ability to talk with users working on similar projects as well as connect to other chat services like Jabber or Google Talk.

In this chapter, you will learn the following:

- What is Sametime Advanced

- What are the software and network prerequisites for Sametime Advanced

- What are the features of Sametime Advanced

- How Sametime Advanced integrates with and enhances your existing Sametime environment

- How to install Sametime Advanced as part of your SSC

- What is Sametime Gateway

- What are the software and network prerequisites for Sametime Gateway

- What are the features of Sametime Gateway

- Deployment options for Sametime Gateway

- Connecting a Sametime Gateway to your existing Sametime environment

Introducing Sametime Advanced

Sametime Advanced is an extended Sametime product that integrates with your existing Sametime Community Servers. Licensing for Sametime Advanced includes Sametime Standard, and the existence of a Sametime Community Server is a prerequisite for the installation of Sametime Advanced.

To make administration and management easier, Sametime Advanced 8.5.2 can be installed alongside the other WebSphere-based Sametime server components and under the management of the SSC.

Sametime Advanced installation files

Sametime Advanced is available from IBM Passport Advantage in the following packages:

Package file	Purpose
CF2Y0ML	IBM Sametime Advanced Server v8.5.2 Multiplatform Multilingual Quickstart Guide
CZYH2ML	IBM Sametime Advanced Server v8.5.2 Windows
CZYH5ML	IBM Sametime Advanced Server v8.5.2 Linux
CZYH6ML	IBM Sametime Advanced Server v8.5.2 AIX
CZYH7ML	IBM Sametime Advanced Server v8.5.2 Solaris SPARC
CZYH4ML	IBM Sametime Advanced Software Development Kit (SDK) v8.5.2 Multiplatform Multilingual

Sametime Advanced ports

The following are the default ports for Sametime Advanced:

Default port	Purpose
9080	Provides default HTTP access to the Sametime Advanced web application
9443	Provides HTTPS access to the Sametime Advanced web application
1883	The port used for MQTT broadcast community alerts and notifications
8883	The port used for MQTT SSL broadcast community alerts and notifications

If you install multiple servers on one machine such as installing Sametime Advanced alongside the SSC, different ports may be assigned. To verify which ports are assigned to your Sametime Advanced server, log into the Integrated Solutions Console (ISC), and choose the Sametime Advanced Server under WebSphere Application Servers. You can then view the ports used by your install under the Communications section of the server page.

Features of Sametime Advanced

Installing Sametime Advanced adds many new collaborative features to your existing Sametime environment. These can be seen as **panels** inserted into the interface for the Sametime Connect Client or Notes embedded client, and are part of the Sametime 8.5.2 client install.

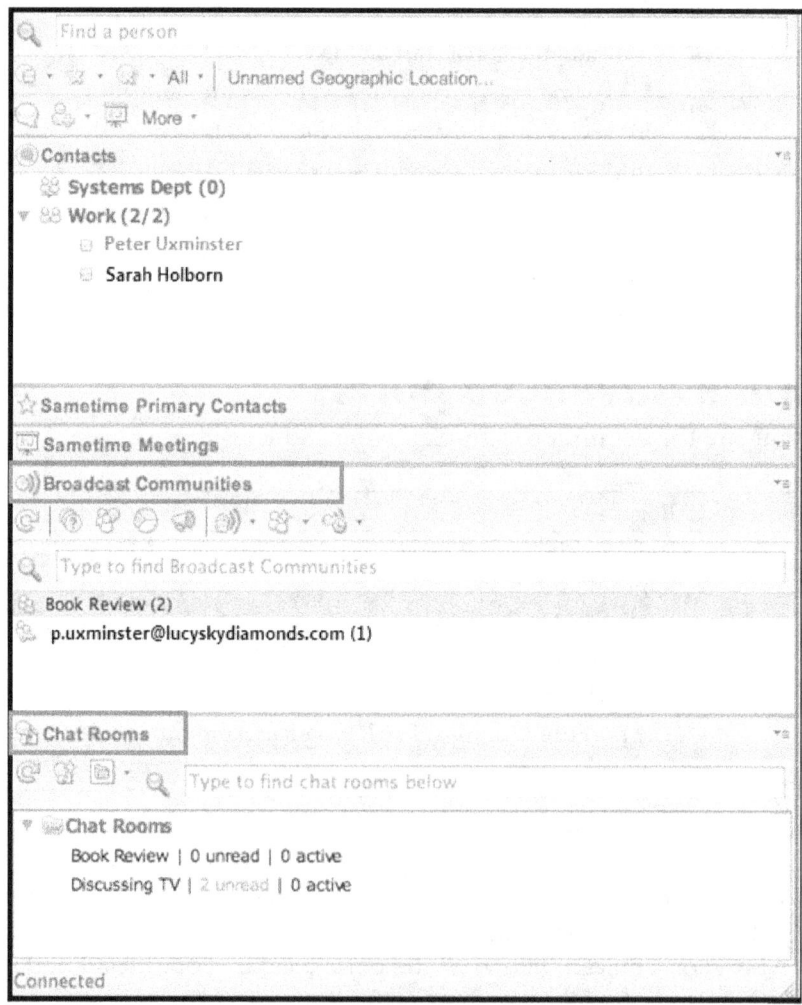

The client features and the related Sametime Advanced preference options can be displayed by changing the following setting of your Sametime `plugin_customization.ini` file, which is found under the `rcp` directory in the Sametime install location:

```
com.ibm.collaboration.realtime/enableAdvanced=true
```

SSC user policies can be created to modify these settings for the Sametime Connect Client and Domino Desktop Policies can be used to control these settings for the embedded Sametime client for the Lotus Notes client.

There is also a web interface available for Sametime Advanced which has a more limited set of functionality than that which is available in the Sametime client.

One of the key features of Sametime Advanced is the ability for users to opt-in to Communities and Chat Rooms of interest to them. If you do not opt-in to a Community, then you are not included in any activities that occur. If you do opt-in, then there are many filtering options to control how and when you get notified. Sametime Advanced is designed to allow you to participate in and contribute to your company's social network on your own terms.

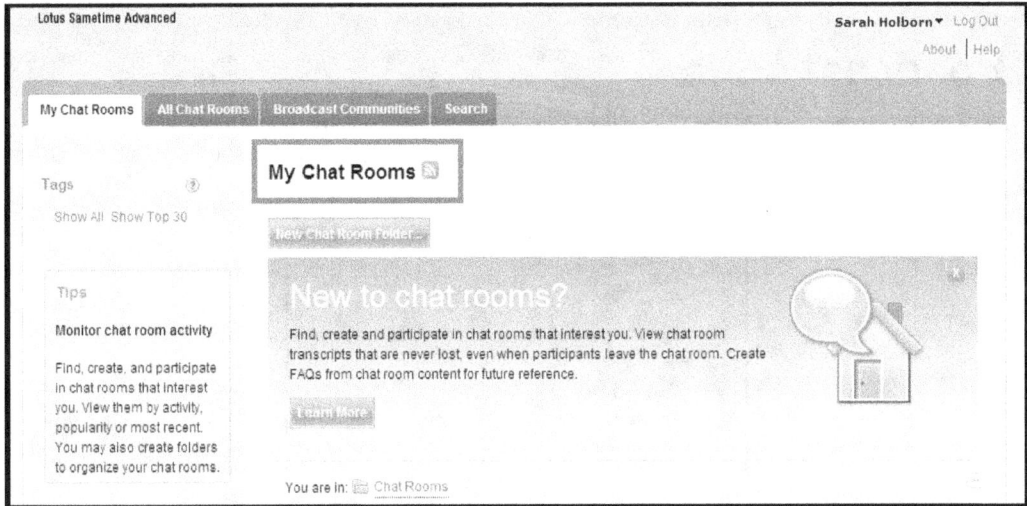

Persistent chats

Instant Messaging is a core Sametime service providing instantaneous connections between people without the formal structure of e-mails. A major drawback to instant messaging is that all the people involved in the chat have to be present and participating at the same time. If one person misses the chat, there is usually no record of the conversations they missed.

Sametime Advanced enables persistent chat rooms where conversations are ongoing, files can be attached for review, and new chat members can read back through transcripts to catch up. Chat Rooms can either be restricted or open based on security needs. Once a user subscribes to a Chat Room, they can easily see the Chat Room activity and if there is anything they need to catch up on.

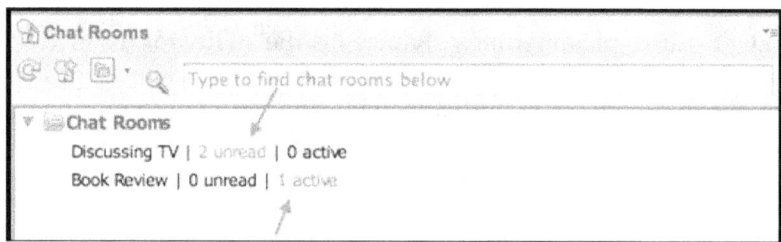

Broadcast suite

Broadcast suites are a range of social networking tools designed to connect skilled people in your company and use real-time communications to gather and share their knowledge with others.

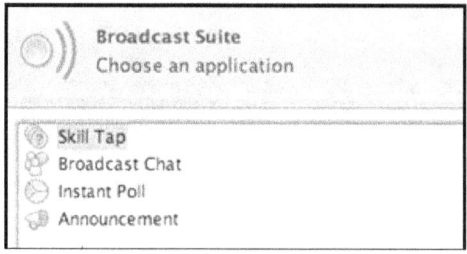

Skill Tap

Skill Tap allows you to ask a community for the answer to a question and search the community's list of previously answered questions for what you need.

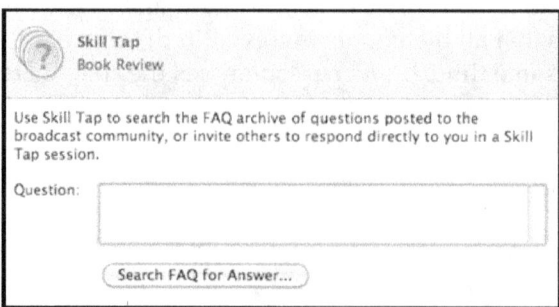

Broadcast Chat

A Broadcast Chat allows you to invite anyone in the community who is available online to join you in an ad-hoc group chat in the Community's Chat Room.

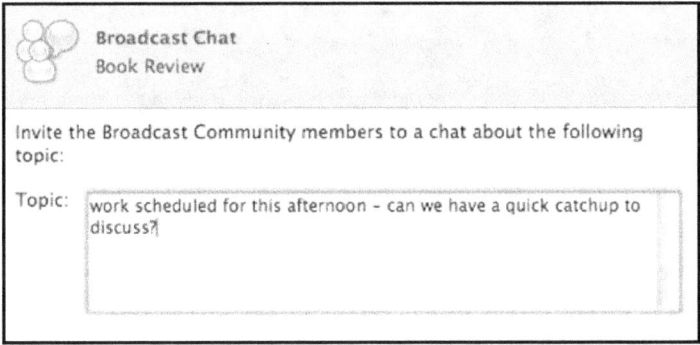

Instant Poll

Instant Poll allows you to create a poll on any topic and send it to your community. The results of the poll are immediately received and tabulated.

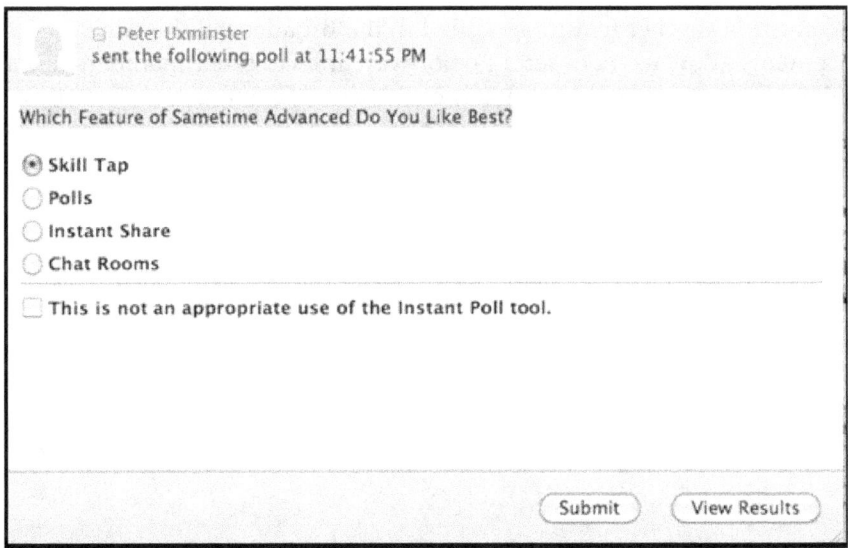

The results are then displayed after participants respond as shown in the following screenshot:

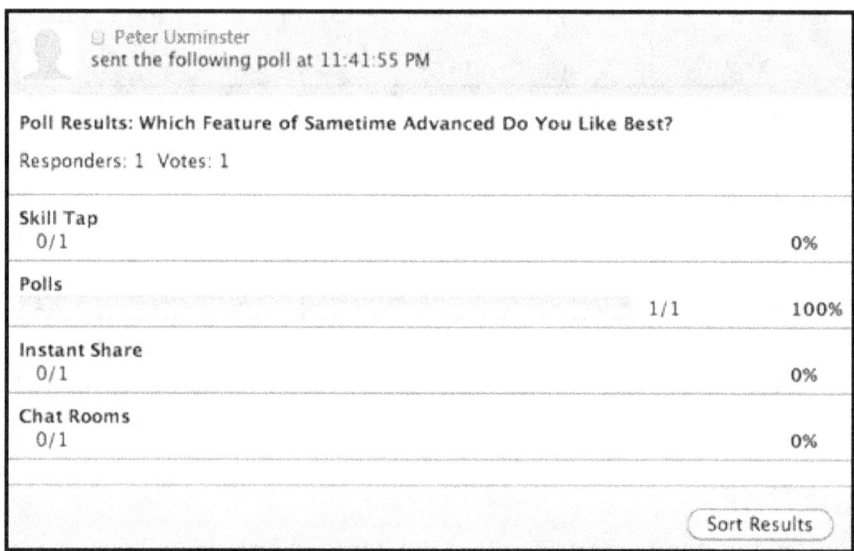

Announcement

Announcement is another feature included in the Broadcast Suite panel. Announcements allow users to send text or web links to other members of the community. Users may use this to notify each other of an upcoming meeting or important event, as in the following example:

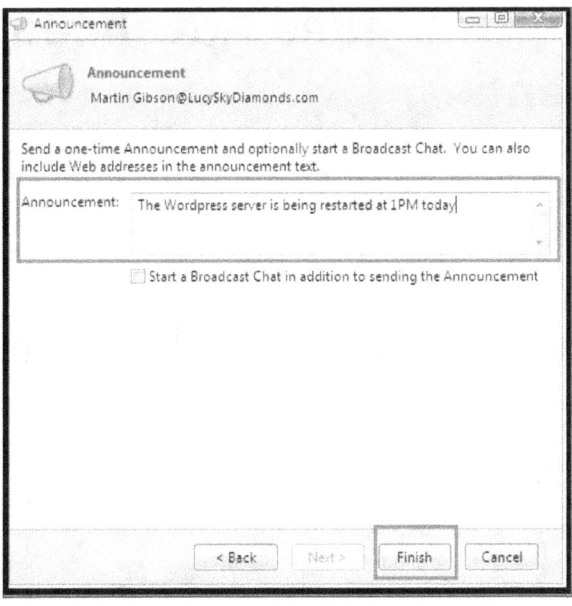

Instant Share

Instant Share is available from your contacts list and allows you to share a single application or your entire desktop with any of your Sametime contacts. Available only within the Sametime Connect or Notes embedded client, the feature is similar to that of Instant Meetings. It uses technology similar to the sharing that is available in the Meeting Center to work but does not require a separate Sametime Meeting server. Instead of creating a full meeting with all the web conferencing functionality, it creates a simple application sharing experience only.

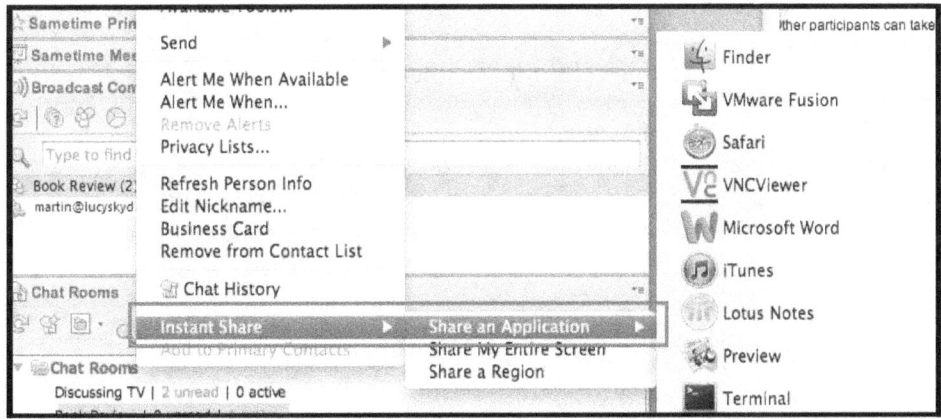

Integrating Sametime Advanced into your environment

Sametime Advanced 8.5.2 is a WebSphere-based application that requires the use of a DB2 database and LDAP for authentication. It can be installed in either stand-alone mode or as part of the SSC, if you are deploying other Sametime components. The full system requirements for Sametime Advanced 8.5.2 are listed at `https://www. ibm.com/support/docview.wss?uid=swg27020283`.

Sametime Advanced requires you to have a Sametime Community Server installed and an LDAP directory for authentication for it to work. It utilizes Single Sign-On (SSO) between the Domino-based Community Server and itself, ensuring that once a user logs into their Sametime Community, they are automatically logged into Sametime Advanced.

Other Sametime components can also be used by Sametime Advanced to enhance its features. The Sametime Proxy Server enables awareness to be shown throughout the browser interface, and the Sametime Meeting Server provides the functionality for Instant Share.

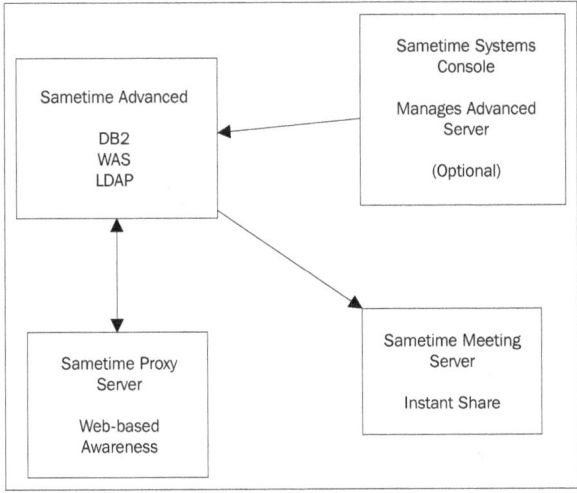

Installing Sametime Advanced

Sametime Advanced can be installed through the SSC, which is a good option to choose if you are managing multiple Sametime servers and want a single consolidated administrative interface. Alternatively, you can install Sametime Advanced as a stand-alone application managed through its own ISC. If you have an earlier version of Sametime Advanced (prior to 8.5.x), it will already have its own ISC. If you are installing through the SSC, then the first step is to create a deployment plan for Sametime Advanced and then use that for the install. Once the deployment plan is in place in the SSC, you can then install the Sametime Advanced package itself.

Creating the deployment plan

You create a new deployment plan for the Sametime Advanced server:

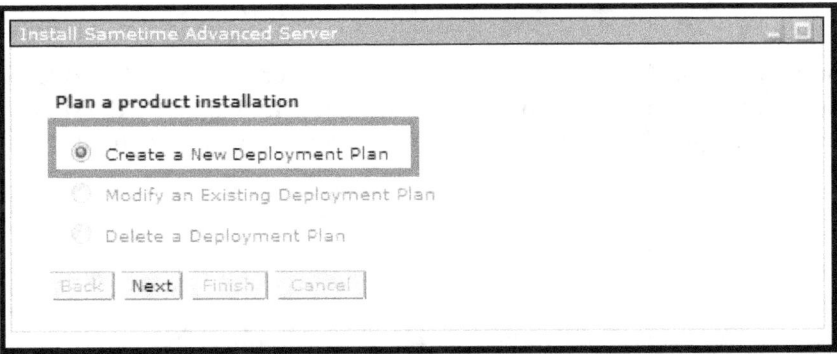

The deployment plan's name can be anything you choose. Your users will never see this name but it will be visible to the Sametime administrator through the SSC. It is usually helpful to use an informative name of some type, such as the location or role of the server.

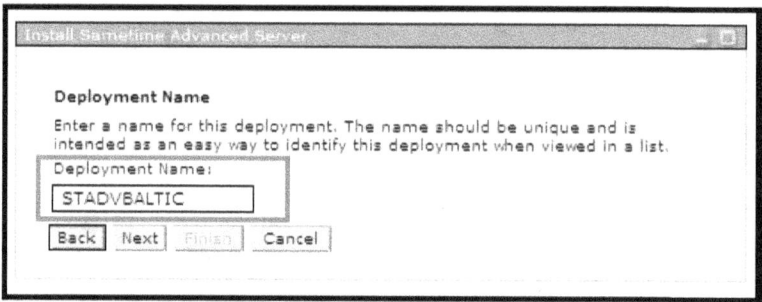

Any WebSphere application needs to be installed into a cell. You can either install Sametime Advanced into its own cell with its own management interface, or into the SSC's cell as either a primary or secondary node. Secondary nodes are only deployed as part of a cluster, so if you were building a cluster of Sametime Advanced servers, you would have a single primary node and multiple secondary nodes grouped together in a cluster.

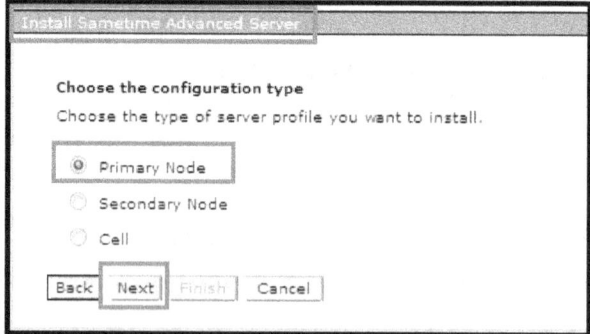

In a default Sametime Advanced installation, the server will be installed as part of the SSC and in the SSC's cell, so its configuration is managed by the same Deployment Manager that is managing the other Sametime components.

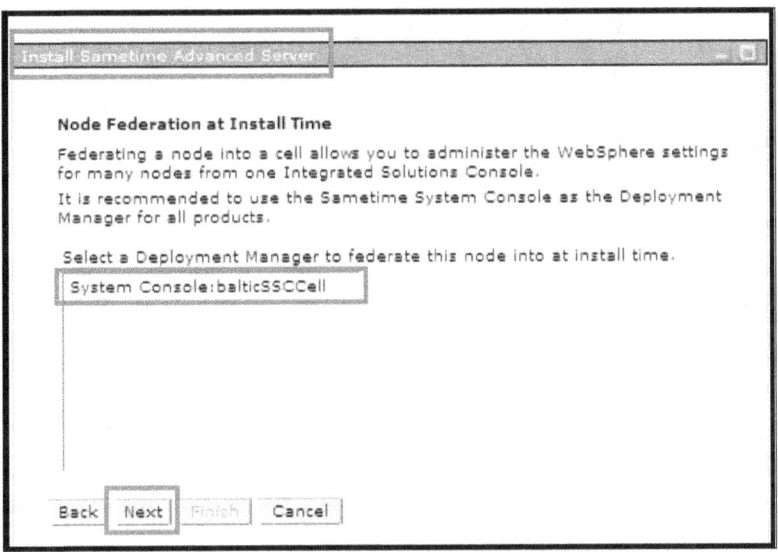

Sametime Advanced has its own user security managed by the Sametime Advanced administrator. There is an option during the deployment plan stage to create a new administrative identity to be used solely for Sametime Advanced settings, but you can choose not to do this in which case your standard SSC administrative account will be used.

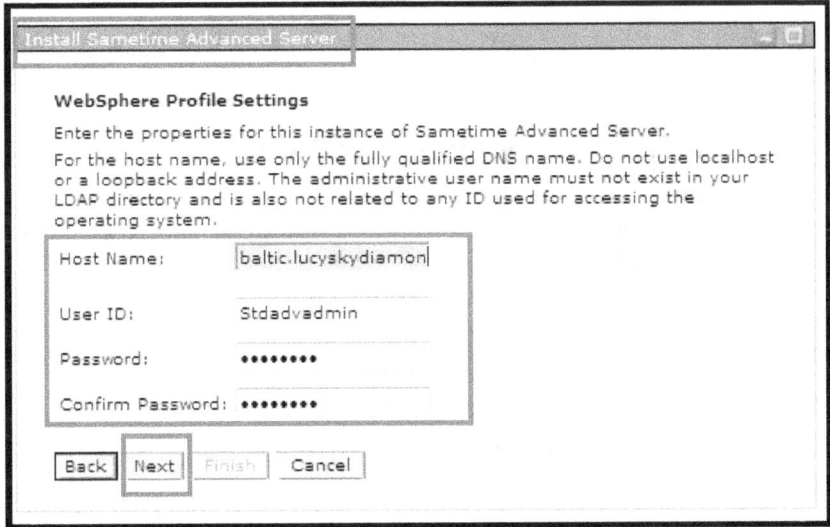

Installing Sametime Advanced software

Once the deployment plan is complete, you can use it to install Sametime Advanced. The server can be installed on a dedicated server or alongside other servers such as the SSC itself. The installer connects back to the SSC and retrieves the deployment profile, using it to configure and complete the install.

Once installed, the Sametime Advanced server should be available through a browser on `http://[hostname]:9080/stadvanced`, although in many installs you will find it installed on port 9081. It is always best to verify through the ISC which ports the server is using. Broadcast tools use port 1883.

The client configuration is completed inside the Sametime preferences, where server name and the ports the server is using are specified. The use of SSO should mean that the user is not prompted again for their credentials upon logging in.

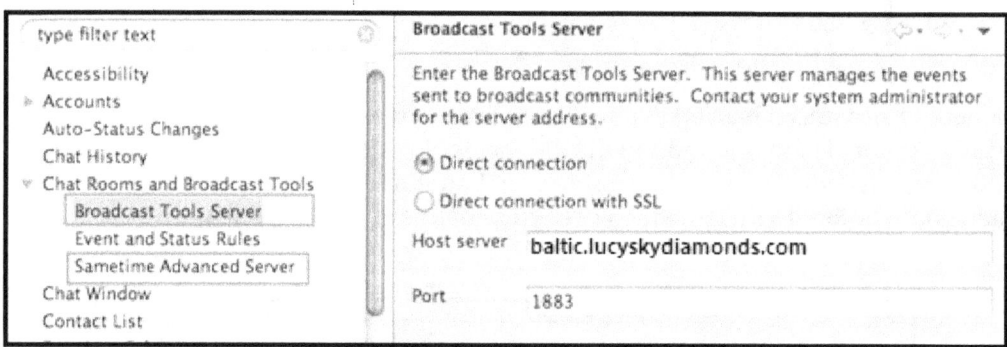

Introducing Sametime Gateway

IBM Sametime Gateway is a stand-alone system for connecting your Sametime Community for instant messaging and presence awareness with other instant messaging communities. IBM Sametime Gateway enables real-time collaboration between your Sametime and:

- External Sametime communities
- Public instant messaging services such as AOL Instant Messenger
- XMPP providers such as Google Talk and Jabber

The Sametime Gateway acts as a broker between those communities and your internal Sametime messaging community. It confirms that the external parties are valid and translates the protocols as necessary. All of this is transparent to the users.

Sametime Gateway can be installed as one server or as a cluster of servers using WAS. Sametime Gateway supports IPv6, but this must be enabled when the gateway is first deployed. Sametime Gateway requires an LDAP server for authentication as well as a DB2 database for storage of system-related files.

Software prerequisites

As always, review the supporting documents that are included in the Sametime download package. They will reference any new requirements regarding software that may need to be installed prior to the installation of Sametime. Additional information about System i requirements can be found at `https://www.ibm.com/support/docview.wss?rs=203&uid=swg21092193`.

Sametime Gateway installation files

Sametime Gateway is available from IBM Passport Advantage in the following packages:

Package file	Purpose
CRE9SML	IBM Sametime Gateway Server v8.5.2 Multiplatform Multilingual eAssy
CZYF9ML	IBM Sametime Gateway Server v8.5.2 Windows IBM i Multilingual
CZG0ML	IBM Sametime Gateway Server v8.5.2 SOL SPARC Multilingual

Sametime Gateway networking

Because the Sametime Gateway connects to external networks like Google and AOL, you will need to confirm that several network ports are open in your firewall to allow communication to those services. One of the deployment methods for Sametime Gateway is to deploy either the Gateway or the SIP Proxy Servers in a DMZ to protect your internal network from possible attack from external sources.

Default port	Purpose
50000	Internal port for communication with DB2
1516	Internal port to communicate with each Sametime Community Server
389 or 636	Port 389 or port 636 (SSL) used to communicate with LDAP server
5269	External port used to communicate with Google Talk or Jabber connections
5061	External port to communicate with AOL or external Sametime communities

Default port	Purpose
5060	External port not using TLS/SSL to external Sametime communities
53	External port to resolve external DNS servers to resolve external community server addresses
5080-5081	Ports required if you are running the SIP proxy

The Sametime Gateway must also be able to access a DNS server in order to resolve public DNS records (A records, SRV records, and PTR records). For example, from the Sametime Gateway, it should be able to resolve the following address with an `nslookup` command:

nslookup sip.oscar.aol.com

nslookup 64.12.162.248

nslookup -type=all -class=all _xmpp-server._tcp.google.com

Features of Sametime Gateway

The primary reason for installing a Sametime Gateway is to expand your instant messaging community beyond your own Sametime environment. The Gateway allows your users to connect to other Sametime communities as well as to external contacts on AOL, Google, and XMPP networks. Communication with external contacts for project or sales-related activities can be an important feature your company or organization may want to consider.

Once the Gateway is set up and connected to the Sametime Community Server in your Sametime environment, Sametime clients will see another option for adding contacts: **Add external user by E-mail address**. Once they choose that option, they can enter the person's external e-mail address and choose an external messaging provider in order to add them to their contact list. Within the Sametime Gateway configuration, you can control whether or not external instant messaging contacts may see awareness of your Sametime Community, as well as control through policies who on your Sametime Community may use the Sametime Gateway.

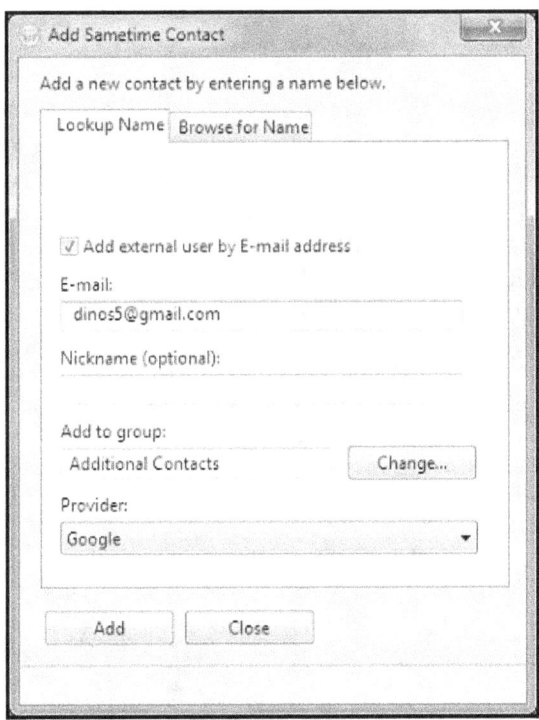

Once the contact has been added, their name will be displayed along with other contacts in the contact list. The only difference is that the awareness icon is specific to their type of connection. Your users should be aware that because awareness updates are network dependent, there may sometimes be a lag in the awareness icon updating once a person logs into the remote network.

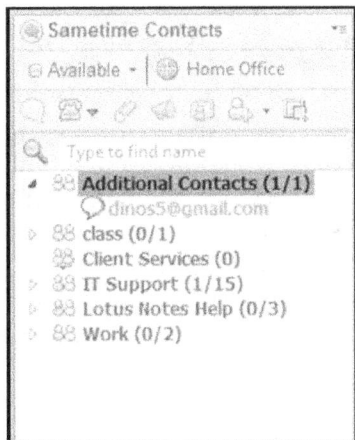

Deployment options for Sametime Gateway

Because the Sametime Gateway connects your corporate or organization's Sametime environment to external instant messaging communities, your security policies may require that you install Sametime Gateway in a fashion that permits limiting the risk to exposure from outside network attacks. Fortunately, the Sametime Gateway is designed with flexibility in mind and allows you to design your environment to fit your corporate firewalls and security procedures.

The Sametime Gateway Server itself needs to communicate with a DB2 server, LDAP server, and your Sametime Community servers. It also may communicate with AOL or XMPP networks such as Jabber or Google.

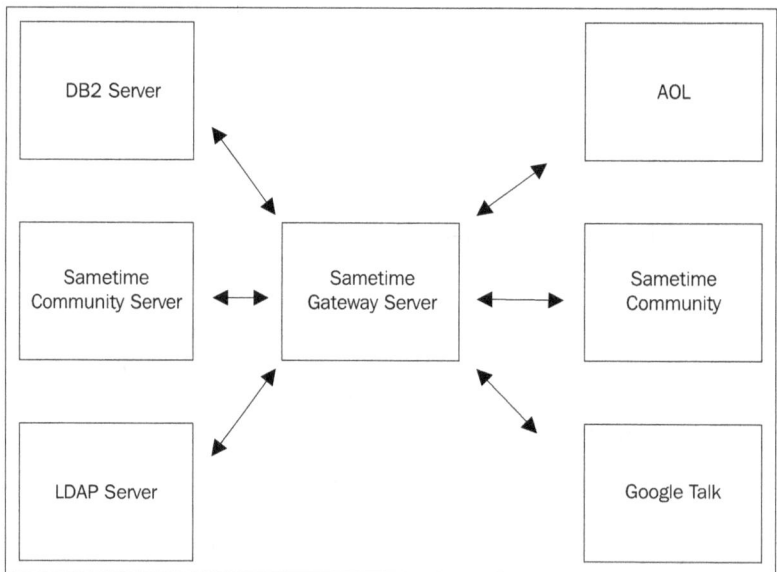

One deployment option is to put a stand-alone Sametime Gateway Server inside your DMZ, while the DB2, LDAP, and Sametime Community servers reside on the internal firewall or protected side of your network. Because the Sametime Gateway Server has its own integrated administrative console, and does not have to connect to the SSC, it can then run inside the DMZ.

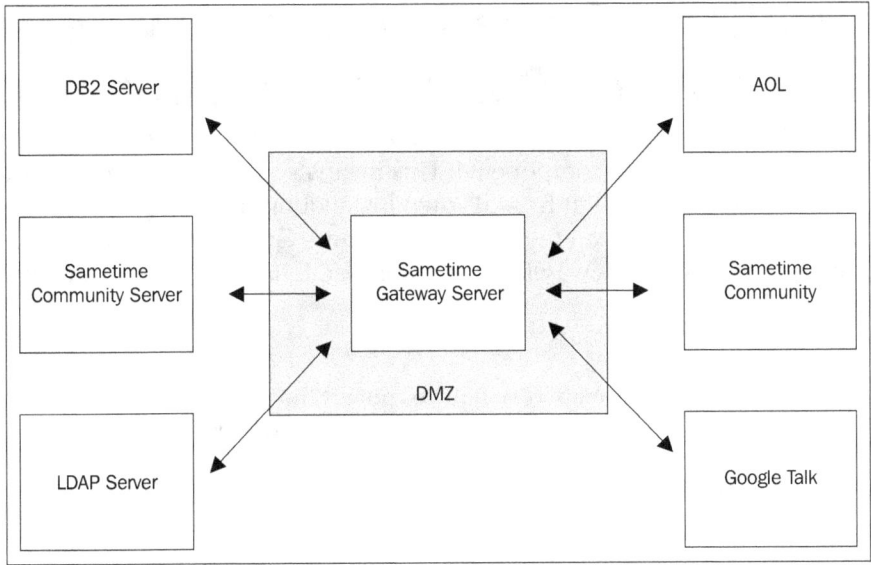

Another method for deployment is to cluster the Gateway Server by installing a separate server for the Deployment Manager and primary node, and then two separate servers for secondary nodes. Additionally, a SIP Proxy Server is used to provide failover to the different clustered nodes. These can all be installed within the DMZ, protecting your DB2, LDAP, and Sametime Community servers from the external network.

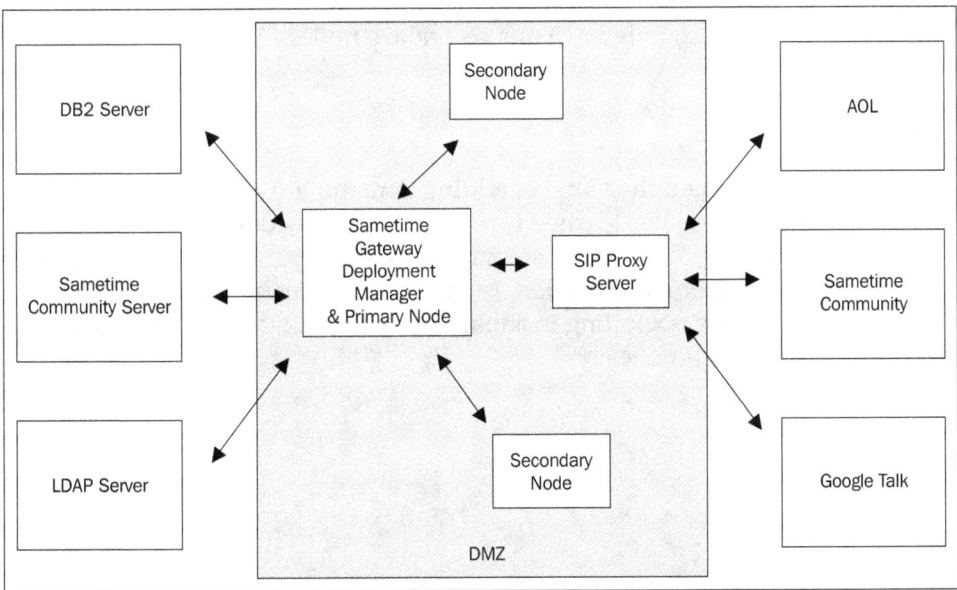

Connecting a Sametime Gateway Server to your existing Sametime environment

It is important to understand that the Sametime Gateway does not have a deployment plan like the other Sametime components. This means you do not begin the install from the SSC. You must install it from its own installation program. Once the installation is complete, you can register the Sametime Gateway with the SSC and administer the Sametime Gateway from there or install it with its own Deployment Manager console.

 For further information on how to connect the Sametime Gateway to the SSC, refer to the IBM Sametime 8.5.2 Installation, Migration, and Configuration Guide at: http://public.dhe.ibm.com/ software/dw/lotus/sametime/st852/st_852_pdfone.pdf.

Coexistence and compatibility

Sametime Gateway 8.0.2 can be upgraded directly to release 8.5.2. But if you have an earlier release, you must perform an interim upgrade to release 8.0.2 before you can upgrade to Sametime Gateway 8.5.2. The install for the upgrade also upgrades WAS from version 6 to version 7. If your Sametime Gateway environment was clustered, then prior to the upgrade you will need to remove each node from the cluster; proceed with upgrading the cluster server and then add them back to the node. In Sametime 8.5.2, you can only have one secondary node.

Summary

In this chapter, you learned the value of adding Sametime Advanced or Gateway to their environment. You also learned how to prepare for connecting Sametime Advanced or a Sametime Gateway system to an existing Sametime 8.5.2 environment and where to go for further information. In the next chapter, you will learn about the various Sametime clients, including installation, customizing install processes, and managing clients through policies.

10
The End User Experience: Preparing for Sametime Client Deployments

So far we have focused on the server aspects of Sametime. But as you know, Sametime includes client software as well. A successful installation, upgrade, or migration of Sametime includes planning for the deployment and management of Sametime clients. We will primarily discuss those aspects of deployment that are new or have changed with Sametime 8.5.2.

- Kadeem's company has several locations and each location uses a different version of the Sametime client. When he upgrades the clients to version 8.5.2, he would like to be able to change the client preferences to a standard set across the company.

- Sam has developed a new plugin for the Sametime client. He would like to keep any actions that his users need to execute to install the plugin to a minimum.

- Tarita is responsible for managing users who use both the Sametime Connect Client and the Sametime Embedded Client. She is interested in preparing new client packages for each group of users.

In this chapter, you will learn the following:

- What Sametime client software is available
- Where do you get the Sametime client packages
- What client versions are available

- How to deploy Sametime client software
  - ° Build new client software packages
  - ° Microsoft Office integration
- How to manage client preferences
  - ° Using the SSC to manage preferences
  - ° Using the Expeditor framework to update Connect Client preferences
  - ° Using the Domino Desktop Policy to manage preferences
  - ° Expeditor preferences
- Audio and video client plugin
- Considerations for upgrading client software

What Sametime client software is available

Your Sametime 8.5.2 environment offers a number of ways to connect users to the Sametime community. These options can be based on desktop configurations, device usage, or administration support considerations.

Sametime Connect

Sametime Connect is the Sametime client that offers the most power and functionality when using Sametime. It runs as a stand-alone client, and is not dependent on any other desktop software.

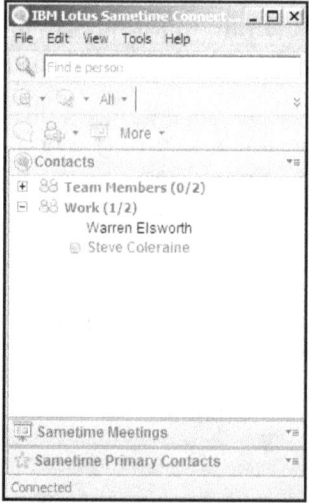

The Sametime Connect Client is a good choice if you want your users to connect and utilize the full range of Sametime features, such as Sametime Advanced and Sametime Meetings.

Notes embedded Sametime client

If you use Lotus Notes, the Notes embedded Sametime client runs as a plugin to the Notes client. When the user starts Lotus Notes, the Sametime client also launches and runs within Notes.

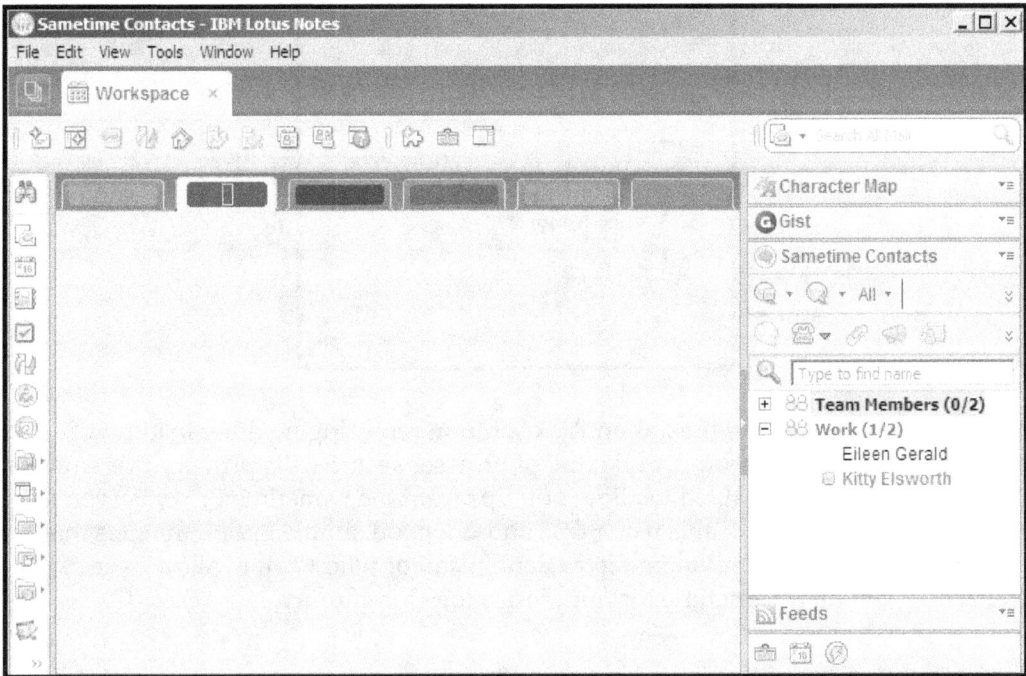

The Sametime client embedded within Notes is a good option for environments that already use Lotus Notes and want to minimize the number of client software packages deployed to the desktop. It offers much the same functionality of the Sametime Connect Client, but from within the Lotus Notes desktop. While the Sametime software is "embedded" as part of the Lotus Notes client, you still have the option to upgrade the Sametime software version independently of the Lotus Notes client version. Additionally, the Lotus Notes packages provided on the IBM Passport Advantage download site contain embedded versions of Sametime.

Sametime browser client

If you do not want to deploy any additional software at all but still use Sametime in your organization, another option for the desktop is to use the browser-based client which comes with the Sametime Proxy Server. This rich instant messaging client has many of the standard features available in the full client, such as rich-text instant messaging, n-way chats, ability to set privacy, status, and add groups. However, it does not provide functionality to make audio or video calls.

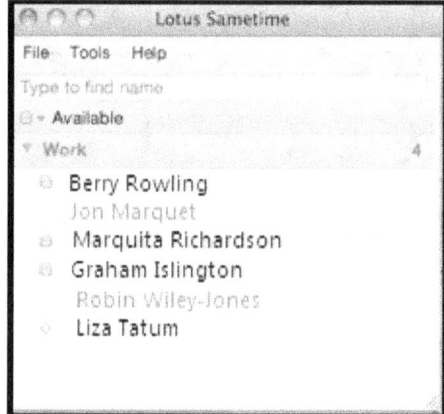

The browser client is designed as an Ajax solution requiring no downloading of additional plugins, software, or relaxing of browser security. Its primary prerequisite is that the browser is enabled to allow pop ups from the Sametime Proxy Server. The browser client is customizable using CSS and is a good simple option for sites that do not want to roll out and maintain a client install or who want to allow external contacts to join their Sametime Instant Messaging Community.

Mobile Sametime clients

For users that are mobile or who need to communicate away from their computers, there are Sametime clients for many mobile devices, such as Blackberry, Windows 7, Nokia, Sony Ericsson, Apple phones and devices, and Android phones and devices. These clients are designed to fit the smaller form factor of mobile devices while still offering core Sametime functionality. The following chapter will delve into the world of the mobile client in greater detail, so we will not cover the mobile Sametime details here.

Downloading Sametime software

The Sametime software for the Sametime Connect and Notes embedded clients can be found on and downloaded from the IBM Passport Advantage site. The part number for the download is CZYF7ML.zip, and it includes the following items:

- Sametime embedded client for Lotus Notes
- Sametime network installation
- Sametime Connect Client
- Optional components (such as Microsoft Office integration, e-mail integration, and spell check dictionaries)
- Sametime/Outlook integration software components
- Sametime/SharePoint integration software components

Once you download the main file, you can decompress and install the parts of Sametime that pertain to your installation plans.

The Sametime browser client is automatically installed when you install the Sametime Proxy Server and connect it to your Community Server. It can be found by directing your browser to http:<proxyserverhost>:port/stwebclient/index.jsp.

Sametime client versions

The Sametime Connect Client is supported on a wide variety of desktop operating systems. The supported operating systems include:

- Mac OS X 10.6.2 Snow Leopard x86-64 and future OS fix packs
- Windows 7 Enterprise/Professional/Ultimate, both x86-32 and x86-64 versions
- Windows Vista Business/Enterprise, both x86-32 and x86-64 versions
- Windows XP SP2 Professional x86-32/x86-64 and future OS fix packs
- Windows XP Tablet PC Edition x86-32
- Red Hat Enterprise Linux (RHEL) 5.0 Update 4 Desktop editions x86-32 and future OS fix packs
- SUSE Linux Enterprise Desktop (SLED) 10.0 SP3/11.0 SP1, x86-32 and future OS fix packs
- Ubuntu 10.04 LTS x86-32 and future OS fix packs
- Internet Explorer 6, 7, and 8
- Firefox 3.0, 3.5+
- Safari 3.2, 4.0

If you plan to install the Sametime embedded client, then it is recommended that you have at least Lotus Notes 8.5.1 FP1 installed. Lotus Notes 8.5.1 FP4 is the preferred version.

Each supported operating system has various hardware and software requirements, along with various optional supported configurations and supplemental software, such as Java and web browsers. To get the most up-to-date information on these requirements, go to the Sametime wiki at the following URL: `https://www.ibm.com/support/docview.wss?rs=477&uid=swg27019598&wv=1`.

Deploying Sametime client software

You have all your Sametime servers installed, and now you are ready for the Sametime end-user software deployment of the Sametime Connect Client or Sametime Embedded client that is used with Lotus Notes. Your organization or company may already be using one or both of these products, but you will want to know how to install the new 8.5.2 client, build a custom install package, and push automatic updates. In the next few sections, we discuss some of your options for accomplishing these goals.

Customizing the client installation package

Sametime provides the ability for you as an administrator to customize the Sametime client installation package specifically for your environment. This allows you to modify features so that they meet your organization's security or login requirements, include extra features such as Microsoft Office integration, or include a custom plugin. You might also have a requirement for adding additional dictionaries or including the Sametime Embedded client in your Lotus Notes installation. All of these options are available to you to build a custom deployment. To customize the installation packages, the following three files are involved:

- `plugin_customization.ini`
- `install.xml`
- `install.addon.xml`

You will find these files in the directories specific to the type of install package you are planning.

The `plugin_customization.ini` file can be modified to include features (plugins) and change preferences for those features. This file is read when the client software starts for the first time. This file cannot be changed after the software is installed, but you can apply preferences using the SSC console or Domino policies as we will demonstrate later in the chapter.

If your plans include modifying the installation package for the Sametime Connect Client, then you will be modifying the `install.xml` file. This file contains the list of features that are included with Sametime Connect. Edit this file and uncomment those features that you want to have included in the installation package. The `install.xml` file is also used to customize network-based installations (file download location or Sametime Welcome page). For example, you can modify the `install.xml` to include the Microsoft Office integration features for Windows-based clients when installing Sametime Connect.

To customize the installation package for the Sametime Embedded client, modify the `install.addon.xml`. This file, like the `install.xml` file, can be edited to include features such as spell-checker dictionaries so that they are included in the Sametime Embedded client when the client software is first installed.

Preparing Sametime Connect Client packages for distribution

Your users can install the Sametime Connect Client from either a CD, download site, or the Sametime Welcome page. After you download the `CZYF7ML.zip` file from the IBM Passport Advantage website, extract it to a temporary location on your server so you can begin familiarizing yourself with the files contained in the package. It includes the client build for the stand-alone client and embedded client for Linux, Windows, and Mac operating systems. It also includes directories for use when building network install packages, optional feature directories, and the `install.xml`, `install.addon.xml`, and `plugin_customization.ini` files for the appropriate OS and client builds.

Creating a Welcome Page download package

In addition to creating a CD image of the Sametime clients, you can also make them available for download from the Sametime Welcome Page URL that is usually hosted by the Sametime Community Server. If you have an earlier version of Sametime, you may be familiar with this website.

To make a package available, you must go through the following steps. First, customize your install package as you did when creating your CD image. This may require you to modify the `install.xml`, `install.addon.xml`, or `plugin_customization.ini` files depending on what type of package you are building. Next, copy the downloaded files into the Sametime Community Server directory: `servername\domino\html\sametime\network-install`. For example: `c:\ibm\lotus\domino\data\domino\html\sametime\network-install`

After you have completed the download, edit the update installer site properties information by editing the `\data\domino\html\sametime\network-install\applet\download.properties` file. The value of the `installer.root.base` value should match the URL of your Sametime Community Server. For example: `installer.root.base=http://st.lucyskydiamonds.com/sametime/network-install`. Save this file.

The last step is to run the **ArchiveCreator** tool to build the downloadable ZIP files. The ArchiveCreator will include all of the customizations you have made. The ArchiveCreator tool can be found in the `\data\domino\html\sametime\network-install\bin` directory. Place the resulting ZIP files in the `servername\domino\data\domino\html\sametime\network-install directory`.

Adding or updating client features

Perhaps you have deployed Sametime, but you have decided you want to extend the feature set your users are using. What are your options for upgrading the clients?

- Push features and updates automatically
- Allow users to choose which updates they will install
- Create zip files for your users to use to install the updates manually

 We recommend the first two options as they are easier to implement and less apt to cause help desk calls.

To enable the automatic push of features and updates to the stand-alone Sametime client, you must first set up the Sametime update site URL. This is done from the SSC, in the **Managed Policies | Instant Messaging** tab. Once the site is set up, the client process will check the update site setting each time a user logs into Sametime. If the update site is configured, the client process will download any features and install them. The user will then be prompted to restart Sametime.

For optional features or plugins, you can create an optional update policy. This is also accomplished using the SSC on the **Managed Policies | Instant Messaging** tab. After this Sametime optional update site URL is configured, the client process checks to see if an optional update site is configured when a user logs into Sametime. If updates or optional plugins are available, the user will be prompted to choose whether or not they want to deploy the option or update the software. The user can also disable checking for further updates. This process cannot be used for deploying Microsoft Office integration.

For Sametime embedded within the Notes client, the behavior for deploying features and updates is slightly different. In that, any plugin must first be converted to a widget and deployed to the Notes client through Domino policies.

Integrating Microsoft Office with Sametime

If you are running Sametime on a Windows or Mac environment, you have the option to allow Microsoft Office (including Outlook and SharePoint) to integrate Sametime as the instant messaging client of choice. This integration installs a Sametime menu bar in the Microsoft application, which allows you to start chats and use other Sametime features.

The following screenshot is an example of how the integration of Sametime and Outlook would appear:

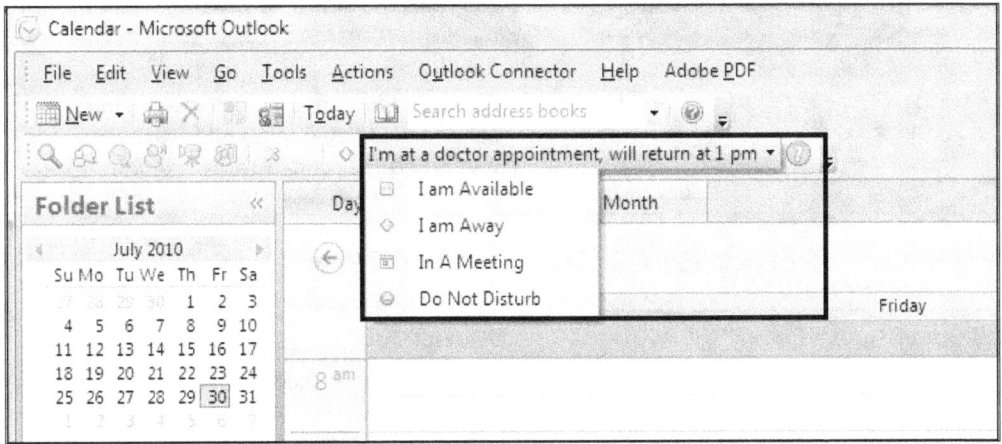

As these features are not activated by default in the Sametime client, you need to edit an XML file to include them in the installation package. If you are installing the Notes embedded client, the `install.addon.xml` file should be modified. The file to modify for a Sametime Connect Client install is `install.xml`. The Microsoft integration features will be commented out. To have them install by default, uncomment the particular lines and repackage the installation files. There is no need to include options that your users will not be implementing, but use caution when modifying the `install.xml` or `install.addon.xml` as you would not want to affect the base installation of Sametime features.

The Microsoft features for the embedded client (`install.addon.xml`) are as follows:

Feature	Description
`com.ibm.collaboration.realtime.exchange`	Provides automatic availability status updates in Sametime based on Outlook calendar entries
`com.ibm.collaboration.realtime.oi.sharepoint.feature`	Provides awareness and instant messaging between Sametime users who are using a SharePoint site
`com.ibm.collaboration.realtime.oi.toolbar`	Provides an action toolbar in Outlook containing Sametime instant messaging actions, including access to the contact list, status, and location information
`com.ibm.collaboration.realtime.oi.webConfTab`	Provides the ability to reserve Sametime meetings from the Sametime tab in Outlook meetings
`com.ibm.collaboration.realtime.oi.smarttags`	Provides Sametime instant messaging actions in Office document Smart Tags menu and the toolbar for Word, Excel, and PowerPoint

The features for the Sametime Connect Client (`install.xml`) are as follows:

Feature	Description
`com.ibm.collaboration.realtime.oi.standalone.feature`	Required: Sametime Connect Client feature (required when you add any Office optional features to the installation file for Sametime Connect Clients)
`com.ibm.collaboration.realtime.oi.smarttags.feature`	Sametime Connect integrator for Office
`com.ibm.collaboration.realtime.exchange.feature`	Outlook calendar availability

Feature	Description
`com.ibm.collaboration.` `realtime.oi.toolbar.feature`	Sametime Connect integrator for Outlook
`com.ibm.collaboration.` `realtime.oi.webConfTab.feature`	Sametime meeting integrator for Outlook
`com.ibm.collaboration.` `realtime.oi.sharepoint.feature`	Sametime Connect integrator for SharePoint

An example of the options included in an `install.xml` is as follows. Two options have been enabled as they are no longer in the commented section of the `install.xml`. The commented section begins with `<!--` and ends with `-->`.

```
<requirements>

<feature action="install" download-size="390" id="com.ibm.
collaboration.realtime.exchange.feature" match="compatible"
mergeaction="add" shared="true" size="461" url=""
version="8.5.2.20110510-1632" />

<feature action="install" download-size="15323" id="com.ibm.
collaboration.realtime.oi.sharepoint.feature" match="compatible"
mergeaction="add" shared="true" size="15733" url=""
version="8.5.2.20110510-1632" />

<!--
The following Sametime features are optional, and may be uncommented
in order to be deployed.

<feature action="install" download-size="17087" id="com.ibm.
collaboration.realtime.oi.smarttags.feature" match="compatible"
mergeaction="add" shared="true" size="20275" url=""
version="8.5.2.20110510-1632" />

<feature action="install" download-size="120" id="com.ibm.
collaboration.realtime.oi.standalone.feature" match="compatible"
mergeaction="add" shared="true" size="89" url=""
version="8.5.2.20110510-1632" />

<feature action="install" download-size="31628" id="com.ibm.
collaboration.realtime.oi.toolbar.feature" match="compatible"
mergeaction="add" shared="true" size="35753" url=""
version="8.5.2.20110510-1632" />
-->

</requirements>
```

Managing client preferences

How often have you, as an administrator, wanted to manage the Sametime settings for your users? Now with Sametime 8.5.2, you have the ability to manage Sametime client preferences either through SSC policies for the Sametime Connect Client or through Domino Desktop Policies for the Sametime Embedded client. Both methods give you the ability to centrally manage and update Sametime user preferences with minimal user interaction, other than requiring them to login or restart their Sametime client. Because you can deploy multiple policies, you can also establish role-based preference sets for your various groups of users based on their specific requirements. You may also designate settings as read-only so that users cannot modify them.

Configuring Sametime Connect Client preferences using SSC policies

A feature included with Sametime 8.5.2 is the ability to configure Sametime Connect Client policies from the SSC. Policies set with the SSC cannot be modified by the user. To use the SSC to set a policy, begin by going to the SSC and click on **Manage Policies**.

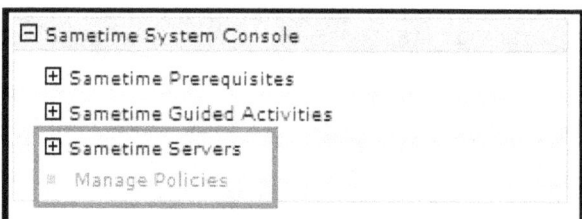

The **Instant Messaging** tab of the **Manage Policies** view provides two preconfigured polices for instant messaging:

- Sametime Instant Messaging Default Policy
- Sametime Instant Messaging Anonymous Policy

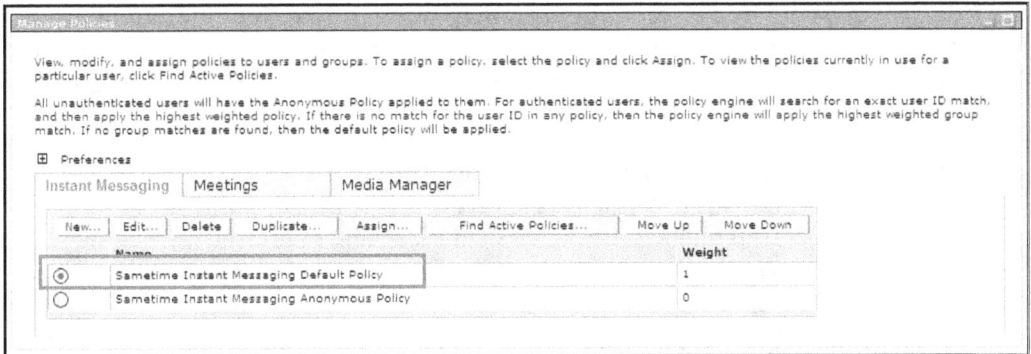

As its name implies, the **Sametime Instant Messaging Default Policy** is assigned to all authenticated users by default. You can, however, create additional policies for individual users or groups of users that take precedence over the default policy. Click on **New** to create a new policy. In our example, we create a policy called **LucySkyDiamonds User Policy**. To begin assigning users to the new policy, click on the **Assign** button.

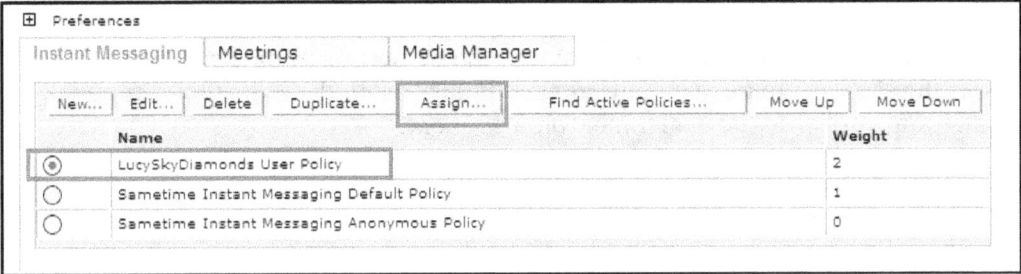

Clicking on **Add Users** or **Add Groups** displays a panel which allows you to choose those individuals who should be assigned to this policy.

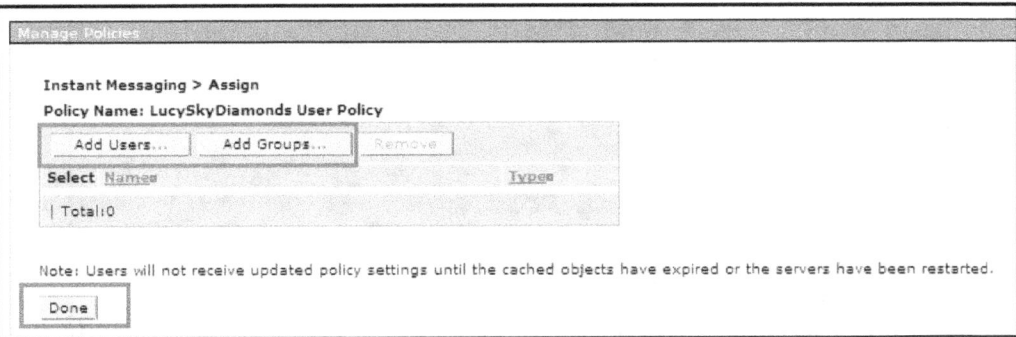

The policies do not go into effect until the policy cache has expired, the Sametime Community Servers have restarted, or the user logs off and logs back into Sametime. The default time for Policy Timeout Cache and Group Membership Timeout Cache is 30 minutes each.

These policy settings are the same ones available through the Community Server's Domino browser administration interface; however, if your Community Server is managed by the SSC, the policy settings applied there will overwrite any settings you have put in place directly in the Domino browser.

Client preferences

If you want to modify specific client options for your user policy, then select the policy name and then click on **Edit**. The following panels are displayed in one long display, but we have broken them up to describe each one individually.

The **Chat** preferences panel allows you to specify whether or not the transcript of chats can be saved by users. Your organization or company may have an information security policy that governs the collection of this type of conversation, and this policy allows you to control that option.

Another important selection on this panel is the **Sametime update site URL (IC)**. This is the site used to push out automatic updates using the Expeditor Framework. This setting applies to the Sametime Connect Client.

The **Image Settings** and **File Transfer** panels allow you to control whether or not you want your users to use custom emoticons or do screen captures, as well as controlling the size of the file they can attach through the Sametime Connect Client. Remember that you can set up these policies for specific groups of users, or make these changes to the global default policy.

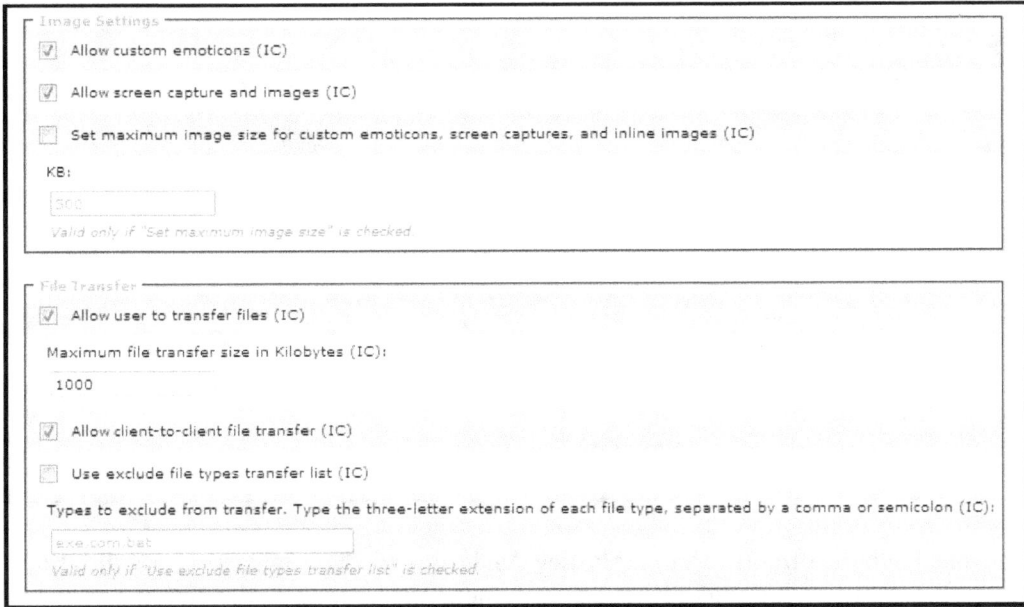

The **Plugin Management** panel allows you to control whether or not the user has the ability to install plugins. You can also set up a standard web page for use for deploying plugins, optional features, or client updates. If you have a large environment, you can set up multiple URL sites and list them in the **Sametime optional plug-in site URL** box separated by a comma or a semicolon.

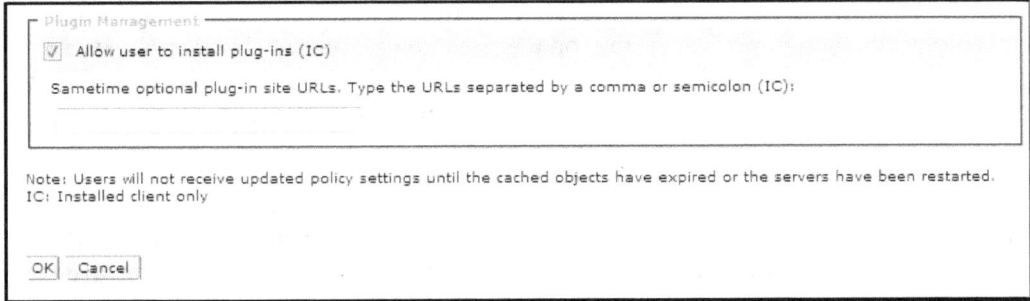

Policy Preferences

If you click on **Preferences**, then you have the option to set when and how the preferences you set with the SSC policy go into effect. The **Cache Timeout** options only apply to the SSC and the Sametime Meeting Center.

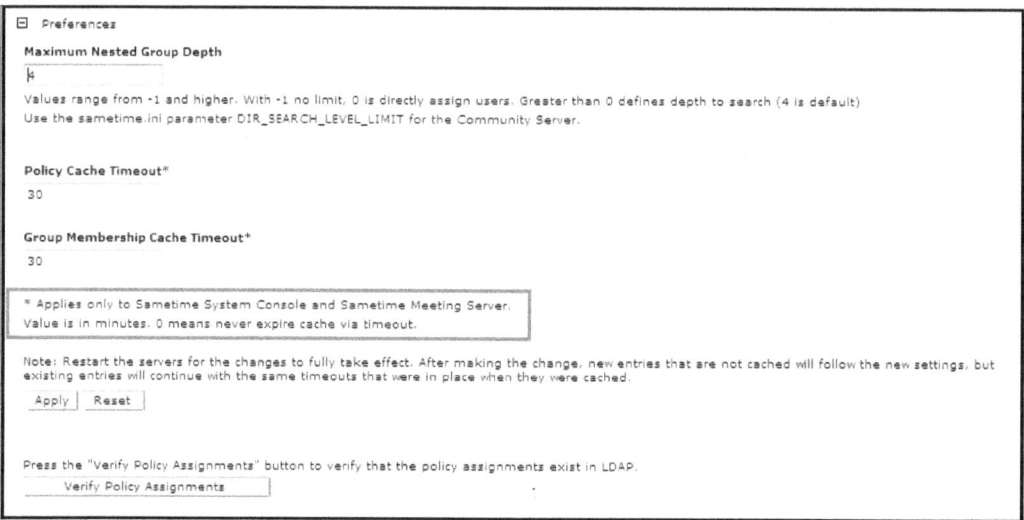

You also have the option to **Verify Policy Assignments**. This is useful for validating any policy changes you make before rolling them out in your environment.

Using the Expeditor framework to update Connect Client preferences

Along with the SSC policies, you can use the Expeditor framework to create a structure for managing preferences using an update website and a `managed-settings.xml` file. With the Expeditor framework, the Connect Client will check for updates each time a user logs into Sametime. Depending on the parameter, you can choose if the user has the ability to modify the preference, when a preference will be updated, and if the client must be restarted in order for the preference to go into effect.

The `managed-settings.xml` file is used to manage and modify Sametime Connect preferences. With policies set with the SSC, you can create multiple sets of preferences for each type of user you may have in your environment. The clients receive the updates either at login time, when the Sametime servers have restarted, or when the cache has expired.

Begin by creating an update website. For illustration purposes, we will create one called `http://stupdate.lucyskydiamonds.com/updates`. When the Connect Client connects to the server, it looks for the `managed-settings.xml` file to see if any settings have changed. For many of the preferences, you can change the setting to `locked="true"`, which will prevent the user from being able to modify the preference. Note that the `managed-settings.xml` file takes precedence over any equivalent preferences in the `plugin_customization.ini` file.

As you can specify multiple policies, you can also set up a policy that references a URL for your test environment. Create a new `managed-settings.xml` file, and apply the policy with the test URL to a subset of users to test the changes you have made.

Here, we have an example of a `managed-settings.xml` file. This file sets the options to hide the **prevent transcript save** checkbox in a chat window and to disable awareness when reviewing chat history. Both options can subsequently be changed by the user by using the following code snippet:

```
<ManagedSettings>
<settingGroup name="com.ibm.collaboration.realtime.chat.
                    logging.ui"
<setting name="allowSaveOverride" value="false" isLocked="false"/>
<setting name="noPersonListLiveNames" value="false" isLocked="false"/>
</settingGroup>
</ManagedSettings>
```

Using Domino Desktop Policies to update Embedded Client preferences

Because the Sametime Embedded Client is packaged as part of the Notes client, you must use Domino Desktop Policies to, if you want to, update or modify Sametime client preferences centrally. Using the Domino Administrator client, **Desktop Settings** are found on the **Configuration** tab. You can select **Policies | Settings** to view the Desktop Policy documents that may be in place in your Domino Directory. Open the appropriate Desktop Settings document you would like to modify, and click on the **Custom Settings** tab. Click on **Managed Settings**, then click on **Edit list**.

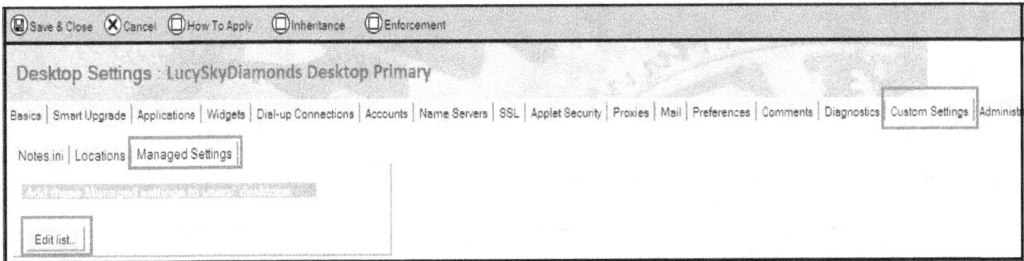

The setting panel allows you to add the Eclipse plugin/preference name, the item to be deployed, and the value of that item. In our example, we are working with the plugin name `com.ibm.collaboration.realtime.location`. The item is **showProfWindow** and the value is **true**. By clicking on **Add/Modify Value** and then **OK**, we add this to the Managed setting for the users' desktop. The Desktop Policy will go into effect the next time the user logs into Notes. The Notes client dynamic configuration will check the Desktop Policies to determine if anything needs to be modified and update any settings as required. You can set up multiple Desktop Policies for individuals or groups of users.

It is important to note that settings made here supplement, but do not override, Sametime policy settings made in the SSC.

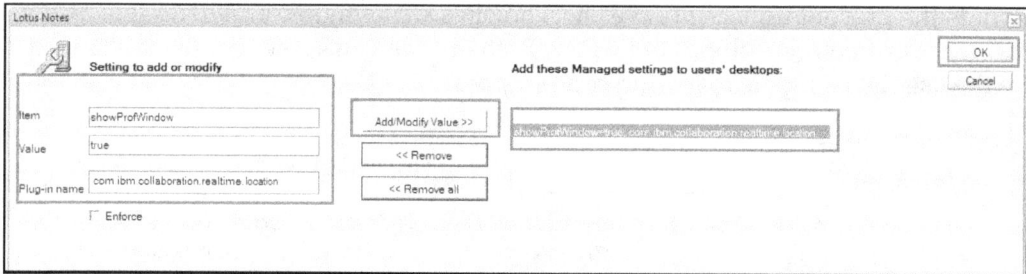

Expeditor preferences

The following is a list of the Sametime plugins that are included with the product. Refer to the IBM Sametime 8.5.2 wiki for further detail regarding the options you can set for each client in each feature group at the following site: `http://www.lotus.com/ldd/stwiki.nsf/dx/Sametime_client_preferences_st852`.

Sametime plugin name	Preference
`com.ibm.collaboration.realtime.accessibility`	Accessibility preferences
`com.ibm.collaboration.realtime.imhub`	Auto-status change preferences
`com.ibm.collaboration.realtime.calendar`	Calendar preferences
`com.ibm.collaboration.realtime.application`	Chat application preferences
`com.ibm.collaboration.realtime.chat.logging`	Chat history preferences
`com.ibm.collaboration.realtime.chat.logging.ui`	Chat history UI preferences

Sametime plugin name	Preference
`com.ibm.collaboration.realtime.chatwindow`	Chat window preferences
`com.ibm.collaboration.realtime.community`	Community server preferences
`com.ibm.collaboration.realtime.imhub`	Contact list preferences
`com.ibm.collaboration.realtime.ui`	External application preferences
`com.ibm.collaboration.realtime.filetransfer`	File transfer preferences
`com.ibm.collaboration.realtime.location`	Location preferences
`com.ibm.collaboration.realtime.login`	Login preferences
`com.ibm.collaboration.realtime.calendar.notes.connector`	Lotus Notes preferences
`com.ibm.collaboration.realtime.meetings`	Meeting preferences
`com.ibm.rtc.meetings.shelf`	Meeting preferences (8.5.x or higher)
`com.ibm.rtc.meetings.appshare`	Meeting Appshare preferences (8.5.x or higher)
`com.ibm.rtc.meetings.ui`	Meeting User interface preferences (8.5.2 or higher)
`com.ibm.rtc.meetings.participants`	Meeting Participant preferences (8.5.1.1 or higher)
`com.ibm.rtc.meetings.polling`	Meeting Polling preferences (8.5.1.1 or higher)
`com.ibm.collaboration.realtime.alertmanager`	Notification preferences
`com.ibm.collaboration.realtime.people`	People preferences
`com.ibm.collaboration.realtime.rtcadapter`	RTC adapter plugin preferences
`com.ibm.collaboration.realtime.telephony.sti.rulesmgr`	Rules Manager preferences (8.5.1 or higher)
`com.ibm.collaboration.realtime`	Sametime Advanced and Telephony—Global preferences
`com.ibm.collaboration.community`	Sametime Advanced—Community preferences
`com.ibm.collaboration.realtime.instantshare`	Sametime Advanced—Instant Share preferences

Sametime plugin name	Preference
`com.ibm.collaboration.realtime.spellchecker`	Spell checker preferences
`com.ibm.collaboration.realtime.telephony.ui`	Telephony, Audio and Video preferences (8.5 or higher)
`com.ibm.collaboration.realtime.update`	Update preferences (8.5.x or higher)

Audio-visual plugin

In order to attend and participate in meetings requiring audio and video using a browser-based Sametime client, you need to install the Sametime audio-visual plugin. This plugin works with Windows and Mac clients that use Internet Explorer or Mozilla Firefox as their browsers.

Normally, your browser will prompt you to install the plugin when you attend your first browser-based meeting in Sametime. A pop-up message will ask you to install the IBM Sametime WebPlayer control. Once the control is installed, you will be able to fully participate in the meeting. This control is 32-bit only and requires a 64-bit browser to be restarted in 32-bit mode.

For detailed information on the particular prompts that occur during the installation, or to learn how to install the plugin prior to a meeting, please refer to the following URL from the Sametime Wiki documentation site:

`http://www.lotus.com/ldd/stwiki.nsf/dx/Installing_and_uninstalling_Sametime_web_audiovisual_plugin_for_browserbased_meeting_clients_sta852`

Considerations for upgrading Sametime clients

When you upgrade your Sametime server environment to version 8.5.2, you need to plan to upgrade your Sametime clients to version 8.5.2 to benefit from the features you are deploying, such as audio and video, as well as ensuring that you are able to take advantage of the latest performance improvements. If your current environment includes Sametime clients running Sametime version 7.5.1 or higher, the clients can upgrade directly to Sametime 8.5.2. The following are some items to keep in mind when planning your client upgrade:

- If you have clients running the Sametime Unified Telephony plugin from a version earlier than 8.5.1, you will need to uninstall the plugin before upgrading. The plugin can be uninstalled using the operating system uninstaller.

- Upgrading the Sametime client software will not upgrade the optional Microsoft Office integration features unless you include them in your new 8.5.2 client package. Otherwise, the older version will continue to be used by the new client installation.

- If you are upgrading Sametime 7.5.x clients, note that the default installation directory for the 8.5.2 release is different than the 7.5.x release. Do not change this as the installer will attempt to remove the 7.5.x files upon completion.

- Sametime 8.5.2 audio and video behaves differently from previous versions of Sametime such that 8.5.2 clients will not be able to use audio or video with 8.5.1 clients and neither of them will be able to use audio with 8.x clients.

Controlling client versions

During an upgrade project, you would want to carefully monitor the versions of the clients connecting to your new servers. On your Sametime Community Server, open the sametime.ini file with a text editor. In the [Config] section of the file, set the minimum client version that can log into the server by setting ST_MINIMAL_CLIENT_VERSION=x, with x being one of the following values:

ST_MINIMAL_ CLIENT_VERSION	Sametime client version
0	All clients may log in regardless of version
6510	Sametime 6.5.1, Notes 6.5, 7.x, and Notes Basic 8.x
7000	Sametime 7.0
7500	Sametime 7.5
7501	Sametime 7.5.01
7510	Sametime 7.5.1
8000	Sametime 8
8010	Sametime 8.01
8020	Sametime 8.02
8500	Sametime 8.5
8510	Sametime 8.5.1

Save and close the sametime.ini file. Client versions are included in the stlog.nsf file. If you have multiple Sametime Community Servers, they should each have the same ST_MINIMAL_CLIENT_VERSION setting, as otherwise there could be login issues.

You may also be familiar with the Sametime Community Server setting—VPS_ALLOWED_LOGIN_TYPES. This setting is also found in the [Config] section of the sametime.ini file and sets the allowed client versions. For more details on how to set this option, see the following tech-note:
https://www.ibm.com/support/docview.wss?uid=swg21114318&wv=1

Another option for migration is to allow logins from those clients that are back-leveled, at least for several weeks to minimize the number of help desk calls. You can also prompt the user with a message and a URL that sends them to the client download site. To manage this process, you will need to modify the following two files:

- sametime.ini (located in the \domino directory)
- stsecurity.ini (located in the \domino directory)

In the [Config] section of the sametime.ini file, include the parameter for allowing logins from earlier clients— ST_FORCE_LOGOUT_OLD_CLIENT_VERSION. If this is set to 0, all logins will be allowed regardless of version. If this is set to 1, clients that do not meet the ST_MINIMAL_CLIENT_VERSION settings will be rejected.

Next, edit the stsecurity.ini file to include the ST_OLD_CLIENT_VERSION_WARNING_MESSAGE setting. If this value equals null, no message will be displayed. But if it is equal to some text message, that message will be displayed to the user after they login to Sametime. You may want to include a URL in the message for the location of the new Sametime software. Finally, you may want to include a brief pause before the announcement is sent to the user, so that the user does not miss the message. In the sametime.ini file, in the [CONFIG] section, add the value (in milliseconds) for the VP_SECURITY_PAUSE_INTERVAL. This will provide a delay before your announcement is displayed.

Summary

In this chapter, you learned about your choices when it comes to Sametime clients, as well as where you can find them on the IBM site. You learned how the Sametime client installs can be customized, and which files in the installation directories contain the customization parameters. You learned how Sametime can be customized to integrate with Microsoft Office. You learned how to set policies for the Sametime clients and how to enforce the policies both on installation and on startup. Finally, you learned how to update Sametime clients from prior versions and how to set your Sametime environment to enforce the Sametime client version levels. In the next chapter, you will learn about Sametime Mobile and about basic features that are offered on the different mobile clients.

11
Collaborate from Anywhere: Sametime 8.5.2 and Mobile Devices

We have discussed the use of Sametime instant messaging and how valuable it is in connecting people in your organization. As you are aware, an increasing number of people are using mobile devices as their method of choice for much of their day-to-day communications whether it is for e-mail or text messaging. With Sametime 8.5.2, Sametime instant messaging can be extended to the mobile device to permit instant messaging on those devices as well. Blackberry, Windows Mobile, Nokia, Android, and Sony Ericsson mobile devices can each run their own locally installed Sametime Mobile client. Additionally, mobile deployment of Sametime for Apple devices, such as iPhones and iPads, is through a custom web application available from the Sametime Proxy Server. In this chapter, we will discuss the steps required to configure Sametime to provide support for these mobile devices. We will also introduce you to the newest clients and features.

- Jess has been asked investigate options for extending instant messaging to mobile devices in her environment. Her company already uses the Sametime desktop client. She believes Sametime Mobile looks like a good option given the number of iPhone and Android phone users she has in the company.

- Simon has deployed a Sametime Community Server in his Sametime environment but is unsure what steps he should take to provide Sametime Mobile download access for his users.

- Chris' organization has several international sites and his organization relies on several phone carriers and handheld device sets. The security officer has asked that he investigate options for securing Sametime Mobile.

- Tim is the Blackberry administrator for his company. He would like to deploy Sametime Mobile and the mobile client to all his Blackberry users.

In this chapter, you will learn the following:

- What is Sametime Mobile
- How to manually configure the Community Server for mobile access
- How to connect Sametime Mobile to the Community Server
- How to configure the Sametime Community Server for mobile downloads
- How to configure the Proxy Server for Mobile device access to Community Server
- What Sametime Mobile clients are available and how they are configured

Sametime Mobile

Sametime Mobile is a set of client software designed specifically to provide instant messaging functionality for mobile devices. The Sametime Mobile family includes clients for the following:

- Blackberry (OS 4.2 to 6)
- Google Android (OS 2.0.1 or higher)
- Nokia S60 E Series
- Sony Ericsson (M600, P990, P1i)
- Windows Mobile 5/6 (Professional and Standard)

The Sametime Mobile client supports many of the key features of the Sametime Connect or Embedded client, including:

- Contact lists
- Client preferences
- Announcements
- Single and group chats
- Emoticons
- Awareness and notification

We also include the Sametime custom web application in this chapter as it provides Sametime instant messaging for Apple iPhone/iTouch/iPad and other smartphone devices. As this is a web application, it does not download software to the mobile device as with the Sametime Mobile client, but does provide similar Sametime functionality.

Configuring the Sametime Community Server for mobile access

In order to provide support for mobile devices, there is some configuration needed for the Sametime Community Server. This is usually completed automatically by the install process for a new Sametime 8.5.2 server. But if you are running in a mixed environment or if your environment does not already have these settings in place, the following information gives you the instructions for manual configuration. To confirm if your settings are already in place in your environment, use a browser to go to the URL `http://<hostname>/mobile` where `<hostname>` is the fully qualified hostname of your Community Server. If that URL returns an error, you will need to complete the following steps.

Create a Website Rule Document

Your first step is to create a URL redirection document that allows Sametime Mobile users to access the Sametime Mobile downloads through a simplified URL. When accessing a download site from your mobile device, you do not want to have to key in a long web address. The URL redirection document helps to streamline the URL that users will enter on their device. An example might be `http://st.lucyskydiamonds.com/mobile`.

Because Sametime Community Server running on Domino must still use **Web Configuration** documents rather than **Internet Site** documents, we will describe how to create the appropriate Web Configuration document. With the Domino Administrator client, select the **Configuration** tab, and open the **Current Server Document** for the Sametime Community Server that will host the mobile downloads. Click on **Create Web** and choose **URL Mapping/Redirection**.

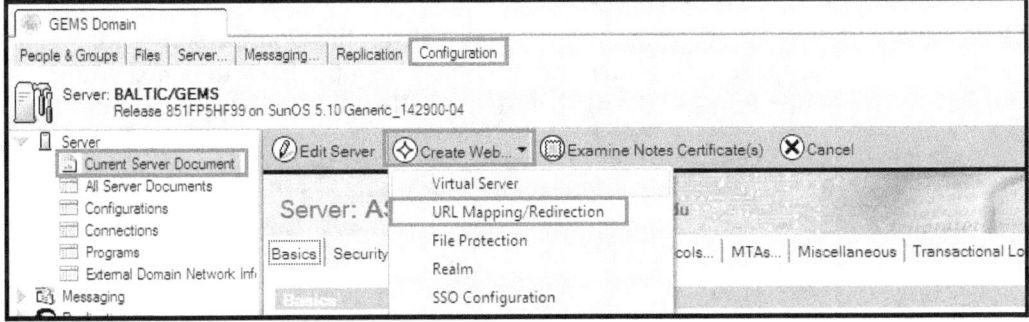

Once the website document opens, on the Basics tab, select **URL → Redirection URL**.

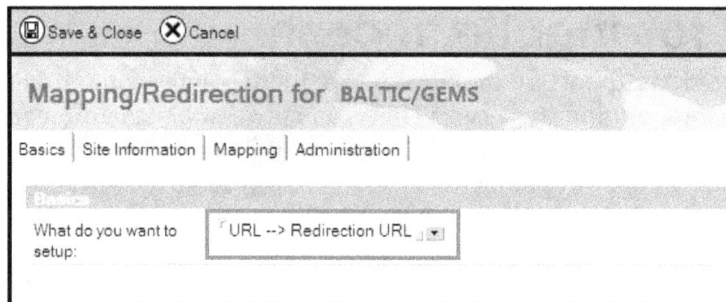

Click on the **Mapping** tab. In the **Incoming URL path** field, enter **/mobile/***. In the **Redirection URL string** field, enter **stcenter.nsf/webmobiledownloads?openview**. Click on **Save & Close**. You will need to stop and start the HTTP Domino server task for this rule to go into effect.

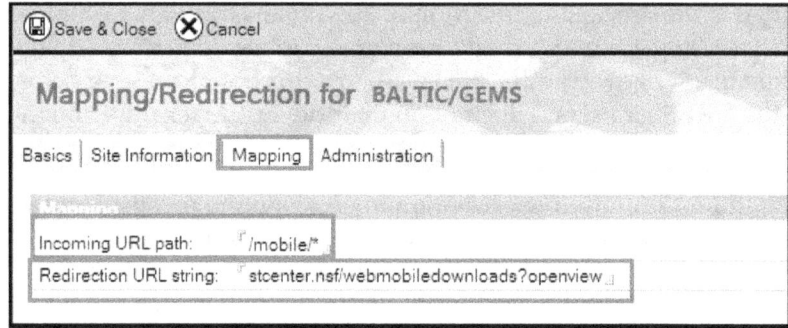

Modify the httpd.cnf file

The next step involves modifying the `httpd.cnf` file on the Domino server to configure MIME support for the client downloads. Open the file with a text editor and add the following items to the file before the **Fallback MIME types** section.

```
AddType    .jad     text/vnd.sun.j2me.app-descripter
AddType    .jar     application/java-archive
AddType    .alx     application/octet-stream
AddType    .cod     application/octet-stream
AddType    .sisx    application/octet-stream
AddType    .cab     application/vnd.ms-cab-compressed
AddType    .cfg     text/Sametime
```

Save your changes and close the file. Once it is edited, the `httpd.cnf` file should look similar to the following screenshot:

```
# Sametime mobile
#
AddType    .jad        text/vnd.sun.j2me.app-descripter
AddType    .jar        application/java-archive
Addtype    .alx        application/octet-stream
Addtype    .cod        application/octet-stream
Addtype    .sisx       application/octet-stream
Addtype    .cab        application/vnd.ms-cab-compressed
AddType    .cfg        text/Sametime
#
#    Fallback MIME types
#
AddType    *.*         www/unknown                    # Try to guess
AddType    *           www/unknown                    # Try to guess
```

The Domino HTTP server task will need to be stopped and started for this change to go into effect. These configuration changes allow for access to a download page that looks similar to the following screenshot:

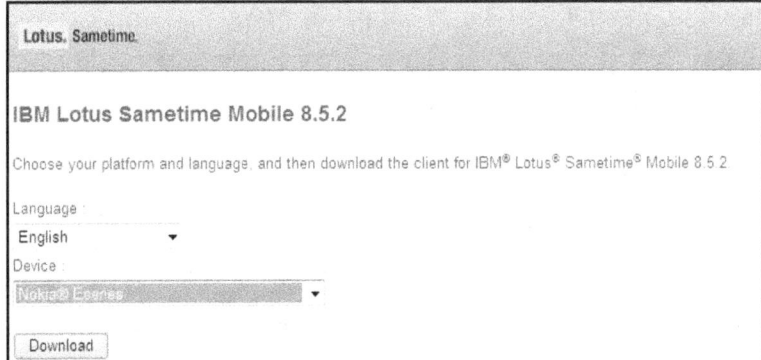

From the mobile device, select the appropriate device from the drop-down list and click on **Download** to begin downloading the software.

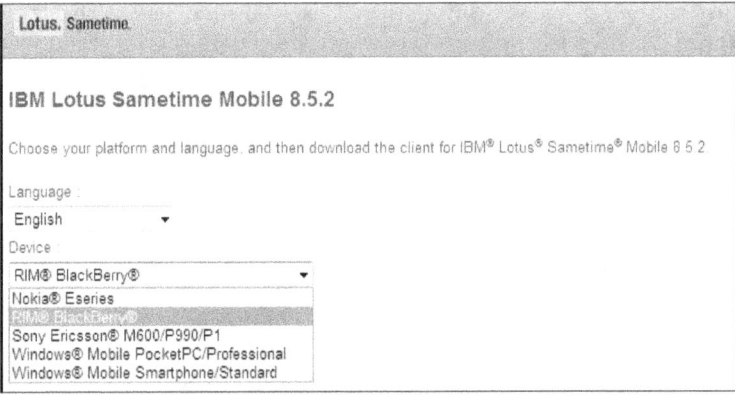

Connecting Sametime Mobile to the Sametime Community Server

There are the following three methods for connecting mobile devices to the Sametime Community Server:

- Virtual Private Network (VPN)
- Direct connection to the Community Server
- Authenticating through a HTTP Proxy

An example of a VPN type connection would be through a connection using IBM Lotus Mobile Connect. Mobile Connect is available for download from IBM Passport Advantage. These types of connections provide for an extra level of point-to-point security. Sametime Mobile is still installed in the same manner, but interaction with the Community Server requires the VPN connection first. An example of a proxy connection would be using Blackberry Mobile Data Services, which creates an encrypted local proxy connection to the Sametime server.

Sametime Mobile users can connect to the Community Server directly using the STLinks protocols. STLinks allows Sametime Mobile clients to connect to the Community Server over port 8082 by default by using 128-bit encryption. If HTTP tunneling is configured on the Sametime Community Server, the connection can additionally be made over port 80. STLinks is also reachable through the Sametime client port 1533. As with any direct server connection, you would want to secure firewall ports to limit traffic for appropriate users and ports.

Finally, the mobile connections can be configured to support a standard web proxy server such as Apache HTTP server or IBM HTTP server. The proxy server must issue standard HTTP 401 or 407 challenge requests. If you are planning to use a reverse proxy server, it must use cookies for authentication. Additionally, plan to configure your server with a SSL certificate obtained from a trusted certificate provider. Many mobile devices do not support self-signed SSL certificates, and therefore will not connect to web services signed with them.

Configuring the Community Server for mobile client downloads

To begin the download configuration, start the Sametime Community Server and log in to the Community web page at `http://communityserverhostname/stcenter.nsf`. Click on **Administer the Server**. In the list of options for administration, click on **Configuration** followed by **Sametime Mobile**. The **Configuration – Sametime Mobile** page displays links for configuring each mobile device download.

The following screenshot shows the configuration page for Blackberry devices. The settings here are those that appear as default on the application when it is installed.

Before making any changes on this panel, you should review the settings of your **Blackberry Enterprise Server (BES)**. It is important to verify if Blackberry MDS is being used, and whether or not the Blackberry client is to be automatically pushed to the devices. If your BES Administrator wants the Sametime client to be auto-deployed to the Blackberries, then an IT policy will need to be created on the BES server for that purpose. You will need to generate a custom IT policy rule with the information generated on this panel that can then be used to populate the rule on the BES server.

Blackberry devices may also be using **Blackberry Internet Services (BIS)** rather than being connected to a BES. If this is the case, these users may still use the Sametime Mobile client and the Sametime download page, but they will not be able to use MDS to connect to the Community Server or have the client automatically deployed to their devices.

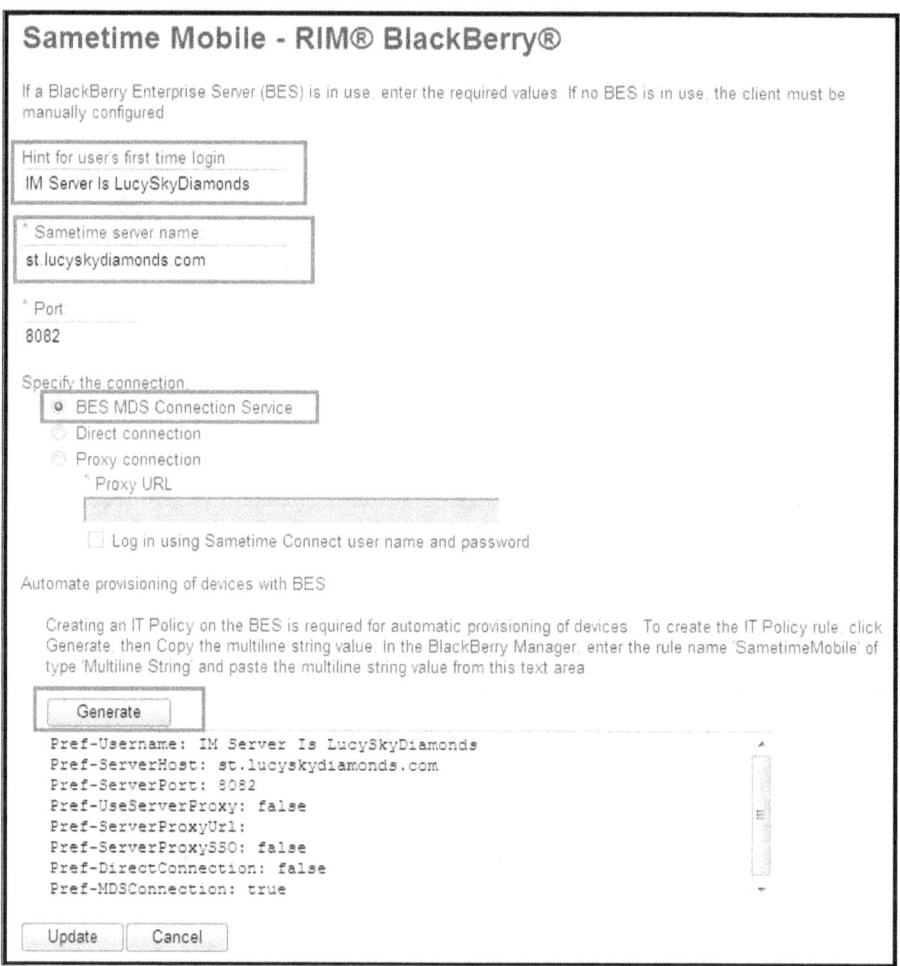

The following screenshot is an example of the configuration page for the Nokia device download. As with the Blackberry download page, you can include the Sametime server name, the port in which the users will connect, and what type of connection will be used. If you are using a proxy connection, you will be required to include the proxy URL string and indicate what credentials should be used to authenticate. These configuration steps will help to minimize the actions that the users have to take once they download the software to their device.

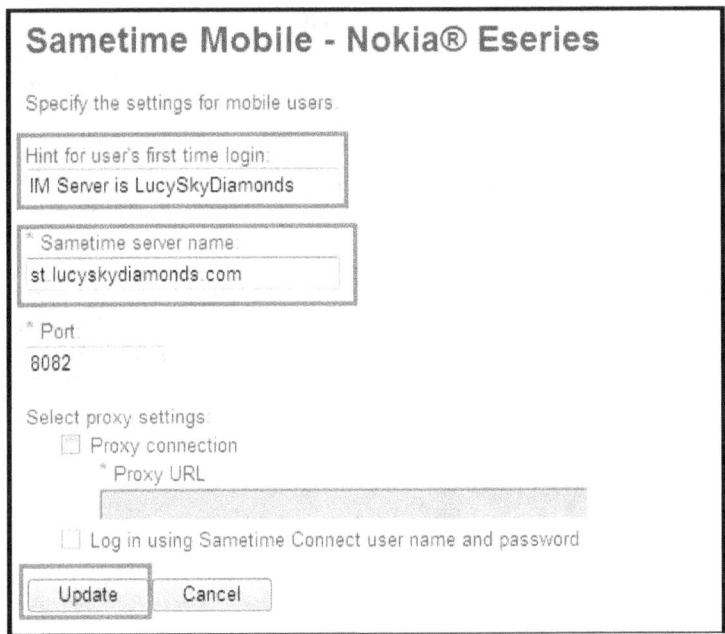

The following screenshot shows an example of the download configuration for Sony Ericsson devices:

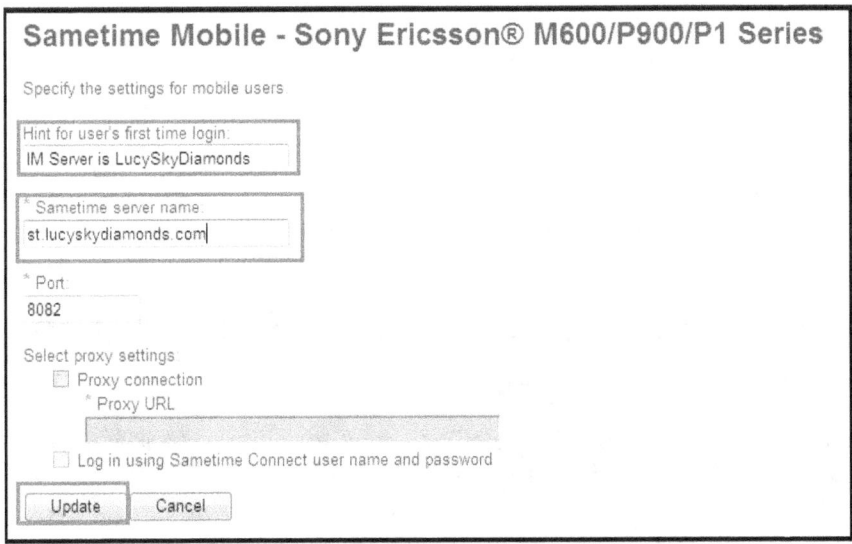

The following screenshot displays the settings for the Windows Mobile download configuration.

 Remember to include information in the **Hint for user's first time login** field as this will assist the user with the first connection to the Sametime Community or Proxy Server.

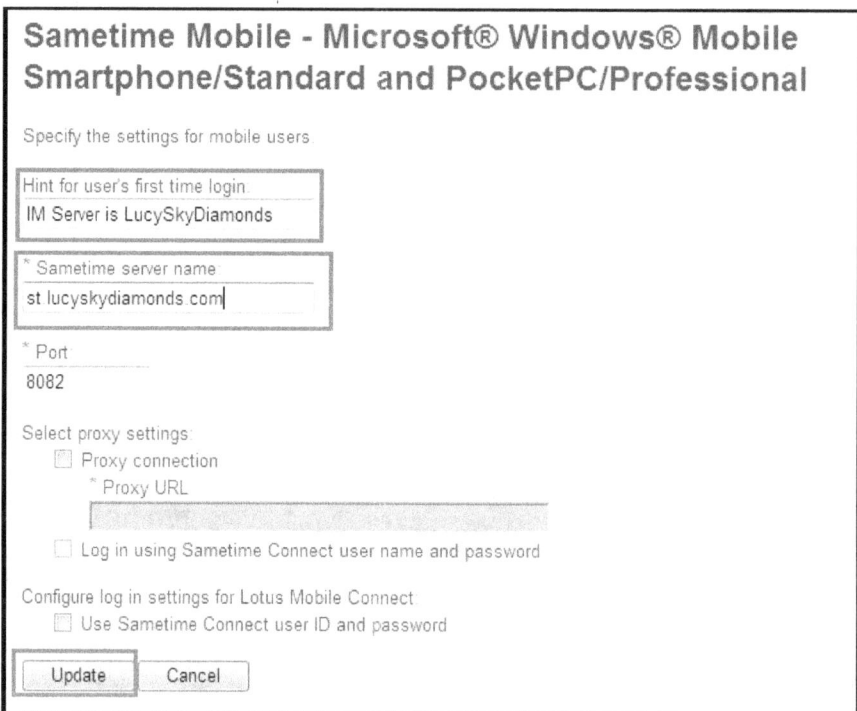

Configuring the Sametime Community and Proxy Servers

Part of the implementation of the Sametime access for mobile devices, especially if you are providing browser-client support, includes using the Sametime Proxy Server to connect to the Community Server. The Sametime Proxy Server will have asked you for a Community Server name during its install, so it will already know the name of the server to which it should connect. However, the Sametime Community Server will not know that the Sametime Proxy Server will be connecting to it. To ensure that your Sametime Community Server will accept connections from

the Sametime Proxy Server, you must add the IP address of the Sametime Proxy
Server as a **Trusted IP** to the Sametime Community Server. This tells the Sametime
Community Server that it is permissible to accept clients and connections that come
from the Sametime Proxy Server.

To configure the Sametime Proxy Server as a **Trusted Server**, you need to modify
the configuration of the Sametime Community Server. You do this by logging into
the SSC and choosing the Community Server you want to modify. The **Sametime
Servers** list contains a link to the Community Server.

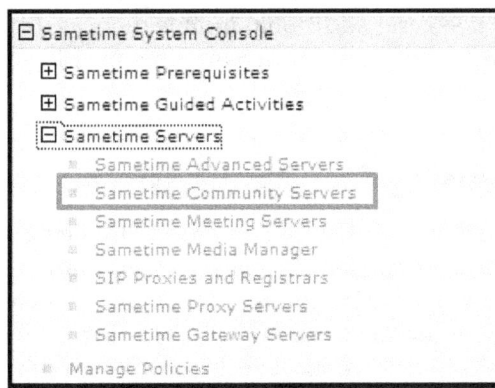

On the **Connectivity** page of the Community Server configuration, there is a section
entitled **Trusted Servers**. This is where you would enter the IP address of the
Sametime Proxy Server which confirms that it should be trusted by the Community
Server for connections it initiates.

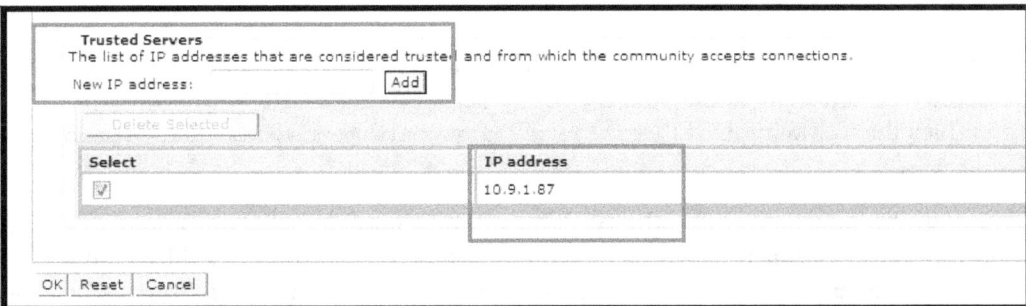

Once your changes are saved, the Community Server will take up to sixty minutes to
accept this change. You could also restart the Community Server for the changes to
go into effect immediately.

If you do not use a SSC to manage your Community Server, you would instead make this change directly in the **Community Connectivity** document in `stconfig.nsf` on the Sametime server. If you do use a SSC to manage your Community Server, you must make the change there as that configuration will overwrite any other configuration changes.

Sametime Mobile clients

In Sametime 8.5.2, one of the most important items was the announcement of support for Sametime on several additional mobile devices including Androids and iPhones/iPods/iPads. Additionally, a Sametime meeting client is also available for Blackberry.

Sametime Mobile for Android

New in Sametime 8.5.2 is the support for Sametime Mobile on Android devices. The new client offers some interesting features. If a user is running the Sametime client in the background, they will now be notified when new messages are received. The use of the camera is now integrated into chats. A user can take a picture and send it to the chat participants, or they can select and include a picture from their picture library into a chat. The new text-to-speech feature will read chat messages aloud, enabling a user to visually focus on something else during a chat exchange. Finally, the Sametime geographic location information is updated from the GPS receiver on the device. More information can be found on the Sametime client for Android User's Guide found at `http://www.lotus.com/ldd/stwiki.nsf/xsp/.ibmmodres/domino/OpenAttachment/ldd/stwiki.nsf/1AA1FBECA6BA5AC8852578A2007868 5F/attach/ATT0XOC5`.

The Sametime Mobile client is installed as an `.apk` file on your Android device. The software is downloaded from the Proxy Server using a URL address that resembles the following URL: `http://st.lucyskydiamonds.com:9080/stmobile/sametime.html`.

To install the Sametime client, the Android must be configured to allow non-Android market applications to be installed. This step is accomplished by going to **Device Settings** | **Select Application** and selecting the **Unknown Sources** box. Some cell phone carriers (in particular AT&T) do not allow non-marketplace or non-trusted applications to be installed.

Once the client is installed, a user would log in with credentials that are authorized for access to the Sametime Proxy Server. The Sametime client looks like the following screenshot:

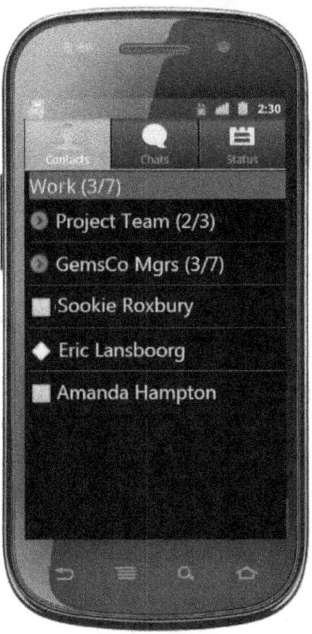

Sametime Instant Messaging client for Blackberry devices

There are now two separate client applications for Blackberry to support Sametime services. The first is the updated Sametime Instant Messaging client for Blackberry devices. Users can install this client by browsing to `http://<hostname>/mobile` on their Blackberry device and selecting the Blackberry install. Once installed, the client will have default settings that have been applied by the Sametime Administrator allowing the user to login.

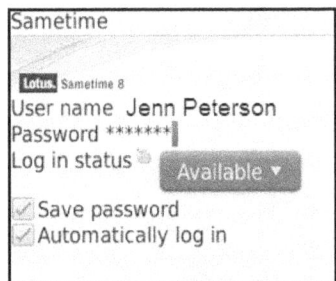

Sametime instant messaging tasks can also be accomplished on the Blackberry using the Blackberry Enterprise Messenger client. However, the Sametime Mobile client offers much better integration with all the Sametime features. This includes support for multiple one-to-one and n-way chats, use of privacy settings, adding of public groups, and status management. Messages received can also be displayed in the Blackberry inbox, providing a single point of reference for all communications.

Sametime Meeting client for Blackberry devices

A new client for Sametime Meetings is now available for Blackberry devices running OS5 or OS6. With this client, Blackberry users can now participate in Sametime meetings. Participation includes joining discussions, seeing participants, and viewing a presentation, application, or document that is being shared. To install the Meeting client, the user first needs to respond to a meeting invitation and attend a meeting. This can be done by clicking on the meeting URL in a calendar invite or in an e-mail from their Blackberry.

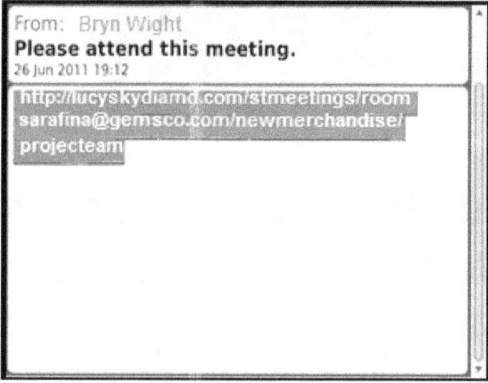

The next screen allows you to install the Sametime Meeting client or go directly to your meeting room.

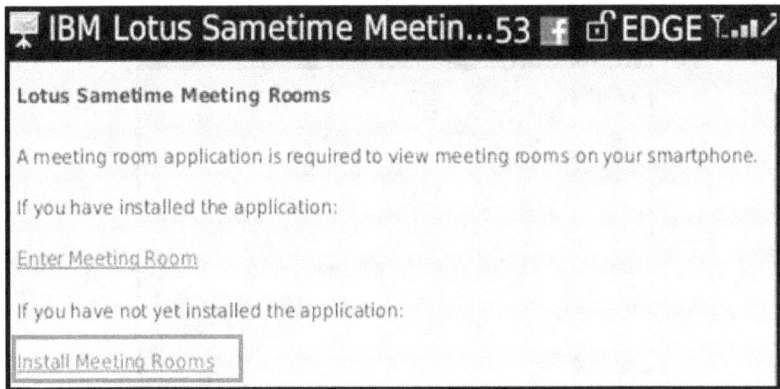

Once the Meeting client is installed, the user can search for the meeting or go directly into it by clicking on the URL.

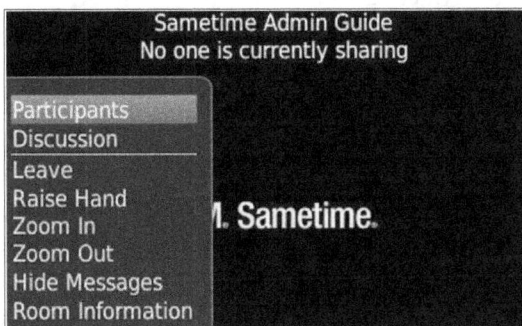

Users can also add additional Meeting Room Servers if they need to access meetings on more than one server.

The following screenshot shows the configuration of the Meeting Room Server login. Note that the Meeting Room Server only accepts e-mail addresses as logins and not names, so the user will have to use their primary e-mail address.

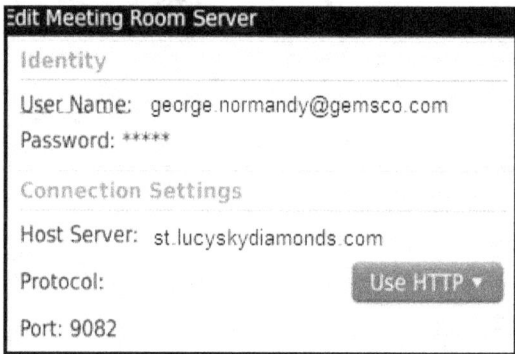

Sametime for iPhone, iTouch, and iPad

Sametime on the iPhone, iTouch, and iPad devices from Apple allows users to chat and have awareness features on the go. While the Sametime browser client does not offer the full functionality of the Sametime Connect Client on a PC, it does offer a useful subset that is most often needed when travelling or away from the office:

- Online status and availability
- Chat
- Emoticons
- Announcements
- Contact and contact management (both for individuals and groups)
- Business card displays

The system requirements for Sametime on these devices are:

- Apple iPhone 3G, 3GS, 4 (2.x or higher OS)
- Apple iPod Touch (2.x or higher OS)
- Apple iPad (2.x or higher OS)

To run Sametime on an iPhone or iPad, a user starts the Safari browser with JavaScript enabled. The Sametime session is run within the browser, pointing to the Sametime Proxy Server within the Sametime environment. To access the sign-on page, enter the URL of the Sametime Proxy Server using a fully qualified domain name along with the port number. An example of a Sametime Proxy Server URL for use with an iPhone would be the following URL: `http://st.lucyskydiamonds.com:<proxyport>/stwebclient/iphone_index.jsp`.

Port 9082 is the default port number when the Sametime Proxy Server is installed. However, the Proxy Server may install on a different port if you are installing multiple servers on the same machine. In our example where several servers are installed together, the default port was assigned as 9084. To confirm the ports in use, log in to the SSC and choose the Sametime Proxy Server under WAS and select **Ports** from the Proxy Server's configuration menu. The port that will be used will be identified as either **WC_defaulthost** or **WC_defaulthost_secure**.

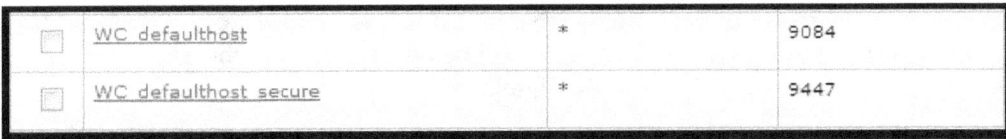

The following screenshot is an example of the Sametime 8.5.2 login panel on the iPhone:

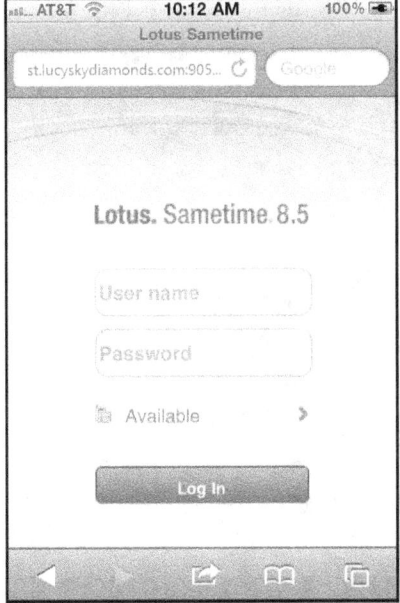

From the Apple device, users can work with their contact lists, as shown in the following screenshot:

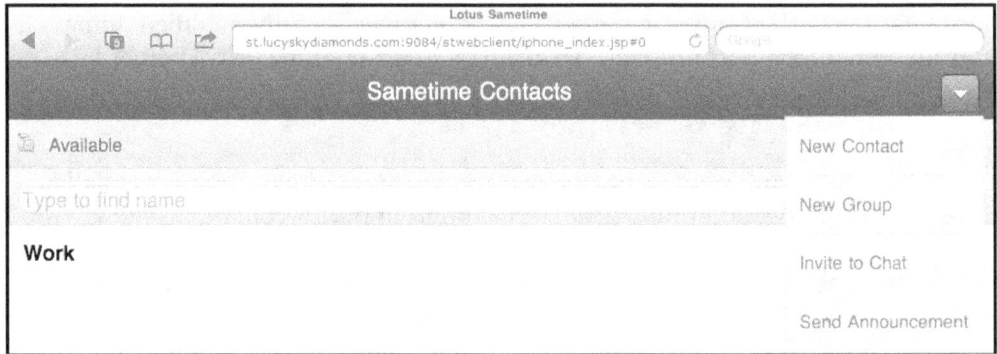

When Sametime loads on the device for the first time, it will take slightly longer than normal. The device is downloading parts of the application and storing them locally. That means that future uses of Sametime will be faster as part of the application is already stored and available for immediate use.

A good tip for using Sametime is to add a bookmark to the site as an icon on your device screen. In Safari, bookmark the home page of the Sametime site, and choose **Add To Home Screen** as the bookmarking location. This puts the Sametime icon on the device workspace, and it can then be quickly accessed in the future.

When using the Sametime browser on the iPhone, there are certain limitations and restrictions that should be remembered:

- The Sametime browser client is only active when it is running in the foreground on the iPhone, iPad, or iPod Touch. If the client browser page is in the background due to running another application, browsing a different page, or in power-saving mode, any messages sent to you will not be displayed or received.

- As the Sametime client is running as a browser application, JavaScript must be enabled in Safari.

- A user must log out of Sametime in order for their status to change to offline and to prevent further messages from being sent to them.

- For scrolling through chat transcripts, a two-finger scrolling action must be used.

[IBM has announced that a native iOS Sametime client, which can be used in lieu of the browser interface, is due for release in late 2011.]

Summary

In this chapter, you learned what Sametime Mobile is and what basic features are offered on the different clients. You learned how to configure the Sametime Community Server for mobile access, and what files on the server need to be updated. You learned how to configure the Sametime Community Server to allow the different mobile clients to be downloaded and installed. You learned about the trust relationship that is configured between the Community Server and Proxy Server to permit browser client access. Finally, you learned about each of the mobile devices and the Sametime feature sets that are supported for each one. In the next chapter, the reader will learn how to monitor, manage, and troubleshoot the various Sametime servers.

12
Managing and Monitoring the Sametime 8.5.2 Server Environment

Congratulations! You have installed or upgraded your Sametime 8.5.2 environment, and it is now in production. As the administrator responsible for the Sametime environment, it is important to know how to review and configure appropriate monitoring and logging for your servers. While you may be required to log Sametime activity, monitoring the servers allows you to stay ahead of any issues that may appear. These issues could be related to performance, connectivity, or other functional aspects of Sametime services.

In this chapter, we will take you through some of the methods and tools that Sametime provides to help you track and troubleshoot potential problems.

- William wants to track his Community Server activity including what clients are being used and how many connected users he has during peak times. He would like to read the Community Server logs to see this activity both historically and in real time.

- Ramona's Meeting Server will not start. She wants to review the WAS logs for the Meeting Server for possible error messages and determine how to fix the problem.

- Marko believes he has configured LDAP correctly for his servers but now users cannot log in. Using the SSC, he wants to verify that WAS can find the users and that the login names being used are correct.

- Femke needs to quickly confirm which servers are up and running in her environment. She would like to use the SSC to review her environment.

- Peter believes his servers are running at capacity, but he needs to confirm what services are being used and which users are accessing them.

In this chapter, you will learn the following:

- How to review user and server activity

- How to monitor and manage Meeting Rooms

- How to troubleshoot LDAP configuration and authentication issues

- How to manage WAS processes

- How to troubleshoot WAS issues

Reviewing user activity

In a Sametime environment, it is important to review which services are being used, which users are accessing them, and when they are being accessed. Reviewing the logs and activity as well as monitoring current performance requires a Sametime administrator to access both Domino (for reviewing Community Server activity) and WAS (for all other server activity).

Understanding Sametime services and peak activity times allows us to plan for growth and manage demand. For instance, monitoring trends for user connections to the Community Server during the day can help indicate if an additional multiplexor is required in the environment. It is important to monitor Meeting Room activity as well. Meeting Rooms take up server disk space. Regularly removing old or unused rooms from the server will free up disk space. At the same time, if there are different types of meetings taking place, tools for planning user policies for Meeting Room usage are available. This would allow you to set variable space limitations or video and audio usage constraints for different user groups.

Reviewing Community Server activity

In a Sametime 8.5.2 environment, a Community Server is usually being managed by the SSC. However, monitoring and logging data for the Community Server is only viewable from the Domino Sametime Administration interface. You would need to check these logs to monitor instant messaging activity. To login, go to the URL: `http://<communityserver>/stcenter.nsf`. You will need to use credentials that have at least **Editor** rights and the role of **[SametimeAdmin]** or **[SametimeMonitor]** in the ACL of the `stconfig.nsf` database on the server. The account you use in the SSC to manage the Community Server will have these rights, but you can easily add other accounts also.

Once logged in, you will see a link on the right-hand side under **Administrator tools** titled **Administer the server**. If you are prompted for another login after clicking on this link, then you do not have the required access levels for `stconfig.nsf` on the server. You will need to update the permissions for your credentials and try again.

On the administrator menu, you have both **Logging** and **Monitoring** options. Initially you should look at the log settings. Keep in mind that all references to Meetings or Meeting activity on these menus refer only to the Domino Classic Meeting Server and not the WAS Meeting Server. These screens are primarily used to review instant messaging activity.

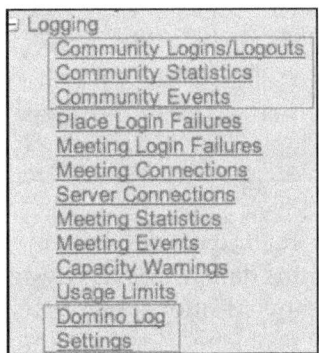

Instant messaging community logging

The menu options for logging include community logins, logouts, statistics, and events. These options show you the activity for instant messaging services. As each user authenticates into their Community Server, the system records:

- The date and time they logged into and out of the system
- The name with which they authenticated
- The IP address of their authenticating client
- The client type (Sametime Connect, Mobile, Embedded) and Sametime version that is being used
- How the user connects to the server

With this information, you can understand not only which users are connecting, but how many users are connecting to the servers. This is useful for planning client upgrades or changes in features through policies. You can also see if there are network connectivity issues for a particular client. The following image shows Community logins and logouts by day.

Logging - Community Server Logins/Logouts

Login/Logout by Time

Time	Event Type	User ID	IP Address	Application Type	Client Version	Protocol Version	Connectivity	Reason
09/10/2011								
05:05:46 PM	Community Login	CN=Lisa Taylor,O=GEMS	192.168.2.11	Proxy 8.5.2 Browser	V8.5.2	30.8520	No Type	
05:32:39 PM	Community Login	CN=Lisa Taylor,O=GEMS	192.168.2.11	UIM 8.5.2	V8.5.2	30.8520	Direct	
05:32:40 PM	Community Logout	CN=Lisa Taylor,O=GEMS	192.168.2.11	Proxy 8.5.2 Browser				User logged on from another IP
05:33:58 PM	Community Logout	CN=Lisa Taylor,O=GEMS	192.168.2.11	UIM 8.5.2				Connection broken
05:36:11 PM	Community Login	CN=Jodi George,O=GEMS	83.54.22.1	UIM 8.5.2	V8.5.2	30.8520	Direct	
05:36:57 PM	Community Logout	CN=Jodi George,O=GEMS	83.54.22.1	UIM 8.5.2				Connection broken
05:37:38 PM	Community Login	CN=Jodi George,O=GEMS	83.54.22.1	UIM 8.5.2	V8.5.2	30.8520	Direct	
05:41:18 PM	Community Login	CN=Jodi George,O=GEMS	83.54.22.1	UIM 8.5.2	V8.5.2	30.8520	Direct	

The source of this report is the `stlog.nsf` database in the data directory of the Community Server. Although this database is not designed for reviewing with the Lotus Notes client, there are many additional views and extensive information that can be used to quickly identify problems. Some common uses of this data include:

- Confirming if a user is logging into the correct server
- Verifying the user's authentication name
- Understanding what client types and versions have been deployed

Domino server logging

To review errors on the Domino server hosting the Community Server, begin by opening the Domino server database `log.nsf`, located in the data directory of the Community Server. For example, you might need to investigate errors related to terminated services or problems with DNS binding on HTTP. The `log.nsf` database also includes events related to authentication regardless of whether the Community Server is configured to use LDAP or the Domino Directory. From the Sametime Administration panel, the log can be opened from the menu using the **Domino Log** option. At a minimum, **Reader** authentication access is required to view the `log.nsf` database.

Logging - Domino Log

The Sametime server uses features in the Lotus Domino server and its associated Web administration pages. You can view the Notes Domino Log in a new Browser Window.

The most commonly used view in `log.nsf` is the **Miscellaneous Events** view. This view is essentially a report of all console output from the Domino server. Another view is the **Replication Events** view. This is useful if you are troubleshooting a possible replication issue. Replication events are particularly relevant to a clustered Community Server environment where databases, such as `vpuserinfo.nsf`, are shared.

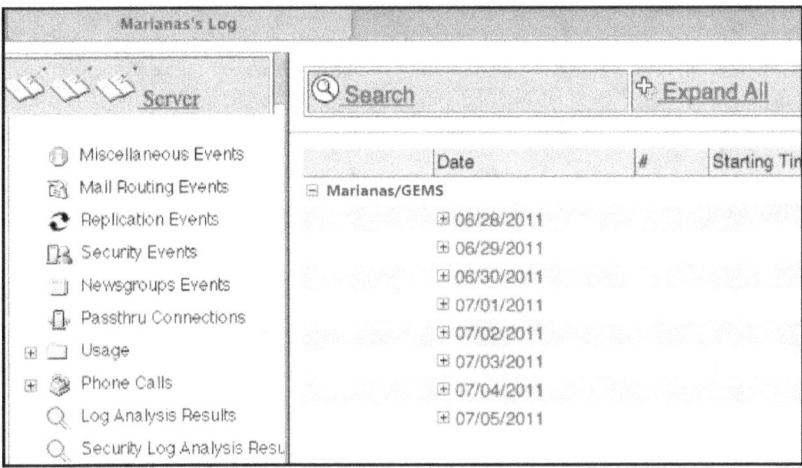

Logging settings

The **Logging - Settings** menu includes options to configure what Community activity is logged, how that log information is stored, and for how long. By default, the server will store Community logins and logouts in `stlog.nsf` and save that information for sixty days. Information on failed logins is useful for identifying security attacks or authentication problems, and can also be included as a logged event.

Another option for logging is to choose to have the log files stored in standard log format on the file system where they can be read and used by other external programs.

Logging - Settings

Capacity Warnings	undefined

⊙ Enable logging to a Domino database. (STLog.nsf)

☑ Remove history after (days). `60`

◯ Enable logging to a text file.

Path to log text file `_____`

The file name format is log[date].txt (For example, log_23_Mar_2001.txt). A new file is created each day.

Sametime Statistics

☑ Write statistics to the log every 60 minutes. This includes Community Services logging of people and chats, and Meeting Services logging of meeting, duration, and participants.

Community Server Events to Log

☑ Successful logins

☐ Failed logins

☐ Community server events and activities

☐ File transfers

Meeting Server Events to Log

☑ Meeting Client Connections

☑ Connections to other meeting servers

☑ Meeting Events

☑ Meeting server events and activities

[Update]

Debugging the Classic Meeting Server

In the event that you need to do some additional debugging of the Classic Meeting Server to troubleshoot a server or client issue, you may need to collect data to submit to IBM for review. To do so may require the addition of specific debug code or parameters based on instructions by IBM support staff. For example, see the following support document for instructions on how to gather data to submit to IBM:

`http://www.ibm.com/support/docview.wss?uid=swg21159758`

Monitoring services

Up to this point we have only discussed reviewing log information which is a window into what happened on the servers in the past. To examine what is happening with current server processes, we will now look at monitoring options.

The Monitoring menu of the Sametime Administration panel includes options to review current server activity, use of services, and server load. The server overview report displays all the individual Sametime Community services installed under Domino and their running state. If a particular service is not running, it may not be indicative of a problem. It may simply be that the service is not being used in your environment. In the following example, the Meeting services are not running because the Classic Meeting Server is not being used. The WAS Sametime Meeting Server is being used instead. Understanding what services you need to have running in your environment and monitoring those services is essential to maintaining a stable environment.

The following screenshot shows a server overview report:

Server - Overview

Services Status at July 5, 2011 4:46:27 PM BST

Service	Status
Domino Application Services (nserver.exe)	Running
Meeting Services (nstmeetingserver.exe)	Not Running
Audio Video Services (stav.exe)	Not Running
Community Services Launcher (stcommlaunch.exe)	Running
Community Services (stcommunity.exe)	Running
Community Services Configuration (stconfigurationapp.exe)	Running
Sametime Places Services (stplaces.exe)	Running
Community Services Multiplexor (stmux.exe)	Running
Community Users Services (stusers.exe)	Running
Community Online Directory Services (stonlinedir.exe)	Running
Community Conference Services (stconference.exe)	Running
Community Directory Services (stdirectory.exe)	Running
Community Logging Services (stlogger.exe)	Running
Sametime T.120 MCU (stt120mcu.exe)	Not Running
Broadcast Gateway Services (stgwservice.exe)	Not Running
Broadcast Gateway (stbroadcastgateway.exe)	Not Running
Sametime Activity Provider (stmsactivityprovider.exe)	Not Running
Sametime Whiteboard Service (stwbserver.exe)	Not Running
Community Buddy List Presence Server (stpresencemgr.exe)	Running
Community Buddy List Subscription Server (stpresencesubmgr.exe)	Running
Community Buddy List Backward Compatibility Server (stpresencecompatmgr.exe)	Running
Sametime Links App Launcher (stlinks.exe)	Running
User Privacy Information (stprivacy.exe)	Running
User Name Resolution (stresolve.exe)	Running
User Connect List and Prefs (stuserstorage.exe)	Running
Sametime Admin (stadminsrv.exe)	Running
Community Chat Logging Services (stchatlogging.exe)	Running
Community Polling Services (stpolling.exe)	Running
Multimedia Processor Services (stmmp.exe)	Not Running
Security Services (stsecurity.exe)	Running
Authentication Server (stauthenticationserver.exe)	Not Running
File Transfer (stfiletransfer.exe)	Running
Event Server (steventserver.exe)	Not Running
Broadcast Gateway Controller (stgwcontroller.exe)	Not Running
Java Service Manager (stservicemanager.exe)	Not Running
Telephony Services (sttelephonyservice.exe)	Not Running
Sametime Policy Services (stpolicy.exe)	Running
Configuration Bridge (stconfigurationbridge.exe)	Not Running
Materials Manager (stmaterialmanager.exe)	Not Running
Logger (stmeetinglogger.exe)	Not Running
Reflector Services (streflector.exe)	Running

Monitoring logins

The **Monitoring - Logins** report is a real-time analysis of Community activity. This browser page will refresh every 30 seconds by default, but there is an option to adjust the refresh and report rate. From this single panel, it is possible to have a constant analysis of Community activity, which helps to isolate performance-related issues and peak demand timeframes.

Monitoring - Logins

Community Server Total Logins

13:43:50	13:43:59	13:44:07	13:44:16	13:44:24	13:44:34	13:44:42	13:44:52	13:45:00	13:45:08
200	172	85	50	10	10	10	40	30	25

Community Server Total Unique Logins (Users)

13:43:50	13:43:59	13:44:07	13:44:16	13:44:24	13:44:34	13:44:42	13:44:52	13:45:00	13:45:08
200	172	85	50	10	10	10	40	30	25

Last Updated: Tue Oct 04 2011 13:45:08 GMT-0400 (EDT)

General server status

The **Monitoring - General Server Status** report includes data on the number of n-way versus 2-way chats that are happening. This report is also useful for identifying performance and load on the server. Based on data found here, you can design the deployment of Media Manager services to provide audio and video capabilities in the Sametime client and in meetings. Again, the reference in these reports to Meeting Room activity and connections refers only to the Classic Meeting Server under Domino and not the new WAS Meeting Server.

Monitoring - General Server Status

Total Active Meetings	50
Scheduled Meetings	10
Broadcast Meetings	10
Instant Meetings	15
Active Meetings without Participants	15

Total Community Logins	123
Unique Logins	40
2-way Chats	50
N-way Chats	10
Number of Active Places	23

Meeting Room Connections	80
Direct Connections	60
HTTP Tunneled Connections	15
Remaining Meeting Room Connections	5

Total Broadcast Connections	78
Direct Connections	40
HTTP Tunneled Connections	38

Broadcast Streams	15
Unicast Streams	5
Multicast Streams	10

Modifying the Community Server connection in the SSC

As we have discussed, the SSC is a WAS-based server that manages all the Sametime server components from a single place. The SSC is configured with an administrative account in Sametime that can manage the Community Server. During the installation of the Community Server using the SSC, the deployment plan for installation asks for an administrative account for the SSC to use. As part of the installation process, it will validate that the account can login to the HTTP interface of the Community Server.

The credentials for the account are stored in the SSC. If at a later time it is necessary to change to a different account or update the password in the stored credentials, this must be done through the SSC. Begin by logging into the SSC and choose **Community Servers** under the **Sametime System Console** menu. The list of installed servers will be shown on the right. After selecting the server you want to update, click on **Edit**. In the following example, the **Community Server** account is being used to connect to the Community Server on port 80 or 443. The password that is stored here can be changed to match an updated password in the LDAP directory or the administration credentials can be changed entirely. If HTTP tunneling is configured on the Community Server, the connection port used here may be 8088 instead of 80.

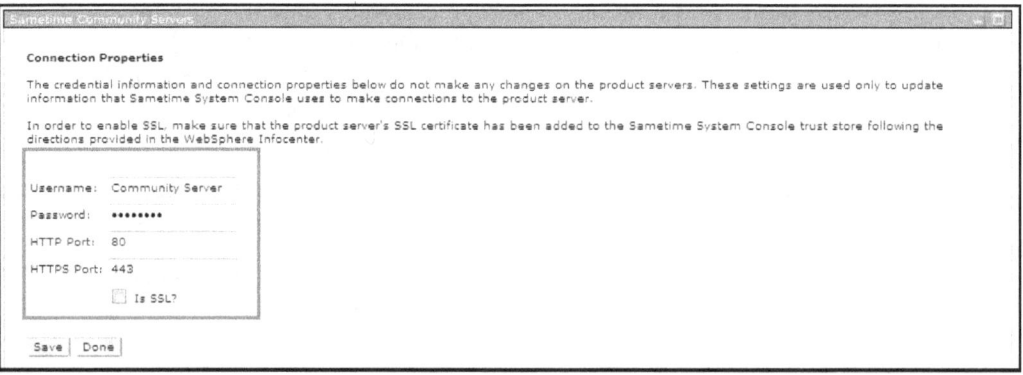

Monitoring and managing Meeting Rooms

Sametime 8.5.2 and the introduction of the new WAS-based Meeting Server has changed the way meetings are created and stored. Prior to version 8.5.2, as well as on the Classic Meeting Server, meetings were created like calendar appointments with a start time and duration.

In the new Meeting Server, meetings are created immediately and available indefinitely. Because they are available indefinitely, meetings can quickly accumulate on a Meeting Server. Even though a meeting does not use up system resources unless it is being used, it is an additional disk usage and potential performance overhead that should be monitored.

To review meetings on a server and how they are being used, use the **Meeting Room Statistics** view from the home page of the Meeting Server.

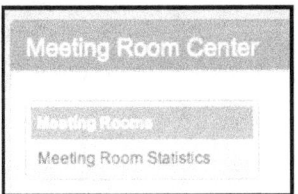

If you cannot see or access statistics on this home page, you will need to add yourself as an administrator for the Meeting Server in the SSC.

Adding Meeting Room administrators

To add additional administrators to the Meeting Server, log in to the SSC and find the Meeting Server application. This can be found under **Application Types | WebSphere enterprise applications**.

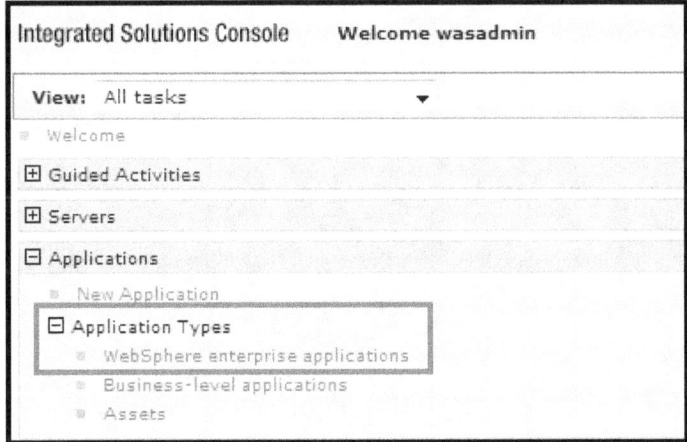

In the example installation, there are several **Enterprise Applications** including the SSC, the Meeting Server, the Proxy Server, and all the components of the Media Manager. The application required for this change is **Meeting Server Administration**.

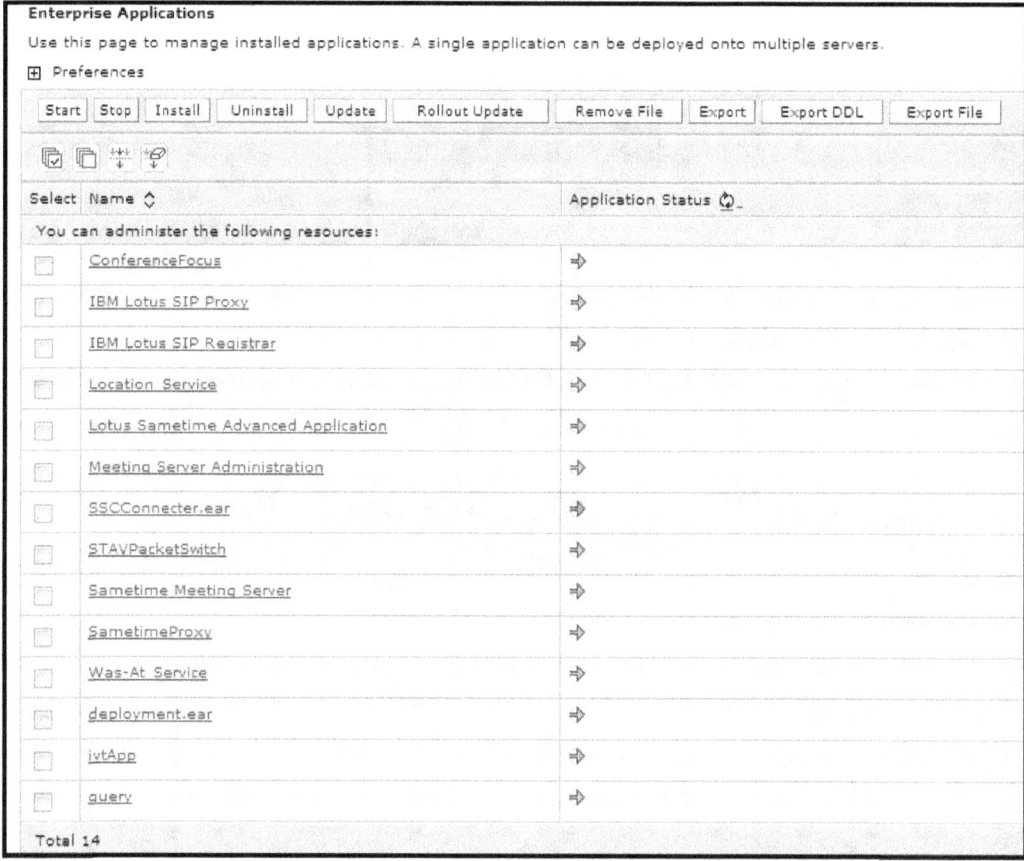

Total 14

On the configuration screen for the Meeting Server Administration application, you want to ignore everything except the link **Security role to user/group mapping**.

Enterprise Applications > **Meeting Server Administration**

Use this page to configure an enterprise application. Click the links to access pages for further configuring of the application or its modules.

Configuration   Runtime

General Properties

✦ Name
Meeting Server
Administration

Application reference validation
Issue warnings ▼

Detail Properties

※ Target specific application status
※ Startup behavior
※ Application binaries
※ Class loading and update detection
※ Request dispatcher properties
※ Security role to user/group mapping
※ View Deployment Descriptor
※ Last participant support extension

References

※ Resource references
※ EJB references
※ Shared library references
※ Shared library relationships

Modules

※ Manage Modules

Web Module Properties

※ Session management
※ Context Root For Web Modules
※ JSP and JSF options
※ Virtual hosts

Enterprise Java Bean Properties

※ Default messaging provider references
※ Stateful session bean failover settings
※ Application profiles
※ Message Driven Bean listener bindings
※ EJB JNDI names

Database Profiles

※ SQLJ profiles and pureQuery bind files

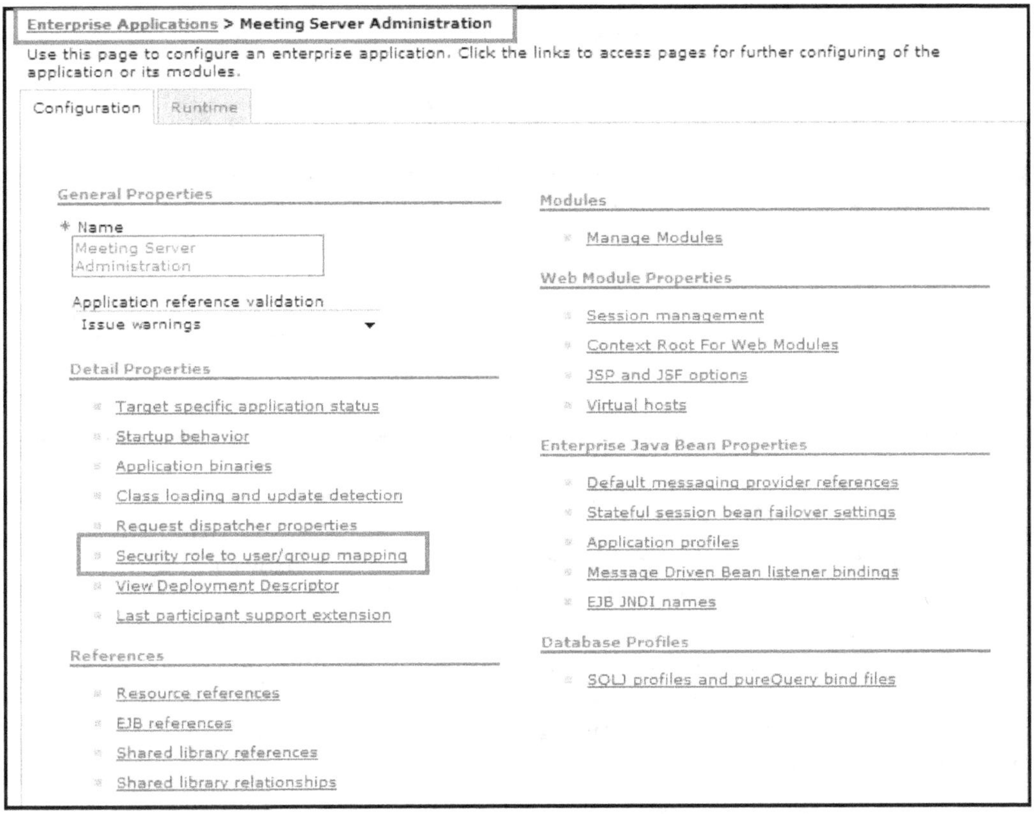

This shows you a list of existing users who have the special **AdminUser** role in this application.

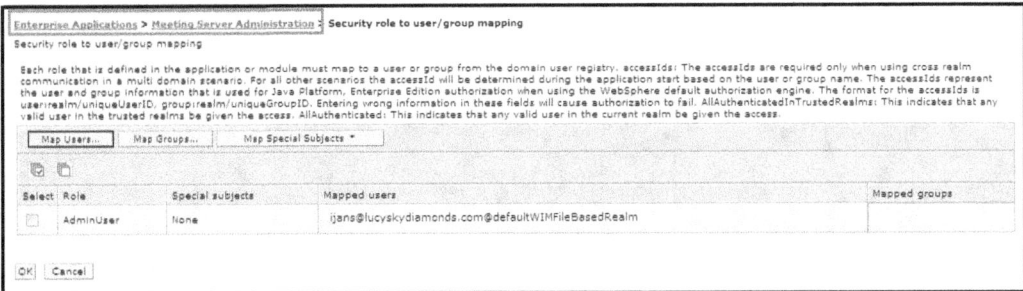

Enterprise Applications > Meeting Server Administration > Security role to user/group mapping

Security role to user/group mapping

Each role that is defined in the application or module must map to a user or group from the domain user registry. accessIds: The accessIds are required only when using cross realm communication in a multi domain scenario. For all other scenarios the accessId will be determined during the application start based on the user or group name. The accessIds represent the user and group information that is used for Java Platform, Enterprise Edition authorization when using the WebSphere default authorization engine. The format for the accessIds is user:realm/uniqueUserID, group:realm/uniqueGroupID. Entering wrong information in these fields will cause authorization to fail. AllAuthenticatedInTrustedRealms: This indicates that any valid user in the trusted realms be given the access. AllAuthenticated: This indicates that any valid user in the current realm be given the access.

| Map Users... | Map Groups... | Map Special Subjects ▾ | |

Select	Role	Special subjects	Mapped users	Mapped groups
☐	AdminUser	None	ijans@lucyskydiamonds.com@defaultWIMFileBasedRealm	

OK Cancel

By selecting the role and choosing **Map Users** or **Map Groups**, you can search for entries in the LDAP directory and assign those as Meeting Server administrators.

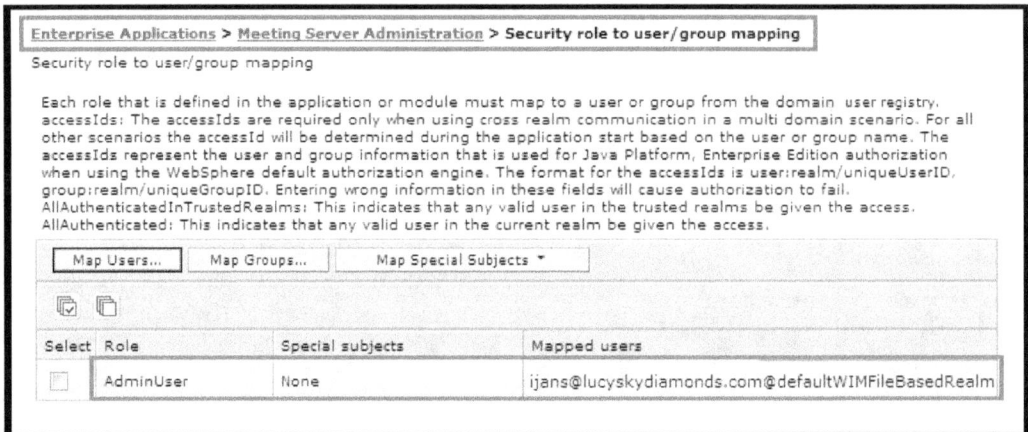

Meeting Server statistics

To view statistics for the Meeting Server, log in through the browser interface. The URL for the browser interface is usually http://<meetingserver>/ stmeetings. As the Meeting Server administrator of your environment, the tasks of oversight, monitoring, and managing the meeting rooms being created are critical. Understanding what meeting rooms are being created and how they are being used will help you keep the server performing at an optimal level, define policies, and plan for future growth.

The following is an example of the summary view of all meeting rooms, including the meetings that are currently active and how much data is stored in the meeting room library (from file uploads, shares, and so on).

Meeting Room Center

Meeting Rooms

Meeting Room Statistics

Meeting Room Statistics

| Summary | Usage By Room | Usage By Owner |

Room summary

All	370
Active rooms	50
Unused rooms	320

Participants Summary

Active Participants	234

Library Summary

Library items	140
Library size	5880 mbytes

In the **Usage By Room** view, statistics are available for usage by owner (the person who originally created the room), the date they were last accessed, and the number of active users. All of the columns in this report can be sorted, making it easy to find those rooms that have remained unused for some time, as well as those rooms with large libraries of uploaded files. Next to each room is a trash icon, which when clicked allows the administrator to delete the room.

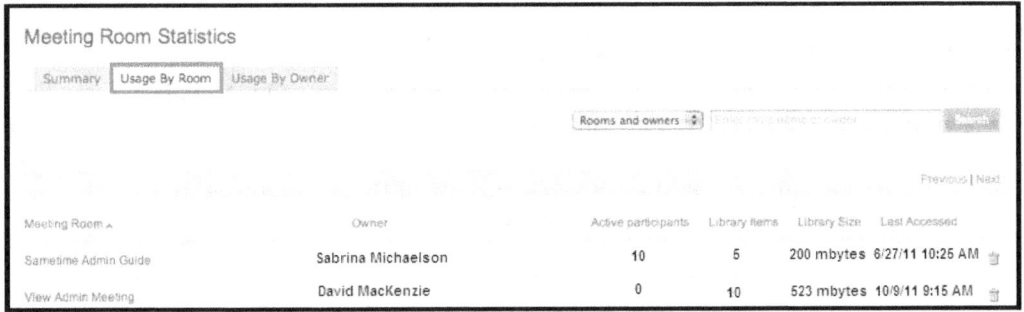

Meeting Room Statistics

| Summary | Usage By Room | Usage By Owner |

Rooms and owners

Previous | Next

Meeting Room ▲	Owner	Active participants	Library Items	Library Size	Last Accessed	
Sametime Admin Guide	Sabrina Michaelson	10	5	200 mbytes	6/27/11 10:25 AM	🗑
View Admin Meeting	David MacKenzie	0	10	523 mbytes	10/9/11 9:15 AM	🗑

It is also possible to review all rooms created by a particular user by opening the **Usage By Owner** view. This view is useful for deleting all rooms owned by someone who has left the company.

Summary	Usage By Room	Usage By Owner				

					Previous | Next

Owner ⌄	Rooms Owned	Library Items	Library Size	
Sabrina Michaelson	10	5	200 mybtes	Delete Meeting Rooms

LDAP troubleshooting

A directory accessible through LDAP is central to all Sametime interactions. The Community Server authenticates users who login against the known LDAP directories. It then creates a SSO token to handle authentication to the other server components such as the Meeting Server. LDAP authentication and a large amount of LDAP traffic is generated from the Community Server. An example of this traffic would be when the server is monitoring presence awareness or displaying nested groups in a buddy list.

A poorly performing LDAP server can impact the entire Sametime infrastructure. For users, poor LDAP performance manifests itself in the form of unreliable presence awareness on the Community Server, slow performing lookups for people or groups, or even failed logins. In most Sametime environments, the LDAP server is the one component other than the operating system itself that falls outside the management of the traditional Sametime administrator. Despite this constraint, there are tools available to Sametime administrators to monitor the LDAP server connections and servers.

Verifying LDAP configuration

When building a Sametime environment, one of the first steps taken before installing any additional servers is to define an LDAP server for use by all the Sametime server components. If necessary, multiple LDAP servers can be defined to provide multiple directories. However, note that multiple instances of the same directory server cannot be defined as this will cause authentication issues due to duplication of user IDs.

To add or federate an LDAP server, the first step is to confirm the connectivity in WAS. From the SSC, navigate to **Users and Groups** and choose **Manage Users**.

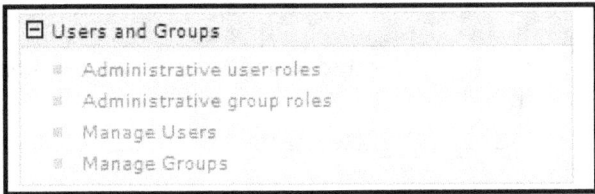

From here it is possible to search for users in all the LDAP directories that are federated. The search can be done by **Last name**, **First name**, or **E-mail** address. It can also contain a wildcard character. The receipt of valid results is a good test to confirm that the query against LDAP server is functioning properly. The e-mail address should be unique in the query results. If there are duplicate entries for the same user ID, that user may not be able to authenticate to the Meeting Server or Community Server.

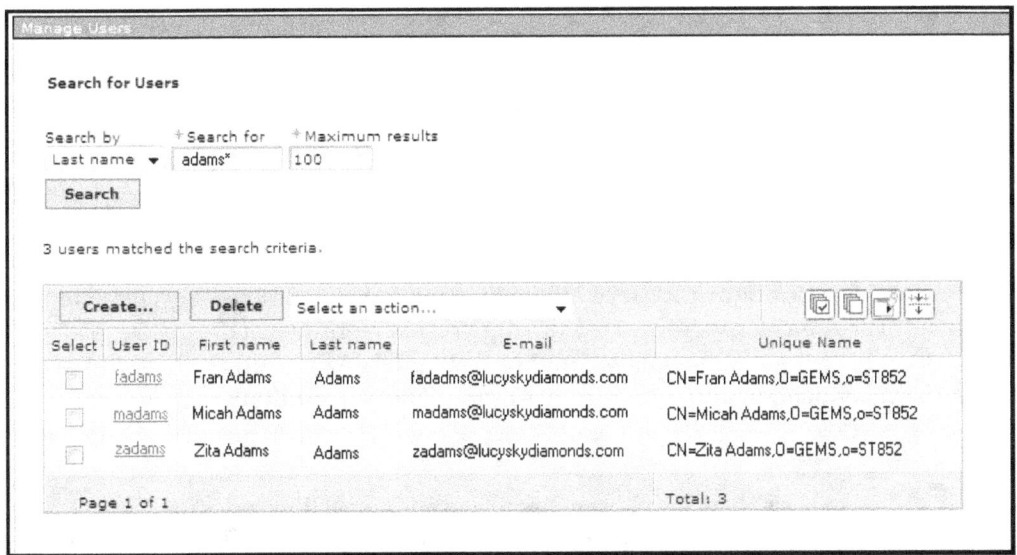

Modifying LDAP configuration

After completing the initial installation and as the Sametime production environment matures, it may be necessary to modify the original LDAP configuration. Reasons for doing this include:

- Supplying new or modified LDAP credentials
- Changing the fully qualified hostname for the LDAP server

- Adding a failover LDAP server
- Modifying the valid attributes for authentication

To make these changes in an existing environment, navigate to the **Security | Global Security** panel and modify the **Federated repositories**. This is where the LDAP server configuration is stored.

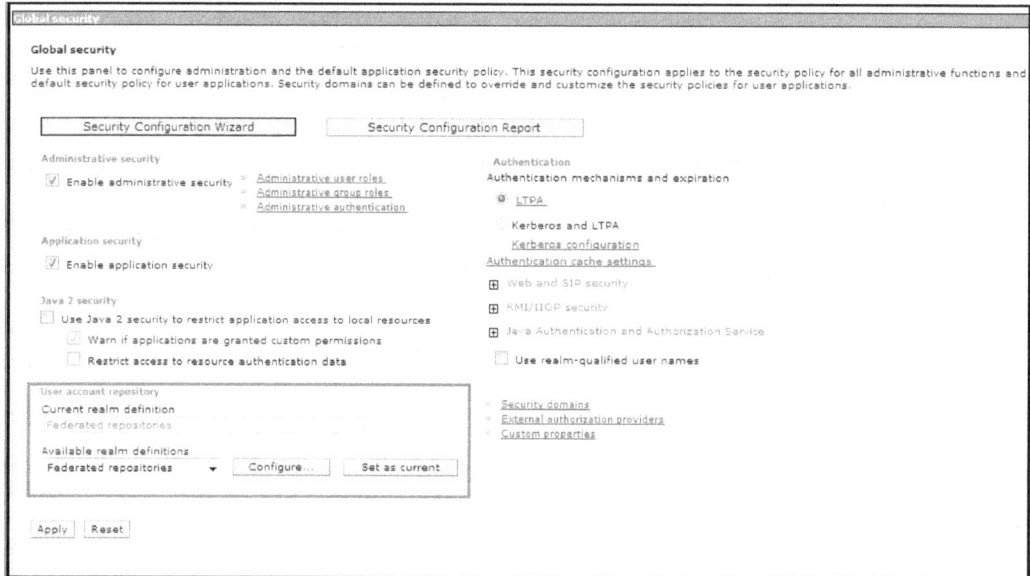

After clicking on **Configure**, a list of all the existing federated LDAP servers will be displayed. These entries were created during your Sametime install process. The `InternalFileRepository` usually contains only the WAS admin credentials used for WAS authentication and SSC administration. The other editable repositories are the LDAP entries.

This is not the panel to use to add additional directories for Sametime. Directories can be added and configured from the SSC panel—**Sametime Pre-Requisites | Connect to LDAP Server**. From this panel, the directories are federated and are then available for editing.

The following screenshot shows a single federated LDAP server which is a Domino Directory served as LDAP. By clicking on the **Repository Identifier** link, the LDAP settings can be modified.

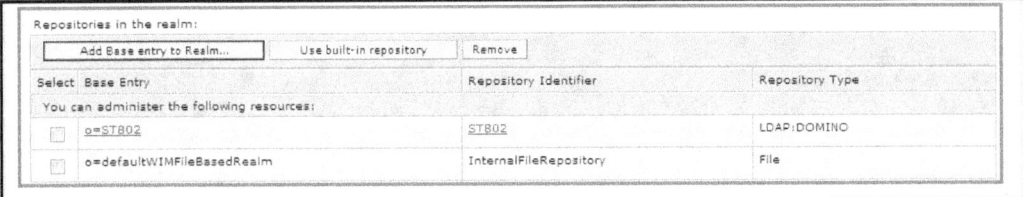

The LDAP configuration screen includes following several options:

- **Directory type** is not usually changed. By selecting the directory source, WAS knows how to construct an LDAP search query to return results for people and groups. Selecting the wrong directory source will result in an incorrect search query and a failure to authenticate.

- **Primary host name** and **Port** are set on the initial server install. If at a later date it is necessary to change the hostname to connect to the LDAP server or switch to a secure port, then these settings would be modified.

- **Failover server** is used to indicate LDAP directory alternates for WAS. Each alternate must have identical directory contents to those being used by the primary server. Failover servers are only used if the primary host is not responding.

- **Bind distinguished name** and **Bind password** are the credentials used to authenticate to the LDAP server and retrieve the directory. If the password for this bind user is changed in the LDAP directory itself, then it must also be changed here or the WAS server will fail to authenticate to the LDAP directory.

- **Login properties** are the attributes accepted as valid for authentication into Sametime. The **mail** attribute must be included and must be listed first. Additional attributes can be added but the value of each attribute must be unique across the directory.

Any modifications made to this panel must be saved to the master repository and the Deployment Manager, and all servers must be restarted.

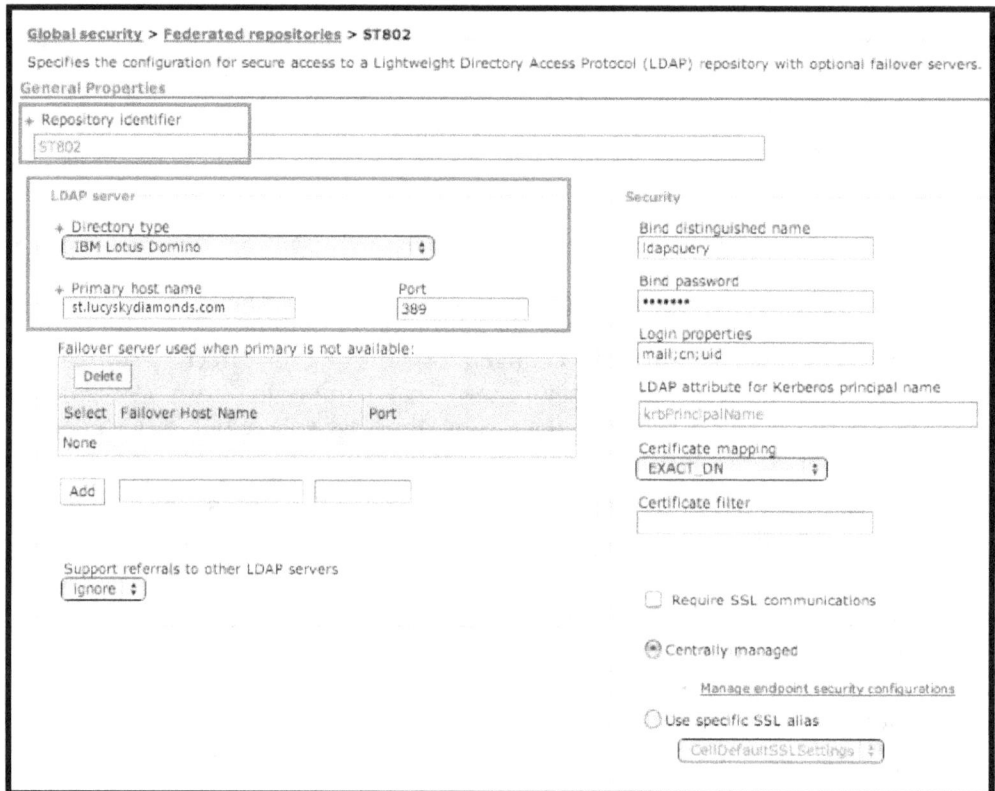

Monitoring LDAP

LDAP is not only a pivotal part of the Sametime infrastructure, it is also an external component often outside the control of Sametime administrators. To ensure the stability of the Sametime infrastructure, it is critical that all LDAP servers are monitored for both general availability and quality of service. There are many third-party tools that are available to monitor LDAP servers and ports. If a Domino server is the LDAP source in the Sametime environment, the built-in **Domino Domain Monitoring (DDM)** toolset can be utilized.

Domino monitoring

If the LDAP server is also a Domino server then DDM probes can be used to monitor the LDAP task for availability and performance. DDM probes are configured in the events4.nsf database on any Domino server running version 7.x or higher. The probes are usually configured through the Domino Administrator application by selecting **Monitoring** under the **Configuration** tab.

Any errors discovered by a DDM probe will be logged in the ddm.nsf database on the monitoring server. In all cases the monitoring server should be the Sametime Community Server as the source of the probe attempting to verify that the LDAP service is available for its use.

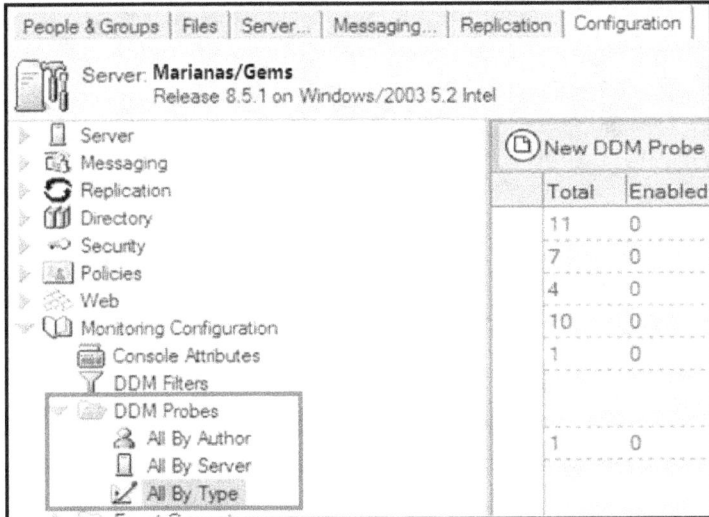

There are three probes that are of potential interest for monitoring LDAP:

- **LDAP Process State** monitors the LDAP task to see if it is running
- **LDAP TCP Port Health** connects to the LDAP ports and performs a simple request to confirm that the task is responding to requests
- **LDAP Search Response** monitors the average response time for searches against the LDAP directory

These are monitoring probes that exist in the events4.nsf database on each Domino server. They are disabled by default. The LDAP Process State and LDAP TCP Port Health probes can be scheduled to run at whatever interval is chosen, but the LDAP Search Response probe runs continuously to monitor the performance of the LDAP task. It is not recommended that all three probes be enabled at one time or that both scheduled probes are set to run continuously, as this would risk overloading the LDAP server with monitoring requests.

LDAP Process State probe

The LDAP Process State probe makes no demand on the LDAP server itself as it does not connect to the LDAP task. It can effectively be scheduled to run at frequent intervals throughout the entire day. In this way a notification would occur if the LDAP task is stopped at any point. If the LDAP task is not running, Sametime users will not be able to log in.

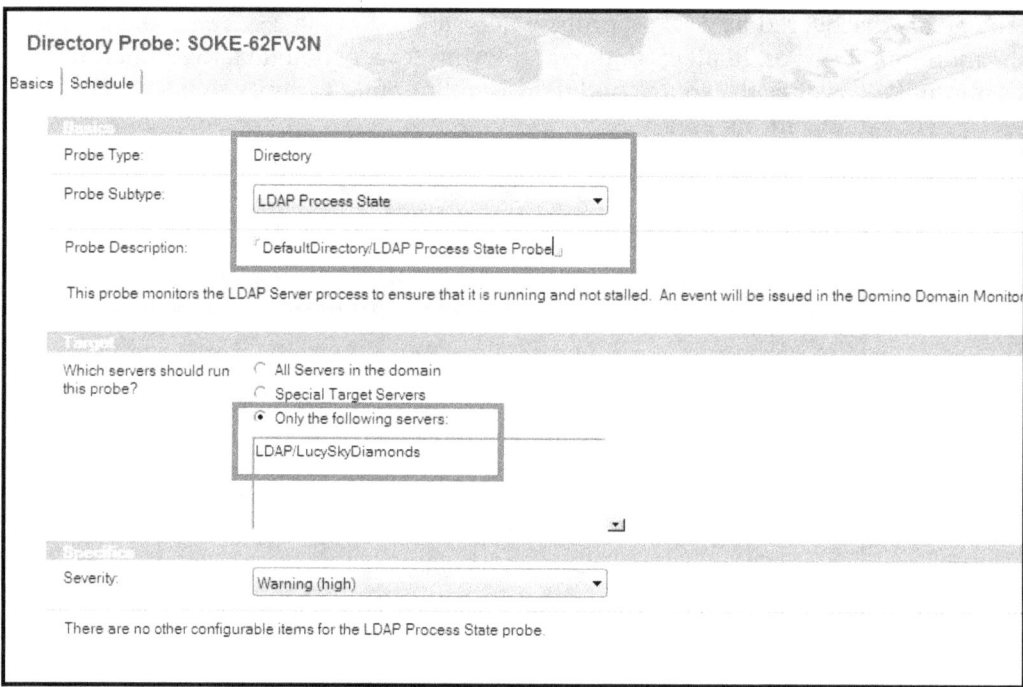

LDAP TCP Port Health probe

The LDAP TCP Port Health probe is useful if it is suspected that the LDAP task in the environment is stalling or failing to respond to queries intermittently. The port health is monitored by connecting to the specific LDAP or LDAP SSL port and initiating a simple request. As it monitors more than just the presence of the task, this probe will also generate errors if there are firewall issues between the monitoring server and the LDAP server. Enabling this probe quickly identifies if there is a wider problem affecting the LDAP task on that server that is preventing it from responding to requests even when it is running. This probe can be scheduled to run multiple times a day, but if run too frequently, it can overload the LDAP server. For example, scheduling this probe to run every minute would fall into that scenario.

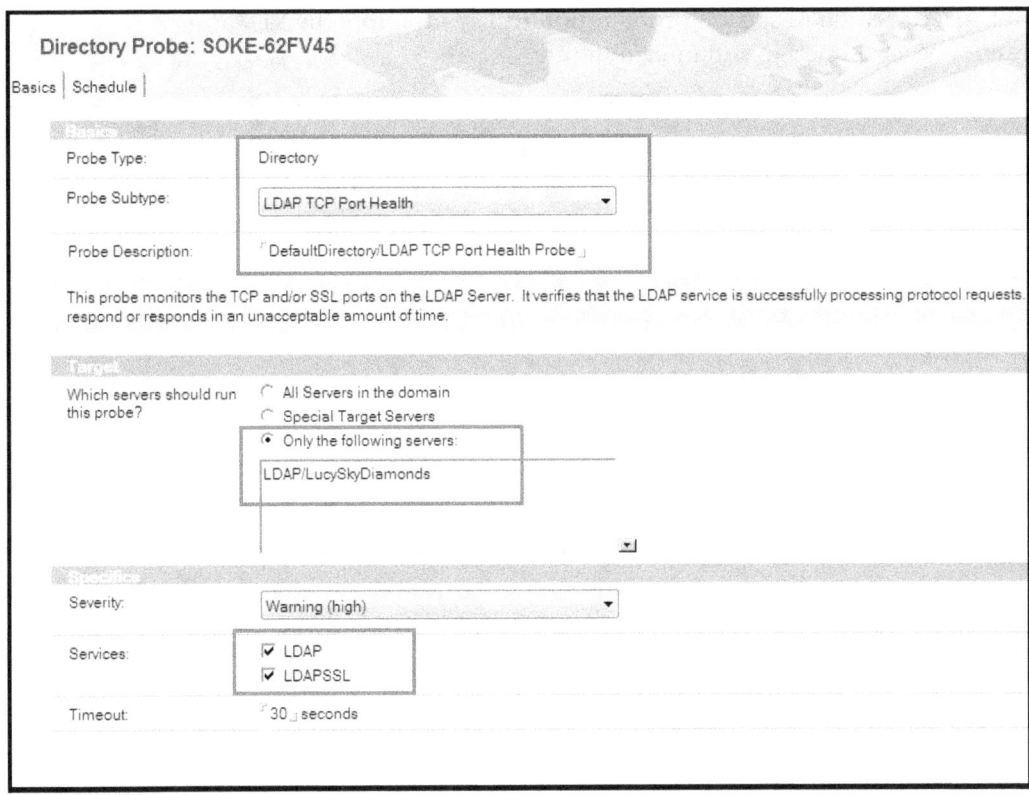

Directory Probe: SOKE-62FV45

Basics | Schedule |

Probe Type:	Directory
Probe Subtype:	LDAP TCP Port Health ▼
Probe Description:	DefaultDirectory/LDAP TCP Port Health Probe

This probe monitors the TCP and/or SSL ports on the LDAP Server. It verifies that the LDAP service is successfully processing protocol requests. respond or responds in an unacceptable amount of time.

Target

Which servers should run this probe?	◯ All Servers in the domain
	◯ Special Target Servers
	◉ Only the following servers:
	LDAP/LucySkyDiamonds

Severity:	Warning (high) ▼
Services:	☑ LDAP
	☑ LDAPSSL
Timeout:	30 seconds

LDAP Search Response probe

The LDAP Search Response probe is used for reporting on the response time that the LDAP server delivers for search requests. In a Sametime environment, a request can be generated by a variety of client activities. These activities include adding users or groups to buddy lists or finding people to invite to a meeting. If the LDAP server is responding slowly to these client requests, users may experience a delay and consider that a Sametime problem. In environments where the LDAP server is used by many different enterprise applications, performance problems are often experienced during peak times. This probe allows administrators to track and isolate these performance issues as well as being aware of them as soon as they occur.

The LDAP Search Response probe continuously monitors the LDAP server and cannot be scheduled to run intermittently.

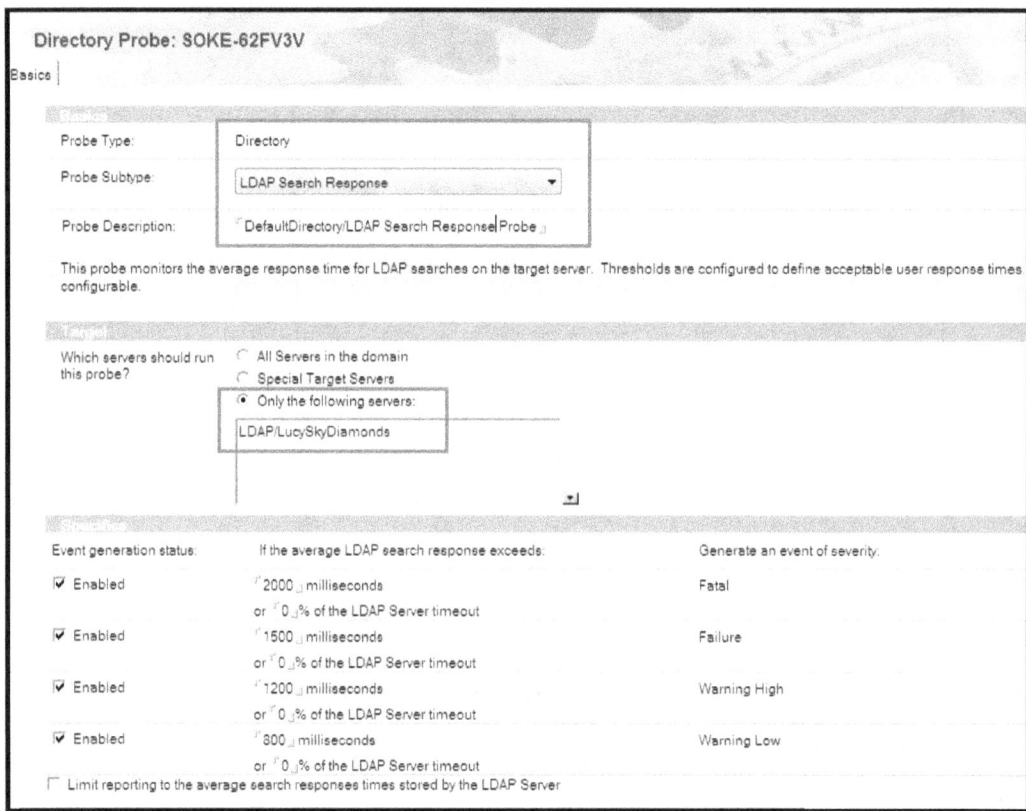

Debugging LDAP issues

Performance issues with LDAP can present themselves as many different but seemingly unrelated problems. These include:

- Inability to log in every time
- Presence awareness not updating properly
- Groups not displaying members correctly
- Search for names not finding any or all of the possible results

LDAP issues are usually a result of request bottlenecks on the LDAP server. In other words, too many requests are coming in for the server to handle. This may be a networking or availability issue, but it could also be caused by attempting to search a large LDAP directory or by performing a large number of concurrent searches. These LDAP problems can occur on any LDAP server platform. Although there are platform-specific tuning changes that IBM recommends for different LDAP servers, there are some general items that should be reviewed first.

Enabling LDAP debugging on the Sametime Community Server permits the review of detailed LDAP authentication requests, resolutions, search requests, and the results returned. Reoccurring problems in the debug logs help to isolate issues. To turn on LDAP debugging, edit the `sametime.ini` file on the Community Server and add the following line under the `[Debug]` section: `VP_LDAP_TRACE=1`. The Sametime services will need to be restarted once this change is in place.

The trace files are found in the **Trace** directory under the Domino program directory on the Sametime Community Server. For example, `C:\ibm\lotus\domino\trace`. The three trace files that contain LDAP debug information are `stauthentication`, `stresolve`, and `stdirectory`.

Community Servers and Sametime, in general, generate a large number of requests against LDAP servers. The LDAP servers often need to be specifically tuned to handle these requests by limiting the number of search results returned or requiring a minimum number of characters before performing a search. Large LDAP directories consisting of thousands of users do not perform well as browse-able directories. For this reason, you can disable that feature in Sametime to prevent your users from attempting to do that. To disable directory browsing for LDAP directories, edit the `sametime.ini` file on the Community Server and in the `[Debug]` section make sure the following parameter is **not** present: `ST_LDAP_BROWSE_ENABLED=1`.

The following IBM wiki document contains detailed information about tuning recommendations for LDAP servers:

`http://www.lotus.com/ldd/stwiki.nsf/dx/Best_Practices_for_using_LDAP_with_Lotus_Sametime#_Toc246828781`

Managing WebSphere Application Server processes

When dealing with WAS applications and servers, it is important that each component is started in the correct order. If you are starting all the servers, it makes little difference whether you start the Meeting Server a few minutes before the Community Server or the TURN Server before the Media Server. However, it is critical that the WAS processes are started in the correct order.

The Deployment Manager for a cell holds the configuration for all server nodes in that cell. The Deployment Manager must be started first so it reads in the updated configuration and has it ready to be accessed by the node agent when it launches. The Deployment Manager server is called `dmgr`.

The node agent is the process that starts the enterprise application server such as the Meeting Server or Proxy Server. It takes the configuration from the Deployment Manager and uses it to start the application server process. The node agent must be started after the Deployment Manager and before the application itself. The server application process must be started after the node agent to ensure its configuration is up-to-date as it loads.

Starting and stopping servers

The first thing to understand when managing a WAS-based system is how the servers are installed and run. As discussed earlier in the book, each Sametime application is simply a server instance hosted by a WAS install. There may be many different server instances such as Meeting, Media, Proxy, and SSC in the same WAS installation. In a Sametime environment, there is often a group of servers being managed by the SSC. Due to the complexity that may be found in some environments, it is important to not only understand the server hierarchy but also how to start and stop the servers.

There are three primary methods for starting and stopping each Sametime server:

- Using a batch file
- Using a Windows service
- Using the SSC to start and stop the server

Batch files

Each Sametime server component installs with its own set of batch files installed into the `bin` directory under its profile. For instance, for a Meeting Server that is installed in the profile `mrkiteSTMPNProfile1`, the start and stop scripts would be found in `<WASDirectory>\profiles\mrkiteSTMPNProfile1\bin` where `<WASDirectory>` is usually `c:\ibm\websphere\appserver`.

Profile names are case-sensitive, so be sure you have checked your syntax before running the script file. There is both a start and stop script in each `bin` directory under each server profile. There is no way to start all the servers from one file unless a new batch process file is written. Each start and stop script can only act upon the servers in that profile directory. There are `.bat` scripts for Windows and `.sh` scripts for Linux. `startServer.bat` or `startServer.sh <servername>` will start the specified server. `stopServer.bat` or `stopServer.sh <servername>` will stop the specified server. An example would be `startServer STMediaServer`.

Following are the server names:

* STConsoleServer — the SSC
* STMeetingServer — the Meeting Server
* STMediaServer — the Media Server (all components)
* STProxyServer — the Proxy Server

There are also specific scripts for starting and stopping the node agents that support each server. These are located in the same directory as the server startup scripts. They are **startnode.bat** or **startnode.sh** and **stopnode.bat** or **stopnode.sh.**

The start and stop node scripts do not need any server name parameters as they are configured to only start the node agent found in that directory. There will only be one node agent in each directory.

Windows services

Having the WAS servers start as Windows services is extremely convenient if everything should be automatically started when the operating system initiates. The installation process will often add the application server as a service, but it does not add the server's node agent or any dependencies. As mentioned earlier, the servers cannot be started unless their node agents are started first.

Modifying, deleting, and adding WAS services is done through the `wasservice` program found in the `bin` directory under your default WAS install. An example would be: `c:\ibm\websphere\appserver\bin`. The `wasservice` program has many required and optional parameters, but for most Sametime servers the parameters used would be just a small subset. We will describe these next.

Adding a service

- **Service_name**: The name under which the service should appear. This can be any descriptive name, but it should be enclosed in double quotes if it contains a space. For example, `"STConsoleServer - Dmgr"`.

- **-server_name**: The actual application server name, such as `STMediaServer`, `STConsoleServer`, or `STProxyServer`.

- **-profilepath**: The location of the profile for the server being added. For example, `c:\ibm\websphere\appserver\profiles\mrkiteSTMSPNProfile1` for the Media Server profile or `c:\ibm\websphere\appserver\profiles\mrkiteSTMPNProfile1` for the Meeting Server profile. All the profile directories are listed under the WAS program directory at `\websphere\appserver\profiles`. Remember that the profile name is case-sensitive!

- **-stopArgs**: The parameters passed with a stop request on the server. For example, the **–username** and **–password** parameters used by wasadmin to manage the server itself. For example, `-stopArgs "-username wasadmin -password mrkitebenefit"`. Note the argument string must be entirely enclosed in double quotes.

- **-encodeparams**: To ensure the credentials given to **-stopArgs** are encoded.

- **-logRoot**: The location of the log directory for the server being added. This is a subdirectory of the `-profilepath` that was already used. For example, `c:\ibm\websphere\appserver\profiles\mrkiteSTMSPNProfile1\logs` for the Media Server.

- **-startype**: How the service should start. It may be **Automatic** or **Manual**.

An example of putting these parameters together—to add the Proxy Server as a service that starts automatically, the syntax would be:

```
wasservice -add "ST Proxy Server" -server_name
STProxyServer -profilepath
c:\ibm\websphere\appserver\profiles\mrkiteSTPNProfile1
-stopargs " -username wasadmin -password mrkitebenefit"
-encodeparams -logRoot
c:\ibm\websphere\appserver\profiles\mrkiteSTPNProfile1\logs
-starttype Automatic
```

Updating a service

If `wasservice` is called again and parameters are passed to an existing service name, the service in question will be updated and not duplicated.

Deleting a service

The command `wasservice -remove` followed by the service name will remove that particular service.

Modifying dependencies

Windows services are added with no dependencies at all so each can start independently. But as discussed earlier, the WAS servers are dependent upon starting in the right order. To ensure this happens, dependencies must be created for each Windows service. This includes the Deployment Manager and each server's node agent. The only way this can be done is by editing the Windows registry directly. To do this, modify the following service configuration:

`HKEY_LOCAL_MACHINE\SYSTEM\CurrentControlSet\Services\<Service name>`

Add a new `REG_MULTI_SZ` key called `DependOnService` and enter the full name of the service that should be started before this one. More information on dependencies can be found here: `http://support.microsoft.com/kb/193888`.

> It is important to note that a service can only be made dependent upon another service if they share the same computer. Making a service dependent upon a service that is installed on a different machine will cause the service to not start.

From within the Sametime System Console

Once the SSC is running, and assuming all servers are installed in the same cell as the SSC, the SSC can be used to start and stop other servers and update the configuration of the node agents from the Deployment Manager. To do this, the node agents for each server must be started. The Deployment Manager (in this case the SSC) cannot start the node agent for another server itself. Let us begin by reviewing where these settings are found in the SSC.

Server | Server Types | WebSphere Application Servers

From **Server | Server Types | WebSphere Application Servers**, all the active servers in the cell are listed with their start state. Individual services can be started and stopped by using the actions buttons on the screen. Starting and stopping each application also starts and stops all its component parts.

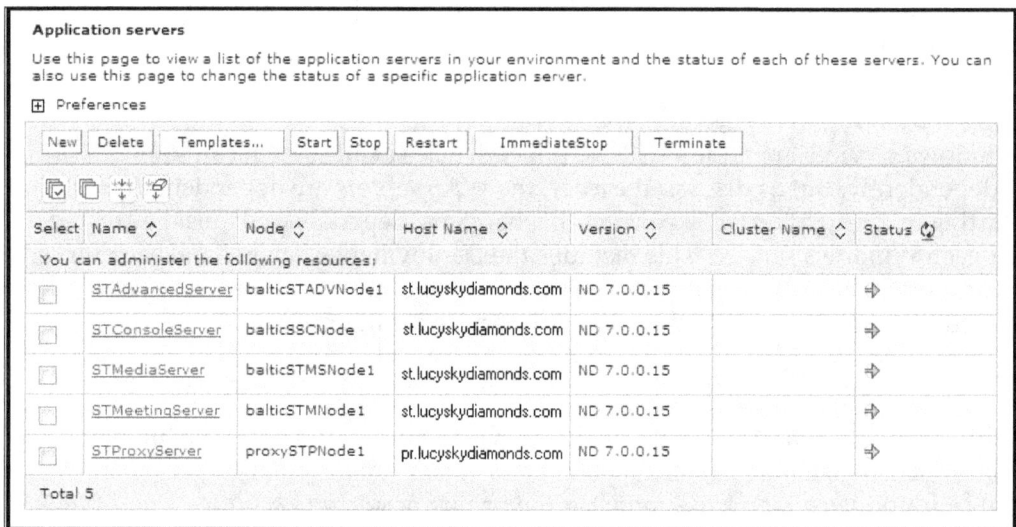

Servers | Applications | WebSphere Enterprise Applications

The **Servers | Applications | WebSphere Enterprise Applications** panel includes all the application components. For instance, in the case of the Media Server, this means the `ConferenceFocus`, the IBM SIP Proxy, the IBM SIP Registrar, and the `STAVPacketSwitch` components. Each of these components can be started and stopped independently from the Media Server application, but the preference should always be to restart the Application Server itself and let it restart its components. This panel would also be used to remove or update a component should you receive a patch, upgrade, or hotfix from IBM.

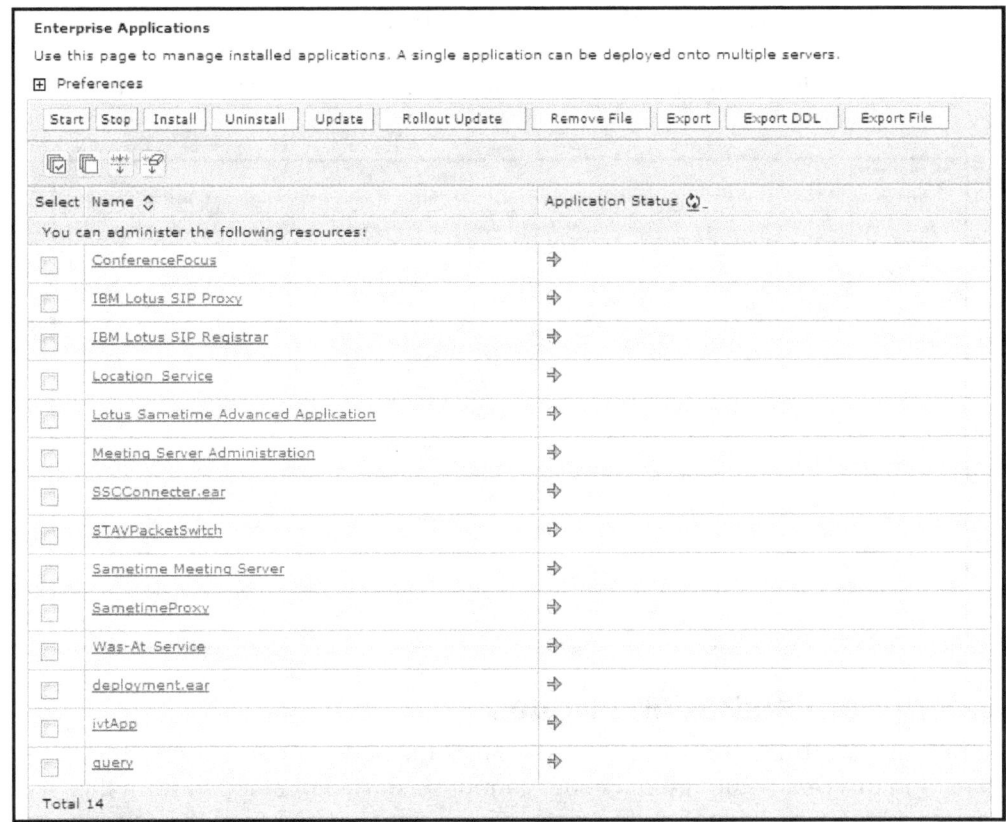

System Administration | Node Agents

The **System Administration | Node Agents** panel lists all the node agents for each server installed in the cell. The panel displays the running state for each node agent and options are included here to either restart just the node agent or restart the node agent and the servers it manages. By restarting the node agent, you ensure it picks up the latest configuration from the Deployment Manager, and that it is ready to update the application server when it next restarts. You would do this if you wanted to ensure the updated configuration was in place, but it was not an appropriate time to restart the server itself. A node agent can represent multiple servers in a single profile. For instance, the node agent for the Meeting Server <name>STMNode1 will restart both the Meeting Server and the HTTP Proxy for that server if present.

It is only possible to use this method to restart node agents if the node agents are already in a started state. This cannot be used to start currently stopped node agents. They would first need to be started using one of the other two methods previously discussed.

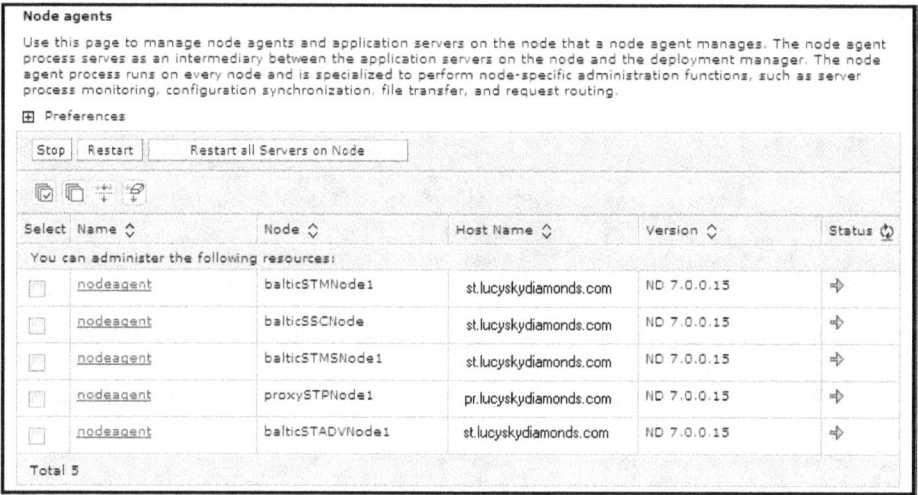

System Administration | Nodes

The **System Administration | Nodes** panel lists the nodes for each application installed in this cell. Although the nodes cannot be started or stopped from this menu screen, it is possible to perform a synchronization which tells the deployment manager to update each node agent with the latest configuration it holds for each server. The icon on the right under **Status** will change if the configuration held by the node agent differs from the one known to the Deployment Manager.

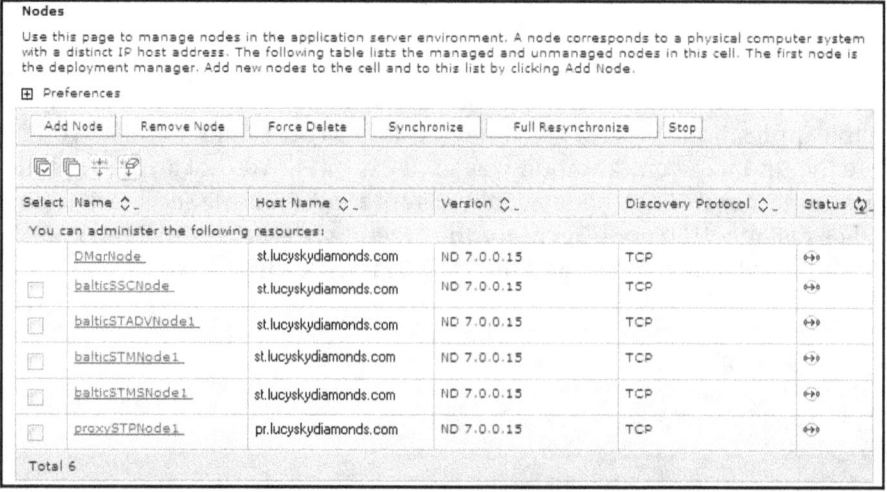

Backing up server configuration

As with any other production system it is important to back up a WAS server. Each WebSphere server's configuration is held in .xml files on the file system of the server where it is installed. Each server has its own configuration files held within the config directory underneath its own profile and within its Deployment Manager's configuration files. For instance, the configuration directory for the Meeting Server might be c:\ibm\websphere\appserver\mrkiteSTMPNProfile1\config. However, some files are held within the Deployment Manager's profile, which in this case would be the SSC.

Compressing files

As all configuration files are in .xml format, a backup can be done by compressing the contents of each profile's config directory into .zip or .tar files. To restore the files you would overwrite the file from your .zip or .tar backup. The advantage of this method is that it is fast and does not alter the ownership or rights of the files being backed up.

In this case, the file backup would occur as a process outside of WAS, so there is a risk that further configuration changes could be happening during the backup process unless the servers are stopped in advance. You must also ensure that both the configuration for the application server and its Deployment Manager are backed up and restored together.

WAS scripts

Although we can use file compression to back up every profile directory and all its subdirectories or each config directory under every profile, there is another way available as part of your WAS install. In each server's profile directory there is a bin subdirectory that contains scripts for performing server functions. Earlier we looked at the start and stop server scripts — startserver and stopserver — stored in the bin directory, and you can also find backup scripts here.

Backup

From within the bin directory for each server, you would run the following command:

backupconfig.bat or backupconfig.sh [drive]:[pathname]filename

There are three optional parameters you should consider using with `backupconfig`:

- The `backupconfig` script stops the servers it is backing up when it runs. This ensures configuration changes are not made during backup. If the servers are to be running during the backup the `-nostop` parameter must be used.

- The `backupconfig` script requires the username and password for each server in order to read its configuration, stop the server, and back it up. The values can be passed to the script using the `–username` and `–password` parameters. Be very careful of storing these in clear text in a batch file.

To back up your Meeting Server without stopping it and without being prompted for credentials, you would use:

```
c:\ibm\websphere\appserver\mrkiteSTMPNProfile1\bin\
backupconfig c:\backups\meetingserver.zip -nostop
-username wasadmin -password mrkitebenefit
```

Restore

The `restoreconfig` script is found in the same `config` directory as `backupconfig`, and applies to the same server profile if it is run from that directory. It will restore the configuration saved in the `.zip` file that was created by `backupconfig` and stop the servers within that node before doing a restore. It will also rename the original `config` directory if it is present before restoring.

It is possible to use the same parameters that were used for the backup to prevent the servers being stopped during restore. If this is done, the restored configuration will not be picked up until after the server is restarted.

```
c:\ibm\websphere\appserver\mrkiteSTMPNProfile1\bin\
restoreconfig c:\backups\meetingserver.zip -nostop
-username wasadmin -password mrkitebenefit
```

Databases

At least two of the Sametime server components use DB2 databases to hold their configuration. Part of the production backup routine should include these databases. By default these would be:

- STSC—Sametime System Console.
- STMS—Sametime Meeting Server. If there are multiple Meeting Servers within the same DB2 instance, they will each have different names.
- STADV—Sametime Advanced Server (only if Sametime Advanced is installed).

The following is a link to an IBM document on DB2 backup options:

```
http://publib.boulder.ibm.com/infocenter/db2luw/v9r5/index.
jsp?topic=/com.ibm.db2.luw.admin.ha.doc/doc/c0006150.html
```

Basic WebSphere Application Server troubleshooting

In a Sametime 8.5.2 environment, the majority of all servers installed now run as applications under WAS, so that the logging and reporting behavior of each server as well as methods for troubleshooting are consistent for any application installed in this environment. The following is a description of how to review WAS servers and guidance on how to troubleshoot potential problems.

Reviewing server status

Reviewing the status of a server can be done from within the SSC (if all the servers are installed in the same cell) or from the operating system. We will first examine how to review status from the operating system.

Operating system review

In each server's profile directory on the file system there is a `bin` subdirectory that contains scripts for performing server functions. Earlier, we reviewed the `startserver`, `stopserver`, `backupconfig`, and `restoreconfig` scripts, but to review our server status we also have the `serverstatus` script. The `serverstatus` script gathers the configuration for a server installed in the profile it is run from if passed the server name. For example, `serverstatus STMeetingServer` will return the running state of the Meeting Server when run from that profile's `bin` subdirectory. You can pass the `-all` parameter to the script to tell it to report on all servers it finds within this profile.

To analyze the running state of a server, the `serverstatus` script will need that server's credentials. The credentials can be passed in the command line with `-username` and `-password` parameters.

For example, to report on the state of all server processes within the Meeting Server profile, you could run the following:

```
c:\ibm\websphere\appserver\profiles\mrkiteSTMPNProfile1\bin\serverstatus
-all -username wasadmin -password mrkitebenefit
```

The resulting output tells you not only which servers exist in this profile but if they are in a STARTED state.

```
ADMU0116I:  Tool information is being logged in file
            c:\IBM\WebSphere\AppServer\profiles\baltic|STMPNProfile1\logs\serverStatus.log
ADMU0128I:  Starting tool with the balticStMPNProfile1 profile
ADMU0503I:  Retrieving server status for all servers
ADMU0505I:  Servers found in configuration:
ADMU0506I:  Server name: meet_proxy
ADMU0506I:  Server name: nodeagent
ADMU0506I:  Server name: STMeetingServer
ADMU0508I:  The Application Server "meet_proxy" is STARTED
ADMU0508I:  The Node Agent "nodeagent" is STarted
ADMU0508I:  The Application Server "STMeetingServer" is STARTED

C:\IBM\WebSphere\AppServer\profiles\baltic\STMPNProfile1\bin>
```

Sametime System Console review

If the application servers are all installed within the same cell as the SSC, then the Deployment Manager used by the SSC also manages those applications. This means that by logging into the SSC you can review the status of all the servers it manages.

Server | Server Types | WebSphere Application Servers

This is a list of all application servers that the SSC's Deployment Manager tracks. Each server is listed with its profile name, the fully qualified hostname of the server on which it is installed, and the status of each server.

Application servers

Use this page to view a list of the application servers in your environment and the status of each of these servers. You can also use this page to change the status of a specific application server.

⊞ Preferences

| New | Delete | Templates... | Start | Stop | Restart | ImmediateStop | Terminate |

Select	Name ◇	Node ◇	Host Name ◇	Version ◇	Cluster Name ◇	Status ⟳
You can administer the following resources:						
☐	STAdvancedServer	balticSTADVNode1	st.lucyskydiamonds.com	ND 7.0.0.15		⇨
☐	STConsoleServer	balticSSCNode	st.lucyskydiamonds.com	ND 7.0.0.15		⇨
☐	STMediaServer	balticSTMSNode1	st.lucyskydiamonds.com	ND 7.0.0.15		⇨
☐	STMeetingServer	balticSTMNode1	st.lucyskydiamonds.com	ND 7.0.0.15		⇨
☐	STProxyServer	proxySTPNode1	pr.lucyskydiamonds.com	ND 7.0.0.15		⇨
Total 5						

If you installed some of your application servers into their own cells, you would need to log in to the Deployment Manager for that cell to review their status. An example of the URL to use would be `https://<hostname:portinstalledon>/ibm/console`. You would only see and be able to review the applications that are installed in that cell.

Reviewing server performance

When designing a Sametime infrastructure, you may be faced with decisions about which servers to co-locate on the same hardware and which ones need dedicated resources. As the infrastructure matures, you may find that demand for services increases. Regularly reviewing server performance helps you plan for future growth.

A review of each server's resource demand is also useful when investigating unexpected problems or unreliability with the Sametime applications. Sametime applications impact different system resources. For example, the Sametime Proxy Server can generate a large amount of network traffic, whereas the Media Manager, which is performing audio and video compression, can require significant processor resources. Identifying a system resource problem on hardware that is used by more than one application does not help resolve the issue unless you can identify which application is at fault.

IBM's performance monitoring tool, **Tivoli Performance Monitor**, is built into the WAS server and is able to monitor each installed enterprise application and its component modules. Monitoring each application with the Performance Monitor consumes server resources, but IBM states that standard monitoring should not consume more than 5% of the system resources. However, there are many detailed monitoring metrics that can be requested from this panel. Unless it is necessary to troubleshoot a specific problem, we would advise that extreme caution and moderation is used when enabling them.

To work with Performance Monitoring, you log into the SSC and navigate to the **Monitoring and Tuning** section.

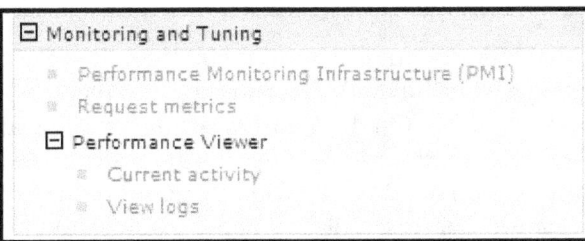

The first step is to enable the **Performance Monitoring Infrastructure** (**PMI**) for the applications that are to be monitored. If a server is not running, it is not available for monitoring. Select **Current Activity** to see which servers are available and which are already being monitored. In this view, it is also possible to select applications and to start or stop their monitoring in real time. This does not start or stop the running of the server itself.

In the following example, monitoring is configured for the key Sametime applications such as Meeting Server, Proxy Server, and Media Server, but not their node agents.

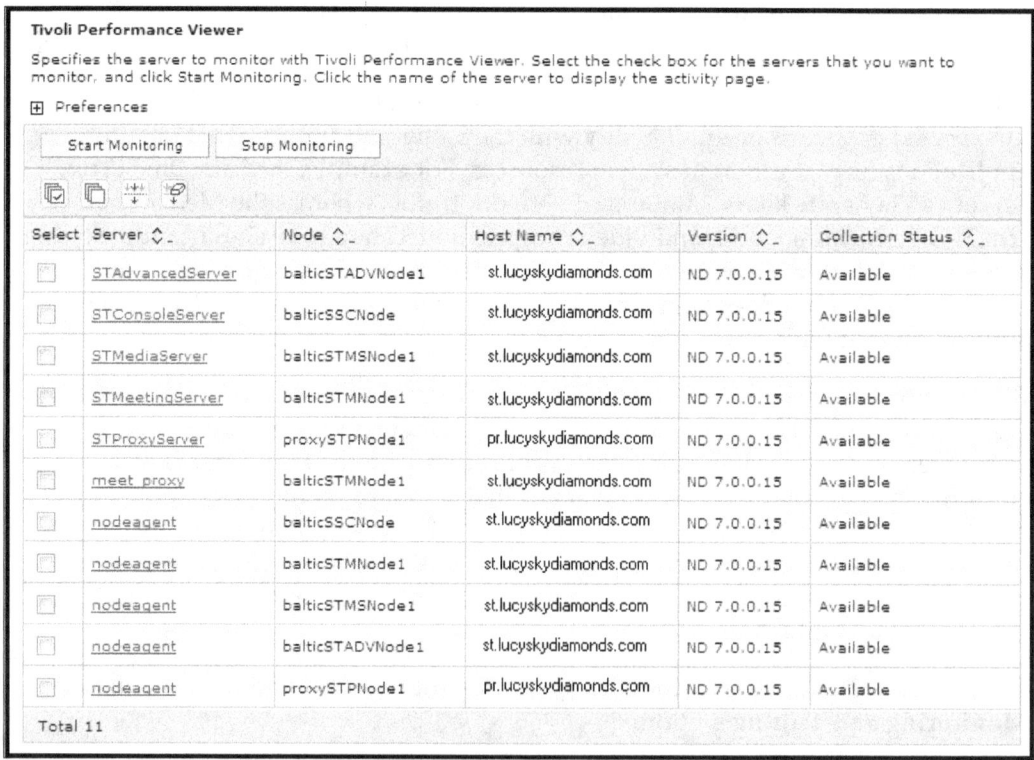

If a server is not available for monitoring and is running, then PMI must be enabled by going to **Performance Monitoring Infrastructure** (**PMI**) and selecting the application that is to be enabled. On the **Configuration** tab of the application settings, check the box for **Enable Performance Monitoring Infrastructure** (**PMI**). After enabling PMI, the application must be restarted by going to **Server | Server Types | WebSphere Application Servers**. Unless you are troubleshooting an application problem, enabling **Basic** monitoring will be sufficient.

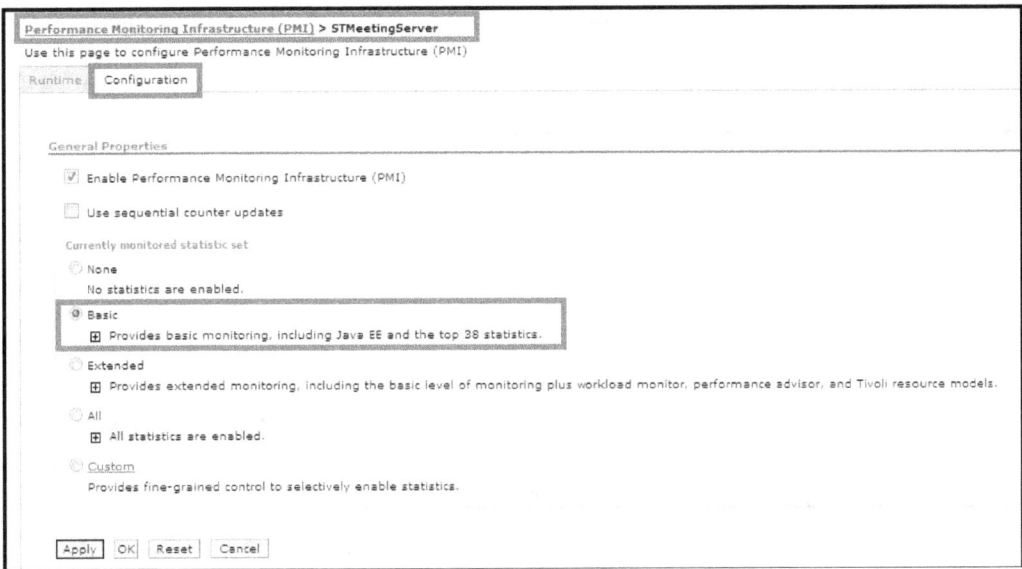

Real-time performance activity

Having enabled monitoring, you can now review the performance of any Sametime application under **Current Activity**. There are two reports on current activity that are useful for you to review: **Advisor** and **Settings**.

In the following example, using the **Advisor** report, a summary of all application resources currently being used is broken down by each process. This is a real-time summary with no historical data. At the bottom of the view is a list of alerts that may require review. Due to the complex nature of the Sametime applications and the WAS infrastructure, use caution when reviewing these alerts and taking action based on them.

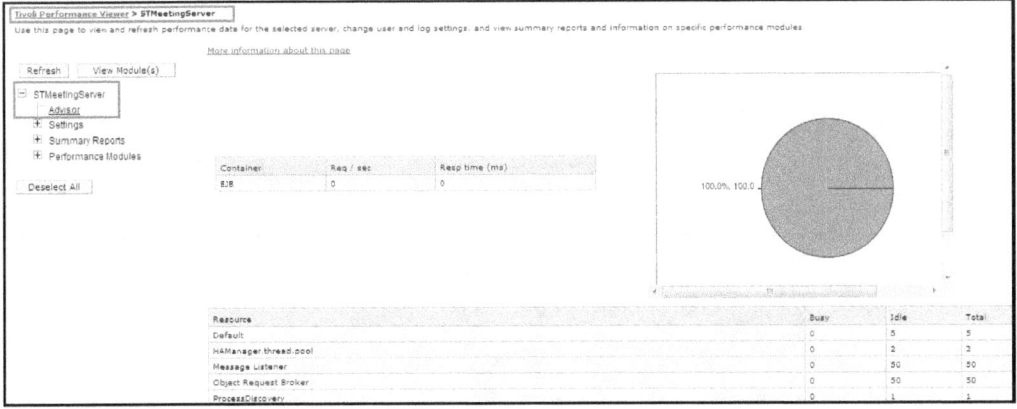

The **Advisor** report displays alerts and tuning suggestions for the Sametime component you are monitoring. Use caution when you consider implementing the suggestions listed here.

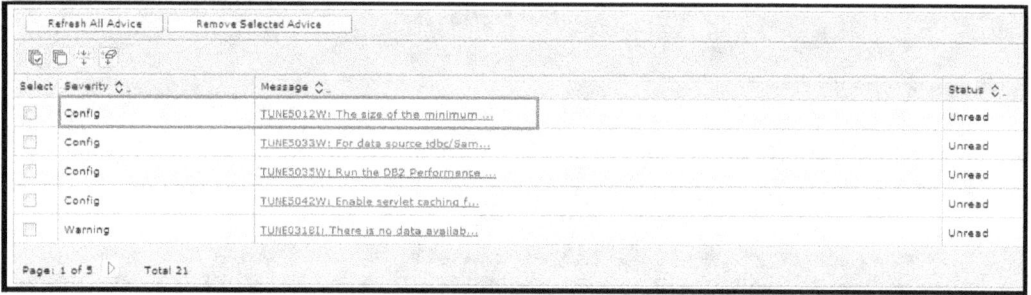

Historical performance activity

To monitor an application over time, you will need to request the generation of .xml logs which will then be available for review. To view historical activity, select **Summary Reports** and choose **Servlets**. Each servlet used by the application is listed along with the number of requests and the average response time. For example, when reviewing the Sametime Media Server, you can see metrics for servlets such as the Conference Manager and the Packet Switcher.

To generate logs of the metrics over time, select **Start Logging** and the system will create .tpv log files on the server in the logs\tpv subdirectory under each server's profile.

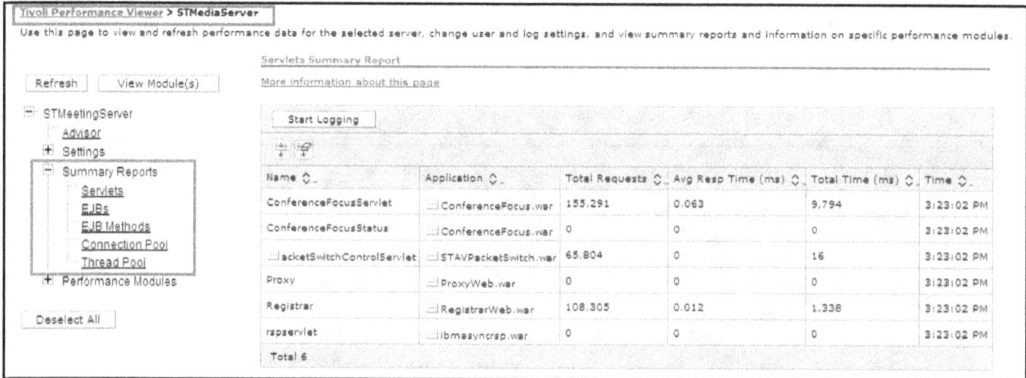

To review the performance log files that have been generated, select **View Log** from the menu and browse on the server to find the log. The log will be in the `log` subdirectory from the server profile in the `tpv` folder. The following example shows one of the logs for the Meeting Server. You can add other logs to view as they are generated and saved to the file system over time.

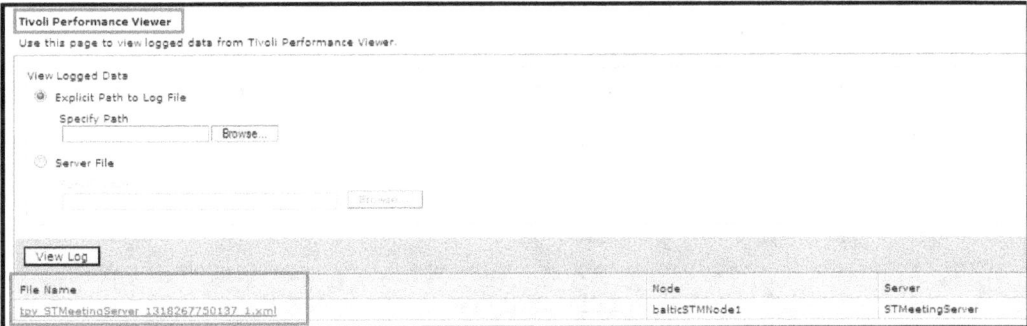

Where to look for log information

Every WAS server generates its own logs as it runs and stores them within its profile directory structure. Under each server's profile, there is a `logs` directory where all logs are saved in standard log format under each server name.

On the file system

The logs for the Sametime Meeting Server in your install would be found on the file system under:

```
c:\ibm\websphere\appserver\profiles\mrkiteSTMPNProfile1\
logs\STMeetingServer
```

There are four key logs that are of initial interest to you:

- `startserver.log` — the activity that occurs as the server is started. If a server is failing to start, this is where to look first to begin troubleshooting.

- `stopserver.log` — the activity that occurs as the server is stopping. If the server does not stop cleanly or fails to start with an error saying it did not stop cleanly, examine this log first.

- systemout.log—this is the equivalent of the console output. All server activity in real time is written out to this log. For example, if one of the running application features is not working or users are failing to login, review this log first.

- systemerr.log—is the record of all errors being generated by the server application. A sudden growth in log file size is an indication of a serious problem which should be reviewed.

When looking at WAS logs, it is important to learn how to interpret each line. The following are two lines from a log file:

```
[06/06/11 13:04:33:817 BST] 00000000 ManagerAdmin I  TRAS0018I: The trace
state has changed. The new trace state is *=info
```

```
[06/06/11 13:04:33:942 BST] 00000000 AdminTool   A ADMU0128I: Starting
tool with the mrkiteSTMPNProfile1 profile
```

The log in the example is showing the date and time an event occurred, the process in which it occurred, and a status report represented by a letter and a message. The lines also have a status of I and A. In all WAS logs, the statuses include:

- A—Audit
- I—Information
- W—Warning
- X—Error
- F—Fatal

When the logs are opened in a log viewer, the statuses are aligned and it is easy to see error warning lines. When errors occur, it is important to scroll up in the logs to find the first instance of an error or warning line, as this will often be the initial cause of the problem you are attempting to resolve. Always read WAS logs from top to bottom, and not bottom to top.

In the Sametime System Console

The SSC also provides a way to view logs for the WAS-based servers from one location, although only the systemout and systemerr logs can be viewed from here. To work with the logs for a particular server, select that server in the **Logging and Tracing** list.

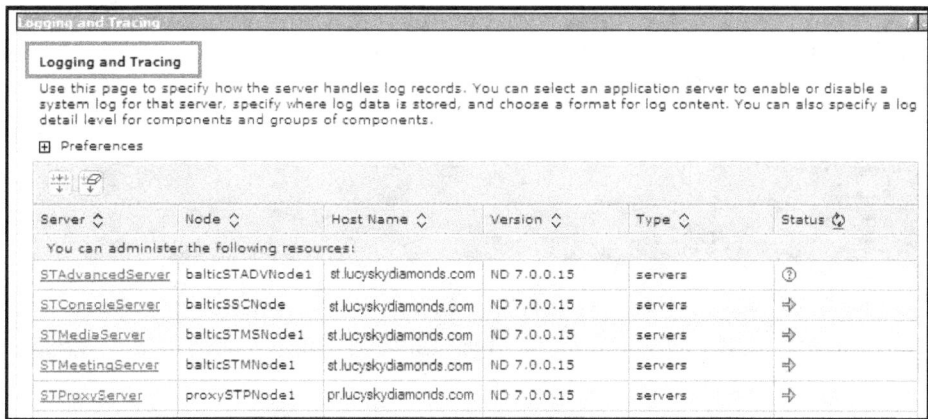

The following are the options for managing the logs for an application server. This example shows the STMeetingServer. The two options that are of interest to you are **JVM Logs** and **Change Log Detail Levels**.

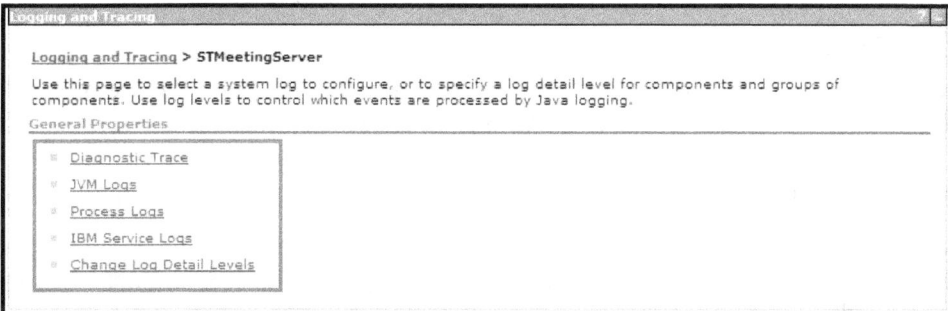

Selecting **JVM Logs** allows you to view the systemout.log and systemerr.log in real time as they are being written.

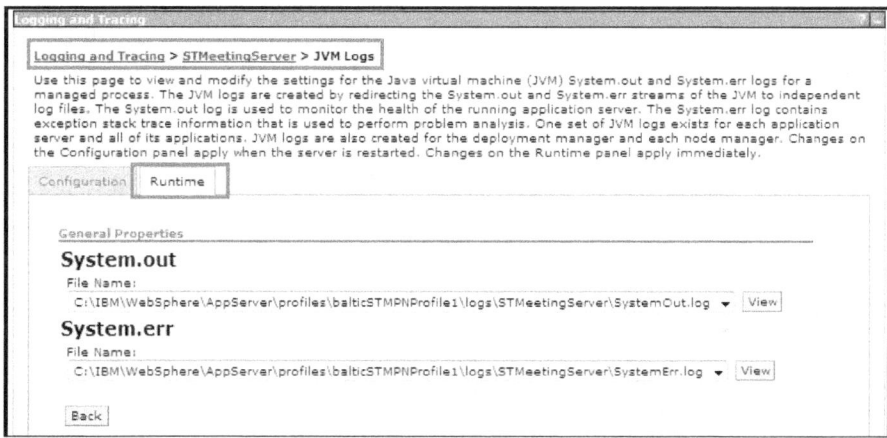

Selecting **View** opens up the log in a viewer, making it easy to read and to quickly spot problems. You can move within the log by retrieving a specific range of lines to review and clicking on **Refresh**.

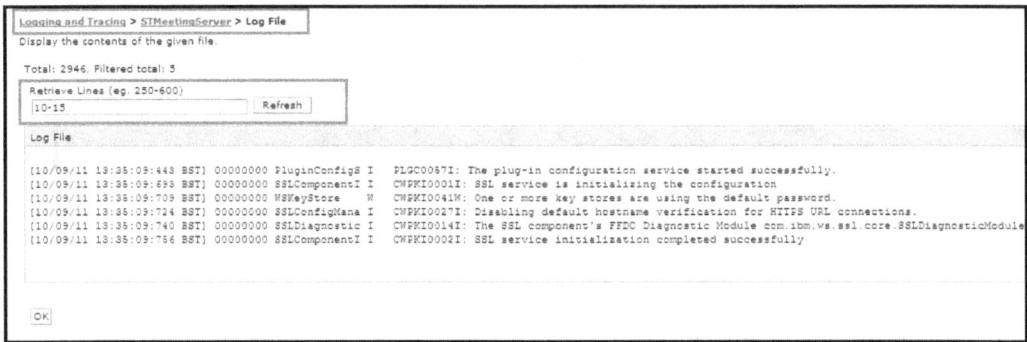

Collecting and reviewing debugging information

In some instances, when troubleshooting a problem, you may want to see more detailed log information. On install, each server is preconfigured to write log information at **info** level only. You can adjust the detail level each server writes to its logs, but this does require a restart of the server that has been changed.

If you want to adjust the logging detail to a higher level of diagnostic tracing (**finer** or **finest**) you can do so under **Troubleshooting | Logging and Tracing**. Bear in mind that detailed logging can create an enormous amount of data which will consume space on the server hard disk and should only be used for analysis of a specific problem and then should be immediately disabled.

Select the server to be reviewed and then choose **Change log detail levels**. The server will be set to log all components (*) at **info** (informational) level. If the word **info** is replaced with **finest**, the server will generate all levels of logging detail.

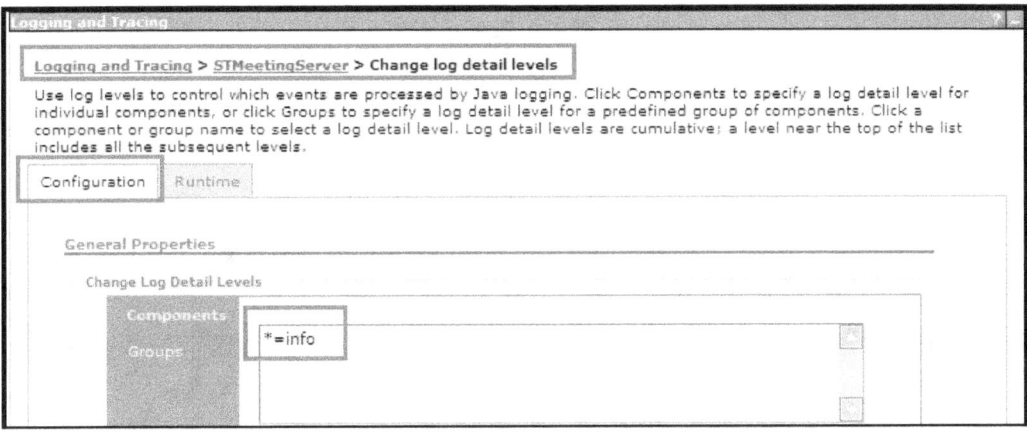

In the event that you are working to troubleshoot a complex issue, you may need to collect log files, profiles, and configuration data to send to IBM for review. To do so, you can use the WAS Collector tool. The Collector tool can be found in the `c:\ibm\websphere\appserver\profiles\hostname_profilenumber\bin\collector.bat` directory. This tool will package the necessary files as Java archive files or JAR files for you to send to IBM support.

Summary

At the end of this chapter, you have learned how to monitor system usage, manage Sametime server processes, and LDAP server usage. You also learned how to configure server processes for Sametime-related connectivity and how to perform basic troubleshooting. In Appendix A, several worksheets are provided for you to assist with preparing and planning for the Sametime server installation.

A

Sametime 8.5.2 Installation Worksheets

This appendix includes some sample worksheets that you can use for planning and installing Sametime. As the Sametime server installation involves the interdependencies on components among the servers, we have provided some sample worksheets to help you organize your installation and deployment. Worksheets that we have included include details for the following:

- Sametime cells/nodes
- Sametime DB2 instances
- Sametime administrator passwords
- Sametime installation preparation checklists

Sample worksheets

The following are sample worksheets for preparing, planning, or for use during the installation of the Sametime server environment. These can be used as a reference and later as part of your server documentation.

Sametime server hostnames

You will have to frequently refer to the fully qualified domain name of your Sametime server during your install and will not be able to change the hostnames you choose post installation. You should arrange to have these added to your domain name server prior to the installation.

 Note that the Meeting Server and Proxy Server cannot have the same fully qualified hostname. Also, all servers need to share a domain for Single Sign-On to work across the environment.

Sametime server hostnames	
SSC server:	
DB2 server:	
LDAP server:	
Sametime Community Server:	
Sametime Proxy Server:	
Sametime Media Manager Server:	
Sametime Meeting Server:	
Sametime Advanced Server:	
Sametime TURN Server:	
Sametime Bandwidth Manager Server:	

Sametime server information

Frequently, the Sametime or Domino administrators may not be the people managing the operating system of the Sametime servers. However, during the installation process, you may be required to restart the operating system. In addition, as you build the deployment plans for each server, you will be prompted to set an administrative username and password. This worksheet lists the operating system, administrative user ID, and passwords that you may use to log into the different server operating systems.

Sametime server information			
Sametime server name	Operating system	Admin user ID	Admin password
SSC server:			
DB2 server:			
LDAP server:			
Sametime Community Server:			
Sametime Proxy Server:			
Sametime Media Manager Server:			
Sametime Meeting Server:			

Sametime server information			
Sametime server name	**Operating system**	**Admin user ID**	**Admin password**
Sametime Advanced Server:			
Sametime TURN Server:		N/A	N/A
Sametime Bandwidth Manager Server:			

LDAP Server

The Sametime server architecture references an LDAP server throughout the installation process. Be sure that prior to installation, you have the proper hostname, bind credentials, and port necessary to access the server.

LDAP server	
Deployment name:	
Hostname:	
Bind credentials:	
LDAP base query:	
Bind credential Password:	
Port:	
LDAP server type:	

Sametime server components

During the Sametime server installation, you will have many instances where you have to refer to the DB2 server, the SSC server, or many of the other Sametime servers. We are providing worksheets here for use during the server and the related DB2 database installation and configuration. Although we have listed only one table for DB2 server details, the full Sametime installation requires DB2 databases for many components. If you choose to install these databases on different DB2 servers or instances, we suggest you duplicate the following table as necessary.

DB2 server	
Hostname:	
DB2 admin ID:	
DB2 admin password:	
Port:	
SSC DB name:	

DB2 server	
Meeting DB name:	
Advanced DB name:	
Gateway DB name:	

SSC server	
Hostname:	
DB2 database name:	
SSC/WAS admin ID:	
SSC/WAS admin password:	
Node name:	
Cell name:	
WAS app profile name:	
Port(s):	

Sametime Community Server	
Deployment name:	
Hostname:	
SSC hostname:	
SSC admin ID:	
SSC admin password:	
Port:	
HTTP Tunneling enabled: Yes/No	

Sametime Proxy Server	
Deployment name:	
Hostname:	
Node name:	
Cell name:	
WAS app profile name:	
Admin ID:	
Admin password:	
Port:	
Proxy IP to add to Community Server:	

Sametime Media Server	
Deployment name:	
Hostname:	
Node name:	
Cell name:	
WAS app profile name:	
Admin ID:	
Admin password:	
Port:	

Sametime Meeting Server	
Deployment name:	
Hostname:	
Node name:	
Cell name:	
WAS app profile name:	
Admin ID:	
Admin password:	
Port:	
DB2 database name:	
DB2 hostname:	

Sametime Advanced Server	
Deployment name:	
Hostname:	
Node name:	
Cell name:	
WAS app profile name:	
Admin ID:	
Admin password:	
Port:	
DB2 database name:	
DB2 hostname:	

Sametime Gateway Server	
Deployment name:	
Hostname:	
Node name:	
Cell name:	
WAS app profile name:	
Admin ID:	
Admin password:	
Port:	
DB2 database name:	
DB2 hostname:	

Sametime Bandwidth Server	
Deployment name:	
Hostname:	
Node name:	
Cell name:	
WAS app profile name:	
Admin ID:	
Admin password:	
Port:	
DB2 database name:	
DB2 hostname:	

Sametime TURN Server	
Hostname:	
Path to `stavconfig.xml`:	
Port:	

Sametime Install package names

As the Sametime install package includes several different files, you may want to create a worksheet or checklist that allows you to keep track of the package name, file name, and its purpose.

Sametime package names	
Package name:	**Purpose:**

Because the installation may be dependent on your server operating system, we have not included the file names. But you may find the list of all the package numbers needed for a Sametime 8.5.2 Standard installation at the following website:

```
https://www.ibm.com/support/docview.wss?uid=swg24029128
http://tinyurl.com/sametime-a001
```

Summary

In this chapter, several worksheets have been provided for you to prepare and plan for the Sametime server installation.

B
Sametime 8.5.2 Related Resources

This chapter includes resources for those Sametime topics not covered specifically in other areas of the book.

Topics to be covered include:

- Customizing the Sametime client
- Sametime client plugins and/or widgets
- Sametime SDK
- Resources for learning about Sametime clustering or partitioned servers
- Migrating from Domino Directory authentication to LDAP
- Integrating SPNEGO with Sametime
- Sametime Unified Telephony
- Resources for Sametime documentation
- Sametime Gateway Server
- Where to find help when using the SSC
- Resources for training and certification
- The Sametime song

Customizing the Sametime client

One of the things that many companies like to do is "brand" the Sametime client so that it has their logo on the sign-on screen. If you need to make that type of customization to your Sametime Connect Client, you can use the information in the "Your Co branding for IBM Lotus Sametime 8.0 and later using the Connect client" article on the developerWorks site at the following site:

```
http://www.ibm.com/developerworks/lotus/library/sametime-branding/
index.html
```

```
http://tinyurl.com/sametime-b001
```

You can also customize client messages and what features are downloaded for the Sametime client package. Refer to the following website for more information:

```
http://www.lotus.com/ldd/stwiki.nsf/dx/Creating_custom_client_
features_sta852
```

```
http://tinyurl.com/sametime-b002
```

Sametime client plugins and/or widgets

A plugin is a program or set of programs created to add functionality to a larger software application. A widget is a stand-alone application that may run with a larger software application such as Sametime. You may hear these terms used interchangeably, but they mean quite different things. The Sametime SDK can be used to write to these extensions.

An example of a plugin is the Sametime wallpaper plugin found at the following site:

```
http://www.epilio.com/web/wallpaper.htm
```

```
http://tinyurl.com/sametime-b003
```

For more information on adding a widget to Sametime, refer to the following website:

```
http://www.notesdesignblog.com/NotesDesignBlog/NDBlog.nsf/dx/
we-are-adding-widgets-support-to-sametime-need-your-opinion.
htm?opendocument&comments
```

```
http://tinyurl.com/sametime-b004
```

Sametime SDK

The Sametime **Software Developer Kit (SDK)** provides a toolkit that allows you to build extensions for Sametime, as well as integrate Sametime into your own applications. The Sametime Meetings Remote Client SDK provides Java APIs that expose Meeting Center capabilities such as creating and deleting meetings. Refer to the following websites to access the developer kits.

IBM Sametime SDK:

```
http://www14.software.ibm.com/webapp/download/nochargesearch.
jsp?q0=&k=ALL&S_TACT=104CBW71&status=Active&b=Lotus&sr=1&q=sametime+s
dk&ibm-search=Search
```

```
http://tinyurl.com/sametime-b005
```

Sametime Meetings Remote Client SDK:

```
http://www.ibm.com/developerworks/lotus/downloads/sametime_remote_
client_sdk.html
```

```
http://tinyurl.com/sametime-b006
```

Sametime clustering or running on partitioned servers

As your Sametime environment grows, you may require a clustered server environment for your Community Server. For information on Sametime Community Server clustering, refer to the following website:

```
https://www.ibm.com/support/docview.wss?uid=swg21196034
```

```
http://tinyurl.com/sametime-b007
```

"Lotus Sametime 8.5 - Installing and clustering servers with the Sametime System Console" video can be found at:

```
http://www.lotus.com/ldd/stwiki.nsf/dx/Video_Installing_and_
clustering_servers_with_the_Sametime_8.5_System_Console_
```

```
http://tinyurl.com/sametime-b008
```

If you must install Sametime on partitioned servers, please refer to the following support document that explains support for that option:

```
http://www-01.ibm.com/support/docview.wss?uid=swg21095988
```

```
http://tinyurl.com/sametime-b009
```

Migrating from Domino Directory authentication to LDAP

If you are currently using the Domino Directory for authentication for Sametime and are preparing to install Sametime 8.5.2, you may be considering what steps are necessary to change the authentication from Domino to LDAP. This is especially true if you are planning a migration of existing Sametime users. Some resources for this process can be found at the following links mentioned:

How to change your Sametime server from Domino to LDAP after installation:

```
https://www.ibm.com/support/docview.wss?uid=swg21181284
```

```
http://tinyurl.com/sametime-b010
```

Upgrading the IBM Sametime client embedded in IBM Lotus Notes client to Sametime 8.5.1:

```
http://www.lotus.com/ldd/stwiki.nsf/dx/Upgrading_the_Sametime_client_
embedded_in_Notes_to_Sametime_8.5.1#Converting+your+Sametime+environm
ent+from+Lotus+Domino+to+LDAP+authentication
```

```
http://tinyurl.com/sametime-b011
```

A key part of this process is the name conversion that must take place for the buddy lists stored in the `vpuserinfo.nsf` on the Sametime Community Server:

```
http://publib.boulder.ibm.com/infocenter/sametime/v8r5/index.
jsp?topic=/com.ibm.help.sametime.v85.doc/config/changing__names_in_
contact_and_privacy_lists.html
```

```
http://tinyurl.com/sametime-b012
```

You should proceed with caution when making the name conversion and buddy list changes and of course have a backup of the original file. There are some tools available to help you with managing buddy lists. One of them can be found from Epilio at:

```
http://www.epilio.com/web/BLControl.htm
```

```
http://tinyurl.com/sametime-b013
```

Integrating SPNEGO with Sametime

For additional documentation relating to **Simple and Protected GSS-API Negotiation Mechanism (SPNEGO)** and integrating it with the SSC as the authentication server, visit the following website:

```
http://www.ibm.com/developerworks/lotus/documentation/
spnegowithsametime852/
```

```
http://tinyurl.com/sametime-b014
```

SPNEGO enables the SSO mechanism for Microsoft Windows clients that are part of an Active Directory domain. If you need assistance with troubleshooting SPNEGO authentication, review the following web document:

```
http://www.lotus.com/ldd/stwiki.nsf/dx/Configuring_and_
troubleshooting_SPNEGO_authentication_with_Lotus_Sametime
```

```
http://tinyurl.com/sametime-b015
```

Sametime Unified Telephony

We have not covered anything relating to Sametime Unified Telephony as it would require many additional chapters to discuss deployments, planning, sizing, and vendor options. For an overview of Sametime Unified Telephony and how it connects to Sametime Standard and the Sametime clients, refer the following website:

```
http://www.ibm.com/software/lotus/products/sametime/telephony.html
```

```
http://tinyurl.com/sametime-b016
```

As you will see, Sametime Unified Telephony extends your VoIP network or existing telephony system to your Sametime users. As this involves not only the Sametime Telephony product set but also plugins from telephony vendors depending on the implementation, it is best to work with your telephony provider and IBM to plan an implementation and connection with your Sametime environment.

Sametime Telephony Resources for users:

```
http://www.lotus.com/ldd/stwiki.nsf/dx/Lotus_Sametime_Telephony_8_
Resources_for_users
```

```
http://tinyurl.com/sametime-b017
```

Getting Started with Sametime Unified Telephony:

```
http://www.lotus.com/ldd/stwiki.nsf/dx/Lotus_Sametime_Telephony_8_
Resources_for_users
```

```
http://tinyurl.com/sametime-b018
```

Previewing Sametime Unified Telephony 8.5.2:

```
http://www.lotus.com/ldd/stwiki.nsf/dx/Administrators_Previewing_IBM_
Sametime_Unified_Telephony_8.5.2_for_your_users_
```

```
http://tinyurl.com/sametime-b019
```

Sametime Unified Telephony Functional Specification 8.5.2:

```
http://public.dhe.ibm.com/software/dw/lotus/sametime/st852/sut852_
func_spec.pdf
```

```
http://tinyurl.com/sametime-b020
```

Sametime Unified Telephony Installation Guide 8.5.2:

```
http://public.dhe.ibm.com/software/dw/lotus/sametime/st852/sut852_
instal.pdf
```

```
http://tinyurl.com/sametime-b021
```

Sametime Unified Telephony Lite Client Configuration Guide:

```
http://public.dhe.ibm.com/software/dw/lotus/sametime/st852/
sutlite852_config.pdf
```

```
http://tinyurl.com/sametime-b022
```

Previewing Sametime Telephony Lite Client:

```
http://public.dhe.ibm.com/software/dw/lotus/sametime/st852/
sametime852_sut_lite_preview_guide.pdf
```

```
http://tinyurl.com/sametime-b023
```

System Requirements – Sametime Unified Telephony 8.5.2:

```
https://www.ibm.com/support/docview.wss?uid=swg27020284
```

```
http://tinyurl.com/sametime-b024
```

System Requirements – Sametime Unified Telephony Lite Client 8.5.2:

`https://www.ibm.com/support/docview.wss?uid=swg27020285`

`http://tinyurl.com/sametime-b025`

Resources for Sametime documentation

The primary source of IBM-provided documentation is the Sametime wiki. This can be found at `http://www.lotus.com/ldd/stwiki.nsf`. The wiki is a public website and is open for comments and updates by anyone working with Sametime. We have also included the following resources that you may find useful.

Sametime product website:

`http://www.ibm.com/software/lotus/sametime/`

`http://tinyurl.com/sametime-b026`

Sametime 8.5.2 Release Notes:

`http://public.dhe.ibm.com/software/dw/lotus/sametime/st852/rnST852.html`

`http://tinyurl.com/sametime-b027`

IBM Sametime 8.5.2 Installation, Migration and Configuration Guide:

`http://public.dhe.ibm.com/software/dw/lotus/sametime/st852/st_852_pdfone.pdf`

`http://tinyurl.com/sametime-b028`

IBM Sametime 8.5.2 Administration Guide:

`http://public.dhe.ibm.com/software/dw/lotus/sametime/st852/st_852_pdftwo.pdf`

`http://tinyurl.com/sametime-b029`

Best Practices for LDAP and Sametime:

`http://www.lotus.com/ldd/stwiki.nsf/dx/Best_Practices_for_using_LDAP_with_Lotus_Sametime`

`http://tinyurl.com/sametime-b030`

Creating Custom Java Searches for LDAP:

```
http://www.lotus.com/ldd/stwiki.nsf/dx/Creating_custom_Java_classes_
for_searching_the_LDAP_st852
```

```
http://tinyurl.com/sametime-b031
```

Sametime Log File Locations:

```
http://www.lotus.com/ldd/stwiki.nsf/dx/Log_file_locations_st1852
```

```
http://tinyurl.com/sametime-b032
```

IBM Redbooks: Sametime 8.5 Enterprise Scale Deployment:

```
http://www.lotus.com/ldd/stwiki.nsf/xpViewCategories.
xsp?lookupName=Redbooks:%20Sametime%208.5%20Enterprise%20Scale%20
Deployment
```

```
http://tinyurl.com/sametime-b033
```

Get Started Installing IBM Lotus Sametime 8.5.1 – You Too Can Be A WAS Admin:

```
http://www.turtleweb.com/turtleblog.nsf/dx/ST%20&%20WAS%20Admin.
pdf/$file/ST%20&%20WAS%20Admin.pdf
```

```
http://tinyurl.com/sametime-b034
```

Steps for Integrating iNotes with STLinks:

```
https://www.ibm.com/support/docview.wss?uid=swg21319618
```

```
http://tinyurl.com/sametime-b035
```

System Requirements – Sametime Entry 8.5.2:

```
https://www.ibm.com/support/docview.wss?uid=swg27019580
```

```
http://tinyurl.com/sametime-b036
```

System Requirements – Sametime Standard 8.5.2:

```
https://www.ibm.com/support/docview.wss?uid=swg27019598
```

```
http://tinyurl.com/sametime-b037
```

System Requirements – Sametime Advanced 8.5.2:

```
https://www.ibm.com/support/docview.wss?uid=swg27020283
```

```
http://tinyurl.com/sametime-b038
```

Understanding Sametime Architecture:

http://www.ibm.com/developerworks/lotus/documentation/
sametimearchitecture/

http://tinyurl.com/sametime-b039

Sametime Messages:

http://www.lotus.com/ldd/stwiki.nsf/xpViewCategories.
xsp?lookupName=Sametime 8.5.2 Message Catalog

http://tinyurl.com/sametime-b040

Sametime SSL-related resources

Importing the Lotus Domino Server's SSL certificate into the keystore:

http://www.lotus.com/ldd/stwiki.nsf/dx/Importing_the_Lotus_Domino_
servers_SSL_certificate_into_the_keystore_sta852

http://tinyurl.com/sametime-b041

Enabling encryption for Sametime services:

http://www.lotus.com/ldd/stwiki.nsf/dx/Enabling_encryption_for_
Sametime_Services_and_between_Sametime_and_web_browsers_sta852

http://tinyurl.com/sametime-b042

Configuring Security:

http://www.lotus.com/ldd/stwiki.nsf/dx/Configuring_security_st852

http://tinyurl.com/sametime-b043

IBM has recently identified a security flaw in the Sametime Community Server that has led to them recommending you use SSL to secure your environment. See the following technote—http://www.ibm.com/support/docview.wss?uid=swg21569452. It is important to note that you should always use LDAP credentials that have minimal (read) access to your directory and are not used anywhere else.

Additional documentation resources

How to add additional Sametime Administrators:

http://www.lotus.com/ldd/stwiki.nsf/dx/Adding_administrators_sta852

http://tinyurl.com/sametime-b044

How to add a Java class path to the `sametime.ini` file:

http://www.lotus.com/ldd/stwiki.nsf/dx/Adding_paths_for_the_new_
class_to_the_sametime.ini_file_sta852

http://tinyurl.com/sametime-b045

Recommended maintenance activities for Sametime environments:

http://www.lotus.com/ldd/stwiki.nsf/dx/Recommended_maintenance_
activities_for_Sametime_environments

http://tinyurl.com/sametime-b046

Lotus Sametime 8 `sametime.ini` file settings:

http://www.lotus.com/ldd/stwiki.nsf/dx/lotus-sametime-8-sametime.ini-
file
http://tinyurl.com/sametime-b047

Sametime TURN Server resources

Troubleshooting Sametime TURN Server and TURN Server Debug Settings:

http://www.ibm.com/support/docview.wss?uid=swg21507564

http://tinyurl.com/sametime-b048

Sametime support and fix list resources

Of course, sometimes servers do stop working and you may need to refer to either the support site or fix list for assistance. The following are those sites:

IBM Support Portal:

http://www.ibm.com/support/entry/portal/Overview

http://tinyurl.com/sametime-b049

Sametime Fix List:

http://www.lotus.com/ldd/stfixlist.nsf

http://tinyurl.com/sametime-b050

Sametime Blog resources

Notes Design Blog:

http://www.notesdesignblog.com/NotesDesignBlog/NDBlog.nsf

http://tinyurl.com/sametime-b051

Sametime Design Blog:

https://www.ibm.com/connections/blogs/SametimeBlog/entry/check_out_
the_sametime_design_blog2?lang=en_us

http://tinyurl.com/sametime-b052

Sametime Gateway Server

The IBM Sametime Gateway Server integrates your Sametime network with external instant messaging networks such as Google and AIM. For additional information on how to prepare for a Gateway Server implementation, refer to the following resources:

Planning for a Sametime Gateway Server:

http://www.lotus.com/ldd/stwiki.nsf/dx/Planning_a_Sametime_Gateway_
installation_st852

http://tinyurl.com/sametime-b053

IBM Sametime Gateway 8.5.0/8.5.1 sizing guidelines:

http://www.lotus.com/ldd/stwiki.nsf/dx/IBM_Lotus_Sametime_
Gateway_8.5.08.5.1_sizing_guidelines

http://tinyurl.com/sametime-b054

Installing and Administrating the Sametime Gateway (A Consultant In Your Pocket Guide), Chris Miller, C Miller:

http://www.amazon.com/Installing-Administrating-Sametime-Gateway-
Consultant/dp/B00262M45E

http://tinyurl.com/sametime-b055

Additional resources

We have also a few "odds and ends" we want to include as we think they may be useful. One is the SNAPPS tool for chat logging, and the other is the GSKIT (formerly known as iKeyman) for managing SSL certs. To download the GSKIT file set requires an IBM user ID and password. As a manager of a server environment that authenticates with LDAP, we have also included a link for a free LDAP browser as well as some documentation for understanding the Domino LDAP server.

SNAPPS Snapshot for chat logging:

`http://www.snapps.com/snaweb.nsf/0/D8B4302106BC41E086256E8C0079D852`

`http://tinyurl.com/sametime-b056`

IBM GSKIT:

`https://www14.software.ibm.com/webapp/iwm/web/reg/pick.do?source=gskitupdt &lang=en_US`

`http://tinyurl.com/sametime-b057`

Softerra LDAP browser:

`http://www.ldapadministrator.com/download.htm`

`http://tinyurl.com/sametime-b058`

IBM Lotus Domino LDAP server:

`http://publib.boulder.ibm.com/infocenter/domhelp/v8r0/index.jsp?topic=/com.ibm.help.domino.admin.doc/DOC/H_ABOUT_THE_DOMINO_LDAP_SERVER.html`

`http://tinyurl.com/sametime-b059`

Help! I need somebody! Where to find help when using the SSC

When working with the SSC, you may occasionally have questions about a field or panel. For additional information, you can click help from several locations. For example, from the main WAS panel, in the upper right-hand corner, **Help** is always available in the toolbar.

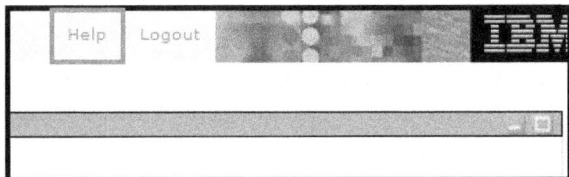

In each WAS panel, there is also a **Field help** and **Page help** displayed.

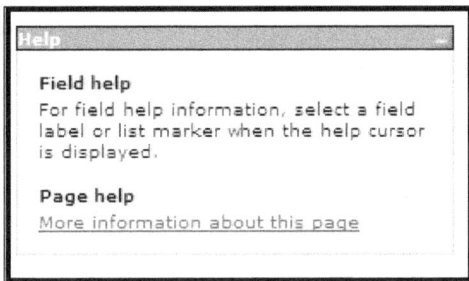

Certification and training resources

As a Sametime administrator, you may choose to pursue certification. IBM provides a certification track just for you. Visit the following website to find information about program preparation and test requirements:

http://www.ibm.com/certify/certs/14011703.shtml

http://tinyurl.com/sametime-b060

IBM also offers a number of classes targeted for Sametime administrators as well as Sametime users and they can be found at:

https://www.ibm.com/software/lotus/training/sametime.html

http://tinyurl.com/sametime-b061

IBM Lotus Sametime 8 Essentials: A User's Guide, Marie L. Scott and Thomas Duff, Packt Publishing:

http://www.amazon.com/IBM-Lotus-Sametime-Essentials-Users/dp/1849680604/ref=sr_1_1?ie=UTF8&qid=1310833347&sr=8-1

http://tinyurl.com/sametime-b062

The Sametime song

If you need a bit of a break after all the work of installing and upgrading Sametime, drop-on over to Mary Beth Raven's website and check out the latest Sametime song titled "Sametime Me":

```
http://www.notesdesignblog.com/NotesDesignBlog/NDBlog.nsf/dx/in-
honor-of-sametime-8.5.2-shipping-some-geeky-new-lyrics-and-another-
sametime-song.....htm
```

```
http://tinyurl.com/sametime-b063
```

And of course, there is still the original Sametime song!

```
http://www.lotus.com/ldd/stwiki.nsf/dx/Sametime_Song
```

```
http://tinyurl.com/sametime-b064
```

Summary

In this chapter, you learned about additional resources for Sametime including customizing the client, certification, and training resources and a little bit of fun—the Sametime song.

C
Sametime 8.5.2 Network-Related Resources

This chapter provides network-related resources pertaining to the installation, configuration, troubleshooting, or tuning of Sametime 8.5.2.

Topics covered in this chapter include:

- Required ports for Sametime servers
- Running with IPv6 addressing
- Understanding NAT and Sametime
- Troubleshooting or tuning your network for Sametime
- Additional monitoring and tuning resources
- Sample network configurations

Required ports for Sametime servers

The following tables include those ports that are required for the various Sametime components. Unless otherwise stated, they refer to TCP ports that should be open for traffic in and out of the firewall. An "x" in the following columns signifies that the port specified is used on the client side of the Sametime environment.

Sametime System Console ports		
Default port	Purpose	Used by Client
8700	Provides default browser access to the SSC.	
8701	Provides HTTPS browser access to the SSC.	
9080	Port used by the Sametime Community Server to access the SSC HTTP port.	

Sametime System Console ports

Default port	Purpose	Used by Client
9443	Port used by the Sametime Community Server to access the SSC HTTPS port.	
50000	SSC database port used by installation manager utilities, post-registration utilities, and Sametime Meeting Server.	

Sametime Community Server ports

Default port	Purpose	Used by Client
80	The Sametime Community Server listens for the SSC on port 80.	
Alternate HTTP port (8088)	If HTTP tunneling on port 80 is configured during the Sametime Community Server installation or afterward, the Domino HTTP server, on which the Sametime Community Server is installed, must listen for HTTP connections on a port other than port 80.	
389	The Sametime Community Server connects to the LDAP server on port 389 if configured to connect to an LDAP server.	
443	The Domino HTTP server listens for HTTPS connections from the SSC on this port by default. This port is used only if you have set up the Domino HTTP server to use Secure Sockets Layer (SSL) for web browser connections.	
1352	The Domino server, on which Sametime Community Server is installed, listens for Notes clients and Domino server connections on port 1352.	
9092	Port 9092 is the Event Server port on for the Sametime Community Server and is used for server connections between Sametime components.	
9094	Port 9094 is the Token Server port on the Sametime Community Server and is used for server connections between Sametime components.	

Sametime Community Services (CS) ports

Default port	Purpose	Used by Client
1516	Port 1516 is used by CS to listen for direct TCP/IP connections from the Community Services of other Sametime Community Servers. This port must be open for chat, awareness, and other Community Services' data to pass between the servers.	
1533	The Community Services listen for direct TCP/IP connections and HTTP-tunneled connections from the Community Services clients (such as Sametime Connect and Sametime Meeting Room clients) on this port.	X
80	If HTTP tunneling was configured on port 80 during the Sametime Community Server installation, the Community Services clients can make HTTP-tunneled connections to the Community Services multiplexer on port 80. But the CS multiplexor listens for HTTP-tunneled connections on both port 80 and 1533. The CS multiplexer simultaneously listens for direct TCP/IP connections on port 1533.	X
8082	When HTTP tunneling support is enabled, the CS clients can make HTTP-tunneled connections to the CS multiplexor on port 8082 by default. Community Services clients can make HTTP-tunneled connections on both ports 80 and 8082 by default. Port 8082 ensures backward compatibility with previous Sametime releases. In previous releases, Sametime clients made HTTP-tunneled connections to the Community Services only on port 8082.	X

Sametime Classic Meetings ports

Default port	Purpose	Used by Client
554	The Sametime Classic Recorded Meeting client attempts a direct RTSP TCP/IP connection to the Recorded Meeting Broadcast Services on the Sametime Community Server on port 554.	X
1533	Port 1533 is used by the Sametime Classic Meeting Room client when the user attends an instant or scheduled meeting through a web browser.	X
8081	The Meeting Room client uses port 8081 to connect with the Meeting Services on the Sametime Community Server.	X

Sametime Proxy Server port

Default port	Purpose	Used by Client
8880	The SSC accesses the Deployment Manager SOAP port. This is used for server-to-server communication and the port may vary depending on how WAS is configured.	
9080	The Sametime Proxy Server port for accessing the web and mobile clients. Port may vary depending upon installation.	X
9081	Secure Sametime Proxy Server port for accessing the web and mobile clients. Port may vary depending upon installation.	X
80	Port on which the Sametime Proxy Server will be accessible if a WAS proxy is deployed in front of it. Used for browser-based and mobile clients.	X
443	Secure port on which the Sametime Proxy Server will be accessible if a WAS proxy is deployed in front of it. Used for browser-based and mobile clients.	X

Sametime Media Manager Server ports

Default port	Purpose	Used by Client
9080	Port 9080 is an HTTP port used for the management of audio/video calls. In a cluster, HTTP ports are proxied through a WebSphere Proxy Server.	
42000-43000	Sametime Media Manager Packet Switcher routes audio data through a range of ports starting with 42000 through 43000. It uses values as needed in increments of two. If encryption is enabled (SRTP), the numbers to be used will be odd numbers.	X
46000-47000	Sametime Media Manager Packet Switcher routes video data through a range of ports starting with 46000 through 47000. It uses values as needed in increments of two. If encryption is enabled (SRTP), the range starts with an odd port number.	X
5060 and 5061	The Conference Manager and Packet Switcher are SIP applications, and therefore use WebSphere SIP container ports.	X
5080/5081	The SIP Proxy Registrar uses these ports for client registration.	X
8880	Port 8880 is used for server-to-server communication. The SSC accesses the Deployment Manager SOAP port.	X

Sametime Meeting Server ports

Default port	Purpose	Used by Client
443	In a single node environment using HTTPS that bypasses the WAS Proxy, the Lotus Sametime Meeting Server listens for data from the Lotus Sametime Meeting Room client over this connection.	X
80/443	Meeting server deployed with WAS Proxy will listen on these ports for client connections.	X
9080	Port 9080 is used in a single node or multiple node environment when Lotus Sametime Meeting Server listens for data from the Lotus Sametime Meeting Room client over this connection when HTTP bypasses the WAS Proxy.	X
9443	In a multiple node environment using HTTPS, the Lotus Sametime Meeting Server listens for data from the Lotus Sametime Meeting Room client that is passed through the WAS Proxy.	X
8880	Port 8880 is used for server-to-server communication. The SSC accesses the Deployment Manager SOAP port.	

Sametime SIP Proxy and Registrar ports

Default port	Purpose	Used By Client
5080-5081	SIP messaging uses these ports in a Media Manager deployment where the SIP Proxy and Registrar runs on a separate virtual host.	X
5060-5061	Ports are used in a multi-server Media Manager deployment where the SIP Proxy and Registrar runs on a separate host.	X

Sametime TURN Server ports

Default port	Purpose	Used by Client
3478	UDP or TCP Port for basic STUN/TURN handling. This port should be open for internal and external access.	X
49152-65535	UDP Ports for dynamic packet allocation. These ports should be available for internal client access.	X

Sametime Packet Switcher (MCU) ports (internal use)		
Default port	Purpose	Used by Client
39000	UDP audio port for the MCU in single port mode.	X
40000	UDP video port for the MCU in single port mode.	X
42000-43000	UDP audio ports for the MCU in multi-port mode.	X
46000-47000	UDP video ports for the MCU in multi-port mode.	X

Running Sametime with IPv6 addressing

An introduction to IPv6 can be found on the following website:

```
http://technet.microsoft.com/en-us/library/bb726944.aspx
```

```
http://tinyurl.com/sametime-c001
```

IPv6 is still not in widespread use across intranets and the Internet at large. For that reason, it is recommended that unless you require IPv6 in your environment; turn off IPv6 before you begin your Sametime install or migration to version 8.5.2.

If you must use IPv6 networking, note that some components of a Sametime server require the use of an IPv4-formatted loopback address. Therefore, to insure that your servers function without potential network issues, do not disable IPv4. Be sure to run both IPv4 and IPv6 addressing.

As stated previously, IPv6 addressing must be enabled at the time of the server install as it cannot be enabled after the server is already installed. For the addressing to work correctly, IPv6 addressing should also be enabled on the client workstation. If your intranet is transitioning to IPv6 networking, this is one more reason to run both addressing schemas to prevent user connectivity issues.

A good article describing IPv6 in the Windows server environment can be found at:

```
http://technet.microsoft.com/en-us/network/bb530961.aspx
```

```
http://tinyurl.com/sametime-c002
```

"Best practices for moving to IPv6" article can be found at:

```
http://www.lotus.com/ldd/stwiki.nsf/dx/best-practices-for-moving-to-ipv6
```

```
http://tinyurl.com/sametime-c003
```

Understanding NAT and Sametime

Network address translation (**NAT**) is the method for modifying the IP address information of IP packet headers in transit across a routing device. This is generally done to prevent internal IPs from being viewable to external network devices. Routers manage the translation so that when requests come back, they are translated back to the internal or private IP addresses. Because Sametime client connections, especially those using audio and video, require a client-to-client connection, a technique called NAT transferral is used to maintain connections traversing NAT gateways. The Sametime TURN Server acts as a NAT transversal server and provides this capability so that if your users are attempting to connect to your Media Server outside your NAT'ed network, they will be able to successfully connect. An example of a TURN Server topology can be found at:

```
http://www.lotus.com/ldd/stwiki.nsf/dx/TURN_Server_topologies_st852
```

```
http://tinyurl.com/sametime-c004
```

We discussed the TURN Server in earlier chapters. However, we provide some additional resources here for understanding how to troubleshoot a TURN Server:

Troubleshooting a Sametime TURN Server:

```
http://www.lotus.com/ldd/stwiki.nsf/dx/Troubleshooting_a_Sametime_
TURN_Server_st852
```

```
http://tinyurl.com/sametime-c005
```

Troubleshooting or tuning your network for Sametime

In the event that you may need to troubleshoot network issues or tune your network for Sametime, we have provided some resources for you. Especially after an installation or migration, you may find that servers and/or clients are not connecting and, therefore, may need to troubleshoot what may ultimately be a network issue. One tool that is good to have in your administrator's toolkit is the Wireshark Network Analyzer. This allows you to "sniff" network traffic to see what is occurring during a network transmission. Of course, check with your network administrators to see if they permit this type of tool before you start analyzing network traffic.

What clients are connecting to your servers and how to tell:

```
https://www.ibm.com/support/docview.wss?uid=swg21114318
```

```
http://tinyurl.com/sametime-c006
```

Troubleshooting network problems on Domino:

http://www.lotus.com/ldd/stwiki.nsf/dx/Troubleshooting_network_
problems_on_Domino_sta852

http://tinyurl.com/sametime-c007

How Sametime establishes a connection with other Sametime servers:

https://www.ibm.com/support/docview.wss?uid=swg21206752

http://tinyurl.com/sametime-c008

Checking for port conflicts:

http://www.lotus.com/ldd/stwiki.nsf/dx/Checking_for_port_conflicts_
between_the_SIP_Proxy_and_Registrar_and_the_WebSphere_proxy_server_
sta852

http://tinyurl.com/sametime-c009

Wireshark Network Analyzer:

http://www.wireshark.org/

http://tinyurl.com/sametime-c010

Sametime Meeting Server audio/video tuning

If you are considering deploying the Sametime Meeting Server with audio and video capabilities, you may need to tune both your Sametime servers and your network to address the bandwidth usage that may occur as meeting room usage increases. Deployment of the Sametime Bandwidth Manager will help you manage your audio and video traffic across the network and track usage; however, there are also some resources for tuning the Sametime servers for this specific need and these are as follows:

Managing the video bit rate:

http://www.lotus.com/ldd/stwiki.nsf/dx/Managing_video_bitrate_st852

http://tinyurl.com/sametime-c011

Managing UDP ports for voice/video:

http://www.lotus.com/ldd/stwiki.nsf/dx/Managing_UDP_ports_for_voice_
chat_and_video_calls_sta852

http://tinyurl.com/sametime-c012

Managing multiple audio/video streams:

http://www.lotus.com/ldd/stwiki.nsf/dx/Managing_multiple_audio_and_
video_streams_sta852

http://tinyurl.com/sametime-c013

Changing the default number of maximum users:

http://www.lotus.com/ldd/stwiki.nsf/dx/Changing_the_default_number_
of_maximum_users_sta852

http://tinyurl.com/sametime-c014

Deploying meetings to external users:

http://www.lotus.com/ldd/stwiki.nsf/dx/Deploying_meetings_to_
external_Internet_users_st852

http://tinyurl.com/sametime-c015

Sametime audio and video network bandwidth requirements:

http://www.lotus.com/ldd/stwiki.nsf/dx/Sametime_Audio_and_Video_
Network_Bandwidth_Requirement

http://tinyurl.com/sametime-c016

Additional monitoring and tuning resources

As every administrator knows, you should monitor and occasionally tune your servers. We have included some additional resources that may help you with monitoring server availability and performance and these are as follows:

http://www.ibm.com/developerworks/lotus/library/sametime-watchit/
index.html

http://tinyurl.com/sametime-c017

Server tuning in general:

http://www.lotus.com/ldd/stwiki.nsf/dx/Tuning_st852

http://tinyurl.com/sametime-c018

IBM Server.Load: The new IBM Sametime workloads:

http://www.ibm.com/developerworks/lotus/library/sametime-workloads/
index.html

http://tinyurl.com/sametime-c019

Using the Watchit Tool to measure performance in your Sametime 8.5.x production environment:

```
http://www.lotus.com/ldd/stwiki.nsf/dx/Using_the_Watchit_tool_to_
measure_performance_in_your_IBM_Lotus_Sametime_8.5.x_production_
environment
```

```
http://tinyurl.com/sametime-c020
```

Optimizing Name Lookup:

```
http://www.lotus.com/ldd/stwiki.nsf/dx/Optimizing_Name_Lookup_Network
```

```
http://tinyurl.com/sametime-c021
```

Troubleshooting the Sametime 8.5.2 Proxy Server—Web Connectivity Issues:

```
http://www.lotus.com/ldd/stwiki.nsf/dx/Troubleshooting_IBM_
Sametime_8.5.2_Proxy_Server
```

```
http://tinyurl.com/sametime-c022
```

Troubleshooting the Sametime 8.5.1 Media Server client:

```
http://www.lotus.com/ldd/stwiki.nsf/dx/Troubleshooting_the_IBM_Lotus_
Sametime_8.5.1_Media_Server_Client
```

```
http://tinyurl.com/sametime-c023
```

Tuning for Sametime Advanced 8.5.2:

```
http://www.lotus.com/ldd/stwiki.nsf/dx/Tuning_Sametime_Advanced_
sta852
```

```
http://tinyurl.com/sametime-c024
```

Sample network configurations

As your Sametime network grows, you may want to consider adding other Sametime components, clustering, or load balancing. Or your intranet at large may change and you may need to reconfigure Sametime to work with a DMZ or different proxy server. We have provided some resources here that we think might be helpful.

Leased-line example with Bandwidth Manager:

```
http://www.lotus.com/ldd/stwiki.nsf/dx/Example_1_Leased_lines_st852
```

```
http://tinyurl.com/sametime-c025
```

Cloud-based example with Bandwidth Manager:

```
http://www.lotus.com/ldd/stwiki.nsf/dx/Example_2_Clouds_st852
```

```
http://tinyurl.com/sametime-c026
```

DMZ and Sametime Meeting Servers:

```
http://www.lotus.com/ldd/stwiki.nsf/dx/Deploying_meetings_to_
external_Internet_users_st852
```

```
http://tinyurl.com/sametime-c027
```

Installing and setting up a stand-alone community services multiplexor:

```
http://www.lotus.com/ldd/stwiki.nsf/dx/Installing_and_setting_up_a_
standalone_Community_Services_multiplexer_sta852
```

```
http://tinyurl.com/sametime-c028
```

Installing a cluster of Bandwidth Managers:

```
http://www.lotus.com/ldd/stwiki.nsf/dx/Installing_a_cluster_of_
Bandwidth_Managers_st852
```

```
http://tinyurl.com/sametime-c030
```

Network topology examples for Bandwidth Manager:

```
http://www.lotus.com/ldd/stwiki.nsf/dx/Network_topology_examples_
st852
```

```
http://tinyurl.com/sametime-c031
```

TLS (Transport Layer Security) support:

```
http://www.lotus.com/ldd/stwiki.nsf/dx/TLS_Transport_Layer_Security_
Support_sut852
```

```
http://tinyurl.com/sametime-c032
```

Summary

In this chapter, you learnt about information relating to network-related resources pertaining to the installation, configuration, troubleshooting, or tuning of Sametime 8.5.2.

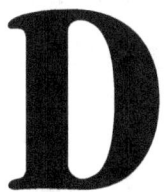

WebSphere Application Server-Related Resources

If you are approaching Sametime 8.5.2 administration with a background in Domino, you might be somewhat overwhelmed with all the new concepts and skills required by WebSphere Application Server. You can use the following links to accelerate your WAS learning and gain the necessary skills you need going forward.

Overview of IBM WebSphere Application Server (WAS) concepts for IBM Lotus Sametime administrators:

```
ftp://public.dhe.ibm.com/software/lotus/info/training/WAS_Concepts_
ST.pdf
```

```
http://tinyurl.com/sametime-d001
```

WebSphere Application Server V7.0: Technical overview:

```
http://www.redbooks.ibm.com/abstracts/REDP4482.html?Open
```

```
http://tinyurl.com/sametime-d002
```

System Administrator skills for IBM WebSphere Application Server 7:

```
https://www-304.ibm.com/jct03001c/services/learning/us/pdfs/was_v70_
sa.pdf
```

```
http://tinyurl.com/sametime-d003
```

WebSphere Application Server V7 Administration and Configuration Guide:

```
http://www.redbooks.ibm.com/abstracts/sg247615.html?Open
```

```
http://tinyurl.com/sametime-d004
```

IBM WebSphere Application Server Introduction for Lotus — this course is
designed to introduce you to WAS, explain its characteristics and benefits,
and show how it relates to Lotus products that run on it.

```
ftp://ftp.software.ibm.com/software/lotus/info/training/waslorlotus.
pdf
```

```
http://tinyurl.com/sametime-d005
```

The developerWorks Technical Library for WebSphere Administration —
developerWorks publishes articles that dive-deep into technical topics, such as
how to build and administer a WAS environment. This is an excellent resource that
continues to grow over time.

```
http://www.ibm.com/developerworks/views/websphere/libraryview.jsp
```

```
http://tinyurl.com/sametime-d006
```

```
http://www.ibm.com/developerworks/websphere/zones/was/ /
```

```
http://tinyurl.com/sametime-d007
```

WebSphere Application Server Discussion Forum — tap into the expertise of the
WAS community in this discussion forum:

```
http://www.ibm.com/developerworks/forums/forum.jspa?forumID=266
```

```
http://tinyurl.com/sametime-d008
```

Troubleshooting WebSphere Server information — IBM Support Portal:

```
http://www.ibm.com/support/entry/portal/Troubleshooting/Software/
WebSphere/WebSphere_Application_Server
```

```
http://tinyurl.com/sametime-d009
```

WebSphere Application Server Certification — if you are interested in pursuing
professional certification in WAS, information about the IBM certification program
can be found at the following site:

```
http://www.ibm.com/certify/certs/ws_index.shtml
```

```
http://tinyurl.com/sametime-d010
```

Index

F

failover method 135
features, Sametime 8.5.2
  audio and video services 37
  mobility 37
  new lightweight client 36
  performance improvements 37
  persistent meetings 37
  telephony 38
features, Sametime Advanced
  about 298, 299
  broadcast communities 300
  Instant Share 303
  persistent charts 299, 300
features, Sametime Classic Meeting Server
    49
features, Sametime Community Server 42
features, Sametime Gateway 310, 311
features, Sametime Media Manager 60
features, Sametime Meeting Server 52
features, Sametime Mobile client 340
features, Sametime Proxy Server 58
features, telephony solutions 71
federated repository 109, 250, 259
file locations, WAS
  /bin directory 106
  about 100
  appserver 100
  config directory 103, 105
  logs subdirectory 102, 103
  profiles directory 101, 102
  WebSphere home directory 100
firewall ports, TURN server 241, 242

G

General Server Status report 367
Google Talk 31, 308
Greenhouse site 279
Group Membership Timeout Cache 328

H

hardware requisites, Sametime 8.5.2 141,
    143
horizontal clustering 136, 145

HTTP 401 or 407 challenge requests 344
httpd.cnf file
  modifying 342, 343
HTTP Proxy 344

I

IBM Connections 7, 131
IBM Connections Business Cards
  Embedded Sametime client 279
  Sametime Proxy Server 278, 279
  stand-alone Sametime client 279
  using, for Sametime 277, 278
IBM DB2 9.5 Limited Use 48, 53, 65
IBM Fix Central website 48
IBM HTTP server 344
IBM Installation Manager 161
IBM Java Virtual Machine (JVM) 17
IBM Lotus Notes 7
IBM Passport Advantage 160, 297, 317, 344
IBM Sametime SDK
  URL 415
IBM Tivoli Directory Server 54
IBM WebSphere Application Server. *See*
    WAS
IBM WebSphere Application Server 7
  URL, for system Administrator skills 439
iKeyman 146
iNotes mail client 134
install.addon.xml file 321
installation files, Sametime Advanced
  about 297
  CF2Y0ML 297
  CZYH2ML 297
  CZYH4ML 297
  CZYH5ML 297
  CZYH6ML 297
  CZYH7ML 297
installation files, Sametime Gateway
  about 309
  CRE9SML 309
  CZG0ML 309
  CZYF9ML 309
installation log files, Sametime 245
installing
  Bandwidth Manager DB2 database 228-232
  Bandwidth Manager Server 228

R

S

Thank you for buying
IBM Sametime 8.5.2 Administration Guide

About Packt Publishing

Packt, pronounced 'packed', published its first book "Mastering phpMyAdmin for Effective MySQL Management" in April 2004 and subsequently continued to specialize in publishing highly focused books on specific technologies and solutions.

Our books and publications share the experiences of your fellow IT professionals in adapting and customizing today's systems, applications, and frameworks. Our solution based books give you the knowledge and power to customize the software and technologies you're using to get the job done. Packt books are more specific and less general than the IT books you have seen in the past. Our unique business model allows us to bring you more focused information, giving you more of what you need to know, and less of what you don't.

Packt is a modern, yet unique publishing company, which focuses on producing quality, cutting-edge books for communities of developers, administrators, and newbies alike. For more information, please visit our website: www.packtpub.com.

About Packt Enterprise

In 2010, Packt launched two new brands, Packt Enterprise and Packt Open Source, in order to continue its focus on specialization. This book is part of the Packt Enterprise brand, home to books published on enterprise software – software created by major vendors, including (but not limited to) IBM, Microsoft and Oracle, often for use in other corporations. Its titles will offer information relevant to a range of users of this software, including administrators, developers, architects, and end users.

Writing for Packt

We welcome all inquiries from people who are interested in authoring. Book proposals should be sent to author@packtpub.com. If your book idea is still at an early stage and you would like to discuss it first before writing a formal book proposal, contact us; one of our commissioning editors will get in touch with you.

We're not just looking for published authors; if you have strong technical skills but no writing experience, our experienced editors can help you develop a writing career, or simply get some additional reward for your expertise.

IBM Lotus Sametime 8 Essentials

ISBN: 978-1-84968-060-8   Paperback: 284 pages

Master Online Enterprise Communication with Lotus Sametime 8 with this IBM Lotus Sametime User book and e-Book

1. Collaborate securely with your colleagues and teammates both inside and outside your organization by using Sametime features such as instant messaging and online meetings

2. Make your instant messaging communication more interesting with the inclusion of graphics, images, and emoticons to convey more information in fewer words

IBM Lotus Sametime 8 Essentials
A User's Guide

Marie L. Scott   Thomas Duff

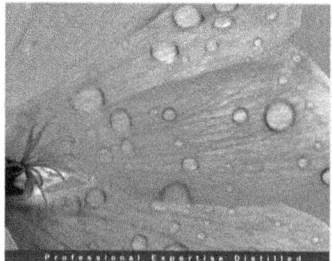

Application Development for IBM WebSphere Process Server 7 and Enterprise Service Bus 7

ISBN: 978-1-847198-28-0   Paperback: 548 pages

Build SOA-based flexible, economical, and efficient applications for IBM WebSphere Process Server 7 and Enterprise Service Bus 7 with this book and e-Book

1. Develop SOA applications using the WebSphere Process Server (WPS) and WebSphere Enterprise Service Bus (WESB)

2. Analyze business requirements and rationalize your thoughts to see if an SOA approach is appropriate for your project

Application Development for IBM WebSphere Process Server 7 and Enterprise Service Bus 7

Swami Chandrasekaran   Salil Ahuja

Please check **www.PacktPub.com** for information on our titles

professional expertise distilled

PUBLISHING

IBM Lotus Notes 8.5 User Guide

Professional Expertise Distilled

IBM Lotus Notes 8.5 User Guide

Foreword by Ed Brill
Director, Product Management, IBM Lotus Software

Karen Hooper

IBM Lotus Notes 8.5 User Guide

ISBN: 978-1-849680-20-2   Paperback: 296 pages

A practical hands-on user guide Book and e-Book with
time saving tips and comprehensive instructions for
using IBM Lotus Notes 8.5 effectively and efficiently

1. Understand and master the features of Lotus
   Notes and put them to work in your business
   quickly

2. Contains comprehensive coverage of new Lotus
   Notes 8.5 features

3. Includes easy-to-follow real-world examples
   with plenty of screenshots to clearly demonstrate
   how to get the most out of Lotus Notes

Professional Expertise Distilled

**IBM Lotus Quickr 8.5 for
Domino Administration**

Keith Brooks   David Byrd
Mark Harper   Olusola Omosaiye

IBM Lotus Quickr 8.5 for Domino Administration

ISBN: 978-1-84968-052-3   Paperback: 252 pages

Ensure effective and efficient team collaboration by
building a solid social infrastructure with IBM Lotus
Quickr 8.5 with this book and e-Book

1. Gain a thorough understanding of IBM Lotus
   Quickr 8.5 Team Collaboration, Repository, and
   Connectors

2. Recommended best practices to upgrade to the
   latest version of IBM Lotus Quickr 8.5

3. Customize logos, colors, templates, and more to
   your designs without much effort

Please check **www.PacktPub.com** for information on our titles

www.ingramcontent.com/pod-product-compliance
Lightning Source LLC
Chambersburg PA
CBHW081713220526
45468CB00008B/1830